DATE DUE

DEMCO 38-296

Development
and Democracy
in India

Development
and Democracy
in India

Shalendra D. Sharma

LYNNE
RIENNER
PUBLISHERS

BOULDER
LONDON

Riverside Community College
Library
4800 Magnolia Avenue
Riverside, CA 92506

HC 435.2 .S494 1999

Sharma, Shalendra D., 1958-

Development and democracy in
India

To my mother,
and to the memory of my father,
Rishi Deo Sharma (1930–1997)

Published in the United States of America in 1999 by
Lynne Rienner Publishers, Inc.
1800 30th Street, Boulder, Colorado 80301
www.rienner.com

and in the United Kingdom by
Lynne Rienner Publishers, Inc.
3 Henrietta Street, Covent Garden, London WC2E 8LU

© 1999 by Lynne Rienner Publishers, Inc. All rights reserved

Library of Congress Cataloging-in-Publication Data
Sharma, Shalendra D.
    Development and democracy in India / Shalendra D. Sharma.
    Includes bibliographical references and index.
    ISBN 1-55587-810-5 (alk. paper)
    1. India—Economic conditions—1947– . 2. India—Economic
policy—1980– . 3. Rural development—India. 4. Democracy—India.
5. India—Politics and government—1977– . I. Title.
HC435.2.S494 1999
338.954—dc21   99-26091
                                                          CIP

British Cataloguing in Publication Data
A Cataloguing in Publication record for this book
is available from the British Library.

Printed and bound in the United States of America

The paper used in this publication meets the requirements
of the American National Standard for Permanence of
Paper for Printed Library Materials Z39.48-1984.

5 4 3 2 1

Contents

Acknowledgments

This project was initiated when I was a doctoral student in the Department of Political Science at the University of Toronto. It was a great privilege to attend Canada's premier educational institution. The tremendous support I received from the university, and the professionalism and intellectual rigor of its faculty, provided a conducive learning environment. My greatest intellectual debt goes to Jonathan Barker, Richard Sandbrook, Nanda Choudhry, and Milton Israel. This distinguished "committee" of two political scientists, an economist, and a historian provided me with all-encompassing support and generous offerings of time and wisdom. At the University of Toronto I was also fortunate to benefit from the insights of Peter Russell, Joseph Carens, Richard Day, Robert Matthews, Gerald Helleiner, Cranford Pratt, and Nibaldo Galleguillos.

I would like to thank the following friends and colleagues for their support and guidance over the many years it has taken to complete this project: Atul Kohli at Princeton University, Akhil Gupta at Stanford University, Hari Sharma at Simon Fraser University, Mohammad Ayoob at Michigan State, Sumit Ganguly at CUNY, Leo Rose at UC Berkeley, Myron Weiner at MIT, Pashaura Singh at the University of Michigan, Amita Shastri at San Francisco State University, Zaheer Baber and Farid Alatas at the National University of Singapore, Quansheng Zhao at American University, Tijjani Mohammed-Bande at Usmanu Danfodio University in Nigeria, and Ilan Kapoor and Okon Akiba at York University in Canada.

I am also indebted to many friends and institutions in South Asia. In Bangladesh I could always count on the generosity of Nural Hussein Choudhury at Rajshahi University. Abdul Matin of Aligarh Muslim University was always gracious with his help. His acute knowledge of the Indian countryside and expertise in fieldwork greatly helped me in my field research. Shri Upendra Chaudhary and Saidur Rahman worked under difficult conditions to help me collect reliable data and insights into rural life. Shri G. D. Jain of the Indian Administrative Service was generous with his time and provided vital contacts. To these friends and many others who wish to remain anonymous and to the hospitable people (whose patience and generosity I often stretched to the limits) of Vikaspur and many other villages, my sincere thanks. In Delhi, P. C. Joshi at the Institute of Economic Growth, K. N. Kabra at the India Institute of Public Administration, Rajni Kothari at the Center for the Study of Developing Societies, and colleagues at Hindu College opened many doors. I sincerely thank them.

This book would not have been possible without the financial support of a number of generous benefactors. I am grateful to the University of Toronto Doctoral Fellowship, the Ontario Graduate Scholarship, the Social Sciences and Humanities Research Council of Canada, the World Bank, and the University of San Francisco for their generosity.

The University of San Francisco (USF), which has been my home institution since 1993, has provided a supportive, stimulating, and collegial environment in which to teach and research. I would like to extend my deep appreciation to Dean Stanley Nel for the exemplary leadership he has provided the university. I owe him a special debt of gratitude for his guidance, stern encouragement, and unfailing support, and for helping me advance my academic career. Similarly, my warmest thanks go to Associate Dean Gerardo Marin, who has unhesitatingly given his time, advice, and support. To Nancy Campagna my many thanks for her unbounded generosity and kindness. I am also deeply grateful to my colleagues at USF for their intellectual and moral support: Barbara Bundy, Horacio Camblong, Miriam Feldblum, Tony Fels, Hartmut Fischer, Andy Heinze, Roberta Johnson, Tetteh Kofi, Lewis Klausner, Uldis Kruze, Pedro Lang-Churion, Man Lui-Lau, Michael Lehmann, Lois Lorentzen, Eduardo Mendieta, Elliot Neaman, John Pinelli, Annie Rochelle, Stephen Roddy, Vicky Siu, and Stephen Zunes. Professor Emeritus Richard Kozicki, my mentor and friend at USF, has been a source of inspiration, and I greatly value his warm friendship and wise counsel; seasoned Asia hand that he is, he will understand when I say that he has been my true *guruji*. At USF I have benefited immensely from the superb research assistance of some exceptional students. I owe special thanks to Bhagman Singh, Tom Curteman, Javier Huete, Seo Hyun Kim, and Juan Callejas, and, more than they may admit, Guido La Volpe, Giovanni Segni, Cyrus Fama, and Adrian Pantoja. The administrative support I have received from Cheryl Czekala, Marie Baillargeon, John Severance, and Krysten Elbers has been truly exceptional.

As someone who has used several of their texts as required readings in my courses, I am honored that this project was accepted by Lynne Rienner Publishers. At every stage I received superb editorial guidance from Bridget Julian, and it is safe to say that this would have been a much weaker text without her incisive comments and keen editorial eye. I thank her for her professionalism and understanding and for not giving up on me.

Finally, the support of my family has been indispensable. None of this could have been possible without the lifetime of toil and sacrifice my parents made for my education. I dedicate this work to my mother and to the memory of my father. My only regret is that my father did not live to see the completed book. I thank my sister, brothers, and our large and growing extended family (especially Sharlene, Renita, and Ashlina) for their unflinching support and unceasing generosity. Special thanks go to Masterji Shiu Prasad and Kamla *fua* who selflessly gave the gift of education to an entire generation of students within the crumbling walls of an open-air village school. Special thanks to Satendra (Bobby) and Indra Singh for all their support and generosity. My greatest debt, however, is to my wife, Vivian; her quiet confidence and courage has long sustained me. My heartfelt thanks to her and our son, Krishan, for always standing by me when it has mattered the most, and for sharing all the joys of life together.

Introduction

In politics we will have equality and in social and economic life we will have inequality. . . . How long shall we continue to live this life of contradictions? How long shall we continue to deny equality in our social and economic life?

—B. R. Ambedkar, speech in the
Constituent Assembly, 25 November 1949

In his address to the expectant nation on the eve of India's independence, Prime Minister Jawaharlal Nehru eloquently noted that "the service of India means the service of the millions who suffer . . . it means the ending of poverty, ignorance and disease and inequality of opportunity." Echoing the hubris and triumphant certitude of the nationalist elite that had vanquished three centuries of colonial rule, Nehru pledged that the fundamental task of the new political leadership was to "build the noble mansion of free India where all her children may dwell and prosper."[1]

To the architect of the grand design, the intrinsic legitimacy and the tolerant pluralistic culture of a representative democratic polity was indispensable to building the "noble mansion." Nehru, the quintessential renaissance man, remained unequivocal: only a democratic state (which under Indian conditions he envisaged as an archetypal liberal democracy derived from the syncretism of the Indic civilization and Western rationalism) based on legal principles and guided by the ethos of purposive constitutional deliberation had the capacity to expunge the feudal-colonial legacies and carry out thoroughgoing national reconstruction. Moreover, only an authentic liberal democratic polity, which through its representative institutions and constitutional-legal devices prescribed accountability and imposed limits on state power, was endowed with the political-institutional wherewithal to mobilize popular acceptance of the government's development programs and to "plan" national economic development in the manner that avoided the painful vicissitudes of capitalism and socialism.[2] Rejecting the ready-made

1

exegesis propagated by proponents of capitalism and communism, Nehru stubbornly opted for the heretical "third way . . . which takes the best from all existing systems . . . and seeks to create something suited to one's history and philosophy."[3] Such a balanced and gradualist pathway to modernity (and prosperity) was seen as in keeping with the cherished Gandhian ideals of nonviolent social transformation and a step closer toward realizing the imagined egalitarian Gandhian teleology based on "each according to his needs, from each according to his capacity"—euphemistically called the "socialistic pattern of society."[4]

Following independence in 1947, India's nascent democratic state embarked on a herculean undertaking: to democratically transform a hierarchically institutionalized, overwhelmingly agrarian order of great antiquity and heterogeneity, burdened with the problems of extreme scarcity, and what Ashis Nandy (1983) has evocatively termed the "pathological anxieties of post-colonialism," into a "modern India" guided by the Nehruvian ideals of secularism, democratic socialism, and social justice. Seeing itself as an exemplar and the legitimate custodian of social order and the repository of the public good—indeed as the only authentic embodiment of universality and progress—no jurisdictions were to be beyond the reach of this interventionist democratic state. In its assumed role as modernizer, mediator, reformer, and nation builder, India's democratic state inaugurated a series of ambitious national development plans that over the past five decades have irrevocably transformed the socioeconomic, political, and normative landscape of the subcontinent, albeit not necessarily in the ways the state had originally intended.[5]

How has India's democratic state interacted with and shaped its society and political economy? What explains the perennial discrepancies between the state's developmental intentions and goals and the actual outcomes? Specifically, why have five decades of democratically guided programmatic state interventions committed to building an egalitarian, socialistic society (the so-called noble mansion) not been realized? More puzzling, and indeed the central paradox of Indian democracy, is why in spite of a profound revamping of the rules of the political game under democratic tutelage—through which the poor and unlettered masses and myriad hitherto underrepresented groups were mobilized, politicized, and substantially empowered with their representatives occupying some of the highest positions in government—the state has failed to utilize its administrative-bureaucratic apparatus and this broad base of support to implement meaningful reform. Why in a country where the poor make up an overwhelming majority of the citizenry, and yet where political participation is open and reasonably fair, have the masses failed to effectively influence public policy or help guide development strategies in a direction that reconciles economic growth with redistribution? Indeed, India's democratic regime's failure to mitigate the "poverty problem" is vividly reflected in the stark fact that poverty remains as pervasive as ever, with roughly 40 percent or some 350 to 400 million Indians living under variously drawn poverty lines, a proportion that has not changed since independence in 1947.[6]

This study examines these questions with reference to rural India, against the experience of some fifty years of democratic nation building. It chronicles and evaluates the origins and content of the Indian state's developmental and reformist policies, marking "critical junctures" in the state's half century of sustained interventions in the countryside.[7] However, what sets this study apart from earlier accounts is that it examines these questions through the conceptual lenses of the "state-in-society" approach.[8] Such an eclectic approach provides a more subtle understanding of both the palpable and pronounced divergence between the state's developmental goals and the actual outcomes, as well as the ramifications of the state's policies on the political economy of rural India.

Drawing from a rich corpus of literature, as well as my own extensive fieldwork data, this study presents a blend of analysis, comparative synthesis, and reinterpretation of and theorizing about research on the complex relationship between democratic governance and economic development in a "low-income country" setting that is often at odds with standard interpretations.[9] First, it challenges the conventional "economic" assumption that "it is only through rapid economic growth that India will be able to reduce poverty."[10] Second, it contests the monocausal rigidities of utilitarian and rational choice approaches, including those that attribute reformist and distributive failures to "misguided policies" and to the inherent pathology or "cruel choice" between democracy and development. Third, it provides correctives to the state-centric explanations (which *inter alia* emphasize shallow political institutionalization, the exceptional developmental capacities of "strong," meaning authoritarian, in contrast to the weak and fortuitous capacities of the "soft" or democratic regime types) as the root cause of India's malaise. And fourth, it argues that the kaleidoscope of reductionist behavioral and society-centered approaches (which tends to view democratic states as either ineffectual neutral arbiters or "power brokers" or captives of the dominant classes) are deeply flawed in explaining India's political economy. In contrast, this study, in highlighting the mutually conditioned interactions among the multilayered structures that make up the "state" and "society," illustrates how India's rural development experiment and, in particular, the failure to reconcile economic growth with distribution, have been fundamentally shaped by the exigencies of state-society interactions.

Patterns of State-Society Interactions

Alfred Stepan (1978, xii) has conceptualized the state as a centralized, administrative, bureaucratic, legal, and coercive system headed by an executive authority "that attempts not only to structure relations between civil society and public authority but also to structure many crucial relations within civil society as well." Yet, as Timothy Mitchell (1991, 81) aptly notes, "the state . . . should not be taken as a free-standing entity, whether an agent, instrument, organization or structure, located apart from and opposed to another entity called society." Since the state is inextricably enmeshed in a complex set of relations with society, the boundaries between the state and society are often ambiguous and porous. Yet, the state has a certain salience, in particular, its own identifiable "interests" and programmatic "goals" that it vigorously pursues or attempts to pursue. Integral to the needs of the modern state is its perennial quest for universality and legitimation, its imperative to maintain its sovereignty and hegemony, and the intrinsic impulse of regime incumbents to retain jurisdiction and power.

A generally agreed upon definition of what constitutes "civil society" remains elusive. For Hegel, who presented a state-centric view of *bürgerliche gesellschaft* or civil society, only under the universality of a legal-rational state, the "actual reality of the ethical Idea," could civil society experience that second "moment" of the spirit, in which atomistic individuals pursued their particularistic interests, and realize its own true potential. In contrast to the Hegelian teleology, Alexis de Tocqueville in his classic *Democracy in America* presented a society-centric view of civil society, claiming that a free and vigorous associational life and a heterogeneous society not only permitted limits to impersonal government prerogatives and constraints on arbitrary state power, but also served as the agency for creating public accountability and participatory government. If there is a common thread to these divergent views, it is that civil society is an arena occupied by a constellation of loosely bundled ensembles of private and particular interests that are institutionally "independent" (or at least have some spheres of autonomy) from the formal precincts of state tutelage and control.

Depending on the levels of economic development and social differentiation, civil society may encompass a myriad of vertically segmented and crosscutting interests, including voluntary associations (like professional and trade unions, community organizations, and ethnic, kinship, or religious affiliations), market relations (business and economic classes), and cultural groups. In the Indian context civil society, like the many avatars of the Hindu god Vishnu, is a creature of manifold forms, orientations, and consciousness revolving around a plethora of usually inchoate and heterogeneous solidarities based on ascriptive familial, ethnic, regional, religious, communal, linguistic, and caste identities, as well as class and interest-based affiliations and networks.[11] Despite its heterogeneity and particularistic concerns, the constituent elements of civil society may simultaneously associate, affiliate, or disengage on the basis of perceived congruent interests. However, the elements' internal cleavages and parochial and potentially antithetical concerns can also provide considerable basis for hostility and conflict.

The patterns of interaction between state and society are protracted, multifaceted, and mutually conditioning—or what Frederic Wakeman (1975) in another context has characterized as "dynamic oscillation."[12] The panoply of constituencies that make up the vast realm of civil society continuously renegotiate their ties and allegiance with the state. However, this does not imply that state-society interactions are irreconcilable zero-sum competitions or that a symbiotic structural functional relation exists between the two. Rather, as Joel Migdal (1988) notes, relations between state agents and citizens are characterized by deep ambivalence and contradictory impulses, resulting in a wide spectrum of interactions that ebbs and flows as the protagonists attempt to devise and exercise a range of strategies to deal with the shifting political and socioeconomic circumstances. State pronouncements, trajectories, machinations, violations, and predations may provoke a range of societal responses—ranging from active partnership and collaboration, discrete reciprocity, purposive negotiation, sullen acquiescence, steadfast agitation and confrontation to strategic evasion, collective withdrawal, and, wherever possible, quiescent disengagement.

Understanding this intimate interconnectedness and the permeability of the state and society, and how the reciprocal bargaining, negotiations, and conflicts between them fundamentally influence and shape the patterns of socioeconomic and political change, affords a more poignant understanding of the subtleties of democratic governance and economic development in postindependence India. If anything, such a perspective forces us to recognize that "national development" or "developmental outcomes" are not simply the result of autonomous state actions or some sort of state-dominant class alliance, but are historically contingent upon the more incremental and protean patterns of state-society interactions.

State and Society in India

Seen through the prism of the state-society approach, the legacies of state formation and the resultant patterns of state-society relations carry important consequences for governance and economic development. The scholarly consensus that democracies are responsive and accountable to their citizens and societies is a truism, but it is important to recognize that the disjunction that always existed between India's democratic state and society has in recent years considerably widened, creating real problems for both governance and development. This study attempts to make the case that the fragmentation within both the Indian state and society and the erosion of institutionalized forms of political mediation between them, besides aggravating the "crisis of governability," have also hindered national development, in particular, reformist and redistributive development.

Over the past five decades, the Indian state has vigorously sought to institutionalize "stateness" by expanding its power and reach beyond the social formation of which it is inextricably a part. Like other successor postcolonial states it has demonstrated a formidable capacity for its own reproduction. The state has become a ubiquitous feature of the nation's political landscape, its jurisdiction and administrative-institutional presence reaching into the remotest rural hinterlands. Yet, the state's instrumental hegemonic trajectory and omnipresence have not made it omnipotent. To the contrary, the state's quantitative expansion has not been matched by a commensurate qualitative increase in autonomy and capacity.[13] That is, even as the state has expanded its size and dominion and acquired an unprecedented centrality, its writ does not seem to run very deep. In fact, the state has become increasingly attenuated and segmented, with its reach and capacities severely constricted.

What explains this paradox, and what have been the ramifications for governance and economic development? Many scholars have pointed to how the Indian state's inability to escape from its more unpropitious historical legacies undermined efficacious state building from the outset and how, in the postindependence period, the discretionary top-down state building resulted in feeble political institutionalization and subsequent speedy "deinstitutionalization." We also have a more nuanced understanding of the exigencies of India's "soft" democratic state, especially how its capture and co-optation by the dominant classes and castes undermined its reformist and distributive capabilities. Pranab Bardhan presents a devastating indictment of India's democracy, arguing that it conveniently serves the interests of the three dominant proprietary classes: industrial capitalists, rich farmers, and professional bureaucrats. The industrial capitalists have been the beneficiaries of the government's import substitution policies, industrial licensing system, and restrictions on foreign investment. Rich farmers have benefited from the government's support programs for agricultural products and from subsidized inputs (e.g., electric power, irrigation, fertilizers, diesel fuel) and subsidized credit. And the bureaucratic elite has gained political power and income through its control over what has become an elaborate system of patronage and rent seeking. Although these classes have some competing interests (the private sector, for example, resents many of the bureaucratic controls, and rural and urban groups clash over prices of agricultural produce), the dominant coalition is held together because none of the classes is powerful enough individually to impose its will upon India's polity and economy, and all three welcome state subsidies.

According to Bardhan this "alliance of domination" has had an adverse effect on the country's overall development because, as the dominant classes are brought under a growing network of subsidies and patronage, the state's resources for economic development and social welfare have dwindled. He argues that this process has not only contributed to a deceleration in public revenue and capital formation but has also severely eroded the state's capacity to meet even its most basic developmental and distributive goals. Thus, to Bardhan, India's elite-dominated democratic polity is the root of the problem. Beneath the veneer of constitutional government, democratic governance serves the functional needs of the political and economic elites—providing an arena for interelite accommodation and thus enables them to utilize the instruments of the state to entrench their power and privileges. While India's democratic regime has served as an arena for conflict resolution and provided a resilient mechanism for relatively stable governance, it has nevertheless also found it difficult to muster the political autonomy necessary to pursue its reformist and distributive agenda.

Yet, for all its limitations, India remains the world's largest constitutional democracy, with a functioning parliament, a political regime of laws and institutions, an independent judiciary and respect for legal conventions, a free press, freedom to join or affiliate with political parties, and relatively free and fair competitive elections in which millions of voters cast their ballots.[14] Over the past half century the "deepening of democracy," reflected in the spread of democratic ideas, competitive politics, and universal suffrage, has spurred unprecedented political activism among formerly acquiescent groups and served as an effective vehicle for the political empowerment of the country's hitherto excluded and subordinate groups. Over the past two decades a broad yet expedient alliance of the lower castes and classes collectively referred to as the "Other Backward Castes"or OBCs[15] (estimated to constitute between 40 to 45 percent of the populace), the *dalits* (between 20 to 25 percent),[16] Muslims (between 12 to 15 percent), and other nonelite groups and communities mired in generations of neglect and oppression have pushed their way into the political arena, translating their numerical preponderance into political power. Today their representatives, who are usually quintessential personalist leaders well versed in the rustic vernacular and the idioms, mores, and manners of their constituents, occupy some of the highest offices in the land. Their political organizations and parties—such as the Bahujan Samaj Party (BSP),[17] the Samajwadi Party, the Rashtriya Janata Dal in the northern "Hindi belt," the Dravida Munnetra Kazagham (DMK) and the All-India Anna DMK (AIADMK) that have ruled the southern state of Tamil Nadu since 1967, and the Telegu Desam Party in Andhra Pradesh state are formidable political machines—when not constituting governments are instrumental in determining the nature and fate of governments. As the old certitudes of the Hindu order, in which the low-caste "inferiors" were expected to show ritualized deference to their propertied "superiors," have crumbled into dust, so has the "top-down" mobilization by the upper castes and classes of the "passive" low-caste vote banks. This sharp erosion of political dominance by the upper castes is nothing short of a quiet revolution that has transformed India's former top-down elitist political system into a truly representative form of majority rule.[18]

Today neo-Tocquevilleans such as Robert Putnam (1993, 182) confidently assert that "Tocqueville was right: Democratic government is strengthened, not weakened when it faces a vigorous civil society." This is similar to what is said by radical analysts like Paulo Freire, who in his renowned *Pedagogy of the Oppressed* argues that such empowerment of civil society under majoritarian democracy would "liberate" it from its debilitating parochial identities and interests and facilitates the development of greater social cohesion and common civil consciousness and solidarity. The assumption is that as yesterday's political outsiders displace the traditional political class and turn into incumbents, they more readily use the instruments of state and the organized "power from below" to serve and protect the interests of their constituencies. Liberated from its many burdens, an empowered civil society thus collaborates more effectively for mutual benefit (and overcomes collective action problems) and compels regimes to move expeditiously in promoting balanced self-reliant and sustainable development models—variously labeled "human-centered development," "participatory development," and "basic-needs development."

However, India's mobilized and empowered civil society—that ultimate agency and guarantor (in the Tocquevillean sense) of public accountability and civil probity—has on the whole failed to perform its anticipated progressive mission. To the contrary, the complicity of civil society in abetting socioeconomic inequalities and political divisions and exclusion cannot be overstated. What explains this anachronism? Neo-Tocquevilleans would no doubt stress the obvious, yet understated fact about Indian society—what Mohandas Gandhi called that "layer upon layer of inbuilt resentment, inequality and oppression"—that it is sorely lacking in what Putnam in another context has termed "social capital." That is, although India is blessed with a robust civil society and a rich and vigorous associational life, the patterns of associationism usually correlate to the narrow caste, ethnic, regional, and communal chauvinisms, including patriarchy, class domination, and other tyrannies, which have deep roots in civil society. These cleavages have prevented the development of the ancillary networks of civic reciprocity and engagement, or what Putnam calls "civic community" or "civicness," necessary for the articulation and aggregation of interests, effective collaboration, and good governance. Not surprisingly, despite India's resilient democratic institutions and relatively long experience with constitutionalism, political participation (especially voting) continues to be a collective behavior rather than the exercise of individual choice as envisioned by liberal theory. Thus, to the neo-Tocquevilleans, the shallowness of social capital has prevented the representatives of the state and civil society to create forums in and through which they can identify and agree to common goals.[19]

However, this study will argue that neo-Tocquevilleans only provide part of the answer. It was Samuel Huntington (1968) who long ago recognized that societies with highly active and mobilized publics and low levels of political institutionalization often degenerate into instability, disorder, and violence.[20] In India, the high levels of political mobilization in the absence of a strong and responsive state and political parties have served to fragment rather than unite society. Instead of responding to the demands of an increasingly mobilized population, the country's weak political institutions have reinforced, it not exacerbated, socioeconomic and political cleavages. Given this unpropitious social reality, the efforts of so many voluntary associations and nongovernmental organizations to build durable and inclusive, representative institutions that would enable those who share common interests to unite politically and pursue collective interests have not been very successful. The record is unequivocal: the resilience and manipulation of the pernicious sensibilities based on idiosyncratic conceptions of class, caste, kin, community, region, and religion, combined with weak political institutions, have worked in tandem to undermine the ability of the state and civil society to act as constituent parts of a common civic realm or public sphere.

India's democratic renaissance, therefore, has a dark side. Even though the new political awakening has provided unprecedented opportunities for a diverse society once tightly regulated and governed by Westernized political elites and by the strict rules and taboos of Brahminic Hinduism to explore its multifaceted and checkered histories, the problem is that the society seems to have become prisoners of its own discursive frameworks and narrative accounts. The nostalgia for the "politics of identity" has spawned controversial and acerbic "inventions of traditions" and "imagined communities"; it has reawakened and incited parochial emotions and pitched these "communities" against each other, especially in the Hindi-speaking northern and central states. Mirroring this jaundiced social reality, political party competition has increased along caste, religious-communal, and ethnic-regional lines, with such loyalties the most significant determinant of electoral outcomes.[21] Not surprisingly, political parties of all stripes today place partisan interests above the public good, often pathetically outbidding each other (through promises of costly state entitlements and other guarantees), to consolidate their base and garner new support. The trend is unambiguous: the response of the upper castes (which constitute between 20 to 25 percent of the population), including sections of the traditionally stoic business and commercial elites, has been to gravitate toward the formerly obscure pro-Hindu nationalist Bharatiya Janata Party (BJP), whose commitment to "good governance" and "traditional values," not to mention its goal of transforming India into an ascetic and disciplined Hindu nation state, has struck a particular chord with the "besieged" upper castes and the propertied classes, especially in the Hindi-speaking heartland.[22] On the other hand, while the secular or "modernist" Indians who fear the BJP's capricious *Hindutva* or militant Hindu nationalism continue to cling to the incorrigibly "top-down" Congress Party, the latter party's traditional Muslims and "backward caste" and *dalit* "vote banks" have long shifted their allegiance away from it because it is widely perceived as a decrepit and corrupt party. The Congress Party's secular credentials have become badly tainted by its short-term political expediency and ingenious reliance on the "communal card" to garner electoral support. The heterogeneous, vertically segmented low castes and classes, unified largely in their desire to settle scores with their former upper-caste "masters," suffer from many internal contradictions that have made common cause extraordinarily difficult.

Low-caste politics exhibit what Lloyd and Susanne Rudolph (1987) have termed "involuted pluralism." As noted, the OBCs are deeply fragmented and face serious collective-action problems. Indeed, in their strident campaigns against the *manuvadis,* or upper-caste pieties and exploitations, the low-caste political "nomenklatura" rarely invokes universal principles of rights and justice. Instead of demanding that the state accord universal rights, protections, and provisions to all its citizens, especially the "weaker sections," members of the nomenklatura often insist that their particular "communities" and groups are most deserving of state entitlements, be they "caste reservations" or other special benefits. As a result, the various constituents of the erstwhile lower castes, are engaged in the perverse game of pursuing and jealously guarding their own prerogatives and narrow sectarian interests. The immediate pursuit of parochial interests have further weakened the already fragile social and political institutions that can mediate and assist in the reconciliation of particularistic demands. Not surprisingly, such an environment has produced a motley array of mediocre quasi-autonomous and self-serving regional chieftains, machine politicians, political fixers (including criminal gangs of *goonda*s and *dacoit*s), local power brokers, and political freelancers. These leaders typically pose as the embodiment or savior of their "communities," promising to sweep away the detritus of the past and usher in a new order. Yet, unchecked by institutional constraints, they enjoy broad discretionary powers. These political operators are willing to circumvent the institutional-legal procedures and, if need be, maliciously engage in political demagoguery to inflame their communities' and clients' sectarian and factional sentiments. It is important to reiterate that social pluralism is not necessarily antithetical to the formation of an inclusive political community and a generalized public sphere, but in contemporary India weak political institutions and chauvinistic politics have engendered societal fragmentation and alienation rather than integration.

Ironically, from the start, the Indian state became an unwitting accomplice in creating and reinforcing particularistic caste-based identities at the expense of common or "national" citizenship. In its effort to correct the systematic injustices and deprivations suffered by the low castes and other underprivileged communities, the constitution abolished "untouchability" and outlawed discrimination on the basis of caste and religion. The first amendment of the constitution (which became law in 1951) also introduced a wide array of compensatory discrimination programs (India's version of affirmative action) by "reserving" 22.5 percent of all central government employment for individuals belonging to scheduled castes and tribes.[23] Similar reservations were made for admissions in educational institutions, including provisions for privileged access to public entitlements. Over time these reservations have been extended to the OBCs. In the 1980 report of the Backward Classes Commission (also know as the Mandal Commission), chaired by B. P. Mandal, a former chief minister of Bihar and a member of a backward caste, recommended an even wider ranging compensatory discrimination program for 52 percent of the population, including Muslims, classified as "backward." The report's recommendations included that 27 percent of all posts under the central and state governments, and 27 percent of all spaces in government universities and affiliated colleges, should be reserved for the 3,743 castes and subcastes identified as backward. For over a decade this report lay shelved. In 1990 the new OBC-dominated Janata Dal coalition government under then–Prime Minister V. P. Singh announced its intention to implement the commission's recommendations.[24] The decision aroused strong passions, convulsed Indian society (including self-immolations by higher caste students), fueled localized "caste wars," and was instrumental in causing the government's downfall. While implementation was stayed by the Supreme Court, pending a ruling on the constitutionality of the measure, no political party has publicly opposed "reservations" since none wants to alienate itself from the large "backward caste" base. In 1991 the newly elected Congress Party under Prime Minister P. V. Narasimha Rao sought to mollify opposition to the reservations issue by adding a 10 percent reservation for the poor of the higher castes. In November 1992 the Supreme Court upheld the reservation for OBCs, with the vague provision that it be "need based," but struck down the additional 10 percent as constitutionally impermissible. Such public policies and decisions have only served to sharpen caste enmities.

In fact—in what has become a classic case of how noble intentions can turn sour—as the contest over these prized state entitlements intensified, a host of political entrepreneurs has emerged to attempt to corner as much of the largesse and special privileges as possible for itself and its narrow circle of cronies. The late 1980s and onward have ushered in an era of renewed religious and communal discord and intercaste fratricide—as the juridically defined "forward" (or elite classes and castes), the scheduled castes, the "backward," the "other backward," and the "more backward" castes and classes, including the competing religious and regional-focused demand groups, fiercely contested every scrap of the state's largesse. Indian society and polity, it seemed, had been irreversibly re-aligned in ways that strengthened divisive caste, communal, and ethno-regional identities.

Inadvertently, the deepening of democracy has also helped to fragment and debilitate the functioning of the federated Indian polity. This polity is a rather loosely structured and shaky postcolonial colossus stretching all the way from the political center in New Delhi,[25] to the two dozen or so provincial or "state" capitals, and eventually to a Byzantine-like "local government" divided into a complex pyramid of "divisions," districts, sub-districts, municipalities, and finally village *panchayats*. While such multi-tiered federal authority arrangements are common to large subcontinental polities, and indeed democratic conflict management necessitates a sub-stantive distribution of powers between the center and the periphery, India's governing arrangements have shown marked tendencies toward ei-ther overcentralization or overdevolution. This is in spite of the repeated attempts by the central political elites to consolidate and centralize power by bringing into play the full range of unitary powers provided in the con-stitution of India. It is enough to note that such efforts have not been very successful. Thus, contrary to the prevailing assumptions of scholarship that stress the apparent monolithic centralized character of the Indian fed-eral state, the fact is that the Indian state containing numerous shifting, cross-cutting, competitive (and often hostile) centers of power have oscil-lated between excessive centralization to overdecentralization and unin-stitutionalized devolution. The trend in recent decades has been decisively toward devolution.[26] In other words, finding that balance—what the report of the Sarkaria Commission on Center-State Relations called "cooperative federalism" with a much stronger center—has been elusive in India.[27]

Today, half a century after its inception, the Indian state mirrors the complex troubles and vicissitudes of its society. It metaphorically and liter-ally resembles a haphazardly assembled and fragmented network of intricate horizontal and vertical power centers with broad areas of ambiguous au-thority, which it shares with the discrete and relatively autonomous array of interests ambivalently dispersed among labyrinthine branches of the polity and society. Viewed in this context, India's democratic state exhibits what Naomi Chazan and Donald Rothchild (1987) in another context described as "varying degrees of stateness." Around the "core power center" with its sup-posedly higher degree of political-administrative institutionalization and bureaucratic coherence (or "stateness"), the state usually looks authoritative (if not imperious); its pronouncements are seemingly well-calibrated, and its bureaucratic regulation and demands receiving deference, if not wary acquiescence and feigned compliance. However, beyond the political core and outside the center's realm of control (an institutional and geographical space whose internal architecture are subject to constant negotiation), the state's jurisdiction gradually diminishes and the "borders" between the state and society become ever more permeable and indistinct, with the sovereignties flowing and ebbing imperceptibly into one another. Not surprisingly, to keen observers India's federal state, unceremoniously pulled and buffeted from within by society, has become increasingly "reflexive" or lacking in autonomy and self-determination. Dominated, and in some arenas "captured," by the representation of organized, established, and emergent societal hierarchies, the state's original *raison d'être* of liberal cosmopolitism and universalism has been long eclipsed by the debilitating inertia of particularism and the parochial "postmodern" folk culture of the subcontinent.[28]

The nature, form, and structure of a country's political-administrative arrangements have important implications for governance and economic development. This study argues that India's highly segmented and fractured federal polity—with its hierarchy of quasi-autonomous and self-assertive units—though a relatively effective vehicle for maintaining order and stability, is also easily penetrable, ironically through the ballot box, by self-serving particularistic interest groups. These narrowly based class and caste groups, in the name of "group rights," have no qualms in utilizing the state's machinery to promote their particular interests and agenda—to the exclusion of others in society. This has greatly limited the state's ability to guide economic development in the manner conducive to *growth with distribution.*

Yet, a distinguished body of scholarship informs us that accommodative and consensual political parties as vehicles for the articulation, aggregation, and representation of interests have the potential to neutralize and tame the forces of social fragmentation and disorder and to invoke a sense of national pride and citizenship. India, after all, was blessed with such a "machine" political organization in the Indian National Congress (or the "Congress"). Founded in 1885 and embodying a centrist consensus, the Congress as the "dominant party" in a competitive party system since the 1920s served as the thread, or what Rajni Kothari (1970) termed the "ordering mechanism," linking the fluid and continuously shifting constellations of state and society. The prodigious "Congress system" served as an all-embracing, all-inclusive agglomeration of the major political tendencies in the country. As the leader of the party system, the Congress provided the organizational, administrative-bureaucratic, and normative linkages between the political center and the sprawling social periphery, its

14   *Development and Democracy in India*

centrist consensus bringing a measure of coherence and stability to an otherwise fragmented continental polity and society.

Although the Congress never won an absolute majority of the popular vote, India's system of plurality elections in single-member districts enabled the party to win consistently large parliamentary majorities, especially during the first two and half decades following independence. This allowed the party to rule continuously at the center and in most states for all but seven years since independence.[29] The Congress Party's unquestioned dominance in the first two and half decades after independence rested in part on the prestige it retained as the nation's premier nationalist organization; in part on the formidable administrative-organizational capacity of the local, state, and national-level Congress committees; and partly on the intricate patron-client networks and alliances (both within the party and between party factions and nonparty interest groups) that stretched from New Delhi all the way to the tens of thousands of rural hamlets and villages throughout India. These tacit linkages and alliances with the competing constituencies facilitated negotiation and accommodation, and provided the party the capacity to maintain stable majority coalitions and, indeed, relatively effective democratic governance. However, unlike some of the other "one-party dominant systems" such as Mexico's Partido Revolucionario Institucional, Indonesia's GOLKAR, Singapore's People's Action Party, and Malaysia's UMNO, which by virtue of their command of a quasi-democratic electoral system or via administrative fiat established unchallenged and exclusive claim to governance, the one-party dominance in India reflected more the weakness of the opposition than the secure power of the Congress.[30]

The decline and systematic emasculation of the federal and coalition pillars of the venerable Congress system that began imperceptibly in the mid-1960s, gathered steam during the 1970s and 1980s, and culminated in the literal fragmentation of the Congress by the 1990s is the result of forces emanating from both the state and society.[31] These complex processes of "deinstitutionalization" and its implications will be discussed in greater detail in subsequent chapters. It is sufficient to note that the political arena has been filled by a plethora of diverse and assertive political parties—a total of twenty-eight in the Lok Sabha (House of the People, the lower house of the national Parliament) in 1997—including the emasculated Congress,[32] the emergent Hindu nationalist BJP, a coalition of some fourteen explicitly regional and caste-based (including left-leaning) parties forming the United Front,[33] and an equal number of smaller and stridently communal, caste-based, and religious revivalist parties. Indeed, the failure of coherent and inclusive political parties to emerge and fill the political vacuum (by aggregating interests broadly across social groups and political issues) has greatly compounded India's problems of governability and development, especially reformist and distributive development.

While the eclipse of the Congress hegemony has made the national parliament and some two dozen state assemblies more pluralistic and representative of the diversity and numerous cleavages in Indian society, it has also raised enormous challenges for India's political and economic development. The devolution of power and resources to the states, districts, and "local communities," however salutary, does not ensure efficacious democratic governance and programmatic national development. The current wave of devolution or decentralization taking place amid institutional fragmentation and politics based on shifting alliances, splits, mergers, and unstable and precarious political coalitions (even as devolution corrects the excessive centralization of the past two decades) does not portend well for efficacious governance and national development—especially reformist and distributive development. Specifically, contrary to the facile equations of decentralization with participatory governance, the decentralization and devolution of power from the national to the provincial and local levels have hardly brought the government any closer to the people or improved the quality of government and governance. No doubt, while the fragmentation and devolution of power away from New Delhi have empowered myriad constituencies to frustrate and constrain the state's arbitrary prerogatives by simultaneously pursuing what Albert Hirschman (1970) has termed "exit, voice and loyalty," such fragmentation and devolution have also provided greater rent-seeking opportunities to the established and emergent sovereignties, as well as enabling them to devise a repertoire of stratagems to modify and delay, if not surreptitiously jettison, the state's "unfavorable" reformist and distributive measures. More than ever, crucial decisions regarding the allocation of resources at all levels of the polity are heavily influenced by political considerations rather than sound technical and developmental criteria. With considerable fanfare, politicians of all hues make regular visits to their constituencies to inaugurate projects as well as to receive petitions for new ones. Ruling parties routinely, and often with reckless candor, distribute government resources and perquisites to reward supporters and supplicants and create new bases of support while running roughshod over the opposition, including withholding resources from opposition supporters and perceived and real "hostile" groups and communities. Such a system has accentuated deep-seated communal and caste allegiances and antagonisms and has led to widespread graft and corruption, with little resources left over for meaningful human development.

Given the prevailing patterns of state-society relations, how can India resolve its pervasive developmental dilemma? Observers are engaged in animated debate, but there is little scholarly agreement on what constitutes a feasible "political economy of development." In contrast to the neoliberal vision of a minimalist government, the statist models of a developmental state (an archetype derived from the once high-performing East

Asian economies), and antistatist and "prosubaltern" models propagated by the "anarcho-communitarians,"[34] this study argues that the resuscitation of public institutions and the renegotiation of state-society relations—in essence building a democratic developmental state—is an imperative for India.

Methodology, Sources, and Data

In piecing together the following narrative, I have tried my best to account for the great variety of circumstances that may have influenced political and socioeconomic change in rural India. Clearly the enormous geographical, climatic, and agronomic variations; historical experiences; external linkages; and localist norms and values are important to any explanation of change. While these are taken into account to some extent, this study examines the process of change with a specific theme in mind: namely, how the complex interactions between a democratic polity and traditional rural society have influenced and shaped the patterns of socioeconomic and political change in the Indian countryside.

Among developing countries India has the longest series of national household surveys suitable for tracking living conditions of the poor. The thirty-five national surveys (known as the *NSS* or *National Sample Survey*), spanning the years from 1951 to 1994, provide reasonably representative data on household consumption that are also roughly comparable over time because the basic survey method has changed very little. Moreover, basic national (or All-India), state, and district diachronic and longitudinal data on such important indices as land holdings, land use, cropping patterns, size-productivity relations in agriculture, consumer expenditure or wealth among different classes of households, the incidence of poverty, and living conditions are available in various issues of *The Statistical Abstract of India, The Basic Statistics Relating to the Indian Economy, Economic Survey of India,* and *The Agricultural Prices Commission.*

However, macrodata have their limitations. For example, the *Land-Holdings Survey* of the *NSS* gives aggregative estimates on the distribution of operational holdings, but reliable data on landownership (which are far more concentrated than operational units), the extent of tenancy, and lease contracts between landowners and tenants are frequently not available. This is to be expected because the terms of tenancy, and even their legality, are regulated throughout India, thus leading to widespread concealment. Similarly, the *Rural Credit* (or *The Debt and Investment*) *Surveys* of the Reserve Bank give estimates of borrowing by various rural groups, but they do not indicate how such patterns interact with the wider rural economy. Also, macrosurveys are often of variable quality—inconsistent in terms of sampling design and field methodologies, thereby making comparisons difficult. Suffice to say, a reasonable margin of error must be allowed when using such sources. To complement and cross-check the gaps in the macrodata, this study will use the detailed information on the rural economy and society from a wide range of monographs and ethnographic materials. India has a rich tradition of "village studies" (dating to the early part of this century), and over the years the countryside has provided scholars with a mother lode for research. These studies employ a whole range of methodologies and are of extremely high caliber, capturing with sensitivity and in fine detail the rich textures of rural life. Beyond this, and perhaps most important, a number of these studies, by working within a broadly similar framework and focusing on common sets of questions, permit us to make reasonably confident inferences about macro and micropatterns of change in the Indian countryside during the past five decades.

Yet, this mountain of data was not sufficient. I soon realized that "fieldwork" was a must if I was to better understand rural society and its contradictory discourses and how the "local" and peripheral articulated with the "national" or the center. However, what I initially envisioned as a short stay became extended stays stretching over a decade in several districts. I draw readily on the empirical materials painstakingly collected during my field research in several selected villages in the states of Haryana, Uttar Pradesh, Bihar, and Rajasthan, first during the summer of 1988 and again during each of the summers of 1991–1997. The fieldwork was not meant to be exhaustive. Rather, the purpose was to better understand how state-society interactions have influenced and shaped the patterns of change at the "micro," or village, and district level. Aside from conducting extensive economic and political profiling of three villages, I also collected information through structured and unstructured interviews with members of both the state and civil society. Those interviewed included senior politicians, public officials, and bureaucrats from various levels of the government; social activists; landlords; rich peasants; and the "subaltern" (the ordinary Indian peasant). The consideration of insights gleaned from their voices together with the "hard data" has helped me better understand the vicissitudes of rural development and the changing relations between the state and society. Indeed, during this fieldwork, as I crisscrossed the varied Indian landscape from one dilapidated village to the next—from the flat, barren, saltpeter-encrusted plains of Champaran, Ballia, Deoria, Gorakhpur, Basti, and Gonda districts of Bihar and eastern Uttar Pradesh to the lush green and prosperous sugar, rice, and wheat belts of Aligarh, Bulandshahr, Muzaffarnagar, Ghaziabad, Meerut, and Rhotak districts of western Uttar Pradesh and Haryana states—I was introduced to a vast network of social relations that helped me better perceive the economic and political impulses of rural society and the forces that helped to give it shape. I listened to national and local politicians and senior government officials who spoke enthusiastically of the state's achievements in agricultural modernization and poverty-alleviation, and who eagerly showed me the state's "continuing initiatives" in irrigation, transportation, and rural "uplift." I heard the unassuming and cynical peasants who, over countless cups of tea, "reconstructed" the past they had a part in creating and changing, and who spoke so eloquently of their current predicaments and their hopes for the future. All the interviews enabled me to piece together a more coherent picture of the nature of changes that had taken place in rural social and economic structure, as well as the changes in the power configurations among the state, the rural elites, and the various strata of the peasantry. Such close experience with daily reality allowed me to better understand the complex workings of the state; its multifaceted structures, roles, and capacities; and the impact of state penetration into the countryside; as well as to observe the new structural linkages or the terms of coexistence, compromise, and cooperation worked out between the rural society and the democratic state. I became more aware of how these established and emergent hierarchies demanded and received compliance as well as complicity, and why some voices and agendas prevailed while others were ignored or silenced. I could better understand the helplessness and the frustrations of the *majdoors,* that teeming mass of humanity that lived on the fringes of the village, and why their valiant efforts to create protective shells against the demands of the hierarchies were so often unsuccessful. These insights and more that I learned during field research cannot be easily quantified, but as the following pages illustrate they are crucial to the understanding of social change.

Organization of the Study

The book is chronologically organized into seven chapters. Chapter 1 provides a selected review of the voluminous comparative literature on the relationship between "democracy and development" as well as the more general literature on the "political economy of development." The aim is twofold. First, the chapter documents the nature and extent of the poverty problem in India and raises empirical and methodological questions regarding the validity of the conventional view that maintains that rapid economic growth will *ceteris paribus* trickle down and reduce socioeconomic inequalities. Second, the chapter illustrates that much of the literature on "democracy and development" has tended to overlook the role of civil society in multinational states and how the governing arrangements in a democracy affect governance and economic development. Also, it further elaborates the analysis and arguments made in the introduction: that India's developmental record cannot be fully understood without factoring in the legacies of the country's federal-political arrangements, especially how vested and ascendant groups in civil society have bent these arrangements to their advantage.

Chapter 2 examines the evolution and nature of India's democratic polity. Drawing on comparative-historiographical sources it outlines plausible links between the past and present, illustrating the contingent nature of state building in the immediate postindependence period and why such building was overwhelmed in the face of political activism.

Chapters 3 through 7 provide the empirical base to the conceptual framework examining the Indian state's developmental policies and the policymaking process, including the intent of these policies, the problems encountered in implementing them, and the impact of these "policy packages" on the political economy of rural India. Cumulatively, these chapters provide the context in which to explain and evaluate the successes, failures, and mixed legacies of the state's approach to rural development.

Specifically, Chapter 3 examines the Indian state's first major rural reform and distributive program: land and tenure reforms. The issues addressed include why the Indian state opted for such a strategy, how one explains the huge discrepancy between policy intentions and actual outcomes, what effects these measures had on the rural political economy and society, and how the democratic state, its autonomy, and its imperatives were transformed by its own policies and interactions with rural society. Chapter 4 examines the origins and content of the Indian government's second major rural development initiative, the "green revolution" strategy introduced with much fanfare in the mid-1960s, and looks at the nature and extent of state "capacity and autonomy" and the processes of policymaking within a democratic regime, in particular, the role of the emergent political-technocratic elite in engineering the "policy shift." The chapter demonstrates that India's segmented state allowed for a high degree of policymaking autonomy at the highest levels of government and the sharp policy shift because India's policies and programs were compatible with the interests of the powerful political and economic interests. Chapter 5 examines the nature and impact of the green revolution strategy on the political economy of the countryside. The juxtaposition of macro or national empirical trends with the richly textured micro or village case studies vividly illustrates (1) the ways the green revolution has had an impact on the social fabric of rural society and (2) the contradictions of the green revolution—its fundamental failure to reconcile growth with redistribution having aggravated deep-seated tensions in the rural political economy and creating new pressures and challenges for the state. Chapter 6 elaborates the nature and dynamics of these growing pressures and challenges, its political ramifications and the state's response. It outlines how the growing power of the "new agrarianism" or the political mobilization of the ascendant rural caste and class configurations has systematically undermined the reformist and distributive capacities of an already weak state. Chapter 7 provides a comparative analysis of India's political economy from the mid-1980s to the economic liberalization period beginning in 1991 and beyond. It asks what explains why economic liberalization in India has been accompanied by growing economic inequalities, social dislocation, and heightened poverty levels. Contrary to the conventional wisdom, this chapter argues that democracies are not inherently incapable of mitigating or modifying neoliberalism's strict market logic in order to ensure that the fruits of the marketplace are more equitably shared. In further underscoring the core conceptual argument of this study, Chapter 7 argues that the failure to ameliorate the social costs of reform in India lies in the weak and fragmented administrative and institutional capacities of the country's democratic regime and not in democratic governance per se. India's weakness is vividly manifest when compared with the "embedded autonomy"[35] or the remarkable institutional capacities and the developmental resolve of Chile's new democracy or the *concertación* under Patricio Aylwin (1990– 1994) and Eduardo Frei (1994–1997). In fact, the empirical evidence from postauthoritarian Chile (1990–1997) not only compellingly illustrates that democracies can complement neoliberalism with meaningful reformist and distributive programs, but also that *politics matter.* For India and a host of new and transitional democracies the message is clear—building and reinvigorating the state's administrative and institutional capacities are fundamental to resolving the economic challenges.

Notes

1. The selected speeches of Jawaharlal Nehru are reprinted in Gopal (1980, 76–77). An extensive coverage is available in Nehru (1948; 1958).

2. The Constitution of India draws extensively from the British and U.S. legal-judicial traditions in its outline of the principles of liberal democracy. Adopted in 1950, it is among the longest constitutions in the world, with 395 articles and 10 appendixes (known as schedules). It is also the most frequently amended constitution in the world—as of June 1995 it had been amended seventy-seven times. However, according to the noted constitutional scholar Granville Austin (1966, 50–52), what differentiates the Indian Constitution from its western counterparts is that "the Indian constitution is first and foremost a social document . . . that has provided much impetus toward changing and rebuilding society for the common good." The core of its commitment to a fundamental change in the social order lies in the sections on fundamental rights and the directive principles of state policy. The fundamental rights guarantee to each citizen basic substantive and procedural protections. The directive principles instruct the state to promote the welfare of the people by securing and promoting as effectively as possible a social order in which socioeconomic and political justice "shall inform all the institutions of national life." However, the precepts of the directive principles are not justiciable—that is, they are not enforceable by a court as are the fundamental rights. These themes will be discussed in detail later.

3. Quoted in Karanjia (1960, 100–101), the idea of a "third way" goes back to Mohandas Gandhi. By the early 1940s the national leadership had a well-articulated conceptualization of the "third way": specifically that "our aim should be to evolve a political system which will combine efficiency of administration with individual liberty and an economic structure which will yield maximum production

without the concentration of private monopolies and the concentration of wealth and which will create the proper balance between urban and rural economies. Such a social structure can provide an alternative to the acquisitive economy of private capitalism and regimentation of a totalitarian state." This was the first official statement by the national leadership regarding independent India's political objectives and economic program. See Indian National Congress, All-India Congress Committee (1954, 18).

4. The term "socialistic pattern of society" is a rather nebulous concept, which has never been rigidly defined. It seems to embrace a mild degree of Marxism and Gandhism, including an emphasis on nonviolent means of creating a welfare state (Iyer 1993, 375–392).

5. In his insightful study, James C. Scott (1998, 2) documents that more often than not the state's "well-intentioned plans for improving the human condition go tragically awry."

6. Concepts of poverty are subject to various interpretations. Generally, both absolute and relative deprivation are essential variables in understanding the poverty problem. Absolute deprivation relates to the denial of basic needs, relative deprivation to interpersonal gaps in the income distribution in the poor country and to international gaps in the income distribution. These issues are discussed in detail in the next chapter.

7. Following Collier and Collier (1991, 27), "critical junctures may involve a relatively brief period in which one direction or another is taken or an extended period of reorientation."

8. An outline of this approach is outlined in Shue (1988) and in Migdal, Kohli, and Shue (1994).

9. With a GNP per capita at US$320 (1994 dollars), India is identified as a "low-income economy" by the World Bank's *World Development Report 1996* (1996, 188).

10. Such claims have long been promoted by the World Bank in its *India: Achievements and Challenges in Reducing Poverty* (1997).

11. In India "communal" refers to religious, principally Hindu-Muslim, conflict.

12. Frederic Wakeman (1975) provides a useful corrective to the literature that tends to view state-society interactions as a zero-sum game. Using illustration from imperial China, Wakeman shows that even as autocratic states seek full fiscal and coercive power over the countryside, rural society—sometimes representing community interests, sometimes pursuing its own gain—seeks to check the state's intrusion. The tension between integration into the imperial system and seeking autonomy from it is what Wakeman calls "dynamic oscillation." Also see Skocpol (1979) and Shue (1988).

13. Stephan Haggard and Chung In Moon (1983), writing in the context of South Korea, provide a thoughtful clarity. State autonomy refers to the autonomy of the state from not only society in general, but especially from the dominant socioeconomic groups, including the giant conglomerates or *chaebol*. State capacity refers to the state's ability to formulate and implement economic plans, particularly its ability to impose its policy priorities on the dominant socioeconomic groups.

14. During every election, however, there are reported cases of irregularities such as intimidation, "booth capturing," and violence.

15. The term "backward castes" (also referred to in the 1950 constitution as "other backward classes" [OBCs]) is used to refer to an inchoate range of *shudra* subcastes of intermediate ritual status in the Hindu caste hierarchy between the elite upper or "forward castes" and lower "scheduled castes" (SCs) (consisting of

the erstwhile *harijans* or "untouchables" or *dalits*) and the scheduled tribes (STs). The *shudras* are the most numerous, accounting for a majority of Hindus in all regions. The Indian constitution recognizes the "backwards" and the SC/STs as "disadvantaged lower castes" or "weaker sections" and has allowed such remedial solutions as reserving for these groups legislative seats, government posts, and places in educational institutions. But it is important to note that the low castes are not a monolithic group. Divided into literally thousands of cognate *jatis* (or subcastes), they, like the upper castes, are governed by strict rules of endogamy and other rituals and taboos.

16. The *dalits* or the "untouchables" in the Hindu caste order are referred in the officialese as "scheduled castes." They represent the most exploited and the poorest sectors in society.

17. The Bahujan Samaj Party (BSP) is a relatively new arrival in Uttar Pradesh party politics. Launched in 1984, and drawing inspiration from the legacy of *harijan* leader B. R. Ambedkar, the BSP represents the most recent organizational expression of the SCs. The arrival of the BSP as a significant political force in Uttar Pradesh politics was confirmed by the advances it made in state assembly elections. In the 1985 elections it took only 2.5 percent of the vote, but in a series of by-elections held in March 1987, it polled some 25 percent of the vote. By the time of the 1989 elections, the BSP had built an organizational structure across the state and stood in contest in all but thirteen Lok Sabha seats.

18. For a detailed analysis across regions of the emergence of the other backward castes as a political coalition, see Frankel and Rao (1989; 1990).

19. Social capital refers to the institutions, relationships, and norms that shape and determine a society's social interactions. These issues are discussed further in Chapter 1.

20. As Samuel Huntington (1968, 82–83) succinctly notes, a well-ordered civic polity requires "a recognizable and stable pattern of institutional authority . . . political institutions [must be] sufficiently strong to provide the basis of a legitimate political order and working political community."

21. The Hindi satirist Harishankar Parsai captured this reality in a telling literary piece. He claimed that he had convinced Lord Krishna to contest a seat in the state assembly. He writes, "We talked to some people active in politics. They said, 'Of course. Why shouldn't you? If you won't run in the election, who will? After all, you are a Yadav [a dominant OBC], aren't you?' Krishna said, 'I am God, I don't have a caste.' They said, 'Look sir, being God won't do you any good around these parts. No one will vote for you. How do you expect to win if you don't maintain your caste?'"

22. While the Hindus of the upper castes were gradually eased out of political power in the major southern states in the 1960s and 1970s, this process did not take place in the Hindi-speaking heartland until the 1980s. Squeezed by the assertiveness of the lower castes, the upper castes, traditionally supporters of the Congress, have flocked to the Bharatiya Janata Party (BJP) because it is widely perceived as the true protector of their interests. The BJP also provides therapeutic support to the besieged upper castes. It is important to note that the BJP is part of a larger "Hindu family." The parent organization, the Rashtriya Swayamsevak Sangh (RSS), founded in 1925, stands for the consolidation of all Hindus into a united community. The main goal of the BJP, the RSS's political arm, is to unite Hindus politically to achieve national power and to transform India into a Hindu nation-state. The Vishwa Hindu Parishad (VHP) is involved in mass-mobilization activities, while the Bajrang Dal serves as the armed wing—often using violence and intimidation against opponents.

23. Comparable reservations for the SC/STs was also made by state governments.

24. Singh declared that the implementation of the reservations was to correct social injustices, but his political opponents saw it as a cynical move to shore up his support among the backward castes.

25. The government of India is referred to variously as the center, the central government, the federal government, and the union government. Details will be outlined in Chapter 1.

26. As early as the 1960s, Myron Weiner (1968, 58) aptly noted that "it is most unlikely that the center will be able to take power away from the states. Indeed, the trend has been just the reverse: the states have tended to become politically more autonomous and to accept central rule reluctantly."

27. The Sarkaria Commission was set up by Indira Gandhi in 1983 under the chairmanship of retired Supreme Court judge, R. S. Sarkaria. The report recommended "cooperative federalism" in favor of a stronger center.

28. The census of India regards most settlements of fewer than 5,000 inhabitants as a village. Some three-fourths of Indians live in approximately 550,000 villages.

29. The Congress was in power at the center from independence in August 1947 to March 1977, from May 1980 to November 1989, and from June 1991 to May 1996. Its share of the vote has declined steadily from around 47.8 percent at its peak in 1957 to 37.6 percent in 1991, barring the unusual "sympathy vote" of 48.1 percent in 1984 after Indira Gandhi's assassination. It is important to note that in India's first-past-the-post electoral system, elections do not yield representation in proportion to votes received; rather, a candidate wins by obtaining the greatest plurality of votes, not necessarily the majority of votes. Hence, 40 to 50 percent of the popular vote can produce legislative majorities of 60 to 75 percent in Parliament, plus polls can result in a large majority of seats, especially if political parties divide constituencies among themselves, as they often do, rather than compete with each other directly. For example, in the years of Congress dominance, from 1947 to 1967, when the Congress held more than 70 percent of the seats in parliament, it never received more than 50 percent of the vote in parliamentary, or in aggregate, in state assembly elections.

30. In other words, the Congress's "dominance" depended on the outcome of an open first-past-the-post multiparty electoral system.

31. A more comprehensive examination of the factors responsible for the decline of the Congress system is discussed later. Suffice it to say that there are competing explanations. Some have blamed Mrs. Gandhi's "authoritarian personality" for the decline (Rudolph and Rudolph 1987). Others see it as the result of expanding electorate, the growing political activism among formerly acquiescent groups, and the rise of nationalist regional parties. Still others emphasize the inherently pluralistic and decentralizing tendencies in India's democracy. For details see Kohli (1988; 1990).

32. The Congress Party's share of the popular vote shrank from 36 percent in the 1991 election to 28 percent in the 1996 general election. Under the first-past-the-post electoral system, this decline of 8 percent in the popular vote reduced the Congress Party's parliamentary presence from that of a majority party to a minority party. This electoral system gave the rightist Hindu BJP the most seats in Parliament, even though it won only 25 percent of the vote.

33. The United Front formed the national government following the 1996 elections. Its support depended on the "Federal Front," a group of regional parties. Not surprisingly, the United Front's "Common Minimum Program" favored further devolution of power from the center to the states.

34. This is a label first used by Pranab Bardhan (1996) to describe India's left-leaning intellectuals and activists.

35. According to Peter Evans (1995), who first coined the term, states with embedded autonomy are those with coherent internal organization and close links with society.

1

Democracy and Development: The State-Society Approach

What seemed important was not so much which of the dozens of political parties was up or down, or which local candidate from the 15,000 running across India was likely to win. What permeated the mood was something as old as independent India itself—the sheer pleasure of taking part in a basic democratic rite, the business of appointing and dismissing governments, that has survived all of the disappointments that Indians have endured in the past half-century. In a troubled land, democracy means there is hope.

—*New York Times,* 18 April 1996

In few countries of the developing world has the impact of the state on agricultural modernization been as pervasive as in India. Since independence, India's democratic state has intervened extensively in the countryside with a plethora of policy packages aimed at promoting rural development, advancing social justice, and improving the living standards of the vast majority of the its inhabitants—known in official parlance as the "weaker sections of society."[1]

However, the achievements of some five decades of democratically planned economic development fall far short of the goals and aspirations.[2] While the state in its ongoing role as modernizer, intervenor, and mediator has acquired an extensive administrative and institutional presence in the countryside, it has demonstrated a remarkable weakness in implementing its own proclaimed policy goals, especially reformist and distributive goals. For example, land and tenure reforms that have been continuously on the government's agenda since independence have not led to any meaningful redistribution of land to the tillers. Similarly, the wealth generated in the agricultural sector through the extension of generous state subsidies and price supports, and the increased profitability of agriculture as a result of biological and technological innovations (i.e., the "green revolution" inputs), have disproportionately benefited the already well off, with little perceptible gain in the income and living standards of the majority of rural households. On balance, the fruits of economic growth have not "trickled down" to the poor. Instead of mitigating the extent and incidence of rural poverty by providing security of tenure to small and marginal cultivators and improved employment and wage conditions for the landless, state policies designed to promote agricultural and rural development have often further exacerbated socioeconomic inequalities in the countryside.

Moreover, respectable average annual economic growth rates of 3.5 percent between 1950 and 1975, over 5 percent in the period from 1975 to 1990, and over 6 percent since fiscal 1992,[3] and an increase in food grain production at the unprecedented annual growth rate of around 2.9 percent over the period 1950 to 1990—which has given India self-sufficiency in per capita food production (with current public stocks of over 30 million tons of food grain)—have not led to any perceptible improvement in the consumption patterns (or caloric intake) of the urban and rural poor. In fact, net aggregate consumption of food per head has remained remarkably constant since 1950.[4] Mukesh Eswaran and Ashok Kotwal (1994) note that this is due in part to growing income inequalities and the constrained purchasing power of the poor. The most recent available figures (for 1991/92) indicate that the top 20 percent of Indian households have a share of more than 40 percent of the total consumption expenditure (i.e., income minus saving), the top 10 percent have a share of over 27 percent. On the other hand, the share of the bottom 40 percent of households is about 20.4 percent, with the lowest 20 percent having a share of only 8.1 percent (World Bank 1996, 196). The distribution of income is even more skewed than that of consumption expenditure. As a result, the poorest in India are exceedingly poor.[5] All-India estimates indicate that the rural poor spend anywhere between 70 to 80 percent of their total income on basic food items and that about 48.4 percent of the rural population (roughly 300 to 320 million people) live under conditions of poverty because they do not have access to what Amartya Sen (1981) has called "basic entitlements" or an income that would cover their "subsistence minimum" daily caloric and nutritional requirements of 2,050 calories per adult per day. On the basis of the trend in per capita consumption of food grains, Sen creatively demonstrates how economic growth (measured on the basis of income) has failed to trickle down to the poor. He notes that although the demand for luxury goods, in particular Western-made high-value consumer products, is the fastest growing sector in the Indian economy, the rate of growth of food grain consumption (including consumption of coarse grains such as sorghum and millet—the principal item in the poor's budget) increased from only 181.8 kilograms a year to 185.2 kilograms a year between 1954–1958 and 1976–1985, a trivial increase over a twenty-five-year period. This suggests in a compelling way that the income gains from economic development are accruing to the top 20 percent of households, while the poor lack incomes to purchase even basic food grains despite the growing accumulation of grain stocks.[6] One of the cruel ironies of development in India has been that even some of the more ostensible measures adopted by the central and state governments to alleviate poverty through direct redistribution of land, assets, or income, and through the creation of state subsidized "self-help" programs and employment schemes, have at best been slow and piecemeal in their implementation and have seldom reached their target groups. These measures include the "20-point *garibi hatao*" (i.e., abolish poverty) program, the Integrated Rural Development Program, the Food for Work Program, the National Rural Employment Program, the Small Farmer Development Agency, and the Jawahar Rozgar Yojana (probably one of the world's largest antipoverty programs), and numerous other such "pro-poor" programs. It is widely recognized that such programs have been a politically attractive palliative rather than an effective solution to the problems of rural poverty and underdevelopment.

The "Poverty Problem" Debate: Nature and Extent

Despite such compelling evidence, the debate on the nature and extent of the "poverty problem" in India continues to rage. Hence an overview on this debate is necessary. According to the estimates made by the Government of India Planning Commission report (GoI 1963) of 1960/61, over 50 percent, or approximately 211 million people, were living below the poverty line in the sense they lacked the 15 rupees (Rs 15) per capita per month in the rural areas and Rs 18 per capita per month in the urban areas to maintain minimum subsistence needs. The Planning Commission report (GoI 1972) for the early 1970s revealed that the percentage of people living in poverty had remained the same, but in absolute terms their numbers had increased to over 220 million. Estimates by the Planning Commission for 1977/78 placed the proportion of the population below the poverty line in rural areas at 51 percent and in urban areas at 38 percent. These estimates were based on a poverty line of Rs 65 per capita per month (1977/78 prices) for the rural areas, corresponding to a minimum daily caloric requirements of 2,400 units per person, and Rs 75 in urban areas, corresponding to a calorie intake of 2,100 units.

However, the Planning Commission's 1983/84 report (GoI 1985), including a World Bank study *India: Poverty, Employment and Social Services* (1989a), made a startling claim about poverty trends for the 1980s. The reports contended that since the beginning of the 1980s there had been a "clear trend" toward "greater" income redistribution and that the proportion of those living below the poverty line declined significantly—according to the *Seventh Five Year Plan* (GoI 1985) from 48.3 percent in 1978 to 37.1 percent in 1984. The Planning Commission's 1993 *Report of the Expert Group on Estimation of Proportion and Number of Poor* confirmed its 1983/84 findings claiming that by the early 1990s under 30 percent of Indians were living below the poverty line.

This official claim has not gone unchallenged, resulting in heated debates and outpourings of published materials on the "poverty problem."[7] Several analysts have criticized the reports for their "exaggerated conclusions," arguing that the data have been based on the unprecedented assumption that incomes increased uniformly across all expenditure classes and on the "untenable assertion" that all families enrolled in the major antipoverty programs benefited sufficiently to cross the poverty line. Others have pointed out that the poverty ratio fluctuates and that the 1983/84 *National Sample Survey* (*NSS*) took place in an exceptionally good year for agricultural production, which largely explains the lower incidence of poverty. The critics add that at any given time poverty levels reflect the variability in individual incomes, and although the transient component may be large, there also exists a substantial core of the chronically poor that has not changed much over time. B. S. Minhas (1991, 1673) aptly notes:

> The massive reduction in the incidence of poverty in 1987–88, as reported by the Planning Commission is again largely a consequence of the peculiar statistical artifacts used by the Commission. Just as it did with the 1983 NSS data, the Planning Commission has continued to indulge in mindless tinkering with the observed NSS size distribution of consumer expenditure for 1987–88 also. Appropriately computed incidence of poverty in 1987–88 comes to about 48.7 for rural and 37.8 percent for urban India, rather than the artificially low estimate of 32.7 and 19.4 percent reported to parliament by the Planning Commission.

It should also be noted that poverty estimates by the Planning Commission and the World Bank are based on requirements of minimum caloric intake only, to the exclusion of the other basic necessities of life such as clothing, shelter, access to safe drinking water, sanitation, and health facilities. By excluding these variables the official data grossly overstate the so-called improvements—the overall percentage "decline" in poverty levels reflects not only the changes associated with measurement techniques (changes in what is considered an acceptable minimum level of consumption) but also the normal fluctuations in poverty levels between a poor person and someone who is even poorer. Granted, even though precise data on how much poverty is transient and how much is persistent are difficult to gather as poverty levels vary over time (reflecting the variability in family employment and incomes), the fact is that in India there exists a substantial core of chronic and persistent poverty.[8]

Interestingly, using three different measures of poverty—the headcount index, the poverty gap index, and the squared poverty gap index—in an attempt to capture alternative dimensions of poverty corresponding to its incidence, depth, and severity, the *NSS* for 1993/94 reported that approximately 37.0 percent of the rural and 30.5 percent of the urban populations live in poverty. The *NSS* implied a national average of 35 percent living in poverty and sharp regional disparities in poverty levels.[9] In Bihar, for example, the proportion of poor in the rural population was estimated to be 64 percent, in Uttar Pradesh 42 percent, and in the Punjab and Haryana 25 percent.[10]

Finally, a recent World Bank report (1997, iv–v) claims that some five decades of growth in India clearly refutes any presumption of "immiserizing growth"—that is, growth that tends to marginalize and impoverish large sections of the population. This report's statement that "it is only through rapid growth that India will be able to reduce poverty and generate the resources to invest in the health and education of its people" sounds rather hollow in light of the sustained economic expansion of 5 to 6 percent per year since 1992. This growth, the result of the Indian government's ambitious macroeconomic liberalization program (introduced in mid-1991) has failed to ameliorate the poverty problem. In fact, earlier World Bank studies by Gurav Datt and Martin Ravallion (1995; 1996) reported that the Indian government's stabilization and structural and reform measures have led to sharp rises in the prices of such key commodities as rice, sugar, cotton, and gasoline, hurting the poor and increasing the incidence of poverty from 36 to 41 percent of the population.[11] Contrary to such claims, Chapter 7 will document in some detail that the accelerated growth in the postliberalization period has tended to impoverished large segments of the populace and that pervasive poverty persists amid rapid economic growth.

To reiterate: the stark fact is that India's major developmental challenge, the poverty problem, has not been mitigated despite efforts by some to wish the problem away (at least statistically). According to the World Bank (1999), roughly 40.9 percent of India's population continues to live under variously drawn poverty lines, a proportion that has not changed since independence. India, the world's largest constitutional democracy, also has the dubious distinction of being the largest single-country contributor to the pool of the world's poor.[12]

Why Poverty Persists: Economic Explanations

Why is poverty so persistent in a country where "abolishing poverty" has long been the proclaimed goal of the democratic state and an indelible part of the developmental discourse? Is the problem the result of misguided and poorly implemented policies and the resultant insufficient "trickle down," or is it due to bureaucratic log rolling and incompetence? More fundamentally, is India's democratic state up to the task (i.e., does it have the capacity and resolve) of implementing its own professed reformist and distributive policies and programs? If so, how can India's national development, to reiterate Rajni Kothari's (1989, 10) poignant words, be "made just and humane . . . where each individual can achieve their true potential under the general constraints of a democratic-capitalist model of development?" These questions, which constitute the core in the study of political-economy of development have long puzzled researchers, generating a lively scholarly debate and a prodigious volume of literature. The following sections provide a brief critical review of the various perspectives.

Analyses of the poverty problem by development economists have tended to adhere to a number of competing, if not overlapping, positions.[13] According to one view the persistence of mass poverty and underdevelopment is mainly the result of rapid (and uncontrolled) demographic growth. Specifically, rapid population growth has a deleterious effect on the disadvantaged because it reduces employment opportunities and the flow of monetary benefits to the wider society. Hence, significant reduction in population growth is a prerequisite to economic development and poverty alleviation.[14] No doubt, the sheer size and rapid increases in human population in many developing countries have simply overwhelmed the employment generation and social welfare programs and exacerbated the poverty problem, but it is now widely recognized that such a narrow Malthusian hypothesis is flawed. While acknowledging that rapid population growth poses a serious constraint to development and poverty alleviation, critics argue that the negative demographic impact can be significantly reduced with greater levels of labor absorption in agriculture and by the creation of employment in the tertiary sectors of the rural and urban economy. See Bagchi (1982); Booth and Sundrum (1985); Ranis (1979).

Others have put forth the view that the problem of underdevelopment and poverty is essentially the result of low levels of economic growth, in particular, of domestic savings and investment in the developing world. For example, Simon Kuznets (1955), in his celebrated essay "Economic Growth and Income Inequality," concluded that given the close correlation between levels of industrialization, economic growth, and equity, the problem of underdevelopment and poverty is largely a sequential one. He argued that the poverty problem would automatically be alleviated over time as maturing industrialization generates increases in national productivity and incomes—a process that in turn would result in "trickle down" to the wider society. Kuznets's arguments were later elaborated by Walt W. Rostow (1962), who argued that like the industrial North the less developed nations would undergo the same sequence or "stages of economic growth"— evolving from the "low-level equilibrium trap" of traditional society to the critical "take off" stage, and then progressing under "the virtuous circle of self-sustaining growth" to "the age of high mass consumption"—as did their developed and modern Western predecessors. Rostow believed that the Indian economy, given its "healthy savings," investment, and a growing "consumer" middle class was ready for "take off." However, he cautioned that to facilitate "take off," the role of the state should be neutral and minimal (the role best performed by democracies), at best aiding the process of development by occasionally intervening to ensure social quiescence and removing the structural barriers to the percolation of self-generating wealth.[15]

To Nobel Laureate W. Arthur Lewis (1954), underdevelopment and poverty were rooted in the inherent "dualism" of developing nations' economies. Dualism, or the "Lewis two-sector model," viewed the economy of poor nations as divided into the "traditional and modern sectors." The traditional or subsistence rural sector is characterized by zero marginal labor productivity, that is, producing surplus labor that can be gradually transferred (without any loss to the agricultural sector) to the modern urban industrial sector. To Lewis, this labor transfer and the simultaneous growth of output and employment in the modern sector are key to solving the problems of poverty and underdevelopment. The Lewis development model has been criticized for its implicit assumption that the rate of labor transfer and employment creation in the modern sector is proportional to the rate of modern sector capital accumulation, and that a competitive modern sector labor market guarantees the continued existence of constant real urban wages up to the point where the supply of rural surplus labor is exhausted.[16]

Theodore Schultz (1964) provided an alternative to the Lewis model. He makes the case that labor is efficient within traditional agriculture; it is the farmers' aversion to technological innovation that explains the general failure to raise agricultural productivity. There are several reasons for this: modern agricultural technology is expensive for most farmers, the diffusion of new technology is slow given the low educational levels, and technological diffusion is often stymied by the farmers' inadequate motivation. Schultz's policy prescription was for governments to promote technical modernization of agriculture. Implicit in Schultz's arguments was the assumption that market-friendly democratic governments are the most likely to create environments where individual farmers are able to fully maximize their "economic rationality and utility."

By the late 1960s, the concerns of development economics shifted as some of the early optimism about "trickle down," "stages of growth," and the promise of the capital-centered industrial approach to development failed to materialize or produce the desired results. Some concluded that there was an inevitable trade-off between growth and equity and that the "cake" had to first grow in size before it could be better distributed. Others, however, while agreeing that higher growth rates are necessary, posited a complementarity between the twin objectives of economic development (i.e., growth and equity) because of the belief that higher equity levels actually reinforce the growth-promoting process.[17] According to those taking the latter position, the problem was not so much that the "cake" was small but that poorly conceived and haphazardly implemented policies, by squandering the fruits of economic growth, were ultimately responsible for preventing benefits from "trickling down" to the poor or the underprivileged sectors of society.[18]

Over the years a number of these scholars/policymakers, some affiliated with the World Bank and other international agencies, have put forward various policy prescriptions for reconciling "growth with distribution" in the developing world. The "solutions" have ranged from calls for a more open market (i.e., the policy of "comparative advantage") to strategies for "getting the prices right." To Robert Bates (1981) and Deepak Lal (1985) intrusive statism must give way to a wider role for markets and private entrepreneurship, freed from the depredations of rent-seeking *dirigiste* regimes of diverse ideological stripes. Moreover, cutting government spending and streamlining public agencies will promote more efficient production and distribution of collective goods. Others have argued that accelerating growth in agricultural production and productivity is the key to solving the poverty problem. For example, in the Indian case, after noting a close inverse correlation between growth in foodgrains and the incidence of poverty, these experts have claimed that the trick is to raise the growth rate of agricultural production and productivity. According to the noted economist, K. N. Raj (1973), a sustained 3.5 percent growth rate for a period of "several years" will force the trickle-down mechanism to work efficiently in Indian agriculture.[19] Hence, the proponents of this view maintain that although in the short run the reduction of poverty will depend on keeping food prices low and by generating rapid growth in rural and nonagricultural employment, the long-term solution will lie in a broad-based rural development strategy centered around market-guided and productivity-enhancing "green revolution" technology. To policy advisers like Montek Ahluwalia (1986) and John Mellor (1985; 1988) the extension of such "scale neutral" modern inputs as improved or "high-yielding" seed varieties, chemical fertilizer, irrigation, and energy as well as price, credit, and market incentives to "progressive farmers" is essential to achieving sustained agricultural growth. This growth, they add, will be followed by related spinoffs, such as secure and remunerative rural and "off-farm" employment, lower food prices, and resultant decline in poverty levels.

However, as Terence Byres (1988a) notes, the literature may analytically support the validity of "growth with distribution" and trickle-down arguments, but the empirical reality is not so clear. First, the causal relation between higher levels of agricultural growth and decreased levels of poverty is problematic, at least in the case of India. Evidence from different regions of the country shows that the skewed patterns of income distribution (that became fixed during periods of rapid growth) are extremely resistant to subsequent change. This explains why the rural poor have not benefited from a greater abundance of food—that is, the increases in grain production have not forced down the price of food, nor have they led to a significant transfer of incremental incomes that accompanied agricultural growth. Given such evidence, Atul Kohli (1987, 12) aptly notes that "the burden of proving the proposition that higher growth rates will automatically percolate down and alleviate poverty in the near future now more than ever, rests squarely on the shoulders of the believers in trickle down."[20]

There is yet another group made up of the "reform-oriented" economists, who are less sanguine about the technological and market-oriented prescriptions. They have called for the establishment of a new international economic order, with equitable participation in the world economy by the poor nations as a necessary precondition for "humane and equitable" development (Brandt Commission 1983; Gran 1983; Mahbub ul-Haq 1976). They have forcefully argued that poverty alleviation must be treated as an explicit objective of national development and that development strategies must be consciously structured to achieve this objective. For example, Paul Streeten (1981) has long advocated a "direct frontal assault" on the problems of poverty and underdevelopment via massive state-sponsored "poverty alleviation programs." He and others have outlined an agenda for radical institutional reforms, namely, the redistribution of wealth, the adoption of more "integrated" development programs, and investments in human capital through improved nutrition, public health, education, and family planning in order to provide "basic needs" to the poor.[21]

Even though the preceding literature provides important insights into the problems of development and poverty, its failure to adequately take into consideration the political determinants has left significant gaps in the debate. The "basic needs" literature suffers from political naiveté based on the belief that enlightened policy packages by themselves can overcome the entrenched socioeconomic and political structures.[22]

Democracy and Development: Competing Perspectives

There is substantial scholarly consensus around the "procedural minimum" that defines liberal democracy as a form of government under which citizens, via open and free institutional arrangements, are empowered to choose and remove leaders who vie for the people's vote. Democracies are based on the principles of popular sovereignty and competitive political participation and representation. An independent judiciary, regular elections, universal suffrage, freedom of expression and conscience, and the universal right to form political associations and participate in the political community ensure that the government in power adheres to the constitution and the rule of law.[23] Moreover, a democratic state is seen to be responsive to the demands and pressures from members of the citizenry since its right to rule is derived from popular support manifested in competitive elections—or, as Robert Dahl (1971) argues, that government responsiveness to citizens' demands is built into periodically held electoral contests guaranteed by juridically protected individual rights.[24] Given this, classical political theorists of the seventeenth through the nineteenth centuries, including John Locke (1988), John Stuart Mill (1961), and Alexis de Tocqueville (1966), not only viewed democracies as the embodiment of reason and advancement, but also assumed that liberal democracies would greatly empower the laboring and disadvantaged sectors of society to press successfully to redress the gross socioeconomic and political disparities.[25]

The quintessential democrat, Jawaharlal Nehru (1948; 1958), also echoed similar convictions, arguing that the fate of India's "toiling and downtrodden masses" is inextricably tied to the country's "democratic ethos and idea." He argued that India's democratic government, constantly pressured by the formidable political resource of the masses with their numerical strength manifest through the ballot box, would willy-nilly compel the governing political elites to promote public policies that directly or indirectly benefit the poor and the underprivileged.[26]

Analysts such as T. H. Marshall (1964), Seymour Martin Lipset (1959), Karl Deutsch (1961), and Albert Hirschman (1970) have argued that economic modernization and the concomitant structural differentiation, emergence of the urbanized middle and working classes, and expansion of rights and privileges of citizenship give civil society an avenue to advance its material interests through organized collective action. According to Marshall, the great distributive measures of the postwar welfare state, including measures introducing health services, social security, unemployment insurance, and new forms of progressive taxation, have been the result of a "modern contract"—the very foundation of democratic citizenship. Some of these themes have been elaborated in the recent writings of Larry Diamond, Juan Linz, and Seymour M. Lipset (1990), Stephan Haggard and Robert Kaufman (1995), Carole Pateman (1970), and Adam Przeworski (1991; 1996), among others, who have argued that the granting of formal rights of citizenship and the expansion of civil-political liberties under liberal democracies make the preservation of the political and socioeconomic status quo problematic because democracies motivate political leaders to be responsive to the preferences of the majority rather than to a small proportion of the citizenry.[27]

Gabriel Almond and Sidney Verba (1963) examine the relationship between democracy and development from a slightly different angle. Focusing on citizens attitudes and values in five countries, they conclude that citizens in stable democracies are characterized by a particular set of widely shared attitudes and values or "civic culture."[28] That is, the citizens possess a relatively common set of understandings about the appropriate boundaries of government, the sanctity of political rights, and the fundamental duties of citizens to preserve them. Hence, "if there is no consensus within society, there can be little potentiality for the peaceful resolution of political [and economic] differences that is associated with the democratic process." Robert Putnam (1993) elaborates the arguments of Almond and Verba—reflecting a return to the study of citizen values, norms, and traditions and their implications for political stability and economic development. Putnam demonstrates that an active associational life complemented with "networks of civic engagement," or communitarian ethic, translates into "social capital" that helps to resolve dilemmas of collective action and to smooth economic and political negotiations. In the Tocquevillian tradition, Putnam argues that a vibrant political culture is based on trust, compromise, reciprocity, and egalitarian values that are central to promoting economic development and social-cultural advancement. Societies endowed with appropriate democratic norms and traditions (namely, dense "networks of civic engagement and generalized reciprocity") can sustain and promote socioeconomic and political cooperation more effectively, as reflected in northern Italy. In sharp contrast, less civic regions reflect a "Hobbesian equilibrium" characterized by "mutual distrust and deflection, vertical dependence and exploitation, isolation and disorder, criminality and backwardness."[29]

However, such sanguine views of the relationship between democracy and development with equity are not universally shared, because, as Robert Dahl (1995, 46) writes, "In practice democratic systems have always fallen considerably short of the criteria and values that justify democracy." David Apter (1965) warned of the possible incompatibility between democracy and development in the "newly emerging nations." Apter suggested that the formidable task of nation building necessitates self-discipline and societal restraint, hence a free-wheeling and potentially divisive Western-style democracy may not be the most appropriate, especially in economically weak and fragmented multiethnic societies. Samuel Huntington's (1968) classic *Political Order in Changing Societies* and Huntington and Nelson (1976) noted more explicitly the "cruel choice" between democracy and development. According to Huntington, since socioeconomic modernization increases the political participation of citizens without ensuring that their demands can be met, economic development is best promoted under conditions of "a high degree" of political stability and order. In settings where elites lack in the "art of associating together" and institutions are unable to channel the chaos that accompanies modernization, democracy can be counterproductive because it has the potential to open and destroy the already fragile political institutionalization. In such settings popular participation makes democracies ungovernable because pluralism tends to create more divisions and encourage consumption at the expense of investment. Hence, contrary to the "assumptions of liberal, technocratic and populist models . . . in the early stages of development, the expansion of political participation tends to have a negative impact on economic equality" (Huntington and Nelson 1976, 75). In a similar vein, political philosopher C. B. Macpherson (1965) stressed the need to conceive "democracy" in terms of "liberal," "communist," and "underdeveloped" variants. According to Macpherson the last variant was distinct insofar as the relevant society was, as a whole, culturally "not attuned to competition and political pluralism." In such environments, Macpherson (1965, 29) argued that a single dominant regime was not only necessary, but also essential to achieve the goals of modernization.

> To call it democratic is to put the emphasis on ends, not means. It is to make the criterion of democracy the achievement of ends which the mass of people share and which they put ahead of separate individual ends. This of course is the classic, pre-liberal, notion of democracy. The classic formulation of this democratic doctrine was Rousseau, and there are strong echoes of Rousseau in many of the theoretical statements made by leaders in the underdeveloped countries.

Other analysts have also posited an inherent "cruel choice" between democratic governance and economic development, especially in the early stages of modernization, claiming that the "trade-off" renders democracies incapable of promoting sustained economic development or reconciling growth with distribution.[30] For example, Guillermo O'Donnell (1973) aimed to explode the "optimistic equation" that democracy was a natural concomitant of development by forcefully arguing that authoritarian coercion acted as a functional requisite to "economic deepening." O'Donnell presumed an inevitability, arguing that the association between democratic governance and the early import-substitution stage of industrialization in Latin America was premature and would give way to the "new authoritarianism" during the later stage of "industrial deepening." The deepening, or expansion, of domestic intermediate and capital goods industries imposed painful economic restructuring, including repression, of the popular sector, necessitating the maintenance of stability and order by "new" bureaucratic-authoritarian regimes led by an alliance of assertive civil-military technocratic elites. Since the new authoritarianism did emerge in the most modernized countries of Latin America, O'Donnell argued that an "elective affinity" exists between industrial deepening in capitalist peripheries like Brazil, Chile, and Argentina and repressive "bureaucratic-authoritarian rule."[31] Elaborating O'Donnell's thesis, some scholars have stressed the significance of regime characteristics for understanding the capacity of governments to promote economic development—repeatedly linking authoritarianism with successful economic modernization and democracy with failure. With illustrations from Latin America, James Malloy (1987, 249) states that "present economic policy . . . demands decision-making centers able to impose policies resisted by almost all segments of society. This is a task that prior cycles show is beyond the capacity of open democratic regimes in Latin America." Authoritarian rule, which implies efficient technocratic management, less dependence on popular support, and more capacity to override political dissent, is consequently seen as more compatible with economic development than democracy. Jack Donnelly (1984, 257) lucidly summarizes the various arguments put forth by the proponents of the "cruel choice" thesis:

> The exercise of civil and political rights may disrupt or threaten to destroy even the best-laid development plan, and must therefore be temporarily suspended. For example, elected officials are likely to support policies based on short-run political expediency rather than to insist on politically unpopular but economically essential sacrifices. Freedom of speech, press, and assembly may be exercised so as to create or inflame social divisions, which an already fragile polity may be unable to endure; free trade unions often merely seek additional special benefits for a labor aristocracy; elaborate and punctilious legal systems on the Western model may seem to be extravagant anachronisms.

Drawing on the archetype derived from the developmental success of East Asia's high-performing economies, some of these analysts have argued that market-oriented "developmental dictatorships" or "soft authoritarianism" as practiced in South Korea during the Park Chung Hee and Chun Doo Hwan regimes, Taiwan under the Kuomintang, and Singapore may hold the secret of rapid economic development with redistribution. Chalmers Johnson (1987), a most astute observer, argues that regimes embodying autonomous growth-oriented political and technocratic elites are more able in rehabilitating or forging state capabilities and judicious "developmental alliances" than open democratic ones that simply retrench cumbersome and profligate governing structures. As Johnson (1987, 131) states:

> Since 1947, despite its adoption of a formally democratic constitution and the subsequent development of a genuinely open political culture, Japan seems to have retained many "soft authoritarian" features in its governmental institutions: an extremely strong and comparatively unsupervised state administration, single-party rule for more than three decades, and a set of economic priorities that seems unattainable under true political pluralism . . . it has seemed to some that the coincidence of soft authoritarianism in politics and capitalism in economics had something to do with economic performance.

While casual empiricism and the experiences of Japan, South Korea, Taiwan, and Singapore suggest that bouts of hard and soft authoritarianism were critical for growth with redistribution, the question of whether authoritarianism is a *necessary* precondition is open to debate.

Finally, rational choice theorists building on Anthony Downs's (1957) and Mancur Olson's (1971) seminal studies have added yet another dimension to the debate. They ask why, since individual actors are inherently "rational maximizers" who constantly make "self-interested choices," the many underprivileged members of the electorate have not utilized the leverage of democratic governance to demand and extract more material benefits from public officials and the state—the entities with a vested interest in serving their constituents? To rational choice theorists, the related "free-rider" and "collective-action problems" prevent the masses from improving their conditions even under responsive democratic regimes. Specifically, although smaller groups may reach binding agreements to cooperate, collective action becomes progressively more difficult as the number of potential actors increases. According to this logic, members of the majority cannot get their voices heard because they are unable to band together in collective action.[32]

The debate on the relationship between democracy and development in the developing world has resolved little. Rigorous empirical testing to compare economic growth under democratic and authoritarian regimes has produced, at best, inconclusive and contradictory results (Sirowy and Inkels 1990; Weede 1983). Some have questioned the analytical underpinnings of such comparisons, arguing that the "exclusionary" or "inclusionary" nature of a regime is more significant than its authoritarian or democratic underpinnings. For example, Karen Remmer (1985/86; 1990) has noted that exclusionary authoritarian governments tend more toward economic predation than "developmentalism"; hence, democracy per se may not be incompatible with reformist and distributive reform, but exclusionary types of formally democratic rule may be incompatible. Writing in the context of advanced democracies, Peter Gourevitch (1986) and Peter Katzenstein (1984) have also compellingly refuted the facile maxim that democracies are poor managers of the economy: rather, they have lucidly argued that democracies have tremendous built-in resilience, flexibility, and developmental capacity. Gourevitch argues that in hard economic times (he uses the example of the Great Depression) the institutional problem-solving mechanism in democracies allowed for mediation between labor and business. By becoming part of the larger "social coalitions" (that soon included the middle classes and farmers), and eventually becoming embedded in political parties and state institutions, these coalitions were able to ride through the hard times without the institutional breakdowns typical of former authoritarian and totalitarian experiments. Similarly, Katzenstein highlights how the modus vivendi (what he calls "democratic corporatism") established between labor and capital in Austria and Switzerland has enabled these countries to enjoy pragmatic business cycles. Perhaps these complex issues are best understood through detailed country case studies—which recognize each case's unique experiences and distinctive challenges—yet situate each case in broader cross-national comparative perspective—the aim of this study.

Democracy and Development: The Indian Experience

Considering the high mortality rate of democracies in most postcolonial settings, democracy in India has long appeared something of an anomaly. At the time of independence it was widely believed that India was among the least likely of the newly emergent nations to sustain democratic governance.[33] Liberal democracy and the practice of representative government, the skeptics argued (reflecting the hubris of the small Westernized élite that had led the independence struggle), was too alien a system to survive in a subcontinent nostalgic for "imagined traditions" and compromised by irreconcilable fissiparous and centrifugal forces. Indian democracy, they believed, imposed from the top and lacking enduring roots in society, would eventually succumb to the inertia of traditionalism and the divisiveness of oriental despotism. Indeed, the bloody communal riots that followed partition, and the subcontinent's ancient enmities sustained and abetted by a myriad of competing traditions and interests, each with its crosscutting layer below layer of entrenched inequities and resentment, lent credence to the view that India lacked the basic requisite "preconditions" in which the values, norms, and institutions of liberal democracy could be expected to survive and flourish. Yet, this rigidly hierarchal and excruciatingly poor agrarian social order, whose population will cross the billion mark in less than a decade, has so far defied the odds. Not only has India maintained its national and territorial integrity, but for much of the five decades since independence has shown remarkable political stability. It stands virtually alone among the new nations in preserving a relatively open system of parliamentary government and holding (on balance) free, fair, and competitive elections on the idea of a secular nation-state in which all groups and communities may aspire to cultural-religious dignity and ultimately share in economic prosperity and political power.

It was this remarkable "Indian exceptionalism" that led Barrington Moore (1966) to devote an entire chapter to India in his influential study. According to Moore agrarian societies with the entrenched "feudalistic type" of social, economic, and political inequalities stood as an impediment to the rise of capitalism and democracy; in contrast, a vigorous class of town dwellers or bourgeoisie was indispensable to democratic development. In his words, "no bourgeois, no democracy" (1966, 418). He concluded that since India lacked these basic requisites, "peaceful stagnation" was the ultimate price of democracy in India.

It was his frustration with the linear, "positivist" theories (particularly the narrow economic growth models) that led Gunnar Myrdal (1970) to advance an alternative "broad institutional approach" to the study of the problems of economic development in poor nations. In his magisterial three-volume study that is "mainly about India," Myrdal (1970, 229) attributed India's inability to reconcile economic development with redistribution to the exigencies of the nation's "soft state":

> The soft state is characterized by a general lack of social discipline, . . .
> signified by deficiencies in . . . legislation and, in particular, in law observance and enforcement, lack of obedience to rules and directives handed down to public officials on various levels, often collusion of these officials with powerful persons or groups of persons whose conduct they should regulate, and, at bottom, a general inclination of people in all strata to resist public controls and their implementation. Within the concept of the soft state belongs also corruption.

Thus, to Myrdal, the "soft states" of the newly emergent nations (India being the classic example) simply lacked the institutional capacity and political resolve to promote urgently needed economic development. However, instead of linking the state's "softness" to the political and socioeconomic configurations, Myrdal attributed it to the peculiarities-cum-idiosyncrasies of India's cultural-religious traditions, in particular to the "obstructionist Brahmanical institutions" and to the inherent immobilism of the Hindu caste system. The "preconditions" for development that logically followed Myrdal's reasoning were that the erstwhile religious attitudes and the panoply of cultural idiosyncrasies had to be neutralized, if not destroyed, before economic modernization and more equitable sharing of the fruits of development could take place.

In the 1960s and the 1970s, a new generation of India scholars radicalized by the "paradigmatic revolution" in Western social sciences (i.e., the emergence of the dependency approach) and troubled by the "twin crisis" of India's development (i.e., the failure to achieve sustained growth and growth with distribution) began to search for new ways of analyzing India's political economy. These radical critics (some claiming to be neo-Marxists) provided trenchant criticism of the "modernization perspective,"[34] regarding not only the substantive interpretations of the problems of developing countries but also the methodological and ideological grounds—challenging what they considered to be the telelogical, unilinear assumptions of the various modernization and developmental approaches.

Some of these critics viewed India's democracy as a cruel hoax, a system that perpetuated the hegemonic rule of the dominant classes through periodic elections. Others denounced the Indian state as a tool of neocolonial domination. Specifically, the critics claimed that "development" carried out under the auspices of a "comprador-bourgeois regime" (hiding behind the facade of democratic politics), headed by an alliance of the "imperialist metropolitan bourgeoisie," the local comprador classes (i.e., the feudal landed classes), and a weak national bourgeoisie, is inherently incapable of promoting growth with redistribution because it is designed to serve the interests of imperialism and its local allies.[35]

The first significant attempt to transcend the rigidities of modernization and neo-Marxist approaches to the study of India's development experience was Francine Frankel's *India's Political Economy, 1947–1977: The Gradual Revolution* (1978). Her 600-page study revolves around two key questions: (1) Why have reformist and distributive efforts failed in India despite strong commitment by the national political leadership to guide the country toward a "socialistic pattern of society"? (2) Can India's democracy reconcile the goals of economic growth and the reduction of disparities without unleashing the social chaos of a violent upheaval?

In a nutshell, Frankel's central argument is that the constitutional and administrative frameworks of democratic India were designed in the interests of the powerful propertied classes. In the case of rural India, the assignment of significant powers to the dominant-class-controlled state governments over "key subjects as land reforms, agricultural credit, land revenue assessments and taxation of agricultural income" put severe brakes on the possibilities of any "sweeping changes of the social order by action from above" (1978, 81). But, why did the Indian government succumb to the propertied classes? Here, Frankel provides a quintessentially "pluralist" answer.[36] She argues that the predilection of Mohandas Gandhi (and a large section of the Congress elite) for nonviolence and an ideological preference for class conciliation and accommodation with the propertied castes and classes served to greatly limit the postindependence state's capacity to fundamentally reform the hierarchal social structures or successfully implement reformist programs. Frankel carefully documents that government policies were determined by the political compromises made by influential political leaders with the powerful interest groups and factions that made up India's ruling coalition. In the case of rural India the relative power of the propertied interests in bargaining, negotiating, and marshaling votes for political support, and the political victory of the "conservative" forces over the "Gandhians" and "Socialists" in the ruling Congress Party early in the postindependence period, virtually guaranteed that the new policies and institutions would favor the interests of the powerful landowning interests.

Frankel's focus on the ideological underpinnings of the Congress Party and the political elite's coalition with the various interest and factional groups sheds much light on the nature of elite political activity in India. Her detailed discussion of the intraelite and governmental struggles over allocations and over turf lucidly shows that politics in a democracy is often the stuff of forced compromises and squalid bargains—the best deals salvaged in the political agreements made by the various factions that made up India's ruling coalition. Also, her discussion of elite decision-making in terms of the organizational interests pursued by competing leaders, ministries, bureaus, and other agencies within the party/state apparatus is highly informative.

However, there are gaps in Frankel's analysis. Specifically, it fails to adequately capture the complex articulation between the democratic state and society. Frankel's study provides a detailed analyzes of elite political activity and the upper level policy process, but it does not provide much understanding of evolving relationships between the multitiered structures of state and society or why the weaker sections of society—empowered through the "gradual revolution"—failed to make the state promote their collective interests.

Two other studies that make a concerted effort to analyze the relationship between democracy and India's development are by Lloyd and Susanne Rudolph (1987) and Atul Kohli (1987). In directing attention to the centrality of the polity, these studies not only provide correctives to the reductionism of modernization and neo-Marxist approaches but also craft an innovative approach for the analysis of India's political economy. Yet, the studies' excessively "statist" orientation, with its asymmetrical and "absolutistic" view of political power, is not without problems.

To the Rudolphs "India is a political and economic paradox: a rich-poor nation with a weak-strong state . . . [that has] alternated between autonomous and reflexive relations with the society in which it is embedded." India's democratic state is simultaneously "weak" and "strong." It is strong because it controls the commanding heights of the economy and because its political "centrism" (a posture seen as functional for the dominant interests in society) has enabled it to minimize (or better manage) socioeconomic and political conflicts. Its growing weakness, or incapacity "to govern wisely and well," stems from the personalization and centralization of power that occurred during the seventeen-year rule (1969–1984) of Indira Gandhi. Specifically, under Mrs Gandhi, the systematic "deinstitutionalization of the Congress Party and state structures, [the erosion] of professional standards, and procedural norms of the Parliament, courts, police, civil service and the federal system" (Rudolph and Rudolph 1987, 6–7), greatly eroded the autonomy and organizational capacity of state and effectively eliminated the channels through which society's many "demand groups" had long articulated and expressed their interests. The consequence of such destructive actions (carried out to enhance "personalistic rule") was to diminish the state's legitimacy or "moral authority" and compounded the crisis of "governability"—or the state's ability to mediate and reconcile conflicting interests, generate consensus, and deal effectively with the pressing problems of law and order and economic development.

Even though the Rudolphs agree that the Indian state's autonomy and capacity have declined since independence, they reject Bardhan's claim that the decline is rooted in the nature of the dominant class alliance. Instead, they see the problem as stemming largely from the "wasting of political assets" and from the dismantling of Congress Party institutions by self-serving and unscrupulous leaders. For the Rudolphs, the solution to the problems of economic stagnation and the growing crisis of governability is to rebuild the legitimacy and effectiveness of the democratic state. That is, the currently weak state can once again regain the relative autonomy (or the centrist posture it enjoyed during the Nehru years) by reintroducing "principled politics" and by rebuilding institutional and political structures along the lines of the Nehruvian state. Only a polity with responsive leadership and strong grassroots organization committed to liberal-democratic parliamentary norms and procedures of governance, and accommodating the political aspirations and economic needs of all the groups in society, can promote political stability, the *sine qua non* for growth with development.

The Rudolphs' *In Pursuit of Lakshmi* has been the subject of much critical review.[37] Rather than provide a comprehensive review I will draw attention to three relevant issues. First, one of the key criticisms leveled against the Rudolphs is that their study is excessively "state-centric and elitist . . . essentially seen from the viewpoint of elites and managers of the system at the apex" (Kothari 1988, 274). To the critics, the Rudolphs' thesis is both methodologically and empirically flawed because it overlooks the role of the "vast social peripheries" by treating society as some residual category in the process of change. In reducing society to a mere aggregation of "fragmented social forces" made up of either sectorally oriented "demand groups" or caste and *jati* clusters, the Rudolphs underestimate the power of the dominant social structural forces, namely how the forces' control over a formally democratic polity has enabled them to legitimize accumulation and dominance. The second and related criticism is that in viewing Indian politics largely in terms of the roles and actions of individual leaders, for example, devoting much intellectual energy in denouncing the role of Mrs. Gandhi, the Rudolphs underestimate the socioeconomic determinants of politics. To be sure, Mrs. Gandhi's actions weakened the Congress Party and left a deep imprint on the country's political landscape, but it is also important to note that Mrs. Gandhi came to preside over a party that was already deeply factionalized at the top and rapidly losing its old coalitional base on the ground. Subsequent chapters will show that the decline of the Congress Party has occurred in tandem with significant socioeconomic changes and the emergence of social groups and classes no longer willing to be passive "vote banks" for the elites and eager to assert their interests in an open democratic polity. Finally, at the conceptual level, the Rudolphs overemphasis on powerful leaders and intraelite power struggles (reminiscent of the "plural state" approach) and their deliberate eclecticism in their characterizations of the political system as "strong" or "weak" fails to capture the deeper determinants of state-society relations.

Kohli's valuable study not only avoids many of the analytical pitfalls of the Rudolphs' study but, to date, is the most coherent exposition of India's developmental problems presented from a statist viewpoint. Kohli argues that in theory democratic states, through their claim to legitimate control of the representation of various social interests, have considerable potential to determine and shape political and socioeconomic relationships between the state and society. Moreover, given the state's control over public resources, its capacity to mobilize interests and intervene actively through coercion, legitimating, and to co-opt or accommodate, it has the potential to enjoy a high degree of continual autonomy from any given class or interest.

However, Kohli is cognizant of the fact that in reality complete state autonomy is hardly the norm. He argues that the ideological orientation of the state leadership, the organization of state power or "regime types," and the composition and structural relationship between the state and the dominant classes are some of the important varying conditions that affect the state's capacity to act autonomously vis-à-vis society. As these variables are continuous and vary in degree, so does the capacity of political authorities to define and implement state goals. But, for Kohli, in the final analysis the variations in state autonomy and capacity depend fundamentally on "the type of regime wielding state power" (p. 28). He argues that in the case of India the "nationalist-democratic regime" that took power in 1947 (and has ruled the country since) was too closely tied to the dominant classes and thus did not have the political nor the organizational capacity to confront and "tame" the powerful propertied interests. Specifically, "as anti-colonial nationalism falls into the background and interest groups compete for state resources" (p. 34), the capacity of states governed by nationalist-democratic regimes to extricate themselves from political and socioeconomic ties so as to restructure the economy and society declines. The state and regime lack the will and capacity to confront the propertied classes, and this political weakness "is, in turn, not merely a function of the omnipotence of the propertied groups. It is in part related to it, but it is also independent of it" (p. 226). Thus, for Kohli the failure to achieve growth with distribution in India is rooted in the weakness of the democratic regime. He argues that only a strong autonomous developmental state, or a state with strong and stable leadership, a pro-poor ideology, and a closed organizational structure with disciplined cadres (such as the CPM [Communist Party–Marxist] regime in West Bengal) can facilitate economic development with redistribution in India.

Kohli's analytical emphasis on the state and regime type as important independent variables has great merit. Indeed, a considerable body of comparative research has shown that the varying regime types that control state power can significantly condition the patterns of socioeconomic development. Kohli makes a strong general case to illustrate that India's political arrangements have been singularly unsuited for distributive intervention. His analysis of the reformist performance of the Indian state in comparison with that of three provincial governments in India, namely, the governments of Karnataka, West Bengal, and Uttar Pradesh, with each functioning under a different regime type "within the larger constraints of democratic capitalism," is highly instructive and further reinforces his position that the organization of politics (i.e., the regime characteristics of the state) do matter in shaping the patterns of national development.

Yet, the overemphasis on regime type has its problems, however. In the case of India, where a wide array of ideologies, economic interests, and political coalitions are encompassed by the broad category of "nationalist-democratic regime," regime types as an independent variable offers only a limited basis for understanding how and why particular policies are chosen and the implications for development and reform. Also, in devoting too much attention to the organizational structure of the state and regimes, Kohli often undervalues the role of nonstate actors in the formulation and implementation of public policies. That is, although the state may be the single most consequential actor in most polities, it does not act in a vacuum; more often than not what it does is conditional upon society. Thus, what counts in the formation and implementation of policy is not only the regime characteristics but also the political-institutional linkages between the state and society. As the critics of statism have argued, the degree of state autonomy cannot be derived solely from regime types without weighing the independent organizational, political, and economic resources of social groups and classes. Karen Remmer (1990, 316) notes that

> a growing body of research has generated considerable skepticism about the importance of regime variations for understanding policy performance. Not only are policy choices constrained by socioeconomic realities, but the similarities and differences among nations appear to be far too complex and multifaceted to be captured by simple distinctions of types of regimes. As a result, knowing that a regime is civilian rather than military, democratic rather than authoritarian, or even inclusionary rather than exclusionary establishes only a limited basis for making predictions about policy outcomes

Moreover, Akhil Gupta (1989, 795–796) has aptly noted "a deep-seated elitism . . . in conceptions of political-economy that does not systematically integrate the lowest levels of the political system . . . [therefore] denying agency to the subaltern." This point is particularly relevant in the Indian context, where the state is far from strong and autonomous but imperfectly consolidated, weak, and retreating. In such an environment, a preoccupation with the upper reaches of the state (i.e., "regimes types") may obscure or at best reveal only a part of the complex and multifaceted drama of socioeconomic change. This problem is vividly highlighted in Ross Mallick's (1994) recent study. Mallick criticizes Kohli and others for portraying a false epistemology of the "Left Front regime" that has governed the state of West Bengal for some two decades as a "developmental success" in terms of promoting growth with redistribution.[38] To the contrary, Mallick argues that West Bengal's "progressive" Left Front regime has failed most egregiously in three core reformist and distributive areas. First, in the failure to enact land and credit reforms, Mallick compellingly shows that the Left Front's Land Reform Act netted only 184,049 acres in excess of land ceiling in its major phase, and that the area redistributed as a percentage of cultivable land by 1985 was only 0.55 percent, well behind a number of states in India. Second, the regulation and protection of tenants under Operation *Barga* ("Sharecropper Protection") is a farce. Marshaling a wide array of evidence (some based on official surveys), Mallick notes widespread intimidation and eviction of poor and small tenants, including the payment of illegal rents to the rich peasantry and their backers, even in the Left Front strongholds of Burdwan and neighboring districts. Third, minimum-wage legislation designed to help the rural majority and the "poorest of the rural poor" (i.e., the landless agricultural workers) has remained ineffectual. Mallick writes that in fact wage demands have been suppressed (*NSS* data indicate that the prevalence of bonded labor in West Bengal remains among the highest in India), and that pro-poor programs are rife with corruption and patronage and are poorly implemented by the state. Overall, the "exploitation of agricultural labor under the Left Front appears to be the worst in India" (p. 75). Finally, Mallick adds that the most oppressed strata of West Bengal (indeed Indian) society, the low castes and "untouchables," who represent over 12 million people, or 22 percent of the state's population, have received low priority. Allocations to special "uplift" programs to help the untouchables are among the lowest in all-India terms, and even blatant atrocities against the untouchables have not produced official outrage or punishment of those responsible. But why have Kohli and others have failed to see the seemingly obvious? According to Mallick the problem lies in their narrow analytical focus. By focusing exclusively on "states," "regime types," and "political elites," and ignoring the lower reaches of the polity and the weaker social constituencies, these researchers have been duped by state officials—in large part due to the analysts' own uncritical acceptance of the official story. The state-society approach outlined in the next section hopes to avoid these problems.

Conceptualizing the State-Society Relations

In the social science literature there is no consensus on the definition of the "state." In fact, over a hundred different conceptualizations have been suggested by scholars representing various ideological and epistemological persuasions (see Easton 1979). According to Theda Skocpol (1979), who speaks for many, the state as a set of administrative, legal, and coercive organizations is the principal institutional locus of political power in most settings. Through its nationalist-populist and/or organic-statist ideologies and manifold structures and institutions, which include *inter alia* the central executive branch, the legislature, the bureaucracy, the judiciary, the army, and the police, the state tries to formulate, implement, adjudicate, and enforce the laws and policies, not to mention engage in "revenue extraction" from its society, to promote and enhance the calculus of its power: territoriality, nationality, sovereignty, and regime longevity.

Despite the state's assumed pivotal position, recent research has compellingly shown that the focus on the "state" may not be universally valid. In most developing world settings, where states are imperfectly consolidated, with diminishing capacities, and increasingly disengaged from the economic realm, states can no longer claim to have sole and universal jurisdiction or be seen as the final arbiters of economic and political authority. This is particularly the case in societies with a large agrarian social base. Rural communities firmly embedded in a textured web of familial, kinship, caste, community, and clientage relationships, with deep historic ambivalence toward the state, are tenacious defenders of individual and collective interests—what James Scott (1976) has referred to as the "moral economy of peasant society"—and not easily "captured" despite repeated interventions by democratic, or authoritarian, or even the "all-penetrating" totalitarian regimes to bring them under control.[39] To the contrary, traditional nexuses of power and dominance in the countryside (even in an attenuated form) have remained resilient despite the "modernizing" and coercive thrusts of states. In fact, states have found their capacity as claimants limited by the strategic negotiating strength of societies, some of which have remained substantially outside the authoritative reach of their states.[40] Nowhere is this more evident than in India.

The foundations of the new Indian state were intensely debated in the Constituent Assembly (elected indirectly from the various provinces in 1946) during the years 1947–1950. The result was the Constitution of India, adopted on 26 January 1950, proclaiming India a sovereign federal democratic republic under a parliamentary system of government. The 395 articles and ten appendixes (known as schedules) in the constitution make it one of the longest and most detailed in the world. Following a British parliamentary pattern, the constitution embodies the Fundamental Rights, similar to the United States Bill of Rights. The Fundamental Rights guarantee to all citizens basic substantive and procedural protections. These civil rights take precedence over any other law of the land and include individual rights common to most liberal democracies, such as equality before the law; freedom of speech, association, assembly, and religion; the right to constitutional remedies for the protection of civil rights such as habeas corpus; and the right to property. In addition, the constitution outlaws the traditional Indian system of social stratification based on "casteism" and "untouchability" and prohibits discrimination on the grounds of religion, language, race, ethnic background, sex, or place of birth—and includes the right of "minorities" to establish and administer their own educational institutions and to conserve a distinct language, script, and culture. An interesting feature of the constitution is the Directive Principles of State Policy, which delineate the obligations of the state towards its citizens. The precepts of the Directive Principles are not justiciable; that is, they are not enforceable by a court, as are the Fundamental Rights. The Directive Principles' admirable goals (some say vague platitudes) such as the injunction that the state "shall direct its policy towards securing . . . that the ownership and control of the material resources of the community are so distributed to subserve the common good" or that "the state shall promote the interests of the weaker sections of society" are there to guide the government in framing new legislation.

The key institutions of national governance are the executive, composed of the president, the Council of Ministers (headed by the prime minister), the Parliament, and the highest judicial system in the land, the Supreme Court. It is important to note that although the Indian constitution formally vests executive power in the president (also the head of the state), the president exercises these powers on the advice of the Council of Ministers headed by the prime minister.[41] Hence, power in both theory and practice is concentrated in the hands of the prime minister, the de facto head of the Indian executive. Theoretically (and in practice), it is the prime minister who determines the composition of the Council of Ministers and assigns departmental portfolios to the "inner circle" or the cabinet, made up of between fifteen to twenty individuals. In India the nature and composition of the Council of Ministers and cabinet has varied according to the prime minister in power. The prime minister's office is also supported by a "secretariat," a large body (currently over 300 strong) headed by a principal secretariat, senior bureaucrats, technocrats, economists, politicians, and their assistants.[42]

India's Parliament, the country's supreme legislative body, consists of a bicameral legislature made up of the Lok Sabha and the Rajya Sabha (the Council of States, the upper house of the national Parliament). The Lok Sabha in 1995 constitutionally had 545 seats, and with the exception of two members that are nominated by the president as representatives of the

Anglo-Indian community, all seats are popularly elected on the basis of first past the post, similar to the system in the United States.[43] Seats in the Lok Sabha are allocated among the states on the basis of population, each state divided roughly into several electoral districts made up of around 1.5 million people. The usual term for an elected Lok Sabha is five years, and under the rules of the constitution it must meet at least twice a year with no more than six months between sessions. However, the president may dissolve the house and call new elections if the sitting government loses its majority in Parliament. The Rajya Sabha, on the other hand, like the United States Senate is a permanent body and meets in continuous session. It has a maximum of 250 members, and all but twelve are elected by the state legislative assembly for six-year terms.[44] The Rajya Sabha (like the British House of Lords) permits more extended debates. Home to a large number of India's elder statespeople, it is designed to provide stability and continuity to the legislative process (that is, it is not subject to dissolution as is the Lok Sabha). Nevertheless, since it rests on the confidence of the popular assembly, the authority of the Rajya Sabha in the legislative process is subordinate to that of the Lok Sabha.

Decisionmaking on public policy in India is concentrated at the highest levels of authority, with the prime minister, his inner cabinet, and high-level officials and bureaucrats, via their control of the various ministries of government, taking the initiative. The government of the day has primary responsibility to draft legislation and introduce bills in Parliament—in either house—albeit financial bills for taxing and spending (known as money bills) can only be introduced in the Lok Sabha. The central government is aided in its activities (known as Public Services) by some 17 million central government employees, 5,000 of whom are officers of the elite Indian Administrative Service.[45] Finally, the Supreme Court as the highest legal tribunal is the ultimate interpreter and guardian of the constitution and the laws of the land.[46] Headed by a chief justice and twenty-five associate justices, the Supreme Court ensures that all legislation passed by the central and state governments are in conformity with the constitution, and the constitutionality on any enactment is determined under the power of judicial review by the Supreme Court, which has original as well as appellate jurisdiction.[47]

While India's federal system has vested many powers of legislation in the central government, the constitution has also provided for enumerated powers divided among the union or central government, the provincial or state governments, and the so-called local governments. Below the central government are twenty-five state governments and six union territories, with populations ranging from 400,000 for the union territory of Sikkim to 140 million for the largest and most populous state of Uttar Pradesh. Although states do not have their own separate constitutions, they are governed by the provisions of the constitution, which specifies that all the states have similar governmental structures and provides for a popularly elected bicameral or unicameral legislature in each state and territory, headed by a chief minister responsible to the legislatures.[48] A governor for each state and territory is appointed by the central government, and has the power to dissent from a bill and refer it to the president of India and to appoint, with the approval of the legislature, the state's chief minister. The strength of the central government relative to the states is further apparent in the constitutional provisions (laid down in the seventh schedule of the constitution) for central intervention into state jurisdictions. The center has exclusive authority over matters of national importance—the ninety-seven items includes defense, foreign affairs, transportation, communications, interstate trade and commerce, and finances. Moreover, article 3 of the constitution authorizes Parliament, by a simple majority vote, to establish or eliminate states and union territories or change their boundaries or names. The central government can dismiss any state government through the president's rule. The center also exerts control over state governments through the financial resources at its command: in a real sense it "acts as a banker and collecting agent for the state governments" (Hardgrave and Kochanek 1993, 130). Under the rules of the constitution, financial resources flow from the central government to the states through a system of discretionary divisible taxes and grants-in-aid—making the states dependent on the center for their regular budgetary needs as well as their capital expenditures. The central government also allocates and distributes substantial "development funds and grants" through its five-year plans. The resources available under the plans are substantial, given the center's exclusive control over taxable income and foreign financial flows.

India's democratic federal state exhibits all the features of a highly institutionalized modern unitary government.[49] However, despite the constitutional powers of the central government, the provincial governments are not without significant constitutional powers. In the words of B. R. Ambedkar, the chairman of the constitution-drafting committee, "The states of the union of India are as sovereign in their field which is left to them by the Constitution as the Center in the field which is assigned to it" (Palmer 1961, 97). Under the constitution states have exclusive authority of sixty-six items, including public order, welfare, health, education, local government, industry, agriculture, and land revenue. In regard to the agricultural sector and land revenue, the constitution, in assigning primary responsibility to the state governments (while placing constitutional and legal limitations on the powers and jurisdiction of the central government), reduced the center to providing guidelines, leaving the actual task of translating rural development policies into legislation, including their implementation, to the state governments. In other words, the development of the rural sector has depended in large measure on the actions of the state governments. In fact, Paul Appleby (1953, 21), who at the request of the government of India conducted a comprehensive review of the country's administrative system, was astounded to discover how much the center was dependent on the states for the actual implementation of major national programs and how little real authority the center seemed to have in the vital areas of policy and administration. He has lucidly captured this paradox: "No other large and important government . . . is so dependent as India on theoretically subordinate but actually rather distinct units responsible to a different political control, for so much of the administration of what are recognized as national programs of great importance to the nation."

Below the state governments exist an array of formal and informal governance structures known simply as "local self-government"—ordinarily understood as the administration of a locality (a village, town, city, or any other area smaller than a state) by a body representing the local inhabitants. The idea behind local self-government, articulated most forcefully by the 1957 *Mehta Study Team Report,* argued that local self-government, or "democratic decentralization," could play a vital role in the process of political legitimation and offer a means for developing a sense of participation in the citizenry.[50] The report (GoI 1957, 10–12) claimed that

> so long as we do not discover and create a representative and democratic institution, which will supply the local interest, supervision, and care necessary to ensure that expenditure of money upon local objects conforms to the needs and wishes of the locality, invest it with adequate power, and assign to it appropriate finances, we will never be able to evoke local interest and excite local initiative in the field of development.

The district is the principal formal subdivision within the states.[51] In 1990 there were 476 districts in India, varying in size and population, the average running at about 4,000 square kilometers and containing an average population of approximately 1.8 million. The district collector, a member of the Indian Administrative Service, and the state-government-appointed district judge (who is in no way subordinate to the collector) are the most important government officials in district administration. Districts are further subdivided into *taluqs* or *tehsils* comprising anywhere between 200 to 600 villages. The *taluqdar* or *tehsildar* and the occasional village *patwari* (accountant) are the most important government (state) representatives at this level, responsible for overseeing government programs, maintaining land records, and collecting revenue. Finally, to provide effective channels of political and economic participation article 40 of the constitution directs all levels of government to engage in the "democratic decentralization of Indian administration" by reviving and creating "traditional village councils for self-government" or *panchayati raj,* and to "endow them with such powers and authority as may be necessary to enable them to function as units of self-government" (GoI 1952, 6–7). Most states have since introduced a fairly institutionalized system of *panchayati raj,* a three-tiered system that has vested extensive responsibilities for community and rural development in three locally elected bodies. At the base of the system is the popularly elected village council or *gram panchayat;* followed by village council chairs (the second tier), elected by the village council, who serve as members of the block council or *panchayat samiti*[52]; and the third tier, the *zila parishad,* congruent with the district, that includes all the *samiti* chairs in the district. The *panchayati raj* received constitutional status following the passage of the seventy-third amendment in 1992. The amendment stipulates that all *panchayat* members be elected for five-year terms in elections supervised by the state election commission.[53]

India's federal arrangement is a political paradox: it is no doubt unitary, seemingly highly centralized and autonomous. However, behind the state's imposing pyramid lie complex networks of competing institutions and structures that cut across formal lines of authority, making the seemingly monolithic Leviathan also weak, decentralized, and easily permeable from within and outside.[54] More appropriately, "the degree of stateness," the nature and extent of centralization or decentralization, state strength or weakness, varies markedly. That is, the Indian state is highly centralized and autonomous vis-à-vis foreign policy or national security but decentralized and fragmented vis-à-vis the vast countryside. In concrete terms this means that while the broad objectives of national rural development are determined at the political center, the form and the prospects of such strategies are negotiated and laid down in the numerous district and village communities. This is not to imply that the competition for political power and authority among the center, the states, and the localities necessarily results in a zero sum. After all, India's nation builders viewed the state and local governments not as rivals but as aids and extensions of central authority. Rather, the nature of India's democratic federalism and the vastness and complexity of the agrarian base—which at its core retains a certain imperviousness to central penetration—make the central government, on the one hand, quite capable of impressive initiatives in land reclamation, rural infrastructural development, water and irrigation control, and expansion of green revolution technologies, and, on the other, quite inept in implementing reformist and distributive measures.[55]

The Indian state reflects features that Anthony Giddens (1985) in another context has associated with "traditional states." Such states are very different as "social systems" from modern ones. These traditional states are able to generate both authoritative and allocative resources through the intersection of city and countryside, but they are fundamentally segmental in character and can sustain only limited administrative authority. Such states have frontiers rather than boundaries (given their relative weak level of system integration); they do not actually "govern," if this means to provide regularized administration of the territory they claim as their own. At best, such polities are mainly limited to governance of conflicts in dominant interests within society.

This became apparent to me during my fieldwork. I realized that beneath the veneer of a rational constitutional order, legal procedure, and formal bureaucracy, India's democratic polity operates in the countryside essentially along neopatrimonial lines—with a shifting mixture of traditional and modern idioms of socioeconomic and political organization enjoying discretionary control over broad realms of public life. Specifically, around the political core (or the so-called center), with its supposedly higher degree of administrative institutionalization and bureaucratic coherence ("stateness"), the state looks authoritative, with its pronouncements seemingly well calibrated and its bureaucratic regulation and demands garnering wary acquiescence and feigned compliance. However, beyond the political center and the state's realm of control its jurisdiction gradually diminishes, and the "borders" between the state and society become increasingly permeable and indistinct, with sovereignties flowing imperceptibly into one another. At the heart of the sprawling rural universe—states, districts, and villages—the state becomes almost indistinguishable from the informal hierarchies of power and dominance. Over the course of my fieldwork, I came to appreciate that behind the state's imposing pyramid there are complex networks of competing institutions that cut across the state's formal lines of authority. In other words the state, as it spreads out from the political center, tends to dissolve or taper off sharply at the levels below the district. As the reach of the state declines and its overarching structures and institutions become gradually intertwined and embedded in the traditional, informal hierarchies of power and authority, there is a simultaneous diminution in the degree of its autonomous capacity, authority, and influence. In the village, block, and district (and even in some states), the formal and informal structures of rule and governance become woven into the same tapestry, a process that over time has further reduced central authority and eroded its efficacy in the countryside. Under these conditions, local notables and seasoned political brokers (some located ambivalently between state and society) have been able to extend their powers, actively pursuing the interests of their constituencies as well as their own individual imperatives by deflecting or delaying certain central directives and demands made against them, in particular, demands to implement reformist and distributive programs. Through stratagems of collaboration, patronage dispensation, building of supportive coalitions with clientele groups, and opportunistic manipulation of the formal apparatuses of the state (e.g., the courts, bureaucracy, police, various political and administrative structures), the local notables and power brokers have legitimized their power and authority and enhanced their rent-seeking capacities. Beyond the pale of law there are also stratagems of control centering on the blatant manipulation of cleavages within the village society, ranging to outright violence against the poor.

Given the preceding, this study suggests that India's rural development experience can be fruitfully understood by disaggregating the state,
viewing it as one more organization within society rather than as some
omnipotent agent standing above and apart from it. While states help mold
their social surrounding (sometimes dramatically), they are also continu-
ally molded by societies in which they are embedded. The boundaries joining the two are often blurred, and the nature of the interaction frequently
cuts across that boundary in the form of multilevel alliances and coalitions
climaxing in periodic domination by the state, and at other times results
in temporary and reluctant accommodation. Therefore, highlighting the
permeability of the boundaries between state and society—in particular,
how the patterns of segmentation or structural differentiation within the
state and society have evolved and impinged on each other—allows a nuanced understanding of the complex embroidery of forces linking the
polity and the sprawling rural communities. Such highlighting also shows
how these overlapping structures of power and dominance have worked,
often in tandem, to undermine distributive and reformist efforts. These issues are the subject of the next chapter.

Notes

1. The most commonly used way to measure poverty is based on incomes or
consumption levels. A person is considered poor if his or her consumption or income level falls below some minimum level necessary to meet basic needs. This
minimum level is usually referred to as the "poverty line." However, what is necessary to satisfy basic needs varies across time and societies. Thus poverty lines
vary in time and place, and each country uses lines that are appropriate to its level
of development. Given this, precise empirical identification of the rural poor or
those living below the "poverty line" is a formidable task because of the conceptual issues involved in defining the many dimensions of poverty and the data constraints involved in measuring its incidence. I will try to quantify the "poverty levels" in India in subsequent pages. Suffice it to note that the rural poor constitute
the vast majority (79 percent) of rural households, and the fact that poverty is
widespread and stubborn in India hardly requires sophisticated statistical analysis.
According to the World Bank (1990, 29–31), the poor in India, or those whose income was less than $370, constituted approximately 420 million people in 1985.

2. Following the United Nations Development Program (UNDP) (1996, 1–5),
I define "development" as a process "enlarging people's choices" so that they can
acquire knowledge to lead a creative and productive life and have access to a decent standard of living. Hence, "human development should be the objective, not
simply rising incomes, which are at best instrumentally important . . . human development [being] the end—economic growth a means." Hence Paul Streeten's
(1980, 107–110) observation is worth noting: "Development must be redefined as
an attack on the chief evils of the world today: malnutrition, disease, illiteracy,
slums, unemployment and inequality. Measured in terms of aggregate growth rates,
development has been a great success. But measured in terms of jobs, justice and
the elimination of poverty, it has been a failure or only a partial success."

3. The Indian fiscal year runs from 1 April to 31 March.

4. The most widely used measure of poverty in India is the "head-count ratio." This is a measure of *income* poverty and measures the proportion of the population below a level of income defined as a poverty line. The poverty line in India is measured by taking the income (separately for rural and urban areas) necessary to buy a rudimentary food basket that yields a minimum level of calories. The poverty line thus defined, is something of a destitution line, since it takes into account only the expenditure required for food for subsistence, leaving out other components such as shelter, clothing, health services needed for a decent living. The head count ratio is computed on the basis of *National Sample Survey* (*NSS*) data on consumption expenditure: people with an income below the poverty line are "poor," and the proportion of the poor to the aggregate population is the head-count ratio. Given this, studies have found a very strong positive association between rural poverty and the consumer price index—hence the argument that keeping food prices low and simultaneously generating rapid growth in employment are the key to poverty alleviation (Ahluwalia 1986; Mellor 1988). While the incidence of poverty in India fluctuates between 40 and 55 percent, depending on whether food is "cheap" and employment available, it has to be noted that over one-third of the rural populace cannot meet its daily caloric intake even at the best of times (Bardhan 1985; Breman 1996; Eswaran and Kotwal 1994; World Bank 1996a).

5. It is important to note that children and women suffer most under conditions of poverty. A large number of children in India have no childhood, working under appalling conditions as "child labor" (Weiner 1992). India's female population continues to face greater malnourishment and less education than men. The sex ratio is disturbingly male biased, at 929 females per 1,000 males. Generally lacking land, women remain locked out of the formal financial system and are constrained in their ability to acquire capital assets or working capital. These and other inequalities continue to constrain attempts to improve labor productivity, reduce fertility, alleviate poverty, and promote economic growth (Agarwal 1994; World Bank 1996a).

6. An excellent discussion of the paradox of growth without redistribution is by Pratha Dasgupta (1993).

7. M. S. Adiseshiah (1985); Pranab Bardhan (1985); Mukesh Eswaran and Ashok Kotwal (1994); Rajni Kothari (1987); and John Mellor (1988), as well as various papers in Srinivasan and Bardhan (1988); Tendulkar (1985); and Vaidyanathan (1988) provide a comprehensive overview of these debates.

8. In fact, a World Bank study (1989a, 175) notes that the physical quality of life of the "ultra poor" (a new category), or those whose incomes is more than 25 percent below the current poverty line standard of Rs 90 to 105 per capita per month has not improved, but in fact has worsened. In 1988, the "ultra poor" in rural India were estimated to number about 123 million or 20 percent of the rural population. According to the World Bank (1990, 29), the "extremely poor" alone (in the mid-1980s) numbered approximately 250 million people, or 33 percent of India's total population.

9. For details see World Bank (1997).

10. For details see J. Dreze and P. V. Srinivasan (1996).

11. For similar conclusions see Eswaran and Kotwal (1994); Rao and Linnemann (1996); and Repetto (1994).

12. For details see World Bank (1999, 196). It is also worth noting that over the past fifty years the world's population has more than doubled, from 2.5 billion to 5.5 billion, and the global gross domestic product (GDP) has increased sevenfold, from about $3 trillion to over $22 trillion. Yet, over one billion people, a fifth

of humanity, live in conditions of abject poverty. The vast majority of the world's poor live in Asia, particularly in rural areas. In the Philippines, for example, the percentage of the poor living in rural areas is almost 75 percent. In India, Thailand, and Pakistan it is approximately 80 percent, and over 90 percent in Indonesia, Bangladesh, Cambodia, and Laos. No doubt rural poverty constitutes the most important development challenge facing many developing countries. Nowhere is this a greater challenge than in India. With over 900 million inhabitants (in mid-1993), and a per capita income of $300, India continues to have one of the highest incidences of poverty in the developing world and accounts for about one-fourth of the world's absolute poor (World Bank 1996).

13. The field of development economics is broad, defined by three approaches: neoclassical, neo-Marxist, and structuralist. For an excellent overview and critical analysis of the contributions of development economists see Chenery (1975) and Meier (1989).

14. For example, in the Malthusian tradition scholars such as H. Leibenstein (1954) and R. M. Solow (1956) argued that the faster the rate of population growth, the more rapid the increase in labor supply, compared with capital formation, and the lower the level of per capita consumption. Thus population growth results in a "low-level equilibrium trap." Similarly, in the growth models of W. Arthur Lewis (1954) and John Fei and Gustav Ranis (1964), population growth was seen as having negative effects because it increased the dualism between the agricultural and manufacturing sectors.

15. Economists were not the only ones promoting such unilinear and inherent ethnocentric formulations. David McClelland (1961), a psychologist, argued that the key to successful economic growth and poverty alleviation lay in inculcating within the masses the "psychological need to achieve."

16. For an elaboration of the Lewis model see Fei and Ranis (1964).

17. See Chenery (1974); Srinivasan and Bardhan (1974); Mellor (1976); Ranis and Kuo (1979).

18. See Chenery (1974); Hayami and Ruttan (1985); Lal (1985); Mellor (1976); Johnston and Kilby (1975).

19. Cited in Mellor and Desai (1985).

20. Montek Ahluwalia (1986, 72), India's long-time advocate of "trickle-down," recently stated: "It must be conceded that even on optimistic assumptions, the process [of reducing poverty] would be slow if we relied on growth alone."

21. See Dasgupta (1981); Ghai (1977); Griffin (1974; 1976); and Krishna (1979).

22. Atul Kohli (1987, 39) expresses these sentiments. As he points out, "the refusal to recognize that policies reflect concrete social and political interests led to unrealistic expectations concerning the prospects of alleviating Third World poverty by mere policy advice."

23. Arend Lijphart (1984) has identified as many as nine different types of democratic political systems on the basis of two dimensions of majoritarian-consensus democracy. Terry Karl (1990) has identified three types of democracy—conservative, corporatist, and competitive—on the basis of whether a nation's party system is restrictive, collusive, or competitive. Robert Dahl (1971) used the concept of polyarchy rather than democracy because of his view that no government ever becomes fully democratic. Thus polyarchies are those governments that approach democratic norms and practices. To Dahl a country can be considered "democratic" if there are contested elections based on universal franchise, as well as civil and political freedoms of speech, press, assembly, and organization. Adam Przeworski (1991; 1996) defines it as a system of processing conflicts in which

parties that lose elections accept this outcome and wait for the next election, rather than trying to destroy the regime to attain their goals.

24. The broad definition used here encompasses both the "procedural" and "substantive" textbook definitions of democracy. Procedural or formal democracy focuses on democratic institutions, structures, and procedures, while substantive democracy centers on democratic conditions and how to achieve the substantive goals of democracy like liberty, economic equality, and redistributive justice.

25. For an excellent review and critique see Macpherson (1965).

26. Nehru's ideas on democracy and development are lucidly presented by James Manor (1990) and Stanley Wolpert (1997).

27. To Stephan Haggard and Robert Kaufman (1995) the mediating role of representative institutions, in particular, cohesive party systems characterized by limited fragmentation and polarization, constitute the key to redistributive reforms in transitional societies.

28. The five countries included were Great Britain, Germany (West), Italy, Mexico, and the United States.

29. "A vertical network, no matter how dense and no matter how important to its participants, cannot sustain social trust and cooperation" (Putnam 1993, 174, 181).

30. Irma Adelman and Cynthia Morris (1967; 1973); William Dick (1974); Guillermo O'Donnell (1973); and Krishna Rao (1974) deal with this point.

31. For example, chapters in David Collier (1979) also trace the roots of Latin American authoritarianism in the 1960s to the need to "deepen" the process of industrialization. Implicit in their claims is the argument that only a strong authoritarian state that could "turn a deaf ear" to the interests of the various social forces could adopt such a market-oriented development strategy. In the particular context of Brazil, it was argued that the economic restructuring and the high rates of growth Brazil achieved during 1964 to 1974 would not have been possible without the strong "authoritarian" and interventionist state. See also Cardoso and Faletto (1979); Collier (1979); and Evans (1979). For similar arguments that links the success of market-oriented industrialization in the East Asian newly industrializing countries to a strong authoritarian-cum-"developmental" states, see Deyo (1987); Jones and Sakong (1980); and Wade and White (1984).

32. The limitations of rational choice approaches will be discussed in subsequent chapters.

33. The classic work on this topic is by Selig Harrison (1960), in which he argues that "centrifugal pressures" could ultimately overwhelm the new state, resulting in chaos and "balkanization."

34. The economic growth theories, including the political development literature.

35. For details see Bagchi (1982); Davey (1975); Gough and Sharma (1973); Kurian (1975); Prasad (1985); Roy (1976); Sau (1981); Shah (1973); and Weisskopf (1974).

36. There is variation among analysts who follow the pluralist models, but they share some basic assumptions. For example, South Asianists who adopted the pluralist model in the 1960s, for instance, Rajni Kothari (1964); Lloyd and Susanne Rudolph (1967); and Myron Weiner (1962), assumed that as India moved from "tradition to modernity," or in the direction of a democratic-pluralist polity based on a system of bargaining, compromise, and accommodation, it would spur organized secular interest-group activity and class-based political associations, eventually weakening and transforming the traditional caste-based relationships with more "rational" and sophisticated democratic politics. It was believed that pressures from the progressive modernizing elite committed to the goals of rapid

national development, combined with political mobilization and pressures from below, would inevitably result in a more equitable distribution of political power and the fruits of economic growth. However, Jayant Lele (1981) in his penetrating critique questioned the validity of the pluralists' faith in such a smooth evolutionary process of democratic development as well as their undue optimism in the "percolation thesis." According to Lele, such models fail to examine "the role of the hegemonic classes in democratic societies. The dispersion of the ruling elite leads pluralists to assume that there is no hegemonic class . . . [and] ignores the identity of interests for this dispersed class in the domination of cultural and economic orders" (p. 195). Also, pluralists "ignore as marginal the barriers faced by the disadvantaged groups. . . . The structural barriers to percolation of rewards are much more complex and impenetrable than the pluralists are willing to recognize" (p. 8).

37. See Byres (1988); Gupta (1989); Kothari (1988c); and Varshney (1988).

38. Ross Mallick (1994) singles out Atul Kohli (1983; 1987), adding that his distorted view of West Bengal has been picked up by Paul Brass (1990) and Lloyd and Susanne Rudolph (1987), among others.

39. For a comparative overview see Bratton (1989); Hyden (1983); Migdal (1994); and Shue (1988).

40. Giuseppe Di Palma has noted that civil society remained relatively vibrant even under communist domination in the former Soviet Bloc. He states that "civil society survived . . . not just as a conventional clandestine adversary but as a visible cultural and existential counter-image of communism's unique hegemonic project" (1990, 49).

41. The president of India occupies in the Indian constitutional system the same position as the Crown does in the British Constitution. India's presidents, with a few exceptions, have usually been distinguished elder statesmen (no women so far), who have generally performed their rather perfunctory duties with dignity. The president, who normally serves a five-year term, is also subject to impeachment by Parliament for violation of the constitution.

42. Yogendra Malik (1993, 86) notes that "in some ways the prime minister's secretariat resembles the U.S. president's executive office. It is entrusted not only with preparation of the agenda for cabinet meetings and maintenance of the records of cabinet proceedings but also with coordination of the administration of different departments of the government headed by the members of the council of ministers."

43. Under this system, political parties can gain commanding positions in the Parliament without gaining the support of a majority of the electorate. For example, the Congress Party that has dominated Indian politics until recently never won a majority of votes in parliamentary elections. The best-ever Congress performance in parliamentary elections was in 1984, when the party won 48 percent of the vote but garnered 76 percent of the parliamentary seats. In the 1991 general elections Congress won 37.6 percent of the vote and 42.0 percent of the seats.

44. As in the United States the terms in the upper house are staggered, so that one-third of the members stand for election every two years.

45. Officers of the Indian Administrative Service (IAS) are an elite corps, drawn primarily from the affluent and educated upper castes. In 1990 only about 150 out of a candidate pool of approximately 85,000 recruits received appointments in the IAS.

46. Unlike the United States, India has a single judicial system (not a system of dual courts), with the Supreme Court at the head of the judicial hierarchy, with high courts in each of the states, followed by district courts. According to the constitution, the Supreme Court should consist of a chief justice and not more than

seven other judges—albeit Parliament is authorized to change the number of judges, and has done so.

47. It is important to note that India has a unified judicial system. That is, there are no separate state courts, but each state has a high court that is subordinate to the Supreme Court. The Supreme Court also covers the disputes arising between the central and the state governments, as well as cases involving two or more states.

48. Most states have unicameral legislatures, however Andhra Pradesh, Maharashtra, Tamil Nadu, Uttar Pradesh, Bihar, and Jammu and Kashmir have bicameral legislatures, with the lower house or legislative assembly (the Vidhan Sabha) as the real seat of power. The upper house or legislative council (the Vidhan Parishad) serves as an advisory body.

49. Some have argued that the "Indian union is not strictly a federal polity but a quasi-federal polity with some vital and important elements of unitariness" (Palmer 1961, 94).

50. The team's report is named after its chairman, Balwantray Mehta, an ex-chief minister of Gujarat state. For the report's detail see Government of India (1957).

51. Local self-government is divided into urban and rural categories. The census report of 1961 has laid down definite criteria for determining urban localities: a population of 5,000 or more, density of not less than 1,000 persons per square mile, and at least 75 percent of the working population engaged in nonagricultural occupations. Rural self-government is discussed in the text.

52. A block is a large subunit of a district.

53. An independent election commission established in accordance with the constitution is responsible for the conduct of elections to Parliament, the state legislatures, and to the presidency. The commission prepares, maintains, and periodically updates the electoral roll that indicates who is entitled to vote; supervises the nomination of candidates; registers political parties; monitors the election campaign (including the candidates funding); organizes the polling booths; and supervises the counting of votes.

54. Norman Palmer (1961, 156) noted this some four decades ago: "The strong tendencies toward centralization in India are for the most part self-evident and self-explanatory; the equally strong trends toward decentralization and toward regionalism and localism are perhaps less self-evident and self-explanatory, but they seem to be growing rather than diminishing."

55. This pattern is not unique to India. For example, Kenneth Lieberthal (1995, 169) argues that "despite the authoritarian nature of China's political system, actual authority is in most instances fragmented . . . in this sense the Chinese polity can be considered one of fragmented authoritarianism."

2

Nationalism, Democracy, and Development: The Making of a "Weak-Strong State"

*India . . . has embarked on an experiment in democratic planning which
is perhaps larger and more complex than any in the modern world. Some
have called it a fateful experiment . . . what is on trial . . . is, in the last
analysis, whether democracy can solve the problems of mass poverty. It
is a trial perhaps never before made in such an atmosphere of urgency.*

—Government of India, 1958

The complex society that inhabits the vast land mass today known as
the Indian Subcontinent has never been easy to govern. The recurring
theme in South Asian historiography—from the precolonial times, through
colonialism, independence, and beyond—is one of an unending struggle
by ambitious central authorities to extend their dominion over the heterogeneous and differentiated socioeconomic and political constellations in
their midst.

The actualization of a unitary subcontinental state has varied over the
millennium as power and control shifted back and forth between the various constituents of state and society. The subcontinental polities such as
the expansionist Mauryan Empire (ca. 321 B.C. to 184 B.C.), the absolutist
state of the imperial Guptas (ca. 300 A.D. to 540 A.D.), and the lofty empire
of the Moghuls in the sixteenth and seventeenth centuries stand out as important epochs during which despotic and dynastic states established their
hegemony over much of the subcontinent.

However, governing a vast and diverse region with all its heterogeneity and contradictions was not easy, and even during the best of times central control over the subcontinental polity and society remained tenuous
and constrained.[1] To consolidate their power and expand their control, the
early state builders (like their modern counterparts) were constantly engaged in what can be best described as coercing, manipulating, accommodating, and integrating the complex web of provincial loyalties, local jurisdictions, and traditional sovereignties that simultaneously collaborated

with, resisted, and challenged the political center. The Moghuls' efforts to weave their imperial order into the fabric of society is an excellent illustration of such a process. The Moghuls (like their Mauryan and Gupta precursors) established with Machiavellian cunning elaborate means of penetration and control of society. The highly centralized fiscal, administrative, and bureaucratic apparatus (the *mansabdari* system) and the imperial doctrine of *sul-i-kul* that stressed the role of the emperor, if not the state, as indispensable to order and prosperity were products of deliberate state policy aimed at integrating the diverse communities of the subcontinent into a common economy and polity. However, despite the Moghuls' considerable powers of coercion and calculation, maintaining durable central control proved largely abortive, if not illusory, as the centralized instrumentalities eventually succumbed to the centrifugal tendencies of the various constituents of state and society. State decline was followed by interregnums during which power and control reverted decisively to the regional kingdoms and to the patchwork of local village *panchayats* that since antiquity had constituted the basal units of South Asian society and polity.

State and Society Under Colonialism

By the early eighteenth century, on the eve of British conquest, the Moghul state was already rapidly disintegrating. The political vacuum was filled by the officials of the British East India Company, who amid the social and political chaos were able to establish themselves as the undisputed rulers of the subcontinent. Acknowledgment of the changed political realities came in 1765 when the Moghul emperor transferred the right of *diwani* or revenue administration and collection of Bengal, Uttar Pradesh, Bihar, and Orissa to the British.

The colonial regime was a fortuitous amalgam of what Judith Brown (1985) has described as the "traditional" and the "modern." That is, it built on Moghul rule, incorporating many of the institutional, personnel, and infrastructural legacies of the Moghul state with British ideas and institutions of control and governance. Moreover, by collaborating with and co-opting regional and local notables, namely the *rajahs* (native princes), the *zamindars* (a hierarchy of landed interests), and a host of more predatory parvenus, the colonial regime was able to enhance its authority, extending its reach into the levels of society that lay outside the grasp of its formal structures of rule. Also, the colonial state's impulse toward bureaucratization and "rationalization" and its relentless drive to increase revenues for colonial administration and pay for the costly "home charges" to the imperial metropolis forced it to penetrate society more deeply than its precursors. According to Christopher Bayly (1988), colonial rule was able to establish far more durable political and administrative institutions—and in so doing profoundly influenced state formation and state-society relations in the subcontinent (see Sarkar 1983, 13–22). Specifically, under the viceregal state of the British *raj* South Asian society and economy underwent significant realignments. For example, in an effort to gain the support and cooperation of the native princes and the hierarchy of landed interests who had earlier served as intermediaries-cum-tax collectors for the Moghuls, the colonial state instituted its own revenue and land tenure "settlements" with these powerful groups.[2] The "settlements" varied from region to region, as prototypes of systems for the exploitation of land, labor, and resources, but they shared the common characteristic of introducing "private property rights" in land by vesting full rights of ownership including those of mortgage and sale in the *zamindars*.[3] In return the *zamindars* were to pay fixed installments of revenue to the colonial state and collaborate in maintaining law and order in the countryside.

The introduction of private property rights in land did not transform the landed or *zamindar* classes into enterprising peasant capitalists or "junker-type" landlords. On the contrary, the policies of the colonial state only served to perpetuate and exacerbate rural disparities by further entrenching what Sumit Sarkar (1983, 30–37) has aptly called "parasitic landlordism" and "feudalistic exploitation." For example, the vesting of full rights of ownership, including those of mortgage and sale in individual holders and the growth of a market in land, led to the expropriation of the actual tillers and paved the way for land ownership to become concentrated in few hands. Further, the high and rigid tax revenue demanded by the colonial state forced the *zamindars* and a host of other intermediaries (e.g., moneylenders, speculators) to maximize their incomes (to meet the revenue demands and maintain their opulent lifestyle) by intensifying the "squeeze" on the actual tillers of the land, ultimately driving many into debt and bondage. Moreover, the commoditization of land and labor, the rapid expansion of commercial agriculture, and the resultant closer linkages with urban centers and dependence on metropolitan markets not only made the rural society and economy greatly susceptible to the boom and bust cycles that characterized primary-commodity export systems, but also severely disrupted (and destroyed) the "corporate unity" and self-sufficiency—what James Scott (1976) has called the "moral economy"—of rural society.

Thus, under deleterious colonial economic policies the structure of agrarian society and economy underwent significant changes. As agricultural production became oriented toward commercial crops and foreign markets, the residual pool of grain and other basic foods available to support the needs of the growing peasant population declined precipitously, worsening the conditions of hunger and poverty and sinking large areas of the subcontinent into "a vicious cycle of hunger and famine."[4] Moreover, colonial agrarian policies further cemented the highly unequal landholding systems and rural power relations by promoting increased concentration of wealth and power and differentiation among the landed classes, the cultivating peasantry, and the landless.

At the apex of a multilayered pyramid stood the traditional upper-caste elites of native princes and the "big feudal *zamindars*" who controlled large landed estates and virtually monopolized productive (and much unproductive) land, labor, and capital and other agricultural resources.[5] These "parasitic elites," as the support base and embodiment of the basic props of Pax Britannica, owed their position to the colonial rulers, with whom they jointly maintained "law and order" in the countryside. Next in the agrarian hierarchy were many intermediate layers of landed interests with varying rights to land and resources, ranging from a class of rich peasantry, usually the dominant local landowning and cultivating castes and classes,[6] with control over substantial landholding, to a group of prosperous "tenants," often identified in the literature as "middle peasants," who enjoyed legal protection in the form of fixed rents and permanent and inheritable rights to the land they occupied. Below this class were a mass of small-holding or poor peasants with claim (often tenuous) to a plot of land barely sufficient to provide daily subsistence needs. At the bottom of agrarian society, totaling about 25 to 30 percent of the populace, and drawn disproportionately from the "untouchable" scheduled castes and *adivasis* (tribal peoples) were the class of impoverished poor peasants, sharecroppers, and landless agricultural laborers.[7]

In contrast to the largely export-oriented and stagnant agricultural sector, a limited amount of manufacturing and industrial development took place during colonial rule.[8] Although the colonial state consistently favored British over Indian capital by insulating British trading and manufacturing interests from the pressures of international and local market forces, a small indigenous capitalist class did emerge out of the traditional mercantile communities (especially among the Parsis, Gujaratis, Marwaris, and Chettairs) in the mid-nineteenth century.[9] But systematic discrimination (in both official and unofficial state policy) against indigenous entrepreneurs kept them not only in an unfavorable trading position vis-à-vis foreign capital but also highly fragmented and concentrated among particular families and regions of the subcontinent. It was only after the end of World War I that the nascent indigenous capitalist-industrial classes were given a measure of fiscal autonomy and protection from the "one-way free trade" that enabled them to gain a firmer foothold in the financial, manufacturing, and industrial complexes. Eminent Indian historians, notably, Amiya Bagchi (1982), Sumit Sarkar (1983), and Bipan Chandra (1966; 1988), have argued that the incipient Indian bourgeoisie could never establish a strong and enduring "organic link" with colonial capitalism and thus developed a long-term "contradiction" with it. According to Chandra, the Indian capitalist classes became the chief financial backers of the nationalist movement because the nationalist strategy of reversing the "underdevelopment and de-industrialization of India" and the nationalist commitment to the goals of *swadeshi*—which called for a total boycott of foreign, principally imported, goods—were quite consistent with that of India's nascent capitalists. Moreover, Indian capitalist classes realized that without freeing themselves from the "shackles of colonial subjugation" they would never develop their full expansionist and accumulative capacities.[10]

The other significant class to emerge from colonial rule, or the class that first articulated the idea of "English rule without the Englishmen," was the indigenous Western-educated intelligentsia. Drawn from the traditional high-caste literati and the urbanized middle classes (also disproportionately upper caste), this anglicized urbane elite functioned as doctors, lawyers, and journalists, but mostly as "brown sahibs" (civil servants and petty bureaucrats) in the complex infrastructure of the British *raj*. But limited opportunities for advancement, often open discrimination and exclusion from senior posts, and their overall subordinate position in the colonial hierarchy, gradually changed this class from being what Anil Seal (1968) has described as "collaborators to competitors" for power. Disillusioned with the slow pace of socioeconomic and political reforms, members of this elite were ultimately to spearhead the nationalist movement—first demanding administrative reforms and then *Hind swaraj* (or self-rule) and the end of British rule of the subcontinent.

The Nationalist Movement:
Making of the Modern Indian State

From its inception in 1885 to the early 1920s the embodiment of the nationalist movement, the Indian National Congress (also the INC or the Congress), remained in the words of Barrington Moore (1966, 372) "an essentially upper class club . . . of timid English-speaking intelligentsia." Controlled by an urban-based elite whose advanced education, cosmopolitan travel, and westernized culture had much in common with the colonial rulers, the INC leadership was content to agitate peacefully for political and constitutional reforms within the framework of continued British rule.

As is well known to specialists the INC underwent a decisive change in the 1920s. Under the formidable leadership of Mohandas Gandhi (later canonized as the *mahatma* or "great soul"), the INC was rapidly transformed into a mass-based political movement with the aim of achieving *swaraj* for India. Gandhi's sharp *volte-face* from the earlier INC strategy was a tribute to his political acumen. His sensitive intellect discerned with great clarity that for *swaraj* to be achieved, the anglicized nationalist elite had to first accommodate and politically mobilize the nation's "toiling and unemployed millions," the numerous "little traditions," the "provincial cultures," and the diverse social communities and classes for the cause of Indian nationalism.[11]

Gandhi and his political lieutenants (who included such stalwarts as Jawaharlal Nehru, Subhas Chandra Bose, Vallabhbhai Sardar Patel, and J. P. Narayan) initiated an extraordinary campaign to raise social consciousness and mobilize the masses. They decentralized the Congress Party's organizations and structures and laboriously built its political units at the grass roots by carefully weaving together what Judith Brown (1985) calls the moral and cultural fabric of the world of the peasant with that of the urban-based Western-educated elites. Specifically, the introduction of an annual four-anna (cents) membership fee per person, Gandhi's "towering personality," personal austerities, extraordinary rapport with the masses, and novel mode of social action—which required that Congress Party workers at all levels alternate their political activities with *sarvodaya* (or social welfare and "village uplift" programs) and visibly identify with the masses by adopting the traditional *khadi* (homespun clothes) and conversing in the vernacular—enabled the INC to reach out successfully "to the tens upon millions" and bring the variegated communities and classes into a broad-based nationalist alliance.[12] In 1921, the year Gandhi launched his famous *satyagraha* (the nationwide civil disobedience campaign against British rule), Congress membership had skyrocketed to around two million, with a core circle of party activists and sympathizers in almost every provincial town, district, and village of the subcontinent.[13]

Yet, ironically, even while the INC's strategy of popular mobilization broadened its political base and transformed it into a formidable anti-imperialist force, it also produced countervailing tendencies that significantly weakened it as a political organization (Kohli 1987, 51–72; Moore 1966, 370–410). This resulted in part from the INC's virtually open recruitment policy that did not exercise any real checks on those who joined; in fact, groups and individuals even vaguely sympathetic to the goals of *swaraj* could join the Congress. A lack of established mechanisms of norms and procedure and institutional structures to check the motives or ideological orientation of those who signed on (the only "requirement" being sympathy or support for the anti-colonial cause) opened the INC to penetration by a multitude of organized vested interests, including, in Anil Seal's (1968) provocative words, "opportunists," "careerists," and "mercenaries." Some of these had little, if any, commitment to the announced egalitarian goals of the nationalist movement, but moved into the "Congress system" when it became clear (especially after the mid-1930s) that the INC was the most likely successor to the British raj.[14]

Whatever the full extent of the vagueness and deliberate obfuscation of the INC's mobilization and organization strategy, the most critical factor that weakened the INC as a political organization, simply put, was bad politics. Specifically, even as the INC broadened its support base, the party leadership failed to knit together the mobilized social forces into a cohesive and disciplined political organization. This failure, as D. N. Dhanagre (1975) has noted, stemmed from the fact that in spite of the mass character of the nationalist movement, Gandhi and the Congress leadership remained conservative in political practice (Frankel 1990, 483–504). This conservatism was manifest in both the INC's mobilization strategy and the policy positions adopted by the party leadership. In particular, the Congress leadership's strict adherence to the strategy of class reconciliation and to the principles of "moral politics" based on the Gandhian doctrine of "trusteeship"[15] prevented the party from taking firm and consistent political decisions because it feared that such actions might precipitate class warfare.[16]

Indeed, as Myron Weiner (1967) and Paul Brass (1965) point out, the politics of accommodation and compromise practiced by the Congress elite only tended to reinforce and legitimize the strategic position of the dominant classes and castes. According to Weiner, "party building" involved little more than adapting to local power structures. In the countryside the Congress relied primarily on the support and cooperation of the local landowning interests, in particular the village landlords and the rich and upper strata of the middle peasantry, to organize the party cadres and mobilize the grassroots support for the Congress Party. Weiner (1967, 15) notes that "in its effort to win, Congress adapts to the local power structure. It recruits from among those who have local power and influence. . . . The result is a political system with considerable tension between a government concerned with modernizing the society and economy and a party seeking to adapt itself to the local environment to win elections."

As these links of dependence grew stronger the wider district, state, and national party organizations came increasingly to represent a complex pyramid of hierarchical alliances between the dominant rural interests and the Congress Party. In effect, from very early on the party in structure, process, and policy came to represent the dominant landowning class and castes. Such a political-organizational strategy, what historian Gyanendra Pandey (1978) has called the "politics of imperfect mobilization," not only precluded a challenge to the normative and institutional foundations of the traditional social, economic, and political hierarchies, but also undermined the pressures from below that could have effectively challenged the hegemony of the powerful groups and classes dominating the Congress system.

Not surprisingly, throughout the nationalist struggle the INC leadership, while demanding acquiescence from the popular classes and lower castes, nevertheless tended to respond to the initiatives and grievances of the mobilized *kisan* and *mazdoor sabhas* (peasant and worker associations) with a mixture of distrust and vacillation, seeing a situation to be managed and controlled "from above" by the Congress "high command." Frankel and Rao (1989/1990, 493–494) notes:

> The leaders of the nationalist movement, in following Gandhi, carried out political mobilization from the top down. They relied on rich peasants as intermediaries in the rural areas, and professionals and the trading community in the towns and cities, to reach down to the poorer classes. . . . [Thus] the nationalist leadership not only failed to build links between the diverse religious, caste and tribal communities on the agrarian issue, but they withdrew support from leaders who took up peasant grievances in the name of Gandhi so that the movements were localized as unrelated agitations and petered out.

On a similar vein, D. N. Dhanagre (1975) and A. R. Desai (1966) have noted that even Nehru (the most influential advocate of socialism inside the INC), in placing a higher priority on class accommodation and preserving party unity, even if it meant significant concessions to the dominant class interests, failed effectively to utilize the mobilized peasant/worker political associations to build a dedicated and disciplined party cadre at the grass roots. By not institutionalizing the interests and aspirations of the subordinate classes/castes and communities within the "Congress system" the INC leadership, and especially Nehru, whom Barrington Moore called the "gentle betrayer of the masses," failed to utilize this valuable political resource to build and enhance the party's political autonomy and institutional capacity vis-à-vis the dominant propertied classes.[17] As a consequence, even as the Congress broadened its political base, it grew not into a unified and disciplined political organization but a precarious and loose, elite-dominated, multiparty coalition—what Anil Seal (1968, 2) provocatively characterized as a "ramshackle coalition" of numerous shifting, crosscutting, competitive (and often hostile) centers of power, with conflicting ideologies, petty jealousies, and competing ambitions and interests, unamenable to organizational unity, party discipline, or a cohesive ideology.

During the long years of the nationalist struggle, the fragile unity of the Congress Party was barely held together by the "moral authority" of Gandhi's leadership and the efforts of leading nationalists—men like Jawaharlal Nehru, Vallabhbhai Patel, Maulana Azad, M. M. Malaviya, and Rajendra Prasad—whose substantial experience in politics enabled them to play a balancing act and arrange compromises among the INC, various social forces, and disparate groups and classes that made up the unruly coalition. Numerous commentators have observed that it was the INC leadership's ability at conflict mediation, bargaining, and consensus building with competing interests that laid the groundwork for the creation of a consensual and democratic polity in independent India.[18]

They correctly note that it was the collective wisdom and political perspicacity of men like Nehru and Patel, as well as Rajendra Prasad, Babasaheb Ambedkar, and C. Rajagopalachari, that gave life to the Indian constitution, which not only enshrined the principles and ethos of parliamentary democracy, but did much to augment and transform the rudimentary political and institutional scaffolding of late colonialism into tools for democratic reconstruction. In practice the founding fathers remained committed to the operative principles of parliamentary democracy, rules of civility, political accountability, and respect for constitutional and judicial procedures of governance. This ultimately enabled the founders to forge a united political community, arouse popular passion and allegiance, and assert a solidarity with the masses—providing the capacity to reconcile differences without precipitating political-institutional decline. Beyond this, the Indian founding fathers helped forge an awareness about India that had not existed earlier: that the Indian union was greater than the sum of its parts, its sociopolitical pluralism and religious diversity the source of its strength, and its multitudinous problems best resolved through representative institutions and mediated politics.

As valid as these arguments are, it needs to be recognized that the Congress strategy and the exigencies of democratic politics created its own set of contradictions. That is, while the Congress system's pluralism expanded its power and made it representative, what is often overlooked and needs to be emphasized is that the Congress Party's "promiscuous accommodation"[19] and its open, inclusionary style of politics (that often out of political expediency indiscriminately compromised with the powerful political and societal interests) made the party into a weak political organization with minimal capacity to confront those interests. As so-called revisionist analysts such as Dhanagre (1975), Frankel (1978), and Kohli (1987) point out, the politics of compromise and accommodation that the Congress elites mastered "to [the] highest degree"[20] served fundamentally to sustain old inequalities and legitimize emergent ones. The revisionists argue that the accommodations, bargains, and compromises made within a rigid and hierarchical socioeconomic order not only reduced the Congress Party to a partisan political machine, distributing goods, services, and resources to a carefully selected array of powerful interests, but also made the INC "incapable of generating an autonomous political force to confront and reform [the] social structure" in the postindependence period (Kohli 1987, 58). According to Kohli (1987, 56–58) the INC, from the 1920s onward, can best be conceptualized as a quintessential political movement whose "inclusive ideology, open recruitment, and a weak internal control structure made it into a weak political force suitable for accomplishing only a limited range of goals." Thus, even though the INC's political-organizational form "proved eminently suitable" in mobilizing anticolonial sentiments into a broad-based nationalist movement, these same institutional and organizational characteristics "diluted the capacities of the INC as a tool of social transformation." As the formal structures of the INC became intricately enmeshed in the traditional structure of dominance, its capacity to formulate and implement policies independent of the powerful classes and castes in society declined.

Unlike some other nationalist movements, such as the "reformist nationalism" of Lázaro Cárdenas in Mexico in the 1930s or the "revolutionary nationalism" of the Sandinistas in post-Somoza Nicaragua, which show that there is nothing inevitable about nationalist movements' compromising with and protecting the interests of the dominant classes,[21] the leadership of the Indian nationalist movement (which from the beginning made the politics of class compromise with the dominant interests its *modus vivendi*) failed to translate its extensive popular support into a well-institutionalized and disciplined political organization. Being institutionally weak and fragmented, and increasingly co-opted by the dominant propertied classes, "the INC was not designed to challenge the dominant social interests" and therefore "found it expedient to compromise with the powerful groups and classes in society" (Kohli 1987, 58–59; Moore 1966, 400–410).

Thus the INC, which had loudly proclaimed its goal of creating a socialistic pattern of society, and professed to be the guardian of the interests of rich and poor alike, betrayed early on its tendency to adopt a populist ideology and posture, while in practice compromising with the propertied classes. In consequence, since India did emerge from colonialism under the leadership of the Congress Party, some of these acquired tendencies and incongruities continued to exercise a decisive influence on the country's postindependence political economy.

State-Society Relations in the Post-Independence Period

At the stroke of midnight on 15 August 1947, Prime Minister Jawaharlal Nehru proclaimed independence as the nation's "tryst with destiny," a quest to redeem over two centuries of colonial humiliation and to build a modern and prosperous nation guided by the principles of secularism, central planning, and democratic socialism. The nationalist elite maintained that such objectives could only be attained under the guidance of a strong democratic state that would be an exemplar and social arbiter and play the key role in maintaining political stability and spearheading the nation's strategy of "self-reliant" economic development.

In the immediate postindependence period the political elite's major priority was to consolidate the new democratic state. Despite many constraints that had to be faced, the early years after independence created conditions that momentarily "freed" the new state from established socioeconomic and political entanglements, thereby offering it a greater degree of maneuverability to redefine coalitions, alliances, and policies. In other words, as the rising tide of nationalism swept away the legitimacy and authority of the British raj, the buoyancy and enthusiasm of the times also offered an opportunity, a "breathing space," to use Theda Skocpol's (1979) term, to India's emergent democratic state to enhance its powers and autonomy by transcending dominant structural boundaries.

Specifically, the peaceful transfer of power made for a continuity of political and institutional structures. As the legatee and bearer of the anticolonial struggle, the Congress Party and its leaders, such as Nehru and Patel, enjoyed enormous prestige and popular support. They capitalized on their popularity and legitimacy and enhanced their position by institutionalizing a "top-down" democratic system that further strengthened the legitimization of the new state and gave it greater room to "regulate" the competing interests in civil society and to mobilize popular support for the new regime. Second, with the major divisive issue of the so-called "Muslim problem" solved by the creation of Pakistan, the Congress Party stood politically unchallenged as the lead player in the "one-party dominant system," and the only major nationwide political organization. Third, the so-called steel frame of the British raj, the highly professional and technically efficient bureaucracy, the Indian Civil Service (later the Indian Administrative Service), along with a functioning independent judiciary and parliament provided the new state with the necessary vehicle for administering and maintaining political stability and order, especially during the tumultuous first decade after independence. Furthermore, after independence the new state inherited such key investments as transportation, communications, defense, and some basic industries, notably in the vital sectors of steel, energy, and mining, that only served to enhance national economic power in the society and reduce immediate dependence on foreign capital and expertise.[22] Equally important, the propertied castes and classes, despite their influence and wide representation in the Congress Party, were not always unified enough to make common cause or to effectively challenge the power and legitimacy of the new state. The national bourgeoisie did not directly challenge the new state because as a class it was small in size (and dispersed), and its overall capacities were quite modest. Influential capitalists, including J. R. D. Tata, Purushotamdas Thakurdas, Kasturbhai Lalbhai, G. D. Birla, and A. D. Shroff, who had agreed after the signing of the famous "Bombay Plan" of 1944 to actively support Nehru's strategy of "planned industrialization," were willing to give the new state "a chance" to prove itself.[23] In fact the indigenous capitalists, who had suffered through decades of discrimination at the hands of the colonial state, looked to the new state for protection and economic stimulation.[24] Moreover, the powerful class of "feudal" native princes and *zamindars* who had collaborated with the colonial regime and had lost their colonial patrons were in retreat. Such analysts as Dhanagre (1975), Frankel (1978), and Kohli (1987) have noted that in the euphoric days after independence even the power and influence of the rich landowning peasantry (well entrenched in the state-level Congress political machine) could have been curtailed, or at least moderated. The new democratic state, with its powers now endowed with legitimate authority, and the force of nationalism and potential political power of the mobilized lower peasantry behind it, could have undermined, or at least chipped away at, the vertical political and economic structures and replaced them with new political institutions at the village level—what Frankel (1978, 25) has called "new forms of horizontal class organization among the peasantry." By "utilizing the quintessential political resource—legitimate compulsion," the state could have stood above society instead of compromising with the dominant societal interests (Kohli 1987, 227).

The cumulative effect of these postindependence conditions (both real and potential) produced at a crucial juncture in independent India's history a sort of "hegemonic crisis" (to use Cardoso's term) providing the state some autonomy to "tame" the dominant propertied classes and an opportunity to build and consolidate its social base among the less privileged castes and classes. Indeed, in the immediate postindependence period the state elites embarked on a aggressive attempt to construct and consolidate the instruments and institutions of the emergent democratic state.[25]

State Building and the "Developmental Alliance"

State building and consolidation are complex processes and do not automatically translate into greater state autonomy and capacity for reformist development. In India, despite the apparently favorable (though by no means sufficient) conditions that existed in the early postindependence period, the inheritors of the Indian state once again failed to utilize the conditions history and circumstance had provided to establish the bases of an autonomous democratic developmental state—that is, one capable of transcending, or at least "standing above," the dominant social-structural boundaries and guiding political and socioeconomic development to facilitate economic growth with distribution.

The reasons behind what Atul Kohli (1987, 227) has appropriately called "India's great political failure" are complex. Neo-Marxist analyses have generally viewed the INC (and India's democratic state) as essentially a "bourgeois-landlord organization" designed to preserve and perpetuate the capitalist mode of production. While the influence and powers of the rising national bourgeoisie were not inconsequential, but in overemphasizing the powers of the industrialists and "capitalist classes" in general (which as a group were both unable and unwilling to seize control of the state), neo-Marxist analysis tends to be unduly reductionist. Similarly, the pluralist viewpoint simplistically argues that the proclivity of such important leaders as Gandhi and Nehru for accommodation with the dominant interests, their faith in incremental and peaceful approach to socioeconomic change, and the victory of the "conservatives" within the INC served fundamentally to retard national development in India. Even explanations provided by scholars such as Kohli, who attribute the failure of modern state building to India's weak "nationalist-democratic regime" and its incapacity to utilize "legitimate compulsion" to institutionalize the interests of the subordinate classes within the state structures, are problematic. The Indian case amply illustrates that there were specific conditions simultaneously favoring and limiting state and regime autonomy in the formative postcolonial period. What, then, explains why a more autonomous democratic developmental state failed to emerge in India? In other words, why were the conditions facilitating relative state autonomy—conditions that existed during the immediate postindependence period—not prudently seized upon and utilized by the state elites?

No doubt, the legacies of colonial rule,[26] the privileged position occupied by the propertied classes and castes within the INC, and the ideological predisposition of the Congress leadership toward class compromise with the rich and well endowed are important elements of any explanation, which, however, needs to be complemented. This study suggests that although the Nehruvian state elites actually envisaged a strong centralized federal government, out of "necessity" they readily agreed to a decentralized "parliamentary federalism." As will be discussed, such an agreement was a necessary precondition before the state could strike a tacit "developmental alliance" with the dominant urban and rural socioeconomic and political interests. But what were the forces that propelled the wily custodians of the state to give away so much and agree to preside over a spatially and politically fragmented institutional-administrative governing structure?

The usual references to Gandhian ideals of decentralized development notwithstanding, this study claims that, more than anything else, it was the convergence of interests between the political elites and the industrial and business classes (with the economic interests of the latter and the development goals of the former closely coinciding) that provided the impetus for the *first* "developmental alliance" between the state and the industrial and capitalist interests.[27] After all, the convergence and collusion of shared interests and, at times, complementary "development ideologies" between the political and economic elites were nothing new. Ever since Gandhi's rallying cry for *swadeshi* (economic nationalism) in the 1920s, the Congress elite and the industrial and business classes had shared "cordial interests," with the economic elites actively bankrolling the INC during the long anti-colonial struggle (see Kidron 1965, 65–69; Frankel 1978, 32–35; and Chandra 1966).

During the rapidly changing political and economic circumstances in the postindependence period, particularly as the imperatives of national economic development took precedence over everything else, the state and the industrial classes were inclined to seek even closer cooperation and linkages with each other. But mutual suspicion and distrust persisted on both sides. The national bourgeoisie was still relatively weak as an "organized class" and geographically concentrated, remained leery of Nehru's socialist predilections, especially his fascination with Soviet-style state-guided development, and needed reassurance, if not guarantees, from the new state. Suffice to say, one way of curbing the powers of the center was to create a more decentralized parliamentary federalism—and such an arrangement would suit the economic interests of the national bourgeoisie. As early as 1948, the new state complied. As will be discussed, the Industrial Policy Resolution of 1948 and, less than two years later, the constitution not only gave the propertied interests a privileged position but also vested the state governments with an important constitutional role in the formulation and implementation of industrial policy. Industry was to be jointly developed by the center and the states, with primary responsibilities falling to the state governments. What is important to note is that the closer linkages-cum-alliance between the state and the industrial classes and the subsequent development strategy adopted by the state did not simply result from class domination of the state by the emergent industrial and commercial bourgeoisie. Rather, India's chosen development strategy, though determined to a considerable extent by the state, was nevertheless a shared enterprise evolving from a shared vision that this strategy was the most desirable and feasible means of achieving rapid national economic development.

Institutionalization of the First Dominant Alliance

The Economic Foundations

First, it is important to reiterate that the task of socioeconomic development facing India at the time of independence was overwhelming. India had inherited an impoverished economy that was both extremely poor and stagnating. Under British rule the growth of food production had been negligible. In George Blyn's (1966) careful estimation, from 1890 up to 1947 the output of staple foodgrains per capita actually declined by roughly 26 percent despite the relatively low population growth of 1 percent per year. Not surprisingly, an Indian could on average expect to live for no more than thirty-three years. Further, the almost total absence of growth of per capita income, low levels of capital formation in the public sector, and a technologically backward industrial sector that could barely produce basic goods such as cotton textiles, sugar, soap, matches, and salt (and with an almost nonexistent capacity for the production of basic capital and intermediate goods) stood as major obstacles to national economic growth and development (Bettelheim 1968, 8–54; Bagchi 1982).

Against this backdrop of economic backwardness and stagnation, and faced with the daunting task of economic reconstruction, India's new political leaders declared that the goal of building "national economic self-reliance" was the government's foremost priority. The national political and economic elites agreed that the quest for national self-reliance could best be achieved through a "planned" strategy of modernization of the economy via rapid industrialization and import substitution in which the state would play the central role via its ownership and control of the "commanding heights" in the economy; the indigenous private sector would be guided in the desired direction by the state; and foreign economic interests would play, at best, a marginal and subordinate role, with minimal reliance on foreign capital inflows other than grants and concessional aid (GoI 1956; Bhagwati and Desai 1970).

Prime Minister Nehru, the chief advocate and architect of the strategy of economic nationalism, argued that without industrialization India's economy was doomed to suffer from its peripheral status in the global capitalist economy, and perpetually remain poor and underdeveloped.[28] He gave the modernization-cum-industrialization plan his imprimatur, arguing that the nation's pursuit of self-reliant development was a carefully thought-out strategic plan designed to make India industrially strong and economically self-reliant—which he argued was entirely consistent with the principles and goals of a "socialistic pattern of society."[29] However, he pointed out that because of India's colonial legacy of "deliberate deindustrialization," the process of industrial modernization would be different from that experienced by the early industralizers. Specifically, in India the state would have to assume much of the role that private capital had performed in other settings: the state should have control over important industrial infrastructures like public utilities and basic industries and strict control over the importation of all commodities in order to exclude those not considered central to industrial expansion. The Industrial Policy Resolution of 1948 went to great lengths to outline a preliminary blueprint for future industrial development, as well as clarify the role of the public and private sector in the planned "mixed economy."[30] The resolution gave the central and state governments a virtual monopoly in railroads and the exclusive right to develop minerals and the iron and steel industry, and specified eighteen key industries of "national importance" to be developed under the direct control and regulation of the central government. However, the need to promote India's industries was so great that, in effect, the eighteen key industries the government undertook to develop were industries "in which private enterprise [was] unable or unwilling to put up the resources required, while the rest of the economic arena could be left free for private enterprise" (GoI 1956, 4). In effect, the Industrial Policy Resolution of 1948 was a document of compromise between India's political and economic elites. In March 1950 (shortly after India's constitution went into effect), a quintessential top-down expert committee, the Planning Commission, was established under the general guidance of the provision in the constitution. With Nehru as chairman, the Planning Commission was given the explicit task to further articulate and implement via the five-year plans (the first introduced in 1951) the national leadership's policy directives and developmental objectives.[31]

Critics have noted that in spite of the political leadership's vocal commitments to the reformist or socialistic dimensions of "self-reliant" economic development, the "crash industrialization" strategy adopted by the government was not consistent with the goals of balanced economic development, or the goals of reform and redistributive justice. For example, Ayesha Jalal (1995, 127) argues that "it is hardly surprising that the early fruits of Indian economic development were reaped mainly by the privileged social groups. Committed to rapid industrialization . . . Nehru compromised his socialism and endowed it with the logic of a mixed economy. Nehruvian socialism was perfectly consistent with indirect state support for private enterprise."

The harsh reality was that the new state simply did not have the necessary political-institutional capacity or the economic resources at its disposal to facilitate an ambitious industrial transformation. Presiding over a state still in the process of consolidation (and increasingly penetrated by the dominant propertied interests) and with only modest bureaucratic, political-institutional, and economic capacity—and yet desirous of rapid economic modernization of a "backward economy"—the Nehruvian state elites concluded that the state had few options other than entering into a tacit accommodation with the industrial and business/commercial classes in hopes of releasing the forces of economic dynamism "from above" via public support of private enterprise. Thus, in the end, the compulsions of production won out over the goals of distribution. The "developmental alliance" between "modernist" state elites and the industrial and business classes that began with the Industrial Policy Resolution of 1948 became more firm during the First Five Year Plan, only to be consolidated with the proclamation of the Industrial Policy Resolution of 1956 and the Second Five Year Plan (1956–1961).

The Second Five Year Plan and the Industrial Policy Resolution of 1956—heavily influenced by Nehru's close confidant and the Planning Commission's statistical adviser, P. C. Mahalanobis—spelled out the details of the government's development strategy. The plan's heavy-industry bias was clearly evident as industry's share of the total investment was almost tripled (from 7.6 to 18.0 percent out of a total outlay of Rs 48 billion), while agriculture's share was slashed by nearly half that of the first five-year plan. Overall, the second plan called for "planned industrialization" to be carefully guided in a "mixed economy" involving both public and private ownership. In practice, while the plans greatly expanded the scope of public-sector development they also allocated extensive areas to the private sector, in addition to protecting it from foreign competition. Moreover, private-sector facilities were excluded from expropriation and nationalization, and the state even agreed to provide economic resources for their expansion. Three categories or "schedules" of industries were created. Schedule A, consisting of seventeen industries, reserved for development by the public sector most of the basic and heavy industries. Schedule B contained a list of twelve industries in which public-sector investment would supplement (in the form of equity capital) private-sector development. All other industries, including much of the lucrative consumer goods sector, were open to private-sector development.

Hence, it was the twin imperatives of building national power and rapid economic development via industrialization—what Baldev Raj Nayar (1972) has evocatively called the Indian state's "modernization imperative"—that inclined and, to some extent, necessitated the Nehruvian state elites to compromise, and form a developmental alliance, with the industrial and commercial classes. Moreover, it is important to note that "planned industrialization" did not represent a "movement toward social justice" as some have argued (Ahluwalia 1985; Bhagwati and Desai 1970). To the contrary, it laid the foundations for state-guided capital-intensive industrialization (Byres 1982; Bettelheim 1968, 145–176; Mukherji 1988, 166–195).

Such an arrangement suited the needs of both the state elites and India's budding industrial and business houses. It not only allowed the state to harness the domestic wealth and the managerial and entrepreneurial talent but also buttressed the legitimacy of the political leadership as "progressive modernizers." Furthermore, private capitalists (fully aware that they were not strong enough to promote economic development without massive inputs of public investment and aid) welcomed involvement by the public sector, especially since the state had agreed to operate in risky, capital-intensive industries and provide the much needed financial and infrastructural support to private enterprise. The first two five-year plans (1951–1961) committed the lion's share of the government's financial investment to modernizing the national railroads and related infrastructure, and included insurance, loans, tax breaks, investment opportunities, and, occasionally, even price supports—"services of tremendous importance to private capital" (Nayar 1972, 25–75). Also, the state's commitment to establish a viable national market and its determination to push for import substitution and strict regulation of foreign capital and multinationals in the "national interest" (in practice, dislodging foreign investments and capital from their existing market positions) found strong support among India's rising industrialists, who had much to gain from these nationalistic economic policies. For example, the Foreign Exchange Regulation Act, passed in 1973 to "regulate foreign investment," defined foreign firms as those with over 40 percent of foreign equity. These firms' entry or expansion into most areas was restricted, except for 100 percent export-oriented operations or those that brought advanced technologies into the country.[32] Expansion, in effect, required dilution of foreign equity to under 40 percent, resulting in the virtual halt of foreign direct investment into India. As Pranab Bardhan (1984, 40) has insightfully noted:

> The industrial capitalist class, mainly under the leadership of some of the top business families . . . supported the government policy of encouraging import-substituting industrialization, quantitative trade restrictions providing automatically protected domestic markets, and of running a large public sector providing capital goods, intermediate products and infrastructural facilities for private industry, often at artificially low prices. Since the mid-fifties, the government created several public lending institutions, loans from which form the predominant source of private industrial finance.

Thus, the first dominant alliance between the democratic state and the industrial and business classes was forged to industrialize India. To achieve this goal the state actively pursued a set of policies designed to release the forces of economic dynamism from above, "by public support of private profitability" (Kohli 1987, 64). Under this partnership the state greatly expanded its economic base by creating a public sector that, beginning almost from scratch, grew in a decade to dominate the "commanding heights of the economy." By insulating the private sector from external market competition and providing improved infrastructure and financial incentives, the state helped transform the incipient capitalist classes into a well-organized and powerful social force.[33] Indeed, in the decade after independence the twenty largest business houses controlled over one-third of all corporate assets in the country (Hazari 1966, 36–37); a decade and half later, by 1976, these leading twenty houses had substantially expanded their operations to control nearly two-thirds of the total productive capital in the private corporate sector. Moreover, the small-scale industrial sector was by no means ignored. Over the years it has also grown substantially, and its linkages through subcontracting and ancillary relationships with the big private-sector companies have become stronger.

The simultaneous pursuit of private and state capitalism under the umbrella of economic nationalism and an open democratic polity, therefore, has served the interests of both the state and private capital, further con-solidating the tacit but mutually beneficial developmental alliance. Stanley Kochanek (1987, 1285) has noted that "the decade from 1950 to 1966 proved to be the golden age of private sector development based on close business-government co-operation."[34]

However, as the tacit alliance had matured, so has the conflict, with the state's emphasis shifting from development of the private sector to greater regulation of it. From the mid-1960s (until economic liberalization in 1991), the weak democratic state did what it could "legally" do: incre-mentally erect a whole series of complex and overlapping regulatory rules, orders, and laws designed to better "control" and "manage" the private sector.[35] However, like the genie out of the bottle, India's industrial capi-talists had grown too hefty to be easily controlled and regulated. While these regulatory measures have resulted in some "tensions" and "conflicts" within the dominant alliance, the state and the private industrial/business sectors have on balance adjusted to the new "exchange relationship" of give and take. In Kochanek's (1987, 1284) lucid description of this rela-tionship: "Business (the buyer) went to government (the seller) for bene-fits, and in return paid in the form of resources such as campaign contri-butions, political donations, and jobs for relatives. The political leadership came to depend very heavily on the system as a quid pro quo for securing campaign contributions, and the bureaucracy depended on it for payoffs, employment, power, prestige and patronage."

The state elites, particularly at the national level, enjoy a degree of relative autonomy as they preside and arbitrate over a plurality of con-tending interest groups and classes, but it should be noted that the indus-trial and business classes have been able to set in place an elaborate net-work of formal and informal mechanisms of access to the state. Thus, in practice, regulatory measures have promoted "private interests rather than vague notions of the public interests" (Kochanek 1987, 1284). As Pranab Bardhan (1984, 41–42) lucidly elaborates:

> Even the ostensibly adverse government policy of an elaborate scheme of industrial and import licenses has been allowed to be turned to the ad-vantage of the industrial interests they were designed to control: the richer industrialists, having better connections and better access, have got away with the lion's share in the bureaucratic allocations of the licenses, thus pre-empting capacity creation and sheltering oligopolistic profits. The controlling interest of the public financial institutions in companies has been used more often to take over "sick" or marginal units saddled with large losses. Thus the government not merely finances private in-dustry, it also acts as the risk-absorber of the last resort and a charitable hospital where the private sector can dump its sick units.

Overall, the growth record of India's import-substituting industrializ-ing (ISI) strategy was modest (if not disappointing), in comparison with those of South Korea and other high-performing East Asian states. South Korea's GDP growth rates were 8.7 percent, 9.1 percent, and 9.7 percent in the 1960s, 1970s, and 1980s, respectively, and 10 percent over 1965–1980. Its per capita GDP growth rate was 7 percent over 1960–1981 and 8.5 percent over 1980–1992 reaching $1,700 in 1981 and $6,790 by 1992. Korean industry grew at an astounding 17.2 percent in the 1960s, 17.4 percent in the 1970s, and slowing to a still high 12.7 percent (World Bank 1993). India's growth rate of net domestic product (NDP) from 1956–1957 to 1965–1966 was only 2.9 percent, with industry and manufacturing growing more rapidly at 6.4 and 6.0 percent, respectively. Growth rates from 1966–1967 to 1981–1982 were 4.0 percent, 4.5 percent, 4.3 percent, and 1.3 percent for NDP, industry, manufacturing, and agriculture, respectively. Over 1980–1990, GDP growth picked up to 5.3 percent, while manufacturing growth rate increased to 7.1 percent (World Bank 1996).

The Political Foundations of the Dominant Alliance

Besides laying the economic foundations necessary for planned rapid industrialization, the Indian state also created a legal and administrative framework for economic activity. To use a Weberian term, it established a "property regime" that over the years has been progressively adapted to the distinctive needs of the state and the dominant socioeconomic interests. Beginning with the judicious integration of the princely states into the Indian union, and the Machiavellian political tactics used to oust such opposition groups and parties as the Gandhians and socialists (who split from the Congress in 1948), the state reassured the industrial and commercial classes of its commitment to "nation building" and the ability to provide a stable and predictable political-economic environment, a *conditio sine qua non* for planned industrial-capitalist development.

By far the most important political initiatives aimed at protecting the interests of the propertied classes and castes were those incorporated into the legal, administrative, and institutional framework of the new democratic political order. The Constitution of India offered a complex coverage of legal protection regarding control and ownership of private property, with rights to private property occupying a privileged position in the constitution as a basic and "fundamental right." Article 19 guaranteed the right to "acquire, hold and dispose of property," and article 31 of the constitution stipulated that no property could be acquired for public purposes unless the central government paid full and fair compensation. As discussed in some detail in the next chapter, even the *zamindars* and the former native princes and their successors were also given constitutional guarantees, recognizing their rights to receive tax-free privy purses from the central government, including the "personal rights, privileges, and dignities of the Ruler of an Indian State."[36] This was in sharp contrast to the more egalitarian sections of the constitution, such as the right to "an adequate means of livelihood to all citizens; distribution of ownership and control over the material resources of the community to best subserve the common good; operation of the economic system in order to avoid concentration of wealth and means of production; and the promotion the educational and economic interests of the weaker sections of the people, in particular, the under-represented Scheduled Castes and Tribes." Such sections of the constitution were confined to the *nonenforceable* Directive Principles of State Policy.

Furthermore, as discussed earlier, the legal and constitutional provisions placed strict limitations on the powers and jurisdiction of the central government, particularly on the central government's powers over the rural sector, by assigning primary responsibility of the agrarian sector to the provincial and local governments. Under the new arrangement the central authorities were reduced to providing guidelines, while the actual task of translating policies into legislation and implementation was left to the state and local governments.[37] These "concessions" reflected, in part, the significant political and economic clout of the landowning castes and classes, their representatives in the local, district, and state (*pradesh*) Congress committees, and their ability to control and effectively manipulate the political and constitutional process to their advantage. It is also important to note that this division of powers reflected the growing linkages between the political authorities (especially at the provincial level) and the landed castes and classes. The "vertical alliances" between the Congress Party and the dominant landowning castes and classes forged during the nationalist struggle became even more binding after independence. The Congress Party, lacking a strong political and organizational base among the cultivating peasantry and having only a modest administrative presence in the countryside, continued to rely on the established and emergent hierarchies to organize, on the party's behalf, the rural support base.

Specifically, under the arithmetic of the new electoral politics, the Congress leaders further accommodated themselves to the existing hierarchical power structures in order to win votes. Rural notables, who invariably were members of the dominant landowning classes and castes, enjoyed considerable local discretion and a base of support virtually independent of the Congress Party and increasingly became political intermediaries between the countryside and the outside authorities in the local, district, and national administration and government. These notables became what F. G. Bailey (1963) has termed "brokers" in the rural constituencies, often pursuing particularistic local interests with extra vigor inside (and outside) the state institutions. Their support was courted by the Congress Party because these notables-cum-politicians, through their extensive caste, kinship, and economic ties and their ability to manipulate what Jayant Lele (1981) described as "strategies of patriarchalism and patrimonialism," controlled the rural "vote banks" for the Congress political machine in return for preferential treatment and tangible rewards. Moreover, the landowning rich peasantry (including *zamindars* and former princes) successfully exploited the wide network of traditional vertical ties based on rank, caste, and tradition, not to mention their considerable economic powers, to become powerful "political bosses" with a firm grip on their constituencies. Under such conditions, the Congress Party could only win elections through a deliberate effort to accommodate, cajole, bribe, and reward these power holders into joining the Congress political machine. Indeed, this is how many local notables formally joined the Congress Party. According to Rajni Kothari (1964, 1170) "the Congress system," as a vast, well-greased, hierarchically structured party, attracted "a plurality of elites, sub-elites and groups [that] could both voice their claims and attempt to realize them." Thus, through a complex weaving of the formal and informal structures of governance, the overarching apparatus of the Congress system was able to encapsulate even the most distant hinterlands in its political-institutional orbit.

The cumulative effect of all these sociopolitical and economic changes was to reinforce the strategic socioeconomic and political position of the dominant classes/castes in rural society and tie the Congress Party into a intricate web of "transactional linkages" with the traditional authority groups in the countryside. Clearly, then, the "power-sharing" arrangement worked out between the provincial and central governments "acted as a brake in preventing sweeping changes of the social order from above" (Frankel 1978, 81). Dominated by the landed interests, the provincial governments were not only able to acquire significant powers of administration over law and order, local government, education, and communications, but were also assigned "virtually exclusive control over the governance of the vast rural sector, including such key subjects as land reforms, agricultural credit, land revenue assessments and taxation of agricultural incomes" (Frankel 1978, 81–82). This was of considerable consequence: it not only significantly reduced the central government's control over provincial policies, programs, and implementation, but the constitutional division of power was to become a permanent obstacle to the implementation of land and tenure reforms, discussed in the next chapter.

East Asian Developmental States and India's Weak-Strong State

In their seminal works, Barrington Moore (1966) and Alexander Gerschenkron (1963) illustrate that capitalist industrialization has historically required some sort of an "alliance" between the state and the emerging industrial and commercial/business classes. This was particularly true for "late bloomers" such as Bismarckian Germany and Meiji Japan. Gerschenkron noted that "late industrializers" confronting an established, competitive, and hegemonic international industrial order faced complex problems of economic development and therefore required pervasive state intervention to overcome the political and socioeconomic impediments. In late-industrializing Germany, for instance, capital accumulation and industrialization were spearheaded by an alliance led by a strong interventionist state, private banking, and industrial capital. The state not only harnessed the resources for industrialization but also assumed firm political control over the dominant socioeconomic interests and a direct, coordinating role in economic management and decisionmaking. Chalmers Johnson's study of Japan's Ministry of International Trade and Industry (1982, 17–25) also provides an excellent account of an "autonomous developmental state" in action. He argues that the Japanese state's "embedded autonomy," exemplified by its institutionalized and centralized decision-making structures, its emphasis on "performance" and "plan-rational" technocratic solutions, and the "existence of a powerful talented and prestige-laden economic bureaucracy" allowed the state to act as a surrogate for weak indigenous capitalism, set "substantive social and economic goals," and implement a strategy of rapid economic development based on "industrial rationalization."

Similarly, a growing body of comparative scholarship reveals that postwar East Asia's rapid transition from ISI to export-led growth strategy and the relatively egalitarian pattern of income distribution cannot be attributed to untrammeled market-oriented policies alone, but rather rests on a combination of peculiar social historical conditions and strategic or "targeted" government interventions in the economy.[38] First, East Asia's smooth transition from ISI to export-promotion industrialization was not simply the result of responses to market signals; rather, the foundations of export-led growth was laid in an earlier period of business and entrepreneurial maturation that dated back to the interwar period under Japanese rule in Korea and Taiwan (Cumings 1984; McNamara 1990). Second, while it is true that the impressive performance of East Asian newly industrializing countries (NICs) with respect to rising real wages and income equity is due to its rapid expansion in labor-absorbing (hence, employment-generating) export-oriented manufacturing industries, it should also be noted that the socioeconomic structure and the patterns of income distribution in South Korea and Taiwan were relatively egalitarian even before the transition to export-led growth. This is largely because extensive business/commercial restructuring and comprehensive agrarian reforms had been undertaken in these countries in the 1940s and 1950s by the Kuomintang (KMT) in Taiwan and the Syngman Rhee regime in South Korea (Anderson and Hayami 1988). Third, the East Asian states performed functions that went far beyond the norms of prescribed free-market policy: the market-oriented policies were accompanied by discretionary state intervention that complemented and directed rather than negated market forces. Despite some variations in the patterns of state intervention, the East Asian states through discrete and targeted interventions created an environment supportive of competitive market forces. For example, in the early phase of ISI the states not only acted as surrogates for missing capital markets by procuring domestic and foreign savings and protecting infant domestic industries through tariff barriers and quantitative restrictions, but later played a key role in identifying potentially lucrative niches in the global economy and quickly orchestrating incentives (including tax breaks and subsidies) to encourage domestic firms and export cartels to diversify, invest, expand, and modernize. Moreover, the states, by assiduously following market signals, were able to respond (often preemptively) to externalities, provide crucial market information, and broker relations with foreign investors and creditors. By assuming a catalytic role in the areas of information processing and dissemination (including specialized research and development) and acquisition of technologies, the states were able to foster local mastery (rather than simply transfer) of modern technologies. Also, throughout the different stages of modernization these states provided (i.e., subsidized) the needed infrastructure to industries and businesses by creating a number of industrial parks and export-processing zones. Finally, the activist developmental states, by heavily investing in education (especially vocational training), created a large pool of technically skilled and disciplined workers indispensable to economic modernization, especially export-promotion manufactures. These generalities will resonate better with a more detailed commentary on the role of East Asia's "interventionist, developmental state" in the process of economic development.

The "embedded autonomy" of the Chiang regime in Taiwan and the Park Chung Hee and Chun Doo Hwan regimes in South Korea enabled those states to achieve a relatively high degree of insulation from the dominant interests in civil society and actively shape their economies and societies. A system of elaborate corporatist organization of interest groups—a strategy that granted considerable operational space to market-oriented technocrats and policy elites, and allowed paternalistic collaboration with the powerful business conglomerates (e.g., the Korean *chaebol*) in the private sector—enabled these states to pursue market-conforming methods of state intervention in the economy without precipitating organized opposition from the powerful vested interests. For example, the Park regime's policy of "guided capitalism" launched in 1962 gave the state, via the newly created Economic Planning Board (EPB), chaired by the deputy prime minister, direct management over the nature and pace of industrial development. As Cumings (1984, 29) notes:

The EPB . . . took over from a previous ministry and entire budgeting functions: it decides which industries and firms to promote, which to phase out; it closely supervises both the development and the implementation of planning, along with an official trade promotion agency . . . it surveys the world for needed markets, capital and technology.

Through careful manipulation of financial incentives and disincentives (including regulation), therefore, the Park regime protected infant industries and aggressively promoted exports of labor-intensive light manufactures. The state not only picked winners, it actually made them. Alice Amsden (1989, 18) notes that "to qualify as a regular customer of the government for long-term subsidized credit [and for all other forms of state benefits], objectively necessary, if not sufficient, conditions had to be met. . . . Big firms and small firms, young firms and old firms, *chaebol* and non-*chaebol* had to export."

Moreover, the Park regime (like the KMT in Taiwan) by carefully responding to market signals shrewdly devalued the currency in 1964 and adopted a pragmatic floating unitary exchange rate in March 1965. The establishment of a unitary floating rate and liberalization of import controls, a classic example of "getting the prices wrong," created profitable investment opportunities in targeted export industries, resulting a few years later in an export boom (Westphal 1978). These states further supported would-be exporters by establishing the compulsory quality inspection of export goods (so the few bad apples could not damage the reputation of the other Korean or Taiwanese exporters) and provided exporters with information on foreign standards, tastes, and distribution and marketing systems. In fact, it was the state that placed Korean-made goods in international trade fairs—a strategy that proved useful in checking the problem of product and technological obsolescence, as well as helping Korean firms gain entry to the global marketplace. As if all this was not enough, the states also guaranteed exporters exemptions from business and commodity taxes, easy access to foreign exchange, and assurance of high initial profits, thereby further reducing the manufacturers' reluctance to invest in export industries. Over the course of the 1960s and 1970s these states repeatedly intervened in their economies to enhance firms' competitiveness in the global marketplace by imposing moderate import protection—for example, the effective protection rate for manufacturing was nearly 30 percent in South Korea well into the 1980s. Complementing this, the states' well-trained, efficient, and "meritocratic" bureaucracy (a product of "hard" developmental states' "business-like" institutional and decisionmaking structures) reduced intrabureaucratic log rolling and conflict, and the corporatist control of organized labor and students (and the states' ability to create manufacturing jobs) enabled the states to co-opt and subordinate groups (namely organized labor) from the popular sector.

Robert Wade (1990) essentially concurs with Amsden, Cumings, and Johnson. Wade articulates a "governed market" theory claiming that the East Asian developmental states are not merely "market conforming" in their intervention but "market governing." In other words, there exists a "pragmatic synergy" between East Asian governments and markets that explains their economic and developmental success. Focusing on Taiwan with comparisons with South Korea, Japan, and Hong Kong, Wade provides detailed accounts of how these states have utilized their policy instruments to maintain macroeconomic growth and stability to spearhead export-promotion industrialization. Painstakingly tracing the state's role in different industries and sectors over time, Wade shows, for example, how Asian governments encouraged both high levels of investment and sectoral composition of investment (that could not have been supplied by the market) by managing their financial markets and maintaining control over both the interest rates and the allocation of credit through the state-owned banking system. Further, he provides a detailed account of the "trade regime" (the core of the neoclassical account of export-led growth), arguing that although exporters enjoyed a free-trade regime for inputs, the domestic markets for final products were protected by governmental regulations well into the mid-1980s, and exporters were granted supports (such as relaxed enforcement of income tax payments) that went far beyond a favorable exchange rate. For example, Wade notes that subsidies to Taiwanese exporters in the 1960s were tied to export targets and administered by industry associates that were monitored by state agencies. These associates, which acted as cartels, collected members' dues out of which bonuses were paid to successful exporters. That is, firms were allocated export targets and penalized if they fell short of their performance targets. It is enough to note that under such a demanding state regulatory system, most firms had to perform well, and many did. Through the use of such detailed empirical evidence in the form of case studies and exhaustive reviews of the instruments of government policy, Wade demonstrates how market-guided state intervention—mobilizing domestic and foreign savings for "productive investments," targeting lucrative niches in the global economy, providing incentives to ensure technological and financial innovations, and deliberately responding to market signals to allow firms to minimize risk and exploit comparative advantage—have been central to the economic success of the East Asian NICs.

However, India's disaggregated and weak federal state, which also acted as a demiurge, failed to produce the economic achievements of the East Asian NICs because it lacked the embedded autonomy of the latter. This greatly limited the state's ability to calibrate linkages and forge dynamic symbiotic relationships between civil society and markets. Therefore, although the Indian state continued to expand its role as regulator, producer, and distributor throughout the 1960s and 1970s, including sheltering producers (in both the public and private sector) from market competition, unlike the South Korean or the Taiwanese states it did not have enough leverage to facilitate global market competition by encouraging private capital flows or by expanding export-processing zones and foreign investment—while at the same time gradually removing itself from speculative and unproductive economic activities. In the end, the Indian strategy of import substitution became more than a policy of protecting infant industries, it became a way of protecting inefficient and monopolistic producers. The Indian state, in adopting what Jagdish Bhagwati (1993) has termed "proscriptive economic policies" (unlike the "prescriptive policies" of the economically successful East Asian countries), failed to direct the economy through market signals. Proscriptive policies grant politicians and bureaucrats the power to say no to most private initiatives and create opportunities for self-aggrandizement, thereby spawning quasi-monopoly rents (in forms political contributions and black money), licenses, and in-built inefficiencies.

Although the economic crisis of the mid-1960s laid bare the inadequacies of India's ISI strategy, rather than shift to an outward-oriented export-led industrialization, the Indian state intensified import substitution. The failure of the Indian state to reorient macroeconomic strategy away from ISI to export promotion was rooted in the nature of the country's governing arrangements and the developmental alliance between the state and industrial-commercial interests. This alliance only served to enhance the powers of the propertied classes, while at the same time eroding the political capacity of the state. Specifically, two core constituents of the dominant coalition, industrial capital and the political-bureaucratic state elites, had vested interests in the maintenance of state-regulated import substitution. Since ISI had created a substantially large as well as small-scale protection-dependent private industrial sector, these interests had a stake in the state-controlled ISI model. Similarly the state elites, both politicians and bureaucrats, had strong vested interests in maintaining their discretionary powers in industrial and import licensing and foreign exchange allocation. Furthermore, India's organized labor enjoyed legal protection (while its counterparts in East Asia faced repression), assurance of "permanent employment" under ISI, and the backing of the left wing of the Congress Party that was strongly opposed to even closing chronically unprofitable industrial units, let alone making the shift to export promotion. The Congress Party split in 1969, which saw the defeat of the potentially free-enterprise (right) wing of the party and the victory of left-leaning Indira Gandhi–led Congress, ensured the continuation of the pro-ISI and pro-public-sector strategy of the state.

It was the complex and mutually conditioning mesh of forces from both the state and society that served to dilute the autonomy and capacity of India's state. Specifically, by failing to construct strong and durable institutional and structural capacity of the new state, by failing to "incorporate lower-class bias institutionally within the state" (Kohli 1987, 58), and by compromising with and accommodating to the needs of the propertied classes, the state elites weakened the polity over which they presided. Moreover, the "top-down" developmental alliance, forged by political expediency and the imperatives of building national power, was from the beginning biased in favor of the dominant economic interests. The "development" policies of the state, justified largely in terms of the sole criterion of achieving maximum increases in production, benefited those better situated to exploit profit-making opportunities, namely, the propertied classes. Moreover, as the interests of the propertied classes became incorporated institutionally into the constitution and state structures, these classes not only benefited disproportionately from state intervention but were also able to enhance their political and economic leverage over the state. The Indian case suggests that a state (whether democratic or authoritarian) lacking overall cohesion and discipline, and with weak and fragmented political and institutional structures of administration, cannot provide the necessary "administrative guidance" because the structures are easily penetrated by organized and powerful social and clientelistic forces that then confine the state to operating within an ever narrowing range of choices.

Notes

1. In their recent book, Sugata Bose and Ayesha Jalal (1997, 240) note that "it is now emerging from scholarly research that pre-colonial empires, far from being centralized, bureaucratic autocracies, were flexible, nuanced, and overarching suzerainties . . . the amount of power actually vested in the different levels of sovereignty was subject to historical shifts and downward flows and seepages in periods of decentralization and fragmentation. What was non-existent, even in the heyday of pre-colonial empires, was any notion of absolute sovereignty and its concomitant demand for singular allegiance."

2. In different parts of the country the landed interests were referred to as *chakdars, jagirdars, maqaddam, taluqdars, or zamindars.* Here *zamindar* is used as the generic term.

3. Prior to colonial rule, agricultural production was carried out by self-sufficient cultivators using plots of land over which they had usufructuary rights on a hereditary basis. The land was "owned" communally by the whole village, and plots could not be bought or sold or otherwise transferred privately. However, the village communities were not communistic in the sense of everything being held and used in common. Substantial stratification existed—different families or *jatis* (caste groups) had different rights and privileges vis-à-vis the *zamindars* and the state. For details see Sarkar (1983); Frykenberg (1969); and Thorner (1976).

4. For a good overview see Bhatia (1963); Bagchi (1982); and Sen (1962).

5. Some of these powerful landed interests, as allies of the colonial rulers, enjoyed considerable "autonomy" under the colonial umbrella. While British paramountcy was firmly maintained, about one-third of the subcontinent—or the "princely states"—fell under their direct control. Sumit Sarkar (1983, 64–65) points out that these semi-independent states were nothing more than "petty despotisms"— feudal backwaters harboring the most reactionary elements in Indian society (also see Sen 1962).

6. The dominant landowning and cultivating caste and classes usually have the following characteristics: large population concentration in particular regions and districts, the control and ownership of substantial agricultural land, ritual rank, and a willingness to use their power to assert domination and demand compliance.

7. Landlessness existed in precolonial India, but it was during colonial rule that the size and proportion of landless peasants increased significantly.

8. See Sarkar (1983, 38–44); Chandra (1966); Ghosh (1986); and Jha (1963).

9. To a considerable extent Indian capitalism developed in spite of, in opposition to, and independent of foreign capital. Thus, the Indian bourgeoisie emerged in sectors (such as cotton textiles) that colonial capitalism shunned after 1850 because it was both high risk and unprofitable. For details see Byres (1982); Bagchi (1982, 87–94); and Sarkar (1983, 38–44).

10. See Chandra (1988, 375–385); Patnaik (1972, 210–229); and Jha (1963).

11. Jawaharlal Nehru (1936, 253) wrote that Gandhi "is the quintessence of the conscious and subconscious will of those millions [the peasant masses] . . . he knows his India well and reacts to her lightest tremors and gauges a situation accurately and almost instinctively."

12. According to the Congress Party constitution, an active or "primary" Congress member must "wear khadi, be a teetotaler, oppose untouchability, favor equality of opportunity, believe in intercommunal unity, perform constructive activity, pay a few *naye paise* (Rs. 1 annually and collect another Rs. 10 for the Congress)" (Palmer 1961, 191).

13. Lest the paragraph convey a misleadingly rosy impression, it should be noted that despite the success of the INC in mobilizing the masses, the Congress never succeeded in making itself an all-inclusive body. Many of India's Muslims supported the Muslim League, and the poor, low-status "caste Hindus" gained little more than token representation in the Congress Party. For a critical review see Sarkar (1983) and Krishna (1966, 413–430).

14. Similarly, Robert Crane (1959, 181) noted that "from the time of the first civil disobedience campaign, the internal history of the Congress was the reconciliation of a multitude of special interests and different points of view."

15. It was during his famous Champaran and Kheda *satyagrahas* in the 1920s that Gandhi articulated his doctrine of "trusteeship." Essentially, it emphasized voluntary reform through the moral regeneration of the exploiting castes and classes. Gandhi appealed to the moral and religious conscience of the privileged sectors of society, and expressed the belief that the propertied castes and classes could be "converted" into acting as honorable "trustees" of society in responsible and socially productive use of their wealth and power on behalf of the downtrodden. For Gandhi, trusteeship would not only restore the ancient moral glory of Indian rural life, but also ensure an equitable production, consumption, and distribution of goods and resources. For details see Gandhi's own writings (1957), as well as Majumdar (1962) and Mehrotra (1971).

16. Francine Frankel and M.S.A. Rao (1989/1990, 496) note that "Gandhi's determination to avoid social and economic issues that could lead to class conflict, and the Congress leadership's mobilization of support from the top down, cast politics in the mould of elite accommodation."

17. Similar arguments are presented by D. N. Dhanagre (1975); Atul Kohli (1987, 51–93); and Francine Frankel (1978, 18–27).

18. See Brown (1985); Morris-Jones (1971); and Rudolph and Rudolph (1987).

19. I owe this metaphor to Gopal Krishna (1966).

20. See Frankel (1978, 23).

21. Nora Hamilton (1982, 3) has argued that it was during the Cárdenas administration (1934–1940) that the "ideal of a progressive and implicitly autonomous

state was to a large extent realized in Mexico." The Cárdenas administration carried out far-reaching agrarian reforms by effectively eliminating the power of the traditional landed elites. The regime also challenged the incipient capitalist classes by encouraging the mobilization and organization of urban and industrial workers, ultimately incorporating the major labor unions as well as peasant associations into the government and party structures. However, in the case of India the political elites failed to take advantage of the potential power of the popular organizations and use this political resource to bring pressure upon the propertied interests and move development goals in the direction of economic democracy.

22. Although factory establishments and mines accounted for only 6.5 percent of the national product and employed only 2.6 percent of the labor force in 1950, modern industry was in absolute terms quite important. For details see Weisskopf (1974); and Vaidyanathan (1983).

23. The so-called Bombay Plan was the blueprint for industrialization drawn up by a group of leading Indian industrialists that called upon the state to play an active role in laying the groundwork for future industrialization of India.

24. This argument is made by Thomas Weisskopf (1974) and Prabhat Patnaik (1972).

25. One of the most significant achievements of the new state was the integration into the Indian union of the territories of the former princely states, which had covered some one-third of the subcontinent during colonial rule.

26. The demarcation of responsibilities between the central and state governments was made explicit under British rule with the signing of the Government of India Act in 1935.

27. The "second dominant alliance" with the agrarian interests will be discussed later.

28. In a speech to the special silver jubilee convocation of Lucknow University on 28 January 1949, Jawaharlal Nehru (1958, 368) stated that "we are bound to be industrialised, we are trying to be industrialised, we want to be industrialised, we must be industrialised."

29. It was widely assumed that state-guided industrialization would not only modernize the industrial sector but also pull up the agricultural sector, and that the trickle-down from this growth would generate sufficient employment and revenue to raise per capita income and living standards (Bhagwati and Desai 1970).

30. According to the First Five Year Plan, "in a planned mixed economy, the distinction between the public and the private sector is one of emphasis. The two sectors are and must function as parts of a single organism" (GoI 1952, 9).

31. The task of the Planning Commission is "to assess the nation's resources, draw up a plan to use them with proper priorities and allocation, determine the conditions, machinery and adjustments needed to make the plan succeed, appraise the progress of the plan from time to time and make any recommendations necessary to facilitate it" (GoI 1952, 170). Although the Planning Commission is an advisory body (with the administration and implementation of the development program the responsibility of the center and the states), there is no doubt that the Planning Commission, until recently, wielded extraordinary influence.

32. Despite this, technology import has been strictly regulated from 1970 to 1991. Royalty limits on foreign technology licensing agreements were limited to 5 percent of net value added—effectively 3 percent after 40 percent taxation of royalties. Also, the Indian Patent Act, which gave less protection to foreign patent holders, and restrictive clauses such as bans on exports made technology suppliers less willing to include anything beyond the minimum in the technology package transferred.

33. From 1956 onward there was a major growth of government financial institutions dedicated to serving private-sector industry. For example, the aggregate amount of loans going to the private corporate sector increased from Rs 20.6 crores in 1956 (1 crore = 10 million) to Rs 123.1 crores in 1962 (Gupta 1969, 95; also Bettelheim 1968; Chattopadhyay 1970).

34. For similar arguments also see Bettelheim (1968); Myrdal (1968).

35. The major legislative provisions included the Industries Development and Regulation Act of 1951, with provisions for industrial licensing for producing any new product. The act has been amended frequently to increase the regulatory authority of the government. Until the changes in 1991, the Monopolies and Restrictive Trade Practices (MRTP) Act of 1969 enabled the government to place restrictions on new licenses for larger industrial houses (with assets of over Rs 200 million and Rs 1,000 million after 1985). Such "monopoly houses" required additional clearances over and above the usual industrial licensing procedure under sections 21 and 22 of the MRTP Act.

36. Nehru's objections to this clause was overridden by the "conservative factions" within the Congress Party. Sardar Patel argued that such assurances to the landed gentry were essential to the stabilization of the new political order (Frankel 1978, 80). However, this concession also reflected the reluctance of the state authorities to alienate the propertied classes.

37. Norman Palmer (1961, 179) noted early on that "generally speaking, the States have not provided the resources or carried out the tasks assigned to them in the Five Year Plans, and the Central Government has been unable to hold them to greater accountability."

38. There is vast body of literature on this subject. Important works include those of Alice Amsden (1989); Frederick Deyo (1987); Gereffi and Wyman (1990); Thomas Gold (1986); Haggard (1990); Wade (1990).

3

Rural Development During the Nehru Era: Limits to Reform and Redistribution

Sabhi bhommi Gopal ki.
—Mahatma Gandhi

The motivations for state intervention in the countryside are always complex, but the question of how state authorities define the task of national development and why particular policies are chosen and pursued cannot be isolated from the wider socioeconomic and political milieu. In India (and in many other developing countries), state policies toward the rural sector have been influenced and shaped both by the "development ideologies"[1] adopted by the state elites and by the political accommodations and compromises struck between the national state elites and the various social groups, in particular the dominant landowning classes and castes in rural society.

In India the content and goals of state policies for agricultural and rural development have undergone some important shifts, often paralleling the changes in the political leadership, the development ideologies of political elites, and the nature of the dominant class power and its linkages and alliances with the democratic state. However, while the capacity of political authorities to define and implement the state's developmental goals has varied over the decades, what is clear is that state intervention in the countryside has significantly transformed the agrarian political economy, though not always in directions intended by the national political elites.[2]

The aim of this chapter is to evaluate the Indian state's agricultural and rural development strategy during the Nehru era: from 1947 to 1964, a period that emphasized agrarian reforms and village-level "self-help" community development projects as a solution to the problems of poverty and underdevelopment in the countryside. The following discussion examines the impetus behind the strategy, the complex of forces that gave it shape, the problems of implementation, and its broader political and socioeconomic (in particular, reformist and distributive) ramifications.

It is argued that although the central government was constitutionally and programmatically committed to reducing rural inequalities and the amelioration of poverty by reforming the agrarian structure, nothing signifies as vividly the "governing paradox" and the hiatus between state policy intentions and actual outcomes as the failure of land and tenure reforms. Despite the numerous central policy directives, Nehru and the reformist-oriented Congress elite failed to convince or coerce the state governments—and virtually all the state governments in the period were Congress governments—or for that matter the various levels of local government, to effectively implement the agrarian reform policies. Without the backing of committed and disciplined party cadres, and lacking well-institutionalized political and bureaucratic organizations to authoritatively implement central directives, the center was at the mercy of state and local governments to translate central reformist decisions into reality. However, as noted earlier, the state and local-level political-bureaucratic elites, who were often themselves members of the rural propertied classes and castes, or functioning as representatives of the propertied interests (tacitly if not explicitly), colluded with the rural elite to make a mockery of the reformist policies. Hence, the failure of agrarian reforms was not simply the result of "bad" or "misguided" policies, or poor implementation, but a political failure rooted the makeup of India's democratic polity and in the patterns of state and propertied class alliance.

The Modernization Imperative and the Countryside

The adoption of ISI as the key development strategy by the Indian state following independence had clear ramifications for the countryside. Even as economic development became synonymous with industrialization, state planners and policymakers recognized the pivotal role of the agricultural sector in the overall development process.[3] They understood, for example, that the drive for industrialization required rapid agricultural modernization, in particular, significant increases in agricultural production and productivity. According to the Planning Commission agricultural modernization was a national imperative. A highly efficient and productive agricultural sector would not only help to underwrite industrialization, but also generate agricultural surpluses sufficient to avoid shortages of food grains and other essential commodities. Further, agrarian reforms promised to rid the countryside of unproductive large landholdings and the parasitic or "feudal" landlords who controlled them. Hence, structural reforms, the planners and policymakers argued, by creating a class of efficient and entrepreneurial or market-oriented farmers and smallholder peasantry, would simultaneously spearhead agricultural growth, ameliorate the problems of hunger and poverty, and reduce India's peripheral and disadvantaged position in the global economy. Indeed, the First Five Year Plan (GoI 1952, 60) reflected the importance the national policymakers attached to agricultural modernization:

> For the next five-year period, agriculture including irrigation and power must, in our view, have the top-most priority. . . . We are convinced that without a substantial increase in the production of food and of raw materials needed for industry, it would be impossible to sustain a high tempo of industrial development. It is necessary, however, on economic as well as on other grounds, first of all to strengthen the economy at the base and to create conditions of sufficiency and even plentitude in respect of food and raw materials.

However, while there was general agreement among the state planners and policymakers on the need to modernize the agricultural sector, two quite different perspectives were already well advanced inside the Congress Party on how this was to be accomplished.[4] One school advocated a predominantly "technocratic strategy" based on incentives to greater private investments in modern inputs and the concentration of technological innovation and capital resources for well-endowed areas (i.e., under irrigation or guaranteed rainfall) as the fastest way to achieving increases in agricultural production and productivity. The other line of thinking, advanced by Nehru and the Gandhian and socialist members in the cabinet, the Congress Party, and the Planning Commission, while in agreement with the broad principles of the technocratic strategy,[5] nevertheless questioned its efficacy under the prevailing, highly inequitable agrarian framework (see Malaviya 1954). These self-styled "Congress radicals" identified the basic cause of India's backwardness not in the absence of modern technology per se, but in the persistence of "certain inhibiting socioeconomic factors that prevent the most dynamic forces in the economy from asserting themselves" (Frankel 1978, 95). In other words, Nehru and his supporters argued that under Indian conditions, higher levels of agricultural output depended less on the application of modern capital-intensive technologies than on the elimination of the exploitative *zamindari* or "feudalistic" social and economic relations that inhibited peasant entrepreneurship and efficient farming and production practices. Accordingly, they argued that a transformation of the institutional structures of the agrarian order, or the abolition of the anachronistic "*zamindari* system" via land and tenure reforms and structural changes at the village level via "community development," must be an integral part of the overall program for rural and agricultural development. While both these perspectives have been influential in generating policies for the countryside, the so-called institutionalist strategy emerged as the more influential in the 1950s and early 1960s, only to be superseded from the mid-1960s by the technocratic or the "green revolution" strategy.

The State and the Political Economy
of Institutional Reforms

To Prime Minister Nehru, the Congress National Party Executive, and the Planning Commission, "meaningful" institutional reforms in the country-side were necessary if the state was to achieve its "multiple" economic, political, and social goals of development and reform. However, while the economic goals took precedence, with the central government's policies and prescriptions primarily concerned with the economic goals of achieving rapid increases in agricultural production and productivity (in order to underwrite industrialization), other goals, such as the socialist commitment of the central political leadership to "egalitarian development" by reducing social and economic inequalities and to improve the quality of life of the rural population, were not ignored. Indeed, for Nehru and his supporters there was no contradiction between the reformist and distributive socio-economic goals of rural development and achieving rapid agricultural and industrial growth.

Drawing eagerly upon a Congress Agrarian Reforms Committee report of early 1949 (GoI 1949), whose recommendations formed the basis for subsequent land and tenure reform legislation,[6] Nehru and his colleagues in the cabinet and the Planning Commission agreed that "there cannot be any lasting improvement in agricultural production and efficiency without comprehensive reforms in the country's land system" (GoI 1949, 7). They argued that the system of "extremely inequitable" landownership and tenure arrangements inherited from colonial rule was not only unjust but also imposed severe limitations on the efficient allocation of land, labor, and capital resources. Indeed, the first extensive data on landholdings and tenure arrangements in India, collected during the immediate years after independence and published in the *National Sample Surveys, 8th Round, July 1954–March 1955,*[7] further supported the claim made by the Agrarian Reforms Committee that "extreme inequalities" with respect to land ownership and resources stood as major obstacles to agricultural and rural development.[8]

The eighth *NSS* figures showed (or one can reasonably conclude) that amid regional variations, esoteric usufructuary tenures, complex subinfeudation, and a maze of intermediary rights India's agrarian social structure represented the archetypal feudal order—exhibiting extreme disparities in the ownership and control of land and its resources.[9] It also showed a discernible common pattern with respect to landholdings and the structure of rural stratification.[10] Not only was there an unfavorable land-person ratio of about .92 acre per capita, but also over one-fifth of all rural households (approximately 22 percent) owned no land at all. Another 25 percent owned fragments of land or land of less than one acre. An additional 14 percent owned "uneconomic" or marginal holdings of 1 to 2.5 acres.

Hence, the vast majority of the rural households, roughly 61 percent, made up of the landless, the marginal holders or the land poor, and "sharecropping tenants"—whom Daniel Thorner (1956) classified as the *mazdoors*— either owned no land or small fragments of land that often encumbered in debt remained uneconomic units of cultivation. The *mazdoors,* who overwhelmingly belonged to the low-caste groups, altogether "owned" less than 6 percent of the total cultivated area. In contrast, the "cultivating peasantry," or the *kisans* (in Thorner's classification), who made up some 27 percent of the rural households, either owned or held "occupancy rights" (i.e., leased) to roughly 29 percent of the land. As a class, the *kisans* were the classic middle-caste smallholder peasantry surviving via a Chayanovian type of "self-exploitation." They were given to constant upward and downward mobility, their composition varying from insecure tenants (who often structurally overlapped with the land-poor peasants) to "self-sufficient" peasants with relatively secure rights to the land.[11] The *maliks* (or upper-caste landlords), who made up the upper 12 percent of the rural households, controlled approximately 65 percent of usually the best arable land.[12]

Even though Thorner's categorization of rural class divisions does not always indicate the numerous gradations, and the very eclectic and fluid nature of the *maliks* as a socioeconomic entity, it is important to note that the *maliks* also exhibited marked internal stratification vis-à-vis differential access to land and its resources, in wealth, and in ritual or caste status. For example, in different parts of the country, they varied from the village-level or "petty *zamindars*" to the rich and the upper strata of the middle peasantry or "superior occupancy tenants," who either owned or leased anywhere from 20 acres to several hundred acres of land. This landed stratum, according to Terence Byres (1974, 235), formed "a class of capitalist farmers in embryo, in the womb of the old order." Indeed, it will be discussed later how these relatively secure and privileged tenants of both lower-caste peasant and upper-caste origins, who enjoyed proprietary and inheritable rights to the land they tilled, were among the major beneficiaries of land and tenure reforms (Sharma 1973; Kotovsky 1964; Sen 1962).

The next higher stratum of *maliks* were the "medium *zamindars*," of usually upper-caste origins, who owned or enjoyed proprietary rights to estates ranging up to 2,000 acres or more—estates that extended over several villages. At the apex of the agrarian hierarchy were the big "feudal" *zamindars*-cum-maharajahs, a numerically small but influential elite of high-caste, largely absentee landlords who owned or controlled large estates and were recognized by the colonial government as their rightful owners and revenue payers. Some, like the maharajah of Balrampur, had holdings encompassing some 500 square miles in the sub-Himalayan districts of Gonda and Bahraich. Other big landlords, such as the nizam of Hyderabad and the maharajahs of Darbhanga, Hatwa, and Chotanagpur, controlled "fiefdoms" consisting of several hundred thousand acres of land, the landlords' writ extending over thousands of villages, spanning several districts and, at times, states.[13]

Compounding the skewed distribution of land ownership were the prevailing tenurial arrangements. Although it was difficult to make accurate estimates regarding the "incidence of tenancy," given the regional variations and the "hidden" nature of tenurial arrangements, the eighth *NSS* reported a "substantial incidence of tenancy."[14] The *NSS* data showed that while 20 percent of all cultivators operated "mixed holdings" of partly owned and partly leased land, an additional 17 percent were "pure" tenants cultivating land entirely on lease. Altogether, roughly 25 percent of the total area under cultivation was under one form of tenancy or another. Further, on the question of ownership and control of "non-land assets" such as draft animals, livestock, farm implements, and machinery, the eighth *NSS* data, including the evidence from an enquiry made in six states between 1954/55 and 1956/57 (GoI 1963a), showed that the vast majority of rural households (over 70 percent according to the eighth *NSS*) did not even possess such basic "forces of production" as draft animals, milch cattle, or farm implements such as ploughs, hoes, harrows, and carts.[15]

For Nehru and his allies, all this was further evidence that the problem of rural poverty and the chronic gap between productivity potential and the actual output in the agricultural sector was the direct result of the inequitable and exploitative system of land ownership and tenurial arrangements. Approvingly citing the Report of the Congress Agrarian Reforms Committee (and other evidence such as the Reserve Bank of India's *Rural Credit Surveys*), they argued that the institution of sharecropping tenancy, with the sharecroppers paying in excess of 60 to 70 percent of their total output in rent, was both inefficient as a productive system and exploitative (Malaviya 1954, 36; Jha 1971, 6). Furthermore, they argued, since the tenants and sharecroppers had no legal redress against the disproportionately high rents they were charged (because most lease arrangements were covert oral agreements), the tenants' existence was at the complete mercy of the landlords, who could arbitrarily raise rents; demand such "feudal dues" as *abwab* (extra taxes), *nazarana* (bonus or "gift" in cash or kind given to the landlord for renewing tenancy), or *beth begar* (unpaid or forced labor services); or evict the tenants at will.

Nehru argued that under these circumstances, the vast armies of the landless and land-poor peasants, trapped in quasi-feudal ties and "demoralized . . . bullied and crushed by every dominant interest,"[16] neither had the incentive nor the capacity to become efficient and productive rural producers. On the other hand, the "parasitic *zamindars,*" whom Nehru bitterly denounced as the "the native garrisons of an alien imperialism" and "physically and intellectually degenerate," had no interest or incentive in agricultural modernization or the betterment of rural society (Malaviya 1954, 46). Instead, like "a fifth wheel in the coach, the *zamindars* are not only unnecessary, but an actual encumbrance, and a burden on the land" (Malaviya 1954, 56), because under the existing unequitable and "oppressive" land ownership and tenurial arrangements they effortlessly squeezed the actual cultivators, collecting reliable income from rents and interest on loans, squandering it in unproductive *durbars* (extravagant parties) and other forms of conspicuous consumption.[17]

Further, a powerful economic rationale in favor of land and tenure reforms was the empirically observed phenomenon of the inverse relationship between farm size and land productivity. The Congress Agrarian Reforms Committee put forward the argument (which was also supported empirically by the Farm Management and Rural Credit Surveys) that large *zamindar* holdings were inefficient and unproductive, whereas the small and medium holdings were efficient and productive (GoI 1949; Jha 1971, 20–33). The empirical argument for this claim, based on comparative data from several districts in India and from countries like the United States, Denmark, Britain, and Switzerland, showed that the gross output per acre was higher on the small farms relative to that of the large farms. Predictably, the proponents of institutional reforms used the committee's findings and recommendations to argue that the break up of large *zamindar* estates and land redistribution to the actual tillers would not only provide employment for the large mass of the unemployed rural inhabitants, but also significantly increase the aggregate growth and productive efficiency of the agricultural sector. This would in turn cut down on central government welfare and relief obligations in the countryside.[18]

There were other pressing or "pragmatic" concerns that made the institutional path attractive. For example, Francine Frankel (1978, 111–118), Kamal Kabra (1981), and Michael Lipton (1968; 1977) point out that Indian planners facing frightening demographic givens of an exploding population growth rate, and possessing very limited resources and a prior commitment to the goals of rapid industrialization, had little choice but to support the institutionalist path.[19] Specifically, by early 1954, as the Planning Commission became deeply involved in formulating the design for industrialization under the Second Five Year Plan, it became clear that increases in agricultural production had to be carried out without diverting much resources from the state's priority goal: the creation of basic and heavy industry. Under these circumstances, where the large industrial programs preempted the lion's share of the state's available resources (i.e., the total outlay for agriculture and irrigation in the Second Plan dropped from 34.6 percent in the First Plan to 17.5 percent in the second), and where the state was both unable and unwilling to devote much economic investments to the countryside, there was little possibility of increasing agricultural output by providing rural households with costly capital-intensive production inputs. In other words, agricultural production and productivity had to be increased by the more efficient use of the available land and labor resources, a goal that many in the policymaking circles believed could best be achieved within the context of a reformed and equitable agrarian order.

Finally, political calculations were also an important motivating force for generating support for agrarian reforms. Hung-Chao Tai (1974) provides a comprehensive study of a broad range of contemporary land reform experiments (including India's), and points out that most developing states are attracted to land reform because, as a policy goal, it serves as a "strategic political resource."[20] The Indian case confirms this observation (Herring 1983; Joshi 1973; Kohli 1987). No doubt the commitment of many Congress nationalists to *zamindari* abolition was genuine. Some were deeply distressed by the appalling poverty and exploitation in the countryside. Land reform was a weapon that could once and for all emasculate the traditional rural power structure and spearhead a genuine social revolution in the countryside. For others, it reflected a desire for punitive actions, to inflict some retribution on the hated *zamindars* and their allies who had been an important pillar of colonial rule and had long been identified in the nationalist lore as representing the most "parasitic, corrupt," and unproductive members of Indian society. However, there were many in the Congress Party (especially at the lower levels) whose reformist commitments were ambivalent or nonexistent, but who recognized the potential political and symbolic value associated with the simple, yet potent, Gandhian slogan of "*sabhi bhommi Gopal ki.*" As Herring (1983, 217–238) points out, by forcefully reaffirming (or at least appearing to reaffirm) the new state's commitment to reforming the existing inequitable patterns of privilege and authority in the countryside, many Congress members hoped to enhance their socialist credentials and acquire a firmer political base in the countryside. Also, political calculations and the need to enhance the government's and polity's legitimacy and their prestige as "progressive modernizers" standing for economic modernity and the interests of "the little man" motivated some to assiduously court the peasantry. Also, leaders like Nehru felt that some authoritative action against the rural potentates was a political imperative. There was justified apprehension that if left alone, the landed elites could organize themselves and pose a challenge to the country's democratic regime—as had happened in Pakistan. As Herring (1983, 217–238) notes, by escalating the radical rhetoric the Congress political elite hoped to coax and intimidate the influential rural groups into accepting the new state's authority and its moderate reforms programs for the countryside. Finally, commitment to some sort of reformist agenda was necessary to dissipate and co-opt the opposition, elicit popular support, and forge closer links with the cultivating peasantry and the landless. Samuel Huntington's belated warning (1968, 375) that "no social group . . . is more revolutionary than a peasantry which owns too little land or pays too high a rental" was not lost to the political elites. Winning over the peasants by satisfying their ubiquitous land hunger was one way the Congress political elites hoped to neutralize and undermine the call of the Communist Party of India for militant mobilization of the peasantry for an eventual Chinese-style agrarian revolution (Alavi 1965; Desai 1986). Indeed, the unprecedented electoral victory of the Communists in the state of Kerala in 1957 (the communist ministry was dismissed by Nehru in 1959) made clear to the national Congress elite the urgent need to implement some tangible reforms in the countryside.

Hence, it suffices to note that the cumulative effect of these rationalizations was that the proposals for institutional reforms were incorporated in the First and Second Five Year Plans (1951–1961) as an integral part of the agricultural and rural development strategy (GoI 1952; 1956a).

The Reformist Strategy: Policy and Goals

In the period 1948–1964, after repeated directives, regulations, and decrees from the central government, the provincial governments promulgated a body of legislation designed to reform the agrarian economy and structure in their respective jurisdictions.[21]

These reformist measures can be divided into three roughly overlapping phases. During the first phase, from 1949 to 1954, legislation was passed by several of the provincial governments to abolish the "*zamindari* system," or any such system of "parasitic landlordism" that promoted extreme inequalities and the exploitation of one class by another (GoI 1952; 1963). The planners believed that "*zamindari* abolition" by itself would significantly ameliorate the problems of agricultural stagnation and rural poverty by breaking up the huge "unproductive" estates and redistributing land to the actual cultivators. In the second phase, from 1952 till the end of the 1950s, emphasis was placed on tenancy reforms. The aim was to regulate tenancy rights, provide security of tenure to the "actual tillers," institute "fair" rents, and provide legal measures for the "tenant-cultivators" to acquire permanent, transferable, and heritable ownership rights to the land they cultivated. In the third phase, from 1956 to the early 1960s, legislation was aimed at placing ceilings or an "upper limit" to the amount of land that an individual could hold. The aim was threefold: (1) to restrict land concentration by distributing "excess" land to the direct tillers; (2) to maximize "efficiency of production" by consolidating small and fragmented holdings; and (3) to pool all the excess land to establish "cooperative joint farming," including a few experimental collective farms consisting of the landless and holders of marginal or "palpably uneconomic" holdings. The planners argued that cooperative farming made economic sense in a land-scarce economy, because it would not only make the rural sector more productive but also rehabilitate the rural poor, namely the landless, and regenerate the ethos of the traditional "harmonious" village society (GoI 1956a, 175–180).

Buttressing agrarian reforms were the Community Development Projects (CDPs) launched in 1952 under the joint supervision of the Planning Commission and the newly established central government's Ministry of Community Development. The aim of the CDPs was to stimulate agricultural production and productivity through the mobilization of pressures from below by involving millions of peasants in labor-intensive agricultural production programs comprising all aspects of economic, social, and political goals of planning.[22] Specifically, the planners hoped to bring all of India's villages under the CDPs by the end of the Second Plan. Indeed, by the end of the First Plan, some 120,000 villages (about one-fourth of the rural populace) were already divided into Community Development Blocks (each comprising about a hundred villages), and each village was earmarked for an intensive development effort. Each block was assigned a block development officer, a hierarchy of technical specialists, and village extension workers whose primary task was to provide "practical aid" to the peasants, ranging from technical assistance in such projects as land reclamation, irrigation works, road building, and "educating" the villagers in the use of agricultural technology and "better" farming methods. The villagers, however, had to provide *shramdan* or voluntary free labor (GoI 1952; 1956a). Further, provisions were made for the construction of "social uplift projects" in the villages: schools, community centers, dispensaries, veterinary clinics, roads, deep-water wells, and even libraries. The villagers were expected to pool local resources (in voluntary labor, money, or materials) to qualify for government assistance. The planners hoped that such community-centered development projects that stressed the principles of local cooperation and self-help would set in motion a process through which new norms of cooperative activity and equality would become incorporated into village life.

Backing up the CDPs were a series of "strategies" designed to further harness popular "grassroots" support and participation for the plan policies and to stimulate community-oriented organizational and structural changes at the village level. In particular, the policymakers, harking back to Gandhi's utopian vision of "harmonious self-sufficient" village communities, called for a systematic political and economic decentralization of power, in particular decisionmaking authority away from the "center" to the villages.

Indeed, during the First and Second Plan period, concerted efforts were made to establish "multipurpose village cooperative societies," and the traditional village *panchayati raj* (the three-tier system of local government at the village, block, and district levels) was hastily revived along "new principles" of universal membership and adult suffrage. The planners believed that such an approach to rural reform would, over time, not only shift the balance of socioeconomic and political power away from the upper-caste landed gentry to the actual cultivators, but also avoid the destabilizing effects of class conflict and provide the necessary support from below for the effective implementation of the reform program. In fact, the First Plan went as far as recommending that the village *panchayats* be given statutory responsibility for raising additional resources through a village property tax, plus the responsibility of (1) managing all land, water, and roads in the village; (2) acting as a channel for government assistance to the village; (3) organizing voluntary labor for local community work; (4) protecting tenants from unlawful eviction; and (5) providing full assistance in the implementation of land reforms and community projects. Furthermore, all rural households, including the poor and the landless, were expected to become members of the government-funded cooperative societies. The planners believed that making "moral character" rather than wealth and social status the most important factor in determining the eligibility for *taccavi* (government loans) and providing low-interest loans to peasants, as well as rural marketing and distribution services, would go a long way toward eliminating the powers and influence of village middlemen and moneylenders. The planners felt that village cooperatives, once financially secure, would be able not only to provide the capital and resources necessary for technical advances in agriculture, but in the process revive and strengthen rural communitarian values and ultimately restore the traditional, harmonious corporate character of village society.

The Problems of Implementation: A Preview of the Arguments

In assessing the impact of land and tenure reforms, M. L. Dantwala made this acerbic (and accurate) observation in the early 1960s: "If you ask me what is the most important feature of land reforms I would say it is non-implementation."[23] Indeed, the discrepancy between the policies intentions and outcomes has been huge. It is well documented (even by the Indian government's own reports) that community development and land and tenure reform measures, especially the implementation of "land ceilings" and the consequent redistribution, have been largely ineffectual, if not outright failures.[24]

Therefore, it is not necessary to reiterate the nature and extent of this failure, but to understand the causes of the failure. A brief survey of the vast literature on the topic reveals that the existing explanations tend to adhere to the following, often complementary positions. For example, Wolf Ladejinsky (1977), the noted U.S. agricultural economist, who devoted much of his adult life to the study of India's agrarian problems, attributed

104   *Development and Democracy in India*

the failure (or what he termed "unfinished business") to ambiguous or "faulty" land reform legislation—which left "numerous loopholes"that rendered much of the legislation ineffective.[25] Some have blamed the failure of implementation on administrative and bureaucratic inertia and corruption.[26] Still other analysts have viewed the failures as the result of the two interconnected evils: the "soft state" and the "lack of political will" (Myrdal 1968; Moore 1966; Tai 1974). According to Francine Frankel (1978, 246–250), who presents a more complex version of the argument, the huge discrepancy between "ideals" and "actual outcomes" was the direct result of the constitutional division of power between the center and the provinces. That is, the assigning of significant powers over "rural matters" to provincial governments dominated by rural propertied interests, coupled with the victory of the so-called conservatives in the Congress Party (at the center), resulted in the gradual "retreat from the social goals of Planning." However, scholars like Ronald Herring (1983), while agreeing with Frankel, argue that it was at the village level, where the socioeconomic and political powers of the rural elites were most visibly felt, that the land reform measures were emasculated and ultimately gutted.[27]

Marxist analysts, on the other hand, have focused on the dominant class constraints to land and tenure reforms. Some have suggested that land and tenure reforms were designed only to facilitate the destruction of "feudal" or *zamindari* production and social relations in agriculture. In other words, the goal of the state was only to "complete the bourgeois revolution" in the countryside, not to carry out a sweeping "land to the tiller" type of agrarian reforms. However, such a change could not be effectively carried out because the "comprador alliance" between the state and the "reactionary feudal *zamindars* and merchant usurers" prevented a "thorough-going transformation from one mode to another."[28] Other radical writers have argued that rural reforms failed because the dominant rural castes and classes, given their traditional authority and hegemonic power to manipulate and control the provincial state apparatuses, systematically undermined the reformist measures (Beteille 1974; Joshi 1975; 1982; Thorner 1976).

A few analysts, such as Michael Lipton (1968; 1977), have gone as far as to argue that land reforms could not be effectively implemented in South Asia because of the dominance of the "urban bias" in development planning. More recently analysts like Atul Kohli (1987, 69), in their efforts to integrate the various positions, have argued that "the failure of Indian land reforms . . . resulted from a failure to institutionalize elements of lower-class interests within the state." For Kohli, land reforms were essentially a "political failure" because the Congress elite, in aligning themselves with the rural power configurations ipso facto allowed these elites to capture political power and subvert the reformist policies at will (also see Hasan 1989; Weiner 1967).

In my judgement these varying, and at times competing, explanations provide important insights into the workings of the Indian polity and rural society, as well as their complex relationships and interactions. However, a more comprehensive picture of the politics and policies of the Nehru period can be obtained if these various strands are synthesized in a broader state-society framework. The following section offers a modest, preliminary sketch.

The Failure of Implementation: A State-Society Analysis

The case of India highlights what is common to many of the weak and fragmented democratic and nondemocratic states of the developing world, namely, a political incapacity to translate their proclaimed policy goals, especially reformist and distributive goals, into real implementable policies. Comparative studies have shown that successful redistribution of land, power, and privilege in the countryside requires that the state must simultaneously insulate itself from the pressures and demands of the landed classes and effectively penetrate and establish strong and enduring institutional and organizational links between the governmental institutions and the rural society. In Maoist China and postwar Japan, South Korea, and Taiwan, for example, strong centralized states with embedded autonomy, applying what Samuel Huntington (1968, 381–396) has called "concentrated power from above," were able to carry out significant land redistribution because their institutional autonomy enabled them to successfully exclude the landed gentry from penetrating the state's institutions and structures. In such settings, the state's policies and goals were often swiftly and effectively implemented by an elaborate and well-organized network of dedicated and politicized party cadres, a mobilized lower peasantry, a well-institutionalized and efficacious political-bureaucratic apparatus, and a reformist oriented political-executive leadership. Does this mean that a basic incompatibility exists between parliaments and land reform, and that, therefore, some sort of centralized authoritarian rule is a necessary precondition for land and tenure reform? While casual empiricism may suggest this, careful research have presented a more nuanced picture. Jeffrey Riedinger (1995) clearly shows that the formulation and implementation of agrarian reform policy in the Philippines under the "non-developmental authoritarian" Marcos regime existed only on paper. On the other hand, although the democratic Aquino and Ramos regimes were also characterized by policy ineptitude and failure, they have nevertheless reduced the predatory rent seeking and self-aggrandizement of the Marcos period, and have attempted to rectify the problems of governance by buttressing the capacity of the state and augmenting public accountability. As noted in Chapter 1, Karen Remmer's (1985/86, 81) empirical study of inclusionary and exclusionary regimes in Latin America leads her to conclude that "no exclusionary democracy in Latin America has ever administered a land reform program with a major redistributive impact. All significant land reforms have resulted from inclusionary rule, either of the competitive or non-competitive variety." Stephan Haggard and Robert Kaufman (1995) concur with Remmer. They make a compelling case that centralized executive authority, whether authoritarian or democratic, and backed by cohesive party systems characterized by limited fragmentation and polarization, is the critical variable in formulating and implementing distributive reforms. The case of Mexico under the presidency of Lázaro Cárdenas is particularly illustrative. The Cardenas *sexenio* witnessed a genuine attempt by a reformist group within the political-bureaucratic elite to create a rural society based on an equitable distribution of land and resources, and to reorganize peasant socioeconomic and political life through the *ejidos,* the land-grant collective and communal system. Cárdenas, capitalizing on the legal power of the state and the support of mobilized worker and peasant communities, confronted the power and privileges of the landed elite. By shifting the balance of power of the dominant Partido Revolucionario Institucional (PRI) away from the continuing influence of the Callists[29] and their networks of powerful regional *caciques,* and in favor of sectoral incorporation of workers and peasants, Cárdenas was able to carry out the most sweeping labor and land reforms in Mexico's history. That is, by 1940, the Cárdenas government had distributed more than eighteen million hectares of land to some 800,000 recipients, twice as many as his predecessors had managed to in the preceding twenty years. *Ejidos* now held 47 percent of cultivated land, compared with 15 percent in 1930, the *ejido* population had more than doubled (from 668,000 to 1.6 million), and the landless population had fallen from 2.5 million to 1.9 million (Knight 1991, 256–259). Cárdenas achieved this by mobilizing and linking what would become the "metropolitan" and "peripheral" coalitions in the PRI's national coalitional structure. The national labor movement was mobilized as an official constituency of the party, an act that made it a pivotal part of the party's emerging metropolitan coalition. In the countryside, extensive land reform initiatives were accompanied by the sectoral organization of the *ejidatarios* (middle and poor peasantry who had acquired *ejido* lands, and the landless *campesinos*) and their formal incorporation into the party's structure as "supportive pillars for state action." Cárdenas then spearheaded the reform of the party itself, renaming it the Partido de la Revolucián Mexicana (PRM) and converting its territorial organization to the functional organization of the national peasant, labor, and middle-class groups. With this functional reorganization of the party Cárdenas empowered new socioeconomic groups whose support, loyalty, and political clout strengthened the PRI. This enabled the Cardenista agrarian reform to be conducted not in gradual bureaucratic style but with "terrific fervor," punctuated with dramatic presidential initiatives.[30] Moreover, by adding a new line of cleavage to the previously dominant regional cleavage he also weakened or neutralized those elite groups with power bases in the party's territorial structure.

The experience of postwar Taiwan also provides some instructive lessons. In 1945 (following the Japanese surrender) Taiwan's economy was in disarray. Agricultural production that year was less than half the prewar peak, inflation was in triple digits, and the people faced grave shortages of food and other basic necessities. However, in four short years the agricultural sector witnessed a miraculous transformation, increasing at the annual rate of 19.2 percent between 1946 and 1950, and by mid-1951 agricultural output had surpassed the prewar peak (Fei, Ranis, and Kuo 1979). A number of factors contributed to this recovery: (1) the rapid increase in labor input and crop area complemented by multiple-crop diversification; (2) the introduction of better production techniques, repair of irrigation facilities, and reorganization of farmers' associations; and (3) the implementation of land reforms. It is generally agreed that the successful implementation of land reforms was decisive. Prior to its implementation, over 50 percent of the farmers in Taiwan did not own the land they tilled. Tenant farmers paid exorbitant rents (usually over 50 percent of the crop harvest); consequently, there was little incentive for these farmers to invest in technology or improve farming techniques. The massive land reform program introduced in 1948 and completed in 1953 transformed the inequitable agrarian structure and social relations of production. The program included a three-pronged strategy: the reduction of rents and secure tenure, the selling of public lands to the "actual cultivators," and the "giving of land to the tiller." The new rental fee was set at about one-third of the farmers annual yield of the main crop, and their lease was made more secure—covering a period of six years, with extension after expiry. Also, large areas of public lands were sold to incumbent farmers, the price fixed at a reasonable two-and-a-half times the annual yield of the main crop, to be paid in twenty semiannual installments. The land to the tiller program made it clear that each former landlord would only be allowed to keep three *chia* (about three hectares) of medium-grade paddy field or six *chia* of dry land. Holdings in excess of these amounts were purchased by the government and resold to incumbent tenant farmers, at the set price of two-and-a-half times the annual yield of the main crop. The landlords were paid 70 percent of the land price with land bonds and the rest with shares of government-owned industries. Given the pragmatic and mild nature of Taiwan's land reform program, the argument made by some that such "revolutionary reform programs" require coercion by an authoritarian state is not compelling.

As discussed earlier, India's disaggregated, compromised, and weak parliamentary federalism was ill suited as an instrument for reformist and distributive development. This system simply did not have the political, institutional, bureaucratic, or administrative wherewithal to implement a meaningful land and tenure reform program. Moreover, compounding this problem were the countervailing tendencies toward fragmentation within the Congress system. As the next section illustrates, short-term political expediency won the day in India.[31]

The Congress Party, the crucial link between the Indian state and society, failed to insulate the major organs of the state—the ruling party organizations, the bureaucracy, the decisionmaking and executive machinery, and the lower-level party organizations and structures—from the dominant propertied classes and castes in the countryside. Rather, the party, which over the years had come to build its rural political and electoral support through local notables, many of whom came from the ranks of the rich and middle peasant castes and upper-caste "petty and medium *zamindars*," found it extremely difficult to insulate itself from the pressures and demands of these powerful interests. Moreover, lacking a firm political-institutional base in the countryside independent of the rural elites, or strong organizational linkages with the peasant masses, the Congress leadership did not have very many channels open to it that could be effectively utilized to direct and mediate central government policies, in particular reformist and redistributive policies from either "above" to "below." As Kohli (1987, 69) succinctly notes, the Congress leadership could not "utilize the party as a tool of direct politicization and social transformation, or use it to goad the governmental and bureaucratic levels below the center to follow through the central directives." Therefore, in the absence of such political autonomy and organizational networks there was no force to counter the class power of landed castes and classes.

In fact, so limited was the reach of the Indian state vis-à-vis the countryside that the question of what the central leadership could do about the implementation of land reforms was academic. Having abdicated its powers over most aspects of agricultural policy, including those concerning land and tenure reform enactment and implementation (which now fell within the purview of provincial legislation and administration), the reformers in the central government often found themselves in a highly frustrating position in an emerging postindependence federal democratic system. Reformers like Nehru, lacking the necessary constitutional powers and the support of influential "conservative" colleagues, including Vallabhbhai Patel and India's first president, Rajendra Prasad, could do little but articulate the "broad outlines" of the reform strategy and try to impress upon the provincial political leaders and notables the need to carry out agrarian reforms. However, because neither the central nor the state-level political leadership were agreed on the reform strategy, and since it was left to each state government to determine the "actual policy" and the time frame for implementation, the reform policies predictably were left to the pushes and pulls of the political and socioeconomic forces in each state. As outlined earlier, these forces were formidable. State-level political power was with very few exceptions closely tied to the hierarchical agrarian power structures.[32] Political leaders and functionaries in the states and districts, who were largely composed of and structurally or electorally dependent on the rural propertied classes, tended to be more responsive to the needs of their powerful rural constituency than to the reformers in New Delhi. So, irrespective of the numerous policy statements and repeated directives from the central leadership on the need to pursue agrarian reforms consistent with the "directive principles of state policy" as specified in the Indian constitution, the reformers often had great difficulty in enlisting the support of provincial and district-level politicians and bureaucrats (many of whom were also card-carrying "Congressmen") for effective implementation of the provincial governments' own watered-down reformist measures.[33]

At this point it is useful to reiterate briefly the point made earlier, namely, that although the political leitmotif of central-provincial and local struggle emerged early in India's history, it has remained the dominant *problematic* even after independence. And, despite the exaggerated claims by the central authorities that the Indian state was the quintessence of liberal democracy and modernity, with roots reaching to all of India's far-flung corners, or to the "very salt of the earth,"[34] the reality was that the postindependent state did not (and perhaps could not) transcend the entrenched hierarchies, especially in the vast rural periphery.

As in the past, the continuous, mutually conditioning interplay between the elements of state and society worked in tandem to reduce central state authority and its efficacy in the countryside. India's fragmented democratic polity, institutionally differentiated among three competing levels—on the top, the central government, and below, the provincial and local district and block governing units—each linked to the other by only fragile vertical structures, could not provide an adequate basis for political and economic integration throughout the subcontinent. Instead, this pattern of rule and governance tended to reinforce the de facto limit to the authority and reach of the national political elites and central government institutions. Thus, what the center did control it often controlled indirectly, via individuals and "instruments" who not only represented the dominant rural interests but also inhabited that misty middle ground between the state and society—and thereby enjoying considerable administrative autonomy and discretionary decisionmaking power vis-à-vis the center.

When it came to the actual task of implementing "unfavorable" (reformist and redistributive) statist policies and directives, the wily provincial, district, and local politicos (the so-called link men) and the sprawling Byzantine-like political-bureaucratic apparatus they controlled built defenses against central state penetration and control, often confounding the central planners. To the best of their abilities these Janus-faced intermediaries actively delayed, distorted, deflected, and destroyed inimical or "intrusive" central (statist) policies and directives as often as they faithfully implemented those perceived as "harmless" or "beneficial" to their careers and the powerful propertied interests they represented.

In the course of time these political entrepreneurs and their allies developed a repertoire of strategies and styles to come to terms with the seemingly dramatic changes taking place in their world. In a sense, then, the widespread corruption, malfeasance, nepotism, and favoritism, as well as the routine bullying, the depredations by local tyrants, and the outright vendettas and violence of that period against the hapless poor or landless peasantry, cannot simply be dismissed as the normal despotism of "Indian feudalism," but were all part of the state's and the dominant rural classes' and castes' coming to terms with each other. In the end, using all their savvy, skills, wealth, and control of the rural political and bureaucratic machinery (the "vote banks"), all assiduously built on the diffuse loyalties of caste, kinship, and patron-client relationships, the dominant propertied interests were able to adapt quite well to the emerging socioeconomic and political realities of "modern India." Perhaps these realities, outlined so far in generalities, will resonate better with a few concrete examples.

Agrarian Reforms: Winners, Losers, and Consequences

In theory, land and tenure reforms sounded gloriously transformative, a revolutionizing initiative designed to abolish the entrenched hierarchies and the crushing inertia and parochialism of the countryside. In practice, however, the reforms were full of failures and frustrations, inefficiencies, miscalculations, and double entendres at all levels. Even as the national political elites engaged in a deluge of reformist rhetoric, the "reformist strategy" was simultaneously subjected to continuous legislative tinkering as the state governments enacted laws and legislation with deliberate loopholes and telltale exemptions designed to protect their turf and the powerful propertied interests they represented. By the end of the day the reform strategy had undergone several permutations, weakening its bite and rendering it quite ineffective.

For example, despite the passage of "*zamindari* abolition acts" in several provincial legislatures between 1949 and 1954, the legislation was not very successful in appropriating *zamindari* lands or undermining the position of the *zamindars* as economic elites in the countryside. What "*zamindari* abolition" did achieve with some success was (1) to facilitate the transfer of land from a handful of large absentee *zamindars* to the state governments and to the already well-off village *zamindars* and "occupancy tenants" (i.e., the rich peasantry); (2) to withdraw the juridical-legal and political supports that had allowed the *zamindars* to function as "feudal" overlords; and (3) to goad many large holders into modernizing and becoming entrepreneurially oriented farmers.[35] In other words, the acts abolished the rights of the *zamindars* as superior lords over the land on which the tenants held "legal occupancy rights," and technically removed their arbitrary rights and prerogatives over the tenants' labor and produce. Nevertheless, significant as these changes were, it is important to note that *zamindari* abolition fell far short of an agrarian transformation.

The *zamindari* interests shrewdly utilized the constitutional provisions to their advantage. In the state of Bihar, for example, even as the state legislature passed its landmark legislation to abolish "intermediaries" (i.e., *zamindars*) and secured the approval of the governor-general on 6 June 1949, the landed interests quickly challenged the constitutionality of the legislation, and the state courts issued injunctions restraining the Bihar government from implementing the Bihar Act XVIII of 1949 (see Jannuzi 1974). In due course the reform legislation was repealed and superceded by "new," weaker legislation, the Bihar Land Reforms Bill, 1949—which was eventually passed by the state legislature in 1950 and sent for review by the president of India. As soon as it received the assent of the president, it (now the Bihar Land Reforms Act, 1950) was again challenged in the courts, and the Patna High Court declared that the act contravened article 14 of the constitution. In response, the central government introduced, and the central legislatures passed, the Constitution (First Amendment) Act, which validated the Bihar Land Reforms Act, 1950. This first amendment to the constitution, article 31A, specified that "no law providing for (a) the acquisition by the State of any estate or of any rights therein or the extinguishment or modification of any such rights . . . shall be deemed to be void on the ground that it is inconsistent with or takes away or abridges any of the rights conferred by Article 14, Article 19 or Article 31." Responding to the amendment of the constitution, the *zamindari* interests challenged the constitutionality of article 31A in a suit brought before the Supreme Court. When the Supreme Court declared the constitutional amendment as valid, the landed interests began proceedings to test the constitutionality of the Bihar Land Reforms Act, 1950, bringing a suit to the Supreme Court. Even though, in late 1952, the Supreme Court upheld the validity of the act, it was in vain because the passage of time had given the landed interests ample opportunity to thwart the legislation.[36]

As Frankel (1978, 191) points out, "While [the provincial governments] abolished the *zamindari* system, the provisions stopped well short of expropriating the *zamindars*." Even as the *zamindars'* proprietary rights were vested in state government, they were permitted to keep the "home farms" or land in their direct occupation for "personal cultivation." In most states no ceiling was placed on the size of the "home farms," and, given the vague definition of the term "personal cultivation" (which could mean anything from the *zamindars'* "farming himself or through an agent, employing hired laborers, or [through land] leased to tenants who had no legal recognized rights of occupancy"[37]), the *zamindars* (especially those in villages) were able to circumvent the land reform legislation and retain under their possession unrestricted amounts of land.

In Uttar Pradesh, for example, circumventing the reform legislation was made particularly easy. Daniel Thorner (1956, 20–22) points out that since "manual labor" by the landlord was not used as a criterion for personal cultivation in Uttar Pradesh (given upper-caste prohibitions against physical work), supervision of wage labor or cultivation through personal "servants" or landless "partners" qualified as "self-cultivation." In fact, the main distinction made in the Uttar Pradesh *Zamindari* Abolition Act was between *bhumidars* and *sirdars*. While a *bhumidar* was entitled to transfer his interest and to use his land for nonagricultural purposes, a *sirdar* was denied these rights. A *sirdar* paid as land revenue an amount equal to that which he had formerly paid as rent to landlord, but a *bhumidar* paid at a much lower rate; and to obtain *bhumidar* rights a *sirdar* had to pay a lump sum equal to ten times his previous rental payment (this was subsequently changed to ten times his annual land revenue). These legal categories only served to change the former landlords—who became *bhumidars,* having lost the lands they had rented to tenants but retaining those that they had cultivated themselves (*sir* lands) and their home farms (*khudkasht* lands)—and most of their former tenants became *sirdars*. In effect, the Uttar Pradesh *Zamindari* Abolition Act simply exchanged one form of rural hierarchy for another.

Not only were the *zamindars* able to retain all the *khudkasht* land (i.e., the home farms), they were also conferred full ownership rights with respect to their home farms. But despite the failings of "*zamindari* abolition" it would be incorrect to suggest that the legislation left the agrarian structure unaffected. As Herring (1983, 86–90) correctly notes, *zamindari* abolition was relatively successful in breaking up some of the large feudal estates, in particular, the estates of the "unproductive feudal" *zamindars,* who were usually absentees and too removed from the daily operation of their estates to protect themselves against the machinations of the estate managers or the resident *zamindars* and rich peasants. The small and medium *zamindars* were, on balance, able to hold on to much of the land they controlled,[38] but the major beneficiaries of land reforms were the privileged "occupancy tenants" or the rich peasants and the upper strata of the middle peasantry, who were able to acquire full *bhumidari* or ownership rights to the land they cultivated (see Frankel and Rao 1989, 92–94; Parthasarathy 1979). For example, legislation in the states of Uttar Pradesh, Rajasthan, and Gujarat, and later in Assam, Bihar, West Bengal, Orissa, and Hyderabad (now Andhra Pradesh), permitted these "superior occupancy tenants," who held permanent and heritable rights to the land, to acquire full ownership rights after paying a small compensation to the state governments. By taking advantage of such provisions many of the "superior occupancy tenants" were able not only to keep their landholdings, but in some cases increase the size of the holdings by "resuming" land from unprotected tenants or by purchasing it from landlords.[39] Hence, many were able to enhance their overall economic standing relative to the mostly upper-caste "ex-*zamindars*," some of whom were now left with reduced estates.

However, not all the cultivators benefited from the land reform legislation. The vast majority of the "inferior title holders," the "non-occupancy *raiyats*" or the tenants-at-will and tillers whose structural status varied between that of sharecropper, bonded laborer, farm servant, and landless laborer, were adversely affected.[40] For example, in Uttar Pradesh over 66 percent of poor tenants who were not able to acquire ownership rights either remained *sirdars* or became day laborers (Singh and Mishra 1965, 121–135). Specifically, the provision in the state legislation that allowed the *zamindars* (and the other landed intermediaries) to keep all the land classified as home farms without any upper ceiling limit proved a direct incentive to *zamindars* to evict unprotected tenants from the lands they cultivated. This would prevent these tenants from acquiring protected status and exaggerate the proportion of the estate under "personal cultivation." H. D. Malaviya (1954, 452), a member of the Planning Commission, made this insightful observation of India's land reform experience in the mid-1950s:

> Cases abound where a landlord may have considerable areas recorded as his personal cultivation but may be actually cultivating only a part of it, or none at all. The tenant cultivators on such lands have no rights, and even if rights have been conferred by the new legislation, the landlords see to it that they are evicted before the law becomes effective. The right to *Sir* and *Khudkasht* made the *zamindars* resort to eviction of even the occupancy tenants themselves on a large scale and claim it as their personal cultivation.

Not only were the actual cultivators, in particular the "inferior tenants," denied protection from such violations, the provincial governments, with few exceptions, made virtually no effort to stop such abuses. Rather, they maintained that in order to minimize disruption, the legislated changes were to be adopted voluntarily by the landlords. Wolf Ladejinsky (1977, chap. 44–48) noted that under such circumstances, implementation became little more than a "pious hope." Moreover, the tenants were required to provide incontrovertible documented evidence to support their tenant status and right of occupancy (something virtually no "inferior tenants" had, given the informal and oral nature of tenancy agreements), but there were no institutional mechanisms for the tenants to acquire such evidence, except by asking the landlords to provide the necessary rent receipts and other documentation of status. Predictably the *zamindars*, concerned with their own property prerogatives, were not forthcoming. In fact, in Bihar and Uttar Pradesh (and other states) the landlords simply refused to make available the *jamabandi's* or rent rolls and related village records crucial for determining the rents received and the distribution of holdings between the *zamindars* and their tenants.[41] Further, most provincial governments not only failed to pressure the landlords to release the records, but also to undertake, on their own, the "reconstruction" of land records to correct the irregularities and establish the identity of tenants and the extent of the area under the tenants' cultivation.[42]

Finally, even though provisions in most tenancy legislation allowed the tenants to seek legal redress against landlords who refused to comply with the tenancy laws and against unfair evictions and rental demands, in reality the political-institutional arrangements for achieving fair settlement were hardly in favor of tenants and other lower orders of cultivators. Given the enormously costly and excruciatingly slow judicial process, a collaborationist bureaucracy, and provincial and district civil and revenue courts mired in archaic procedures and rigid formalism (not to mention its open bias for the propertied classes), the threats of landlord retaliation (including the growing incidence of violence against "troublesome" tenants) were sufficient reason to dissuade the vast majority of poor cultivators from lodging complaints, let alone pursue civil suits. Not surprisingly, most poor tenants simply acquiesced to the landlords rather than demanding their legislated rights. And since most tenancy laws provided that tenants could "voluntarily surrender" the holdings they cultivated to the landlords (in such cases no ceiling restriction on the right of resumption by landlords for "personal cultivation" would apply); this only invited the landlords to evict their tenants, if only to prevent them from acquiring the protected status.[43] Fully aware of the local realities and the hierarchies' formidable powers, most tenants voluntarily surrendered: it was, after all, better to forfeit one's tenancy and be hired back as a laborer on the same land than to resist and risk losing all sources of livelihood. Thus, to protect that all-important "subsistence insurance" for the uncertain times ahead the vast majority of poor tenants voluntarily surrendered their rights, only to be hired back as *bargadars, bataidars, naukers,* and *waramdars* (in South India)—in other words as sharecroppers, "servants," and "farm hands"—no longer entitled to ownership rights or legal protection. *Zamindari* abolition and tenancy reforms, rather than aiding and protecting the lower orders of cultivators, in fact sanctioned large-scale violations and arbitrary evictions, thereby depriving poor tenants of what little security they might have enjoyed.[44]

The benefits of *zamindari* abolition were skewed even further to favor the landed interests by providing them with generous compensation packages for their losses in land ownership and revenue income. Compensation was paid at ten times the rental and market value, on a scale inversely proportional to the size of holding. By 1961 it was estimated that roughly

Rs 6,700 million were paid out to the landed interests in compensation grants.[45] Hence, most *zamindars* were not ruined by *zamindari* abolition. Rather, land reforms (or the threat of future expropriation) did alarm the landlords and brought enough pressure on most to "change their lifestyle." Indeed, having been left with considerable economic assets, many erstwhile landlords either sold their lands to the market-oriented farmers or they themselves became "progressive" and entrepreneurially oriented. By the mid-1960s they would emerge as politically and economically more significant. That is, those with superior education, skills, and connections used their compensation grants to "rebuild" their fortunes by taking up new and profitable activities in commercial agriculture, rural business and manufacturing, and, of course, politics.

If *zamindari* abolition and tenancy reforms failed to distribute land to the tillers, the ceiling laws did not fare any better. Indeed, it was the widespread abuses under *zamindari* abolition and tenancy reforms that prompted the central government to exert pressure on the provincial governments to impose ceiling limits on land holdings. First announced in 1953, detailed recommendations for legislation were not made until 1956, and, due to the procedural and legislative delays in enactment, most states did not pass enabling legislation until 1961 or 1962. The landed interests, therefore, had ample time (roughly seven to eight years) to evade the ceiling laws. As Kusum Nair (1961), the pioneer observer of rural India noted, land ceiling evasion was as widespread as it was easy. The landed classes effectively evaded ceiling laws by dividing their estates among "family members" and engaging in other forms of *benami* or fraudulent transfers.

But, more importantly, ceiling laws were simply more difficult to implement. According to the Rudolphs (1987), "the embourgeoisement of the beneficiaries" that resulted from *zamindari* abolition meant that the *zamindars* could now count on the support of the rich and prosperous middle peasants, who as titleholders also had a stake in landownership. Indeed, it was Chaudhuri Charan Singh, the powerful Congress member in the Uttar Pradesh legislature and the state's minister of revenue and finance, and the leader of North India's rich peasantry, who led the forces in the Congress Party first to weaken the ceiling laws (which he criticized as "superfluous" and "irrelevant") and, in 1959, to soundly defeat Nehru's Nagpur resolution that called for cooperative farming.[46]

Moreover, the ceiling legislation contained so many glaring loopholes that the distributive aims of the legislation were systematically diluted and defeated before it got off the ground. For example, the Bihar Land Reforms (Fixation of Ceiling Area and Acquisition of Surplus Land) Act of 1961 declared that any landowners who had not transferred "excess land" before the enactment of the law to their "families" could do so within six months of the law's enactment. As Jannuzi (1974, 68–86) points out, this helped many landowners escape the ceiling laws at will. Also, the legislation kept the levels of the ceilings high in most parts of the country. In

Gujarat, for example, the permissible retention per family varied from 19 acres of perennially irrigated land to 132 acres of other types of land, in Mysore it varied from 27 to 216 acres, in Rajasthan from 22 to 336 acres. In Bihar each member of a family was permitted to hold 20 to 60 acres, in Madhya Pradesh from 25 to 75, in Andhra Pradesh from 27 to 324, and, where a household exceeded five members, additional land was allowed at the rate of 6 to 72 acres per family member. In Maharashtra ceiling limits varied from 38 to 126 acres, in Orissa from 20 to 80, in Uttar Pradesh the ceiling level varied from 40 to 80 acres, in certain parts of Punjab and Haryana from 27 to 80 acres, while in some parts of the country no ceiling was placed on landownership (see Chattopadhyay 1973, 3–24). The deficiencies in the laws, combined with fictitious transfers to "family members," living, dead, and non-existent, were used by many landholders to retain much of the land (see Thorner 1956, 70–71; also Appu 1975; Ladejinsky 1977).

Second, the ceiling laws exempted several categories of farms, especially those organized along capitalist lines, including "mechanized or efficient farms," farms with "heavy investment," "farms engaged in cattle-breeding, dairying and fisheries," "farms under orchards," "lands in possession of educational institutions," "lands under religious trusts," "farms in a compact block," and so on, from the ceiling legislation. So "loose" and ambiguous were the exemptions, that "if one could get good agricultural lands, with occasional fruit-bearing trees planted here and there, recorded as an orchard, the entire area went out of the ceiling provisions" (Chattophadhyay 1973, 11). Not only was there a veritable rage in the planting of "orchards," numerous dummy institutions such as religious "trusts" and "educational institutions" were created overnight to evade the ceiling laws.

Third, as with the *zamindari* abolition and tenancy reforms, the "personal cultivation" clause in the ceiling laws once again allowed landed interests to operate agricultural holdings either with hired laborers or through disguised tenancies, as in sharecropping "partnerships," since in most states the ceiling laws altogether excluded the sharecropper from the tenant status—hence, no protection in law. Quite frequently, ceiling legislation ostensibly designed to redistribute land to the tillers actually worsened the condition of the tenants because it led to resumption of land by the landed classes for "personal cultivation." The result was a "second wave" of arbitrary evictions of tenants under the guise of clauses like "home farms" and "voluntary surrender" of land. Predictably, by the end of the 1970s, for the country as a whole, the "declared surplus" land was 2.4 million acres and the "area distributed" just half of that, or 0.3 percent of the total cultivated area (Balasubramanyam 1984, 92). In Uttar Pradesh only about a tenth, or less than 0.7 percent of the cultivated land, was actually redistributed. On balance, much of the "distributed" land included semiarid wastelands, lands with poor soil, and lands tied up in litigation. In one case there was even land—as an elderly near-landless peasant I interviewed in Vikaspur recalled with humor and cynicism his 2 *bighas* (about .3 acre)—that was under the Ghaghara River. Fourth, local-level *panchayati* government institutions failed miserably to either democratize village decisionmaking processes or implement the center's reformist and distributive policies. In an environment of acute inequality, the dominant landed interests used the *panchayats* they controlled to both stifle central directives and to enhance their own power positions. Since the village and block *panchayats* were often influential in determining how the land was to be redistributed, there was widespread corruption because the village elites made sure their families and favorites got the first crack at the good lands. In fact, the comprehensive Government of India *Report of the Committee on Panchayati Raj Institutions* (1978, 6–7) admitted that

> Panchayati Raj Institutions (PRI) are dominated by economically or socially privileged sections of society and have as such facilitated the emergence of oligarchic forces yielding no benefits to weaker sections. The performance of PRIs has also been vitiated by political factionalism, rendering developmental trusts either warped or diluted. Corruption, inefficiency, scant regard for procedures, political interference in day-to-day administration, parochial loyalties, motivated actions, power concentration instead of service consciousness—all these have seriously limited the utility of Panchayati Raj for the average villager.

The Community Development Programs and village cooperative societies also did not fare any better.[47] By the end of the 1950s there was growing evidence (including reports of the Programme Evaluation Organization of the Planning Commission) that much of the benefits of the CDPs and cooperatives were being appropriated by the landlords and rich peasants by virtue of their economic power and political and administrative control over the *panchayats* and the other newly created institutions.

As Barrington Moore (1966, 394) tersely noted, the CDPs failed because they were based on the "absurd" assumption that it was possible "to democratize the village without altering property relationships." Predictably, normative appeals for self-sacrifice and dedication to the collective interest failed to generate much response. Efforts to mobilize village manpower for unpaid work on "community projects" met with little success because the benefits of projects like irrigation, land reclamation, or soil conservation were disproportionately skewed toward the landlords and the rich peasants. Similarly, "peoples participation" in the construction of social amenities projects, such as community centers, schools, libraries, or drinking-water wells made little sense because caste and ritual hierarchy and customary village practices excluded the lower-caste and poor peasants, sharecroppers, and landless from even entering the upper-caste sections of the village, let alone using the community centers or taking water from the same well. Also, as L. C. Jain (1983) points out, the CDPs suffered from excessive bureaucratization and lack of sensitivity to local needs and diversity. Implemented from above and generally unresponsive to the demands and initiative of ordinary, less privileged peasants, most villagers tended to ignore the community development programs, and by the early 1960s community development as a strategy was out of vogue.

The village cooperative societies failed for the same reasons as the community development programs. Although the number of cooperative societies increased from 105,000 in 1951 to over 212,000 a decade later, with a corresponding rise in the total amount of loans and advances from Rs 229 million in 1951 to Rs 2 billion in 1961, rural cooperatives failed to displace the dominant position of the landlords or the village money-lenders (Bettelheim 1968, 196–200). Gunnar Myrdal's (1968, 1335) penetrating observation needs to be quoted at length:

> Unfortunately the notion that cooperation will have an equalizing effect is bound to turn out to be an illusion. While land reform and tenancy legislation are, at least in their intent, devices for producing fundamental alterations in property rights and economic obligations, the "cooperative" approach fails to incorporate a frontal attack on the existing inegalitarian power structure. Indeed, it aims at improving conditions without disturbing that structure and represents, in fact, an evasion of the equality issue. If as is ordinarily the case, only the higher strata in the villages can avail themselves of the advantages offered by cooperative institutions—and profit from the government subsidies for their development—the net effect is to create more, not less, inequality. This will hold true even when the announced purpose is to aid the disadvantaged strata.

Hence, village cooperative societies became essentially a conduit of subsidized credit to the old and emergent rural rich. Given their privileged economic and political position, members of this stratum were able to capture much of the scarce development resources and enlarge their role as intermediaries-cum-brokers in relationships among the village, the district, and sometimes with the provincial and central authorities.

Reforms and Beyond:
Emergent Trends in the Countryside

From the preceding discussion it can reasonably be concluded that attempts at socioeconomic and political reforms through the institutionalist strategy proved to be largely ineffective. State policies aimed at promoting rural reform and development produced results opposite to those intended—further entrenching (and aggravating) rural disparities and undermining the developmental goals of planning. Indeed, the draft outline of the Fifth Five Year Plan (1978–1983), revealed that the poorest 10 percent of rural households in India had secure rights in land on only 0.1 percent of the land, while the richest 10 percent of rural households controlled over 50 percent of "total assets in 1971–72" (GoI 1978, 11). In fact, several observers of rural India have argued that the central government's agrarian policies during the Nehru era, far from promoting "an efficient peasant-based agriculture" or "socialistic pattern of society," instead laid the foundations of capitalist social and production relations in the countryside.[48] The real legacy of *zamindari* abolition was that in curbing the hegemonic political and socioeconomic power of the traditional feudal *zamindari* elite, it perceptibly shifted the locus of rural power away from the native princes and large feudal landlords to the more entrepreneurially inclined and "market-oriented" *zamindars* and rich peasants. These forward-looking gentleman farmers, or, in the radical lexicon, the agrarian bourgeoisie or "kulaks," have compensated their loss of land and crop rents by diversifying their economic activities (discussed in Chapter 5). Moreover, as their economic and political power have increased, so have their demands for more favorable treatment from the central and state governments. Needless to say, this old and emergent rural elite has also systematically undermined potentially unfavorable (i.e., reformist and redistributive) central directives (discussed in chapter 6).

By the mid-1970s the proportion of the "agriculturalists"[49] in the Lok Sabha had more than tripled—from a mere 14 percent in 1951 to 34 percent in 1971 and to over 40 percent in 1977. This was due in part to the "deepening of democracy" and the push by Congress leadership—and, increasingly, political parties such as the Bharatiya Lok Dal (BLD), the Janata Party, and regionally based parties—to seek allies from the influential rural castes and classes, that is, those with the greatest economic and political resources. In effect, the imperatives of electoral politics, with politicians hungry for the floating rural votes, made the national political elites and parties operate more than ever before through the existing structures of rural power—which effectively meant greater dependence on the rural landed elites. Paul Brass's (1984, 104–105) meticulous study of Gonda and Deoria districts in Uttar Pradesh in the late 1970s and early 1980s is illustrative. He showed that despite more than three decades of *zamindari* abolition, the aristocratic landed families not only continued to control village and district politics, but that their influence extended out of the district directly to the state's chief minister and to the office of the prime minister. In Gonda district the descendant of the former *raja* (aristocratic *zamindar*) owned at least 1,500 acres of prime agricultural land, owned a factory worth Rs 3 *crore*[50] just 2 kilometers from his family palace where he lived in feudal splendor, chose the local Congress candidates for the state legislature and the national parliament, and hobnobbed with the influential politicians, including the prime minister. His counterpart in

Deoria district, while a lesser *zamindar,* is known for delivering "single-handed" the district vote to friendly parties and politicians.

In effect, what occurred was the "traditionalization" of a modernizing democratic polity. India's democratic state goals of citizenship, purposive direction of public policy, and national integration were traditionalized by rural society. That is, traditional politics were resurrected under new auspices. Power had been delegated downward so far, and on such a scale, that it could no longer be easily recovered because the devolution of state power had played into the hands of entrenched local elites. As power and authority became concentrated, personalized, and organized around wealth, caste, faction, and clientage, it enabled vested interests to gain discretionary control over broad realms of public life.[51] By the early 1970s, in all but name, the "national parliament came to act as a commodity lobby to reinforce the substantial voice already enjoyed by the Chief Ministers of the states as spokesmen for agrarian interests" (Kochanek 1975, 83). The central government also came to terms with this reality "by altering its half-hearted confrontational attitude towards the landowners and . . . moving towards an explicit support for agrarian capitalism" (Kohli 1987, 72). Not surprisingly, the Fourth Five Year Plan (1969–1974) was the last of the plans to vigorously reiterate the theme of land and tenure reforms. By the time of the Seventh Five Year Plan (1985–1990), land reform was considered redundant and was discarded as an instrument of state policy. The seventh plan included only a few short paragraphs on land reform; at best, the reform was subordinated to a variety of state funded antipoverty programs.

Today, in most Indian states,[52] and especially in the "Hindi belt" covering the vast geographical expanse from Rajasthan to the gangetic plains of Uttar Pradesh and Bihar, the emergent agrarian elite, though socially and economically diverse—ranging through upper-caste *brahmins* and *rajputs,* peasant castes of *jats* and *bhumihars,* and "backward cultivating castes" comprising *ahirs, yadavs,* and *kurmis* and *koeris*—has been successful in achieving for themselves a political role commensurate with their growing economic power and influence.[53] Their near total dominance of the state, district, and local political and bureaucratic machines, and their support for explicitly pro-*kisan* (pro-rich-peasant) political parties has meant that the socioeconomic interests and power of the rural rich have been protected, if not enhanced. Suffice it to note that the growing economic-political power and influence of these rural elites have concomitantly further limited the range of options available to the Indian state to institute even mild reformist and distributive policies in the countryside.

These complex themes will be elaborated in subsequent chapters. The next chapter examines the political origins of the shift from the institutionalist strategy to the technocratic or the "green revolution" strategy in the mid-1960s. The complex politics of the period tell us a lot about the democratic state's changing economic and development imperatives and the nature of the state's policy- and decisionmaking process. The discussion will also allow us to better evaluate the ramifications of the policies.

Notes

1. The term refers to the ideas, strategies, and models of development adopted by the state elites and policymakers. For details see Grindle (1986, 19–21).

2. It is important to note that unlike the industrial sector, state intervention in the agricultural sector has been based on policy intervention rather than direct control.

3. For a good discussion see GoI (1952; 1956a) and also Balasubramanyam (1984, 78–109).

4. For details see Lewis (1995, 55–131); Singh (1974, 149–196); and Frankel (1978, 71–112).

5. Specifically, Nehru and others were not against agricultural modernization via technical upgrading, but argued that technology must complement structural reforms and not be viewed as the solution to the rural problems. They also felt that traditional agricultural technologies and farming methods must be integrated with modern ones.

6. This committee, also known as the Kumarappa Committee (after its chairman, J. C. Kumarappa), was appointed in 1947 (with Nehru's approval) by the Congress president to formulate the general principles of the reform package. It made a detailed survey of the country's agrarian relations, collecting oral and written evidence numbering over 6,000 typed pages. A useful background is provided in Warriner (1969, 150–165).

7. This data are reprinted in Government of India (1963, Appendix V). A useful summary of the data is also available in Sen (1962, 26–34).

8. Given the fact that land reform legislation had already come into effect in many states when the detailed *NSS* landholdings data were first collected in 1954–1955, these data in all probability reflect underreporting of large holdings to escape the legislation. In other words, inequalities were perhaps even worse than the following data show.

9. For a good background to the discussion regarding the nature of Indian feudalism, see Sen (1962); Sen (1982); Sharma (1965); and Thapar (1961).

10. Daniel Thorner (1956, 35–36) once called the land tenure system in India the "most bewildering in the world." For an excellent survey of the landholding patterns in the various parts of India, and for conceptual clarification of this complex issue, see Alavi (1965); Byres (1988a); Kotovsky (1964, 1–42); and Sen (1962).

11. According to the *NSS,* these groups owned anywhere from 2.5 to 10 acres of land (see GoI 1963).

12. In Uttar Pradesh, for example, 3 percent of the *zamindars* owned 54 percent of the land (Singh and Mishra 1965, 28).

13. It is important to note that the *NSS* of 1954/55 classified landholdings of only sizes 0.00 (or landless) to holdings of over 50 acres. However, in the state of Kerala it was noted that the size of the large *zamindar* estates, in the early 1950s, ranged from 1,161 to 63,130 hectares (cited in Tai 1974, 24). To get a better sense of the size and power of the large *zamindar* estates, see Henningham (1983); Jannuzi (1974); Kotovsky (1964); Metcalf (1967); and Ojha (1977).

122 Development and Democracy in India

14. This is quoted in Frankel (1978, 98). For an all-India overview see Sen (1962, chap. 5).

15. The six states where the enquiries were conducted are Bombay, Madhya Pradesh, Madras, Punjab, Uttar Pradesh, and West Bengal. The case of Uttar Pradesh (the only study I examined in some detail) clearly showed that the disparities were wide. For details see Government of India (1963a).

16. This is cited in Frankel (1978, 109).

17. Warriner (1969, 159) reports that in Uttar Pradesh, on the eve of *zamindari* abolition, the *zamindars* took Rs 191 million per annum from the tenants, paid Rs 71 million as revenue, and kept the balance of Rs 120 million as income. In Bihar the *zamindars* took Rs 120 million a year from the tenants, paid Rs 20 million as revenue, and kept the balance of Rs 100 million as income. For an all-India overview see Malaviya (1954, 90–106); also Sen (1962, 124–132).

18. For details see GoI (1956a, 220–225); also Jha (1971, 34–52); Herring (1983, 130–131).

19. The Second Plan, with its emphasis on import substitution, increased the share of industry from 7.6 percent in the First Plan to 18 percent out of a total outlay of Rs 48 billion and sharply reduced that of agriculture and irrigation from 32 percent to 22 percent (GoI 1980).

20. For similar arguments see DeJanvry (1981); Myrdal (1968); and Paige (1975).

21. It is worth reiterating that the central government enjoyed less leverage over events in the agricultural sector than in industry. Due to the constitutional limitations on the power of the Indian state, provincial governments have enjoyed exclusive jurisdiction over the enactment and implementation of rural development policies, including land and tenure reforms.

22. See GoI (1964); Mellor (1976, 30–32); and Wunderlich (1970, 56–60).

23. Quoted in Warriner (1969, 136). Gunnar Myrdal (1968) came to the same general conclusion, as did Daniel Thorner (1956; 1976) and Francine Frankel (1978).

24. According to Barrington Moore (1966, 395), "Nehru's agrarian program was an out-and-out failure." This view is shared by others, and the literature on this subject is vast. For a sample see Joshi (1975; 1982); Jha (1971); Ladejinsky (1977); and Government of India (1976, chap. 66).

25. For a similar interpretation see Mellor (1969, 30–32); Singh and Mishra (1965); and Warriner (1969: 136–218).

26. See, for example, Malaviya (1954); Jannuzi (1974); Neale (1962); and Uppal (1983).

27. A similar perspective is available in Nair (1961); Sharma (1962); and Wood (1972, 33–42).

28. See Chattopadhyay (1973); Desai (1984); Prasad (1985); Sharma (1973); and Sen (1962, 189–291).

29. The term refers to the supporters of the former conservative president, Plutarco Elias Calles.

30. Alan Knight (1991, 258–259) notes that "in regions of long-standing agrarian conflict the climate changed overnight: beleaguered *agraristas* suddenly found the weight of the 'center' behind them." A classic case was the Laguna. A major center of agrarian conflict and rebellion during the revolution, the region had known constant peasant agitation during the 1920s, despite the hostile political climate. In this simmering dispute, "Cardenas personally intervened [in October 1936], and decreed a sweeping reform whereby three-quarters of the valuable irrigated land and a quarter of the non-irrigated were turned over to some thirty thousand *campesinos*, grouped in three hundred *ejidos*."

31. The same can be said of other countries. For example, in Egypt, where land and tenure reforms have been put on the policy agenda for decades, yet the state lacks the capacity to effectively implement them. For details see John Waterbury's (1983) excellent study.

32. Although the initiative of the central government in forcing land reforms on conservative states is often stressed, it must be noted that the Indian state has also, on occasion, undermined the potential for radical rural reforms in states like Kerala and West Bengal (Herring 1983; Kohli 1987).

33. The fact that the Congress during this period was dominated by members of the upper castes led Ramashray Roy (1967, 375) to evaluate the ramifications: "This means that traditionally entrenched social as well as economic sectors of the society have greater access to positions of power, not only in the party but also in the government, with the result that radical policies of social transformation are bound to be delayed if not sabotaged. The dominance of the vested interests in the Congress, therefore, prevents it from carrying out measures of reforms which may adversely affect the interests of the upper castes." Also see Franda (1968, 129–179); Frankel (1978, 190–191); Jannuzi (1974); and Sharma (1973) for similar analysis.

34. I owe this metaphor to P. C. Joshi (from an interview conducted 28 and 29 June 1990 at the Institute of Economic Growth, New Delhi).

35. F. T. Jannuzi (1974, 53–55) suggests that landlords were not so much concerned about the economic impact of the reforms (because they had their tracks covered), but feared that *zamindari* abolition, by curbing their previously unquestioned authority, would also undermine their social prestige.

36. A fascinating account of the process is presented in Jannuzi (1974).

37. This is cited in Warriner (1969, 162).

38. For details see Jannuzi (1974, 196–199) and Metcalf (1967).

39. For example, Zoya Hasan (1989, 52) in her study of Uttar Pradesh reports that "the number and size of holdings of the rich peasants grew rapidly after 1952. The percentage of rich peasants increased from 9.6 to 25 percent, and the holdings (in terms of area) went up from 39 to 55 percent in the years 1951 to 1971."

40. A comprehensive discussion is provided in Chattopadhyay (1973, 3–24); Sen (1962); and Thorner (1976).

41. For details see Jannuzi (1974); Ladejinsky (1977); and Neale (1962).

42. A drive to register tenants by the Bihar government encountered such violent agitation from the landed interests that the whole idea was quickly dropped. See Jannuzi (1974).

43. It is important to note that the antagonism of the landlord was not so much against the tenant but the latter's protected status.

44. While it was extremely difficult to establish the actual numbers of tenants evicted, the Planning Commission believed the numbers to be substantial in almost every state. Large-scale evictions were also reported by individual researchers. See, for example, Jannuzi (1974); Singh and Mishra (1965); and Thorner (1976).

45. For further details see Kotovsky (1964, 49) and Wunderlich (1970, 52–56).

46. The Congress Working Committee meeting at Nagpur on 6 January 1959 called for an immediate transformation of the agrarian structure through the completion of land reforms and joint cooperative farming. The Rudolphs (1987, 318) point out that "the defeat of the Nagpur resolution marked the end of efforts at the national level to bring about large-scale structural change in Indian agriculture."

47. See Nair (1961, 93–99) and Myrdal (1968, 1339–1346).

48. The literature on the subject is vast. For a summary see Byres (1974; 1981); Sharma (1973); Thorner (1982); Kohli (1987); and Rudolph and Rudolph (1987).

49. The term is used to denote modern or "forward-looking" farmers.

50. One *crore* is equivalent to 10,000,000.

51. Paul Brass (1965, 2) was among the first to note this pattern. He argued that the Congress Party chose "to make adjustments and accomodations, to interact with rather than transform the traditional order. In India modernization is not a one-way process; political institutions modernize the society while the society traditionalizes institutions."

52. The only significant exception to the total dominance of agrarian capitalists in rural India is Kerala. In Kerala, for example, reformist and redistributive intervention on behalf of the poor has demonstrated the potential for fundamental changes in the countryside through democratic and constitutional means. During the mid-1970s Kerala under the "Left Front" government led by the Communist Party passed and effectively implemented a series of reformist and redistributive legislation that abolished landlordism, outlawed bonded labor, and successfully distributed land to the tillers (in particular, to land-poor peasants), as well as enforcing (with relative success) the payment of legally mandated wages and ensured old-age pensions for small farmers. These reforms were successfully implemented because of the extraordinary political mobilization through participatory and democratic means of a broad coalition of smallholder peasants, tenants, sharecroppers, the landless, and urban-based groups such as labor unions and students under the auspices of the left-front government, which for all practical purposes had abandoned the Naxalite-Marxist dogma of violent and insurrectionary class struggle, and functioned electorally as a social democratic party. However, it is important to note that the case of Kerala is anomalous for India. Lest I exaggerate the Kerala experience, it is important to note that the reforms in Kerala have by no means solved the agrarian problems, in particular, the problems of poverty and associated malnutrition and ill health among the poor. Smallholders and relatively larger tenants have been the greatest beneficiaries, and the promised higher wages and other benefits promised to the rural landless are not always successfully implemented. Also, Kerala has not been able to generate agricultural dynamism needed to enhance income and living standards.

53. See Blair (1984); Brass (1980); Das (1983); and Frankel and Rao (1989; 1990, 2 vols.).

4

The State, Public Policy, and Agricultural Modernization

---

*If our dependence on imported foodgrains has to cease, it is necessary
to make far greater use of modern methods of production. . . . A new
strategy or approach is needed if we are to achieve results over a short
span of time. During the last four years as a result of the trials conducted
in several research centers in India on exotic and hybrid varieties of
seeds, a breakthrough has become possible. These varieties are highly responsive to a heavy dosage of chemical fertilizers. . . . The long term objective is to organize the use of high-yielding seeds together with a high
application of fertilizers over extensive areas where irrigation is assured.*

—Government of India, Planning Commission,
Fourth, Five Year Plan: A Draft Outline, 1966, p. 175.

The agricultural policies that the Indian state has pursued since the
mid-1960s have been christened the "green revolution" or the "technocratic strategy" because of its emphasis on technological solutions to the
problems of rural underdevelopment and agricultural stagnation, instead of
the emphasis of earlier policies on institutional reforms. How did a weak
democratic state engineer such a decisive reorientation in macroeconomic
policy, and what have been the socioeconomic and political ramifications?
This chapter outlines the nature and content of the dynamic interactions
between the contending political and societal forces, as well as external
actors, as they helped introduce "a package of policies" with profound impact on the political economy of the countryside. It is argued that in the
chaotic and unpredictable political-economic environment of the mid-
1960s, the interests and imperatives of the dominant rural propertied castes
and classes, and their backers and supporters in the central and state legislatures, were broadly congruent and coincided with those of the new political leadership and the technocratically oriented policymakers in the
central government and bureaucracy. This congruence caused these rural
elements, legislators, and policymakers often to act as a unified lobby
against the proponents of institutional reforms. Specifically, their shared

hostility toward the reformist institutional strategy (albeit with varying
reasons and rationales) resulted in a implicit alliance of convenience
between these forces. As Nehru passed from the political stage in 1964,
these forces' combined influence and the institutional-bureaucratic power
exerted both from "above" (within the central government) and from
"below" (in the state legislatures) ultimately defeated the proponents of
the institutional approach. The preceding provides a necessary context to
the following examination of the impact of the green revolution strategy
on the rural political economy and how the strategy impinged upon state-
society relations, in particular, the state's distributional and reformist
capabilities.

Explaining the Policy Change

A survey of the literature reveals several contending explanations of why
the technologically centered strategy was adopted by the Indian government in the mid-1960s. According to Frankel (1978), Rudolph and
Rudolph (1987), and Kochanek (1968), the dramatic reorientation of agricultural strategy represented a monumental attack on the principles of
Nehruvian socialism and a "retreat from the social goals of planning."
Specifically, the reorientation marked the victory of conservatives in the
ruling Congress Party at the center and in the various state governments—
who then systematically engineered the shift in agricultural policy. Other
scholars have argued that external actors, in particular, the United States
government, the World Bank, and private U.S. foundations such as the
Ford and Rockefeller Foundations, were largely instrumental in influencing and pressuring India's decision- and policymaking elites into adopting
the technocratic strategy (Castore 1982; Goldsmith 1988, 179–198; Ladejinsky 1977; Prasad 1980). Neo-Marxists have provided a different interpretation. While some have argued that the new strategy was a direct result
of "imperialist and neocolonial domination" of India's political economy
(Abrol 1983; Cleaver 1976; N. K. Chandra 1988, 67–81; Weisskopf 1974),
others have emphasized the "organized class power" of the "emergent
landlords and kulaks," arguing that the adoption of the green revolution
strategy was predetermined and thus inevitable, a logical outcome of the
"bourgeois-landlord" state committed to rapid capitalist development and
serving its new patrons: the "bourgeois-kulak alliance" (Sharma 1973,
77–103; Byres 1981; Joshi 1982; Rastyannikov 1981). However, analysts
like Bardhan (1984) and Kohli (1987) have provided important correctives
to the excessively instrumentalist radical interpretations. Atul Kohli (1987,
37–38), for example, has argued that the adoption of "the green revolution
represented a continuity in the unfolding of the basic political economy of
India: a growth-oriented alliance between a heterogeneous political elite

and private enterprise." In contrast to others, Lewis (1995) and Aushtosh Varshney (1995) have argued that the shift toward the green revolution strategy was neither determined by the interests of the dominant propertied classes nor by international actors. While at crucial turning points external agencies and powerful domestic socioeconomic forces greatly influenced the content of the new policy, the primary force initiating and spearheading the policy change was India's technocratically oriented political and decisionmaking elites.[1] These policy elites were not simply "conservatives" representing the dominant rural propertied interests, or individuals blindly following the prescriptions outlined by external advisers and agencies; rather, many took a formative and active role in shaping the content of the new policy because of their philosophy that technocratic solutions were the best (and most feasible) means of achieving agricultural modernization and national development. Varshney (1995) correctly notes that although political calculations clearly determined the choice of some, the intellectual values or "development ideologies" of the ascendant political and policy elites, in particular, their strong conviction in the appropriateness of the technological solutions, played a crucial role shaping the content of the new policy.

The political economy of policymaking and change to India's agricultural strategy presents a tapestry rich enough to provide evidence to buttress these competing claims. Integrating them into a state-society framework, the following illustrates that following Nehru's death in 1964, the ascendant political elites and technocratically oriented policymakers were confronted with a host of serious political and economic problems—which were either directly or indirectly the result of the failure of the reformist-institutional approach to rural development. In particular, the failure to improve agricultural performance or meet the increasing food demands of a rapidly expanding population led to growing food shortages, skyrocketing inflation, and food riots. Moreover, the growing pressures on political leaders from the dominant groups in civil society (in particular, the rural propertied interests) as well as the pressures and growing dependence on foreign aid, coupled with diminishing popularity of the Congress governments in the center and the states, contributed to the rapid undoing of the entire Nehruvian approach to rural and agricultural development. Indeed, within eighteen months after Nehru's death, the new political leadership and its allies instituted a series of far-reaching political and economic initiatives that cumulatively replaced the reformist-institutional approach to development with a technocratic one.

Contrary to conventional thinking, the agricultural policy change in India in the mid-1960s vividly illustrates that democratic governments do have a variable capacity to redefine and reorient public policy, even though the range of options they may have remains contingent on interest-group pressure and state-society configuration.

The Politics of Policy Change

As noted in the previous chapter, the Congress Party did not have a unified economic development policy vis-à-vis the countryside. While Nehru and the Congress "high command,"[2] including the Gandhians and socialists, advocated a reformist-institutionalist strategy, the other group, much smaller and less influential, in the party called for a technocratic strategy to solve the country's agricultural problems. During the first decade after independence, Nehru and *inter alia* the Planning Commission's[3] preeminent authority in determining macroeconomic policies for national development were seldom openly challenged, and criticism of the Nehruvian development approach tended to remain muted (see Brecher 1966; Kochanek 1968). However, from the late 1950s onward, with the defeat of Nehru's Nagpur resolution (which called for joint or cooperative farming) and as the growing, often bitter factional disputes within the party weakened his authority and prestige, the criticism of his approach to national development, in particular, rural development, grew louder.

The first concerted "attack" on the Nehruvian "socialist principles of Planning," as Francine Frankel (1978) aptly puts it, was mounted by the "conservatives" in the inner cabinet, the party, and the government (at both state and national levels). It was led by such men as Finance Minister Morarji Desai and several powerful "state bosses" (many speaking on behalf of the dominant agricultural interests) who opposed land and tenure reforms on political grounds or felt, as Desai was fond of saying, that land reforms and agricultural cooperatives were simply a pernicious attempt by Nehru and the left-leaning Planning Commission to bring communism into India (Brecher 1966). But the so-called conservatives were not the only ones critical of the Nehruvian development strategy. The growing pool of agricultural economists, scientists, and technocratically inclined policymakers and advisers in the government, including the two longest serving ministers of food and agriculture, A. P. Jain (1955–1959) and S. K. Patil (1959–1963), also became critical of the government's development approach on largely economic grounds (Goldsmith 1990; Frankel 1978, 140–145 and 230–235). They felt that the government's overemphasis upon capital-intensive import-substituting industrialization was flawed, as was the exclusive reliance on the reformist-institutional approach to solving the country's agricultural problems. They argued that neither approach met the standards of economic rationality and productive efficiency. Both Jain and Patil not only became critical of what they considered to be the government's excessive reliance on concessionary Public Law (P.L.) 480 grain shipments from the United States[4] but were often at odds with Nehru and the Planning Commission, arguing that greater reliance on market mechanisms, as well as providing incentives to farmers, was necessary if the country was to become self-sufficient in food production and improve the welfare of the poor.[5]

In April 1959 a report by a team of U.S. and Indian experts working under the auspices the Ford Foundation, which was published as an official government document, further supported the position advocated by those calling for a technocratic strategy for the countryside.[6] The report provided what the advocates of the technological strategy considered to be irrefutable empirical evidence for what they had been long arguing: that the stagnant agricultural production was the direct result of misguided government policies. (In fact, the net production of food grains had declined from 63.3 million metric tons in 1954 to 60.9 million metric tons in 1956 and to a low of 58.3 million metric tons in 1958.) By the early 1960s, as professional opinion among the proponents of the technocratic strategy coincided with the interests and imperatives of the political conservatives, the voices calling for a reevaluation of the reformist-institutional approach to rural development grew louder. This combination of forces began to call vigorously for incentives to private investment, including price stabilization, guaranteed prices to farmers, and massive state investments in rural infrastructure, irrigation, and such technological inputs as fertilizers and high-yielding (HYV) seeds as the only realistic way to quickly boost agricultural production and productivity.

In the early 1960s, even as the major planks of the Congress Party's institutional reforms program were facing a crescendo of criticism both from within and outside the party and government, Nehru and the Planning Commission nevertheless held steadfast, defending the government's macroeconomic and sectoral policies and the national development strategy. They rejected the criticisms on grounds that their industrialization-first approach to development was a national imperative and that the modest levels of investment in the agricultural sector were justified because without the effective implementation of land and tenure reforms, and expansion of cooperative farming, "Indian agriculture could never become efficient and productive."[7] In fact, Nehru and his confidants in the Congress Party and on the Planning Commission orchestrated a series of brilliant "counterattacks on their conservatives opponents inside the Congress party" (Frankel 1978, 228). By 1963 several key opponents, including Morariji Desai and S. K. Patil, whom Nehru considered the major obstacles in the cabinet and the party, were purged from their positions and replaced by trusted Nehru loyalists and individuals considered by the prime minister and the party high command as pliant. Not surprisingly, at the annual session of the Congress at Bhubaneshwar in January 1964, the party vigorously reiterated its commitment to the Nehruvian path of development. In particular, it called for greater state intervention in the countryside to stop abuses associated with implementation, as well as to implement more effectively the institutionalist program of land and tenure reforms and agricultural cooperatives as set down in the government's five-year plans.

The immediate consequence of Nehru's death in May 1964 was that the political-bureaucratic institutions he had so assiduously fashioned were significantly reorganized, and the individuals who had helped shape his economic policy and the ideology that underlay their functioning were relegated to the sidelines. This turnabout was swift and decisive. In a matter of eighteen months, Nehru loyalist Lal Bahadur Shastri (who Nehru personally hoped would be his successor), in alliance with the technocrats and influential colleagues within the party, fundamentally reoriented his mentor's development strategy. Indeed, at the time of Shastri's death, in January 1966, the key pillars of the Nehruvian strategy of self-reliant rural development based upon land/tenure reforms and cooperative reorganization in agriculture were virtually abandoned, replaced by an approach emphasizing technological solutions to the problems of rural and agricultural development.

The sharp departure from past policies was fueled by forces emanating from both the state and society, as well as out of a series of independently caused but conjuncturally related events. In May 1964, when Shastri succeeded Nehru as prime minister, the national economy was already caught in an accelerating food crisis. For example, the per capita availability of foodgrains for consumption had drastically fallen to levels of the mid-1950s (Mellor 1976). In the face of acute shortages of essential commodities and the spiraling cost of basic food items, the government was forced to institute a scheme for statutory rationing in several towns and cities as it was confronted with escalating nationwide agitation against food shortages and rising prices.[8] The food crisis of 1964 became even worse in the next year, fueled by an unprecedented 20 percent drop in foodgrain production that followed the two successive monsoon failures in 1965/66 and 1966/67. So severe were the shortages that only massive foodgrain imports-cum-food-aid under the P.L. 480 agreement with the United States, with imports that rose sharply from 3.5 million metric tons in 1961, to 7.5 million metric tons in 1964/65 to 10.4 million metric tons in 1965/66, prevented large-scale famine, hunger, and destitution (Mellor 1976; Paarlberg 1985).

With the economy already vulnerable, the Indian government's problems were further compounded when U.S. President Lyndon Johnson announced that there would be no new negotiations with India for a new food-aid agreement after the expiration of the P.L. 480 treaty in June of 1965. In fact, for two months after the expiration food aid to India was discontinued, and only after much pleading did the U.S. administration agree to restore food aid on a short-term basis—what Johnson termed the "short-tether policy."[9] Although the motivations behind the U.S. policy may have been more political and due to India's strident criticism of U.S. policy in

Vietnam (Paarlberg 1985; Prasad 1980), the reasons given by the U.S. administration were that such "tough-minded" actions were necessary to make the Indian government realize that its "current" agricultural development policies were unrealistic instruments of growth, and simultaneously to "prod" Indian policymakers into adopting rational "self-help" strategies that would improve the country's capacity to increase food production (Lewis 1995; Goldsmith 1988; Prasad 1980). Specifically, the self-help strategies articulated by the team of U.S. and World Bank experts (the so-called Bell mission of 1965) strongly reiterated what the Ford Foundation report had recommended earlier in 1959. This was that the Indian government should either greatly limit or altogether abandon its state-managed institutional model of rural and agricultural development, and adopt more "viable" or efficient policies that ensured "fair" producer and price incentives to farmers, and back the "progressive farmers" with credit, marketing, extension services (particularly irrigation), and adequate supplies of physical inputs such as fertilizers, pesticides, and HYV seeds.

Even though the pressures from the United States government no doubt influenced the policy shift, it is important not to exaggerate their overall impact. Nevertheless, the role of external actors needs to be put in perspective. According to Chidambaran Subramaniam, the minister of food and agriculture from 1964 to 1967 and Dr. L. K Jha, the principal secretary to Prime Minister Shastri from 1964 to 1966, the U.S threats and pressures were both unnecessary and unjustified. In an article he wrote in 1973 Jha argued that the Johnson administration was simply "leaning against open doors."[10] The irrepressible Subramaniam was more blunt:

> Johnson always had a sense of self-importance. If anything good or important was happening in the world, it should be a Johnson initiative . . . he thought the Indian farmer, the Indian minister and the Indian scientist were not adequate, and that he should take a hand in the initiation of this strategy. He reiterated in speeches that India should adopt this new technology, which, as a matter of fact, created problems for me in India. The speeches gave ammunition to those who were attacking me on the grounds that I was following American advice . . . We had already announced and taken these steps and I had to tell people that President Johnson was telling us nothing new (Subramaniam 1979, 53).

As will be discussed in greater detail in the next section, months before the Bell mission started its work (in January 1965), and before its recommendations were made public in October 1965, the Shastri administration had already embarked upon implementing the very kinds of policy recommendations made later by the Bell mission. But before examining the complex of domestic forces that were propelling the Shastri government, caveats need to be noted.

Authors such as Atul Kohli (1987) and the Rudolphs (1987) have tended to view the Shastri interlude as not very important and Shastri as a weak and insecure leader whose vulnerability to domestic and external forces led him to unwittingly abandon Nehru's social and economic goals of planning. However, the recent studies by Lewis (1995) and Varshney (1995) give quite a different picture. One can extrapolate that Shastri was far more politically shrewd and decisive than he has been given credit for. While those around him (including Nehru) mistook his quiet, unthreatening, and unassuming demeanor as a sign of subservience and weakness, Shastri the quintessential *ajatashatru* (i.e., the one without enemies), like the archetypical village *sarpanch* (headman) he fancied himself to be, was a cautious and pragmatic man who knew when to sail close to the wind and when to ease off. Even as he stood in line and paid the requisite *darshan* (homage) to Nehru and his coterie, he was also carefully building coalitions with many of Nehru's bitterest critics and carving a political niche for himself for the hour of reckoning. By the time Nehru came to realize his protégé's true ambitions, it was too late. A political survivor par excellence, Shastri practiced the craft of high politics with considerable skill to become prime minister in May 1964.

Shastri's decades-long experience in politics had given him an intricate understanding of the Congress Party's functioning, especially at the state and local levels. Intuitively he knew well that behind all the sound and fury, the central authorities were embarrassingly compromised vis-à-vis the rural structures of power and dominance. He also knew that even though Nehru and the Planning Commission got their way when it came to policy formulation for the countryside, they repeatedly lost the battle of implementation to the combined powers of the chief ministers, the provincial legislators, and the dominant rural propertied classes. For Shastri, most troubling was what he perceived to be the long-term political consequences of the impasse. He believed that if the widening political impasse between the central and state and district party leaders was not reconciled, it would inevitably erode the political base and legitimacy of the Congress Party and further undermine its ability to guide socioeconomic and political development. Also, Shastri for all his reverence for Nehru never did fully share his mentor's *weltanschauung* of "Fabian socialism." To the contrary, deep down he believed that Nehru's doctrine of socialist transformation of the rural order was simply an impossibility under Indian conditions. And by the early 1960s he had quietly come to accept the "authoritative explanations"[11] given to him by foreign and domestic experts: that misguided state policies (i.e., overemphasis on heavy industry, low levels of investment in the agricultural sector, and poorly implemented rural reforms) were fundamentally responsible for the country's economic crisis. Salvation, he was convinced, lay in renewing the vigor of private enterprise and modernization of the rural economy through rapid diffusion of capital and modern technology.

Given this, it is not surprising that only days after Nehru's funeral ceremonies, Shastri and his allies, now including most of the technocratically inclined experts and policymakers, as well as influential provincial "syndicates" or "party bosses"[12]—men such as Sanjiva Reddy from Andhra Pradesh, S. Nijalingappa from Mysore, C. B. Gupta and Kamalapati Tripathi from Uttar Pradesh, M. L. Sukhadia from Rajasthan, Atulya Ghosh from West Bengal, Bhaktavatsalam from Madras, and Morarji Desai (who gave tacit support)—began to introduce a series of important policy changes. Over a period of sixteen months these policies, even while attempting to maintain an aura of continuity with the past, decisively altered or abandoned the entire Nehruvian approach to rural development.

To achieve this end one of "Shastri's first acts as prime minister was to return them [those ousted by Nehru] to positions of power at the Center" (Lewis 1995, 79–131). Aligned with a new array of forces, he and his close associates launched a quiet yet devastating assault on the Planning Commission, what Varshney (1995) calls "the *bête noire* of the anti-Nehru faction," and the last institutional refuge of many of the Nehru loyalists. In the next sixteen months, this new alignment of forces preempted and defanged opponents within and outside the party by deft maneuvering and political gamesmanship.

Specifically, Shastri redefined the procedures and administrative rules in the policymaking process. First, the members of the Planning Commission were placed on a fixed term of tenure (under Nehru the members enjoyed indefinite tenure). Second, in sharp contrast to Nehru, who as chairman of the Planning Commission concentrated responsibility for all key economic decisions in that body, Shastri delinked the office of the prime minister and other government ministries from the Planning Commission. No longer did individual ministries need to consult the commission on matters of economic policy: the key policy and decisionmaking powers over policy formulation and implementation were shifted willy-nilly to each individual ministry and, by extension, to the chief ministers and legislatures of the states. Similarly, Shastri established an independent prime minister's secretariat with his own team of policy experts. Creating a source of expertise outside the cabinet and the Planning Commission only served further to undermine the policymaking role and, thereby, the influence and power of the Planning Commission (Brecher 1966a, 115–118). Moreover, as Brecher (1966) and more recently Lewis (1995) and Varshney (1995) have noted, the appointment of L. K. Jha, a socialist baiter and one of the sternest critics of the Planning Commission, but also a highly respected economist favoring private enterprise and the market mechanism, as the head of the secretariat significantly reduced the power and influence of the Planning Commission.[13]

The changes at the highest level of the central government and the bureaucracy greatly facilitated the adoption of a new series of policies for the countryside. The appointment of Chidambaram Subramaniam, known for his predilection for science and technology, as the minister of food and agriculture in June 1964 was the first in a series of important steps in that direction. Subramaniam, who is viewed as the chief architect of the green revolution strategy, took to his task with missionary zeal. A long-time critic of the "nonscientific" and "fundamentally inefficient" institutional-reformist model, he now criticized ever more vociferously what he called the "anti-agriculture bias" in development, attacking it as "mere slogan shouting," and arguing that "if we make advancement in agriculture, it has to be based on science and technology."[14]

In a draft paper he prepared for the cabinet upon assuming office, Subramaniam outlined what he considered to be the major problems facing the agricultural sector, as well as policies and programs that could best solve both the immediate and long-term problems of agricultural stagnation and rural poverty. Subramaniam questioned and rejected arguments advanced by the Planning Commission and a Nehru supporter, Finance Minister T. T. Krishnamachari, that food shortages were mainly the result of hoarding by the rich farmers and traders, and that the solution was to extend greater state control and regulation over food trading and distribution, including rationing of available supplies. Subramaniam argued instead that hoarding may have been the immediate cause of the shortages, but the root cause lay in the central government's institutional approach to agricultural development, because in practice the strategy was flawed and thereby an unrealistic instrument of growth.[15] According to Subramaniam it was (1) the low levels of capital investment in agriculture and rural infrastructure, (2) the absence of a stable and fair remunerative price and producer incentives to farmers, (3) the failure to adopt proven scientific and technological knowledge in agriculture, and (4) the government's excessive reliance on the concessionary P.L. 480 grain shipments from the United States that constituted the root cause of the abysmal agricultural performance.[16] Given this, the minister of food and agriculture argued that the immediate task facing the government was to sharply increase agricultural production and productivity, and that the best way to achieve the desired results in a relatively short time was to support individual enterprise and return to the market mechanism. The role of the state was to help create a system that (1) provided higher price incentives to "progressive farmers,"[17] (2) devoted a higher allocation of plan investment resources to agriculture, and (3) made available to farmers the "miracle" HYV seeds, fertilizers, and related extension services so they could adopt optimal farming and productive techniques. According to Subramaniam, since the limits to increasing the area under cultivation as a source of agricultural growth were already reached, only the technologically oriented strategy could rapidly increase production and productivity. Moreover, he argued that the spread of modern technological innovation and the capitalization of "farm enterprises" and the rural economy would not only solve the problems of production and productivity but also the problems of social equity, redistribution, and rural welfare (Subramaniam 1972; 1979; Varshney 1995, 48–80).

Predictably, Subramaniam's prescriptions were almost immediately challenged by the Planning Commission and the finance minister on the grounds that such an approach would be extremely costly to the plan budget and consumers, and spark skyrocketing food prices and social unrest.[18] But as Varshney (1995, 40–65) points out, Subramaniam in a clever move, rather than directly confronting his critics, elicited the support of the chief ministers and (fully aware that the prime minister was also inclined toward his position) requested Shastri to set up an expert committee headed by his chief ally and the prime minister's principal secretary, L. K. Jha, to find a solution to the growing food crisis (also Subramaniam 1979; Dubhashi 1986, 220; Frankel 1978, 257–260). In June 1964 (only weeks after Nehru's death), Shastri did just that, and in September 1964, the Jha committee submitted its report to the prime minister, who to no one's surprise fully endorsed Subramaniam's arguments and policy prescriptions. Further, the Jha committee's recommendation for a 15 percent increase in the procurement price for major foodgrains was immediately granted by the government. And at the committee's request the Agricultural Prices Commission (APC) and the Food Corporation of India were established, with allocative and regulatory powers to ensure that farmers receive fair treatment regarding the procurement and producer prices. In fact, producers were guaranteed before planting that commodity prices would not fall below a certain minimum and that the marketing, procurement, and pricing system would work in their favor (Dubhashi 1986, 220–221). More important, as Varshney (1995) notes, Subramaniam was given the green light to work out the details of his new agricultural strategy (also Subramaniam 1972; 1979).

At the Congress Party's annual session in January 1965, the old Nehruvian guard, in particular, some of the more radical elements now calling themselves the Congress Forum for Socialist Action, mounted what turned out to be the last sustained attack on Shastri and his government's political and economic strategy (Frankel 1978, 266–269). But even as Shastri and his supporters paid lip service to "socialist principles" and a return to the Nehruvian strategy, Shastri, backed by L. K. Jha, the chief ministers, and other provincial notables, quietly encouraged Subramaniam to continue to work out the details of his strategy. Over the next few months the Food and Agriculture Ministry tested some aspects of the new strategy on a pilot basis in various parts of the country. The National Demonstration Program, as it came to be called, was a green revolution strategy in microcosm. The aim was to demonstrate the feasibility and productive capacity of the new technology by trying out the various components of HYV seeds, fertilizers, and water as pilot projects (i.e., on two hectares of land on a thousand different plots) in various parts of the country. Subramaniam felt that such a approach would allow the scientists and other experts to correct technical problems, as well as give the ministry valuable experience in administering the new technology. Moreover, he believed that the demonstrable payoffs of increased efficiency and better returns in yield and prices would rapidly trickle down to other cultivators, regardless of the scale of their enterprise, prompting all cultivators to adopt the new agricultural innovations (Subramaniam 1979, 47–48; also Dubhashi 1986, 151–152).

In the next few months the Agriculture Ministry was buoyed by the good progress of the National Demonstration Program;[19] by the evidence from Indian research stations that the new hybrid varieties of maize, millet, and sorghum performed extremely well under Indian conditions with yields double that of local varieties; and by reported technical breakthroughs in Taiwan and Mexico of new varieties of paddy and wheat with yield levels of 5,000 to 6,000 pounds per acre (almost double the maximum potential output of indigenous Indian varieties). The ministry became enthusiastic about its program for raising agricultural production and productivity.[20] In August 1965 (one month before the release of the Bell Report), the Food and Agriculture Ministry released a comprehensive outline of the new strategy for agriculture. Subramaniam reiterated his claims that "scientific knowledge is available and technological conditions also exist to achieve this goal [of a 5.6 percent rate of growth per annum in output],"[21] provided the government adopted a comprehensive three-pronged strategy of agricultural development. The strategy was to make available at subsidized rates a complete "package of practices" consisting of high-yield varieties of seeds (i.e., wheat and rice); such modern technical inputs as chemical fertilizers, pesticides, and irrigation; and the corollary price/market incentives, extension services, marketing, and transportation facilities to progressive or entrepreneurially oriented producers. The distinguishing feature of the new strategy was that (1) it called for a program of direct payment via credit subsidies to entrepreneurially oriented farmers for the cost of investment in HYV seeds, tubewells, tanks, pesticides, and other technology and inputs, and (2) instead of spreading the new inputs thinly over a wide area, it was decided that development efforts should first be concentrated in "selected areas" with ensured rainfall, irrigation, and related infrastructure to realize the maximum production benefits of the new seeds and technology.

The Food and Agriculture Ministry acknowledged that the foreign exchange component of implementing the new strategy would be very high—an estimated Rs 1,114 crores (about $2.8 billion at the exchange rate of that time), which was over six times the total amount allocated to agriculture during the preceding third plan. Nevertheless, the ministry argued that such an investment was necessary if the country was to achieve self-sufficiency in food and improve the welfare of the poor. Predictably, the Finance Ministry and the Planning Commission found such a proposal unacceptable. They argued that such a large-scale investment was out of the question in a period of mounting expenditures for imports and increased balance-of-payments deficits. In fact, the Planning Commission produced a counterdocument, a preliminary draft of the fourth plan, arguing that shortages in foreign exchange prevented such an expensive outlay.[22] The Planning Commission argued instead that only 54 percent of the capital investment requested by the Agriculture Ministry was sufficient to meet the growth requirements of the agricultural sector.

However, over the next several months several factors intervened to swing the outcome decisively in favor of Subramaniam and his allies. First, the Bell mission's report essentially backed the strategy outlined by the Agriculture Minister. In addition, the U.S. government made the continuation of its food aid contingent on the adoption of a market-oriented technocratic strategy. Also, the sharp drop in domestic food production in 1965 boosted the Subramaniam's position. Finally, the Planning Commission and the Finance Ministry, after the sudden resignation of Krishnamachari on 1 January 1966, became too weak to effectively counter the combined pressures and powers of the central government and the chief ministers and, however reluctantly, gave in to the pressures. Indeed, it was the combined powers of the Shastri cabinet, the new Finance Minister Sachin Chaudhuri,[23] and the chief ministers that later that year brought about the formal approval of Subramaniam's agricultural strategy. Soon afterward the new policy was put into practice, and areas in 114 districts out of 325 (comprising roughly 12 percent of the cultivated area) were selected for an Intensive Agricultural Areas Program.

The sudden death of Prime Minister Shastri on 11 January 1966 and the subsequent election of Indira Gandhi as prime minister (on 20 January 1966) did not in any way alter the newly adopted development path for the countryside. In fact, Mrs. Gandhi did everything to facilitate the new agricultural strategy. Subramaniam was made a member of the Planning Commission and given complete authority over agricultural matters. The victory of the technocratic approach was epitomized in the language of the new draft outline of the Fourth Plan cited at the head of this chapter.

Summary and Conceptual Issues

The rationale behind the policy shift from a reformist-institutional to a technocratic strategy was complex. The preceding discussion has emphasized how the political struggle in the top echelons of the Indian state itself that culminated in the ascendancy of new political leaders and technocratically oriented policymakers greatly facilitated the policy shift. In less than sixteen months after Nehru's death, the emergent political elite substantially dismantled the key elements of the Nehruvian strategy of institutional reforms and cooperative reorganization and substituted a strategy that openly bet on the strong. In other words, technological change, not reformist structural transformation, became synonymous with agricultural and rural development.

This study also underscores the fact that democratic systems are not only very flexible but also quite capable in making dramatic macroeconomic policy shifts. India's political and policymaking elites were not simply forced by events, dominant class pressures, or external agencies, but also had "policy space" or room to maneuver and a relatively high degree of autonomous capacity to shape, influence, and formulate the content, timing, and sequence of policy initiatives. The technocratically oriented state and policy elites played an active and formative role in shaping policy changes and making them politically acceptable to bureaucratic agencies, central and state legislatures, and groups and individuals representing various vested interests. Influential individuals like Prime Minister Shastri, L. K. Jha, and Agriculture Minister Subramaniam demonstrated a considerable capacity to think strategically about managing and neutralizing opposition, taking advantage of opportune moments, and putting together supportive political coalitions in the Lok Sabha and in the provincial state legislatures to build support for their policy packages. In the end, their skill in utilizing the technical, economic, political, and bureaucratic-organizational resources available to them enabled them to successfully defeat their political and policy opponents and to significantly redefine public policy for the countryside.

The role of external actors and the dominant classes and their allies in influencing the policy shift was not inconsequential, but needs to be placed in perspective. External pressure by itself did not bring about the policy change. However, the growing pressures from the U.S. government, the World Bank, and the Ford and Rockefeller Foundations greatly strengthened the hands of those arguing for a market-oriented, technocratic solution to India's rural and agricultural problems. In a sense, then, external actors by "leaning against open doors" acted as a catalyst, facilitating at critical junctures the policy reorientation. Moreover, once the technocratic strategy was formally adopted by the Indian government, foreign organizations and experts provided the much needed financial and technical assistance for its effective implementation.

State elites were not immune from the insinuations and pressures of propertied interests and their allies, but the neo-Marxist argument that the agrarian bourgeoisie were fundamentally responsible for the green revolution strategy sounds rather exaggerated (if not misleading) when scrutinized in the light of the evidence presented. Specifically, such an argument raises an empirical issue. First, the call for and subsequent adoption of the technological strategy preceded the emergence of a class of capitalist or market-oriented rural producers, and, second, the agrarian bourgeoisie, or the "kulaks," as a class were still relatively small, localized, and politically unorganized when the new strategy was formally adopted in the mid-1960s. Hence, state policy was not simply derivative of class relationships; the state elites demonstrated a variable capacity for autonomous decision-making and through it the ability to shape public policy and direct the country's development agenda. The next chapter will elaborate on the agrarian bourgeoisie's assuming economic and political significance a few years *after* the green revolution strategy had been introduced. In the 1950s and 1960s, the rural propertied interests had exerted pressure on the Indian state not through open political confrontation but via subtle means—applying pressure through their allies in the central government and their state and local representatives, the chief ministers, and other influential state and district level legislators. During the 1950s and early 1960s, their energies were more devoted to stalling (and diluting) the central government's reformist policies than to demanding a technologically oriented strategy.

This realignment of forces as manifest in the tacit growth-oriented alliance between the Indian state and rural propertied classes has had important consequences for development, in particular for "growth with distribution," in the countryside. The next chapter examines the broad social, economic, and political ramifications of the new agricultural strategy in the countryside and state-society relations by juxtaposing macro- and microtrends.

Notes

1. In my understanding, the term "political and decisionmaking elites" refers to central government officials who have decisionmaking responsibilities in government and whose decisions become authoritative for society. It is a term I use interchangeably with policy planners, policymakers, and state elites.

2. During Nehru's tenure the national leadership of the Congress Party was called the "high command" because it consisted largely of Nehru's trusted political confidants, men like V. T. Krishnamachari, Tarlok Singh, Gulzarilal Nanda, and P. C. Mahalanobis, among others, who shared Nehru's Fabian socialist outlook and who functioned in conformity with the basic norms of what Paul Brass (1990, 45) has aptly called "Prime Ministerial government."

3. Since the prime minister was also the chairman of the Planning Commission, Nehru's economic positions, generally speaking, became the positions of the Congress Party and the Planning Commission.

4. During the Nehru era India was able to pursue an industrial strategy by relying on grain shipments from the United States. However, Nehru's critics believed that such an approach not only fostered dependence on foreign food but also depressed farm prices at home. It is useful to note that recent studies have shown that P.L. 480 imports depressed the output of wheat by 73 percent in Bihar, 24 percent

in Madhya Pradesh, 33 percent in Punjab, and 28 percent in Uttar Pradesh (cited in Bhatia 1988, 186).

5. See Prasad (1977); Rudolph and Rudolph (1987, 318–319).

6. The report of the Ford Foundation team suggested a shift from the community approach to an entrepreneurial approach to rural development, and that agricultural development be given the highest priority among all the categories of development for the remainder of the Second Five Year Plan and for the entire Third Plan period. Further, it warned of an impending food crisis if corrective measures were not taken (GoI 1959).

7. In a speech to the state agricultural ministers, Nehru went as far as to deprecate the tendency of some planners "to rely far too much on fertilizers for improving production"; he considered this "a dangerous tendency because it took away from the minds of cultivators the use of green manures and other manures used in other countries" (quote cited in Goldsmith 1988, 189).

8. According to Bilap Dasgupta (1977, 30), "between 1961–62 and 1966–67 the foodgrain prices registered an increase of 83 percent, which also led to a 28 percent increase in the price of manufactured goods."

9. In practice, the short-tether policy provided food stocks sufficient only to meet requirements one month at a time. For details see Prasad (1980).

10. See Jha (1973); also Paarlberg (1985), who supports Jha's position.

11. This quote is from Frankel (1978, 247).

12. The state government party bosses were also known as the "syndicate."

13. Brecher (1966, 118) notes that "within a few months Jha became a member of almost every committee at the Secretary level in the Government of India."

14. Chidambaram Subramaniam made this statement at a speech on 28 November 1964. For greater detail regarding Subramaniam's views and the politics behind the policymaking during this period, see the three books (consisting mainly of his speeches and retrospective assessments) written by Subramaniam (1972; 1972a; 1979). An excellent overview of these texts is provided in Varshney (1995).

15. On the question of land reforms, Subramaniam (1979, 28) argued that "unfortunately one could not wait until the land reform legislation was implemented effectively. We had been trying this for over the last ten years but owing to political and other factors it had not proved possible to implement it properly." Hence, given the situation, he asked, "Would you like to have . . . high production and attain self-sufficiency within the country . . . or would you prefer to continue dependence upon food imports indefinitely?"

16. Foodgrain production grew by 2.9 percent per annum from 1950 to 1958, and only by 2.4 percent per year from 1958 to 1964, just slightly above population growth (for details see Balasubramanyam 1984, chap. 5)

17. It should be noted that the term "progressive farmers" does not imply any moral or intellectual superiority, but was used to describe farmers who were willing to adopt modern farming methods. Progressive farmers were invariably rich peasants and enterprising landlords.

18. Subramaniam (1979, 5) noted that "there was a heated debate in the cabinet . . . with particular opposition from Finance Minister . . . T. T. Krishnamachari. He argued the other side; how could we afford to increase food prices, particularly for industrial labour and the urban population? It would lead to much discontent." Also see Varshney (1995, 40–80).

19. Subramaniam (1979, 48) noted that "farmers used to come there [on the pilot plots] on a pilgrimage to see this new wonder and finally, when the harvesting was being done, everybody was amazed that this level of productivity could be achieved on their own land."

20. The Food and Agriculture Ministry argued that in "absolute terms, intensive cultivation based on the new seeds was expected to add 25 million tons of foodgrains to production, out of the 30 million needed during the Fourth Plan. Total output would be boosted from the base level of 90 million tons in 1965 to 125 million tons in 1971" (Frankel 1978, 277; for further details see Mellor 1976).

21. This is cited in Frankel (1978, 275).

22. However, it should be noted that Subramaniam had argued that shortfalls in foreign exchange could be met by encouraging foreign private investment. In particular, he had pointed out that Bechtel International, an American multinational, was prepared to set up five large fertilizer factories in collaboration with the government (Frankel 1978, 281).

23. Subramaniam (1979, 37) notes: "I approached the Finance Minister [Sachin Chaudhuri] for resources for the import of fertilizers. At the time of the controversy, the Finance Minister had been very much opposed to the use of scarce foreign exchange for the import of fertilizers for the new varieties, but by the time I made my approach another Finance Minister had been appointed who was more open to influence. We thus secured the foreign exchange and mounted an important programme for fertilizers."

5

Contradictions of
the Green Revolution:
Growth Without Redistribution

The entrepreneurial approach adopted in the mid-1960s ended with the worst possible result from the point of view of the multiple economic and social goals of planning. The new economic policies appeared unlikely to achieve the goals of economic growth, and they were certain to increase economic disparities.

—Francine Frankel, *India's Political Economy,
1947–1977: The Gradual Revolution*, p. 334

The development ideology or policy preferences of the state elites in the mid-1960s did much to shape the technocratic policy toward the countryside and to establish the agricultural sector's place in national development. The political elites wanted the green revolution technology to expand in order to resolve a number of severe problems such as low agricultural productivity, pervasive rural poverty, and a variety of impediments to industrial expansion. However, the pursuit of agricultural modernization via the new technological strategy did not always produce outcomes intended (or anticipated) by the political-technocratic elites. Contrary to their beliefs the green revolution strategy, far from being a "scale-neutral" instrument within the rural economy, was in fact frequently decisive in encouraging the concentration of resources in the hands of the already well-off landholders, in creating extensive intrastate and intra-regional disparities, and increasing bifurcation and differentiation within rural economy and society. Thus, even as the new strategy greatly increased agricultural production and productivity, it failed to solve (and in some instances even compounded) the problems of rural poverty and socioeconomic tensions. This chapter illustrates that the expansion of the new agricultural strategy paralleled the expansion of agrarian capitalism, a pattern of change with far-reaching consequences for rural political economy and state-society relations. But first some preliminary issues needs to be noted.

The Technocratic Strategy and the Countryside

India's agricultural performance since the inauguration of the new agricultural strategy has been spectacular, confounding those who feared a Malthusian specter of famine. With aggregate foodgrain production doubling since the mid-1960s, the country has achieved food self-sufficiency. In 1965/66 and 1966/67, the nation's total foodgrain output stood at a deficit (in terms of population growth), 72.3 and 74.2 million tons, respectively.[1] However, with the dissemination of technological innovation (improved HYV seeds, fertilizer, pesticides, herbicides), increased investment of capital resources, and more efficient or optimal land use and farming techniques, foodgrain output increased to 95 million tons in 1968/69, to 108.4 million tons in 1970/71, to 133 million tons in 1981/82 and to a record high of 178 million tons in 1990/91.[2] It is important to note that in the period before the green revolution (1947–1966) the increases in agricultural output were almost exclusively due to the expansion of area under cultivation, whereas in the period after the green revolution increases are due also to growth in agricultural production and productivity or yield. Table 5.1 provides a comparative snapshot of the trends in the production and productivity of principal crops over the last three decades (note that the table covers only the period after the green revolution). The aggregate figures show that significant production gains have occurred with the most remunerative foodgrains: wheat and rice. Wheat production marked a 64.7 percent growth in yield between 1969/70 and 1986/87 compared with a 34.8 percent increase for rice. However, the acreage, production, and yield performance of the relatively unappealing coarse cereals, in particular, millet, sorghum, chickpeas, and the coarser varieties of maize, millet, and sorghum, which are consumed by lower income groups, and pulses such as *arhar* or *urad* (a major source of protein), have showed only moderate increases in production.

Tables 5.2 and 5.3 illustrate that the increases in aggregate agricultural production and yield have been accompanied by the sustained expansion of the gross cropped area, in particular, by the acreage expansion of wheat and rice under the HYV program, and by the massive use of *bazaar ki khaad* or inorganic chemical-based fertilizers and pesticides—many of which include DDT, aldrin, methyl parathion, and BHC, or pesticides banned or severely restricted in developed countries.[3] While details are beyond the scope of this study, it is important to note that the green revolution strategy is fundamentally unsustainable. The prevalence of such symptoms as salinization, erosion, waterlogging, and groundwater depletion and pollution, including pollution and resultant degradation from inorganic (and hazardous) fertilizer and pesticides, have had significant negative impact on the ecosystem. The overreliance on one or two crops, what

Table 5.1   **Area and Yield of Principal Crops: 1969/70 to 1986/87**
(post–Green Revolution: base year 1969/70 = 100)

Crop	Year	Production	Area	Yield
All	1970/71	114.1	102.0	110.4
Cereals	1975/76	128.8	104.0	118.8
	1980/81	143.1	104.5	129.3
	1986/87	161.1	104.0	143.5
Rice	1970/71	107.4	101.5	105.8
	1975/76	124.7	106.7	116.9
	1980/81	137.2	108.6	126.3
	1986/87	150.0	111.3	134.8
Wheat	1970/71	132.1	114.9	115.0
	1975/76	159.9	128.8	124.1
	1980/81	201.1	140.3	143.4
	1986/87	244.9	148.7	164.7
Coarse	1970/71	114.7	98.0	117.2
Cereals	1975/76	111.8	93.1	118.2
	1980/81	106.7	88.8	118.8
	1986/87	115.1	83.1	137.0
All	1970/71	104.4	102.5	102.1
Pulses	1975/76	115.3	111.2	105.0
	1980/81	95.8	103.2	95.6
	1986/87	110.2	104.4	107.1
Gram	1970/71	99.7	101.7	98.0
	1975/76	112.9	108.2	104.3
	1980/81	83.2	85.6	97.2
	1986/87	87.3	89.2	97.9

Source: Government of India, Ministry of Finance, *Economic Survey, 1986–87* (New Delhi: Government of India, 1987), 108–110.

Shiva (1989) has called "monoculture," and the rapid loss of biodiversity can only have tragic ramifications for a poor and populous country like India (also see Repetto 1994).

India's achievement in food grain production has been impressive in the sense of providing the country with a reasonable degree of food security and resilience in face of adverse weather conditions, but agricultural modernization has also created undesirable consequences. In particular, it has aggravated interregional disparities in agricultural production. The highest growth rates in foodgrain production have occurred mainly in the six "advanced states" (see Table 5.4). The highest growth rates and productivity gains have been in the wheat and winter rice growing areas of the Punjab, Haryana, and western Uttar Pradesh, areas that are endowed with rich alluvial soil and ensured rainfall, and have been the beneficiaries of

Table 5.2   Area Under HYV and Use in New Inputs: All-India

Year	Gross Cropped Area[a]	Area Under HYV[b]	Fertilizer Use[c]
1950/51	131.8	—	0.1
1960/61	152.7	1.9	0.3
1970/71	165.7	15.4	2.2
1980/81	173.5	43.1	5.5
1984/85	177.0	56.0	8.5
1990/91	N/A	63.9	12.6

Source: Government of India (1992, 42); Rao and Deshpande (1986, 102).
Notes: a. millions of hectares; b. millions of hectares; c. millions of tons.

Table 5.3   All-India: Percentage of Crops Under HYV: 1971–1987

Year	Rice	Wheat	Coarse Cereals
1971/72	41.0	43.0	16.0
1980/81	42.3	37.4	20.3
1986/87	42.8	34.1	23.1

Source: Calculated from Government of India (1988, 125).

massive state investments in flood control, irrigation facilities, and infra-structural development.[4] Similarly, the "favored areas" of Gujarat and Maharashtra (especially areas that specialize in commercial non-food-grain cash crops such as sugarcane, cotton, and tobacco) and the rice-growing areas in the southern states of Andhra Pradesh, Tamil Nadu, and Kerala have benefited from the new agricultural strategy. These advanced states with a share of about 40.5 percent of India's total gross cropped area have accounted for roughly 68 percent of the incremental output of food-grains between the period 1968/69–1985/86. While the spatial and eco-nomic disparities have somewhat narrowed with the extensive diffusion of the new technology, the "backward regions" comprising the states of Assam, Bihar, Orissa, Madhya Pradesh, Rajasthan, and West Bengal ac-counted for only 17 percent of the incremental output while their share in gross cropped area was as high as 41 percent during the same period (Sub-barao 1985, 523–546). Large areas of this region characterized by poor in-frastructure and greater aridity have concentrated on coarse grains and pulses that require less moisture. Table 5.4 provides the annual rate of growth (in percentages) in food grain production in selected states and for India during the period 1970/71–1986/87.

The reasons behind the intrastate and interregional imbalances have been discussed in many studies and need not be repeated here.[5] However,

Table 5.4 Annual Rate of Growth in Foodgrain Production in Selected States
During 1970/71–1986/87

States	Percentage Growth Rate
Andhra Pradesh	3.24
Assam	1.90
Bihar	0.55
Gujarat	3.44
Haryana	3.98
Karnataka	1.43
Madhya Pradesh	1.63
Maharashtra	5.97
Orissa	1.50
Punjab	5.91
Rajasthan	1.31
Uttar Pradesh	3.93
West Bengal	0.46
All-India	2.66

Source: Chakravarty (1990, 138).

the issues that are germane to the empirical and conceptual focus of this study and need further examination are these: What have been the broad socioeconomic and political ramifications of the new agrarian strategy? In particular, what have been the distributional consequences? And how has the strategy impinged upon the interactions between the state and the countryside? These issues are discussed below.

Reconciling Growth with Redistribution

Prior to a discussion of these issues two important qualifications need to be noted. First, unlike many critics who blame the failure of redistribution (and the increasing poverty levels) in India exclusively on the green revolution strategy, I argue that it is not the strategy per se that is an obstacle to development with distribution, but rather the political-institutional context in which it operates. Indeed, the technocratic or market-oriented strategy has been reasonably successful in reconciling growth with distribution in countries like Japan, South Korea, and Taiwan. In those countries, the conditions have included a relatively high degree of equality in rural asset and land ownership (due to sweeping land and tenure reforms), and a strong developmental state was able to create the political-institutional environment as well as introduce an appropriate set of macroeconomic policies conducive to growth-oriented, peasant-based agricultural development (Deyo 1987; Gold 1986; Jones and Sakong 1980). However, as discussed earlier the Indian state has been unable to foster such favorable conditions.

Hence, resource and modern technological diffusion has been slow and benefited disproportionately the rural rich.

Despite the many obstacles to equitable development under Indian conditions, a few recent studies have argued that the "second generation" (or from the late 1970s) effects of the green revolution technology have been positive for agricultural growth and distribution (Ahluwalia 1986; Jose 1988; Mellor 1985; 1988; Prahladachar 1983). Specifically, these authors argue that since the incidence of rural poverty is inversely related to agricultural performance, the increases in growth have led to rural employment, higher wages, and an incremental decline in the incidence of rural poverty. However, a close examination of the evidence leads me to conclude that although these arguments may have some validity, especially in the most high-growth areas such as the Punjab and Haryana, these are exceptions and should not be exaggerated—after all, Ahluwalia's study also demonstrates extensive malnutrition and unemployment among laborers in the Punjab's most dynamic areas (see Chopra 1986 on Kerala; Mencher 1978 and 1980 on Tamil Nadu). Therefore, I am not persuaded by the arguments that these "benefits" are sustainable or that agricultural growth is now "trickling down" to the poor. I will elaborate my arguments with reference to empirical materials from my field data for a high-growth "green revolution" Uttar Pradesh village later in this chapter. Suffice it to say that such factors as the use of labor-displacing technology, eviction of tenants, and rising food prices (without the necessary improvement in "purchasing power parity") usually neutralize the per capita food availability or the short-term "trickle-down" wage increments the poor may make. My argument will be that without the accompanying political-institutional reforms, the "trickle-down" process would continue to be painfully slow, seasonal, and restricted to a few favored areas of the country. However, prior to a more detailed discussion of these issues a brief macro-political-economy perspective is needed to provide some context to the arguments that follow.

As stated earlier, most observers agree that the green revolution strategy has not only increased interstate and interregional economic and agricultural imbalances, but also exacerbated socioeconomic disparities among the different groups and classes in the countryside by benefiting large landowners disproportionately and further economically marginalizing the small and poor cultivators from the process of economic modernization.[6] The Indian Council of Social Science Research (ICSSR 1980, 15), in its authoritative survey of quantitative evidence from various parts of the country concluded that "landowners cornered most of the benefits which resulted in increased disparity between them and the laborers . . . and the relative disadvantage of the small owners vis-à-vis the new technology [has meant that] income disparity among different classes of landowners measured by concentration ratio has increased."

In hindsight it can be argued that such an outcome was inevitable, given the state's incapacity to implement reforms in the countryside and the policymakers' overriding concern with increasing agricultural production and productivity—to the exclusion of issues of equity, poverty alleviation or redistribution. Hence, although much of the green revolution technology was relatively scale neutral in its application, its availability was (and is) generally restricted by inequitable land, income, and credit distribution. Most often, it was the erstwhile zamindars, the rich peasants, and the upper-strata of the middle peasantry who benefited most. For example, in the villages I surveyed in Uttar Pradesh, Haryana, and the "green revolution" districts in Bihar, farmers owning more than 17 acres of irrigated and rain-fed lands, and those with the resources (and connections) to make the necessary investments in chemical inputs and in technological innovations such as tubewells and pump sets in the "backward" or dryer areas, were the major beneficiaries of the green revolution.[7] Also, the dominant castes and classes control of the local *panchayati* and cooperative societies, and control of the district and state political and economic institutions, allowed them access to the information (and dissemination) of the new technology, as well as to the millions of rupees in institutional credit and loans (available under liberal terms) from the state and central government's Rural Development and Cooperative Banks. This in turn encouraged the rural elite to innovate with the new technology and made possible the capital outlays on land improvement, minor irrigation works, and the production costs of the package of HYV seeds, fertilizers, and pesticides. As Andrew Pearse (1980, 181) aptly notes: "A misleading scale neutrality was claimed for the new technology on the basis of the divisibility of seeds and chemicals. In fact, the socioeconomic magnitude of the cultivator is of utmost importance for his economic success, where he must compete with well capitalized large farmers."

As Table 5.5 shows, given the highly inequitable distribution of operational landholdings (which are holdings used by a household regardless of ownership), most cultivators (i.e. the landless, tenants, and small peasant households) were too poor to benefit from the green revolution. Although the quality and reliability of macroaggregate landholding data in India must be taken with the proverbial grain of salt given the widespread concealment and underreporting by large landowners, Table 5.5 nevertheless provides some indication of the overall patterns of land distribution in India in 1971/72. The inequalities are highly visible, with the landless and smallholders forming the bulk of the poor. It should be noted that the landholding data are for the period after zamindari abolition. The high level of inequality bears testimony to the failings of land and tenure reforms and, therefore, the Indian state's limited political capacity to implement its reformist goals.

Given the significant inequalities in the distribution of operational holdings, and within the overall context of a highly skewed resource and

Table 5.5   **Distribution of Operational Holdings in India by Household Size Group, 1971/72**

Size of Holding (in Acres)	% Holdings	% Area Operated
Landless	27	N/A
Smallholders 0.01–2.49	33	10
Middle Peasants 2.50–9.99	29	37
Rich Peasants 10.0–14.99	5	14
Large Landowners 15 and more	6	39

Source: Compiled from Government of India (1976) and Visaria and Sanyal (1977, 245–248).

asset base in agriculture, the benefits of agricultural modernization were limited to a small sector of the rural population. Poor tenants, smallholders, and the lower strata of the middle peasantry made up overwhelmingly of the lower castes, with per capita annual incomes anywhere from Rs 190 to Rs 250, simply could not afford the minimum working capital of Rs 10,000 to Rs 12,000 (in 1970 cost rates) required to switch to the package of new technologies (Ladejinsky 1977, 341–345; Jannuzi 1974; Frankel 1978). Moreover, the Land Development and Mortgage Banks, "which even under the most liberal credit terms required the mortgage of at least two, and more often four to seven, acres of land as security for loans,"[8] ipso facto excluded the vast majority of cultivators who operated small uneconomic holdings of 2 to 3 acres, and those even less well off (the land-poor sharecroppers and the landless), from the process of economic development because they remained outside the eligibility requirements for most institutional or official credit. In fact, given the built-in bias of lending policies and practices, the less well-off peasantry and the rural poor—despite the credit reforms—could acquire credit only through the traditional informal channels at highly usurious rates.[9]

The fact was that under Indian conditions the market-oriented technological policies for rural and agricultural development were not neutral instruments in the rural economy. Rather, by ensuring substantial price and procurement supports for farm commodities and channeling scarce technological inputs (at subsidized prices), as well as government-funded loans and credits at concessional rates, to powerful economic and political interests in the countryside, such policies were decisive in reinforcing and exacerbating rural socioeconomic disparities—or what Marxist (and, indeed, many non-Marxist analysts) have described as the rapid expansion of capitalist forms of production and social relations in the countryside.[10] Some features of the emergent pattern of agrarian capitalism are briefly documented in the following sections.

Patterns of Agrarian Capitalism

While there still remain pockets of traditional, or what some analysts have called semifeudal, agriculture (Bhaduri 1973; 1983; Prasad 1979), India's contemporary rural political economy for the most part operates on a capitalist basis: goods exchanged on the principles of the market; individualistic pursuit of economic self-interest; utilization of "free" wage labor as the dominant form of labor relations; and rapid expansion of commodity production in the countryside (Omvedt 1983; Byres 1981; 1988a; Sen 1982; Thorner 1982). The nature and extent of agrarian capitalism have been well documented in numerous studies, but a brief survey here of some of the literature permits us to better understand the macro- and micropatterns of change that have occurred in the Indian countryside since the early 1970s.

In a series of articles published in the national daily, *The Statesman,* in 1967, Daniel Thorner (1980, 237), an astute student of rural India, made these perceptive observations.[11]

> Before, in the 1960's there used to be in the plains of India only a few pockets of genuinely capitalistic agriculture . . . parts of the Punjab and Western UP, Central Gujarat, Coimbatore and Coastal Andhra. Now for the first time there has come into being in all parts of the countryside in India, a layer thick in some regions, thinner in others, of agricultural capitalists. . . . These capitalistic farmers seem to be the most rapidly growing group in rural India; they may already be the most powerful element.

Thorner's observations were supported empirically by subsequent research. In particular, Utsa Patnaik's (1972) intensive field study, conducted in the early 1970s of sixty-six farms from ten districts covering the five states of Tamil Nadu, Mysore, Gujarat, Orissa, and Andhra Pradesh, concluded that the technologically oriented agricultural strategy was largely responsible for accelerating the expansion of capitalist production relations in the countryside. According to Patnaik, the emergent class of so-called progressive cultivators was actually made up of rural capitalists in the sense that they were commercial farmers operating agricultural enterprises, producing for the market, and reinvesting substantial sums of money on land improvement through irrigation, farm mechanization, and switching to HYV seeds and other high-value crops. This rationalization of production and the enhanced profitability of agriculture also allowed the rural propertied classes to make substantial annual returns on their invest-ments—as much as 200 to 250 percent a year (Patnaik 1972, 10).

Patnaik (1972, 6) classified the emergent class of rural capitalists into four categories: the feudal landlord-turned-capitalist; the dominant land-holder; the rich peasant; and the urban entrant. According to Patnaik, al-though junker-type of landlord capitalism was not a significant phenome-non in the Indian countryside, and while some landlords continued to remain "traditional, unenterprising and extravagant," she nevertheless found growing evidence of many former "feudal" landlords turning into enterprising rural capitalists. For example, she cites

> a big landlord of Mayavaram taluk, Tanjore district [Tamil Nadu] who owned 445 acres of land nominally partitioned between members of his family, but managed as one unit. 115 acres were leased out to tenants, rent being taken at about 60 percent cropshare in the case of paddy, and a flat cash rate amounting to 1/3 to 2/5 of gross value of output in the case of sugarcane. The remaining 330 acres were intensively cultivated on a capitalist basis. 80 acres comprised orchards; the remaining 250 acres, ir-rigated by 18 electric pumpsets, was double and to some extent triple cropped, so that gross sown area amounted to 550 acres. Per acre inputs and consequently output was high; land rent amounted to less than 8% of income from capitalist cultivation, so that the landlord may be re-garded as a landlord turned capitalist.

However, from Patnaik's sample, the rural classes most amenable to capitalist agriculture or who displayed remarkable entrepreneurial and management capabilities were the dominant landholders (seventeen farms out of a sample of sixty-six) and rich peasants (thirty-five out of sixty-six). It should be noted that in Patnaik's formulation the distinction between the dominant landholder and the rich peasantry is minor (and arbitrary): the former plays a supervisory role in actual cultivation, while the latter par-ticipates in manual work on the farm. The remaining eight in the sample turned out to be new urban-based interests that had switched to agriculture because of its growing profitability.

Since the mid-1970s several macrostudies (all-India and state-level) and microstudies (district and village-level) have been published that doc-ument in fine detail the process of capitalist transition in the countryside.[12] These studies provide quantitative and qualitative evidence of expanding capitalist development—albeit, the growth being highly uneven—through-out the vast Indian countryside.

More specifically, there is broad consensus on five points. First, the rural economy operates largely on market principles, with the vast major-ity of rural households tied up in an expanding domestic and global mar-ket and cash relationships. Second, capital is being invested in technolog-ical innovations and production is market oriented, especially in the favored regions where the green revolution technology has taken hold. In fact, the data show a substantial growth in the use of capital inputs such as fertilizers (see Table 5.2), pesticides, herbicides, tractors, diesel engines, and irrigation pump sets by the rural rich. For example, all-India aggregate data show that use of tractors per *lakh* (100,000) of hectares of gross cropped area increased from seven in 1950/51 to 234 in 1978/79, and the use of irrigation pump sets with electrically operated tubewells increased from sixteen to 2,308 over the same period.[13]

Third, the commodification of the rural economy and property system (in particular, rising land and property values) has ushered in far-reaching structural and normative changes in rural society. For example, the salience of the village community as a central unit of social life has been greatly eroded. Traditional or "precapitalist" forms of social, cultural, and economic relations, such as the patron-client (or *jajmani*) relationships between the landlords and their tenants, have been replaced by impersonal, monetized relations. Also, rising land values and the profitability of agricultural commodities have tended to diminish the importance of the more secure customary types of lease, tenancy, and sharecropping arrangements as landed households try to maintain direct control over land in their possession, as well as extend the acreage under their control. Some research, in particular, V. S Vyas's (1970; 1976) study of Gujarat, M. V. Nadkarni's (1976) and Gail Omvedt's (1983) studies of all India and Maharashtra, K. Bharadwaj's and P. K. Das's (1975) study of Orissa, and Nripen Bandopadhyay's (1975) study of West Bengal (all studies focusing on the green revolution areas in these states) found evidence of rapid decline in the traditional forms of sharecropping and tenancy and its replacement by what Omvedt (1983, 38) has called "capitalist tenancy" based on either owner cultivation or "landed tenants." In other words, the landless and land-poor tenants have been increasingly evicted or bypassed in favor of medium and rich peasants, who (given the profitability of agriculture) wish to increase the size of their operational landholdings. Evidence shows that small tenants who are allowed to stay often are required to pay a higher rent in cash or crop share.

Fourth, as the hold of poor households on land becomes tenuous and uncertain, many have turned to wage labor (which is overwhelmingly seasonal, migratory, and temporary) as their only means of livelihood. Several microstudies have shown that the process of rural proletarianization and semiproletarianization has been rapid as well as detrimental to the land-poor and landless peasants. For example, Krishna Raj (1976), basing his calculations on decennial census figures and *NSS* data, estimated that over a seventeen-year period (1954/55 to 1972/73) there had been a sharp increase in the number of landless households and a corresponding decrease of smallholder and family farms (see also Heidrich 1988, 29–66). Raj found that out of a total increase in rural population of 19 million households, the increase in landless households had been 15.3 million. Furthermore, according to the *NSS* between 1971/72 and 1983 the percentage of total casual wage laborers among all rural workers increased from 22 to 29 percent for males and from 31 to 35 percent for females.[14] It should be noted, however, that the rapid growth in rural proletarianization has not only been the consequence of evictions of insecure tenants under land and tenure reforms, or operational concentration of land by the rural rich, but also the result of population growth, the widespread use of labor-dispensing machinery, and the relative underutilization of labor or poor absorption of labor in agriculture and rural industry.[15]

The literature provides ample evidence of a fifth trend, but the widening socioeconomic differentiation among rural households and the nature, extent, and measurement of the differentiation process are extremely complex.[16] Predictably, empirical evidence clearly indicates that rural class differentiation has been most marked in the green revolution areas where the dynamism of agrarian capitalism, in particular, the differential gains associated with the new technology, has been the most marked. However, as both macroaggregative data and microstudies make clear, the process of rural differentiation in the Indian countryside is a far cry from the stark polarization between two antagonistic classes, the agrarian capitalists and rural proletariat as envisaged in classical Marxist theory.[17] Using such different measures of socioeconomic stratification as landownership, size distribution of operational holdings, and control of movable assets (e.g., farm machinery, income, occupation, self-occupation versus selling one's labor, access to off-farm employment), investigators have presented a picture of a highly complex and deeply stratified agrarian socioeconomic order. For example, researchers like Bardhan (1984), Bardham and Rudra (1984a, 167–187), Byres (1981; 1988), Harriss (1982; 1988), Gough (1989), Krishna Rao (1984), Mencher (1978), Omvedt (1983), Patnaik (1987), and Swamy (1976) have identified up to five rural classes: landlords-turned-capitalist farmers, rich farmers (some do not make any distinction between these two classes), family or the "middle cultivating peasants," poor/marginal peasants (including sharecroppers), and landless laborers. Some researchers, by aggregating data from the *Agricultural Census,* the *National Sample Surveys,* the *All-India Debt and Investment Surveys,* and the *Rural Labor Enquiries,* have provided a useful all-India perspective on the changing agrarian class relations. For example, Gail Omvedt (1983) concluded that on an all-India basis, the dominant rural classes are the "kulak type" of capitalist farmers who make up some 15 percent of rural households but who control roughly 60 percent of the cultivated land and related assets. The middle peasantry constitutes about 20 percent of rural households and controls 31 percent of the land and assets, while the poor and landless peasants make up approximately 65 percent of rural households but control only 9 percent of the land and assets. For a similar patterns of rural stratification and disparities see Bardhan (1984) and Swamy (1976).

A few researchers, however, have presented a slightly different picture. For example, the Rudolphs (1987, 335–346), on the basis of the "size distribution of operational holdings" data provided by the *NSS* for 1971/72, have identified four agrarian classes: agricultural laborers, smallholders, bullock capitalists, and large landowners or "tractor capitalists." The agricultural laborers make up 27 percent of the households; smallholders (who control anywhere between 0.01 to 2.49 acres) make up 33 percent of the households and control 10 percent of the cultivated land; bullock capitalists (who own between 2.50 and 14.99 acres) make up 34 percent of the households and control 51 percent of the cultivated land; and the large landowners (15 acres and above) make up 6 percent of the households but control 39 percent of the cultivated land. According to Rudolph and Rudolph (1987, 340), bullock capitalists who are simultaneously "managers and entrepreneurs as well as cultivators and workers" constitute the dominant rural class.

Such empirical anomalies are inevitable given the vastness and diversity of the Indian countryside, the inherent limitations of macroaggregate data, especially the problems of comparability of the data over time, and the fact that the conceptual and empirical identification of socioeconomic classes is to some extent an arbitrary exercise. Nevertheless, there is a general consensus in the literature on the existence of widespread (and growing) inequalities among households in rural areas, rapidly expanding capitalist ethos and market-production relations, and emergence of a hegemonic class of agrarian capitalists (figuratively "bullock capitalists," "kulaks," or "rich peasantry"), which differ from place to place in size and composition as the dominant class in the countryside. These processes are elaborated below with case studies.

Tradition and Power in Rural Uttar Pradesh

How have the changes introduced by the complex of state policies impinged upon the established repertoire of power, dominance, and authority in rural society? In particular, how have the cumulative sequence of changes affected the rural poor? Admittedly, studies focusing on macroaggregate economic trends do not tell us much about the underlying socioeconomic, political, and institutional linkages between the state and society, or how these changing linkages and configurations of wealth and power have affected the patterns of economic growth and distribution. Also, I find that some of the case studies cited earlier in explaining political-economic change in static class variables tend to obscure or oversimplify the exceedingly complex political dynamics of continuing poverty and the multifaceted process of accumulation and appropriation in rural society, and how these conditions of privilege and poverty are perpetuated and maintained. The following sheds light on these issues by drawing on empirical evidence gathered from fieldwork in Vikaspur, a typical Indian village in western Uttar Pradesh, supplemented occasionally with evidence from other villages scattered throughout the vast Indus-Ganges Plain.[18] First, however, a brief survey of some background material is necessary to provide reference points for subsequent analysis.

Eminent Indian sociologists S. N. Srinivas (1967; 1987) and Andre Beteille (1974) have noted that the key to understanding the structures of wealth, power, and dominance in India is to understand the complex and mutually conditioning relationship between caste and class. The close link between the two can be traced to Indian antiquity. The emergence of sedentary human activity in the Ganges Valley (ca. 500 B.C.), the heartland of the Indo-Aryan civilization, gave rise to a complex stratification system that institutionalized and later sanctified the division of labor, wealth, and power in a rigid social hierarchy. These divisions based on *varna* (caste) provided an overarching religious and ritual ranking system that defined one's rights, duties, and obligations in society. Specifically, rigorous criteria of "pollution" and "purity"assigned the upper 20 percent of the population—or those belonging to the highest *varna* order of *brahmins, kshatriya,* and *vaishya*—to a privileged position in society. By contrast, the *shudras,* who constituted the most numerous of the four *varna* groupings and included the bulk of the peasantry and artisans, were deemed socially and ritually inferior. Their *dharma* (or religious duty) was to serve the upper castes with deference and loyalty. At the bottom of the caste hierarchy, roughly 20 to 25 percent of the population had no *varna* standing at all. They were the "untouchables" or "*harijans*" (now referred to as scheduled castes or *dalits*), who were considered so unclean or "impure" as to defile upper-caste persons by touch, or in some cases even by sight. These pariahs, whose hovels were segregated at the outer boundaries of the village, and who ate from broken utensils and wore rags salvaged from cremation grounds of the district, performed the "polluting work" or provided indispensable services to the higher castes.

While the principles of the hierarchical *varna* order has remained essentially unchanged, numerous subcastes or *jatis,* which in some regions number in the hundreds, have become part of the complex caste system. However, despite the complexity and diversity, the numerous *jati* groups are usually represented in the four *varna* orders. Tables 5.6 and 5.7 provide a rough numerical distribution of caste and *jati* groups in Uttar Pradesh. A comparison of the 1931 census and the 1994 census[19] illustrates that the relative proportions of caste groups have hardly changed.

Table 5.6   Distribution of Caste Groups in Uttar Pradesh, 1931

Caste Category	Caste Name
1. Upper or "forward castes" (percentage of population, 20.0)	brahmin thakur bania kayastha
2. Cultivating or middle castes (Percentage of population, 2.3)	jat bhumihar tyagi
3. Lower Shudra or "backward castes" (Percentage of population, 41.7)	yadav kurmi lodh koeri gujar kahar gadaria teli harhai nai kachi others
4. "Untouchables" or scheduled castes (Percentage of population, 21.0)	chamar pasis dhobi bhangi
5. Muslims (Percentage of population, 15.0)	Muslims

Source: Zoya Hasan in Francine Frankel and M. S. A. Rao (1989, 154).

Table 5.7   Distribution of Caste Groups in Uttar Pradesh, 1994 (percentage)

"Forward" or upper castes	
Brahmins	10
Rajputs	7
Bania/kayastha	4
Total	21
"Jats" or middle castes	2
OBCs	39
Scheduled castes	22
Muslims	16

Source: Government of Uttar Pradesh, *Rapid Census* (1994).

Uttar Pradesh, India's largest state, in the middle of the Aryan-Hindu heartland, is a region noted for its deeply entrenched caste divisions. Here, as in the rest of the Indus-Ganges Plain, caste and class have been closely intertwined with cumulative inequalities of status, wealth, and power. At the time of independence, the *brahmins* and the *thakurs* (also referred interchangeably as *rajputs* of the *kshatriya varna*) and *bania* zamindars controlled most of the land, agricultural resources, and the means of production. According to one estimation, brahmins and thakurs owned 57 percent of the land, the intermediate castes, including the "other backward castes" (OBCs), owned 32 percent, the Muslims 11 percent, and the scheduled castes a mere 1 percent (Hasan, 1989a).

The *kayasths* and *brahmins* as the "literate castes" also dominated the civil service and bureaucracy; while the *banias* (an umbrella term extending to all members belonging to the *vaishya varna*) were the bankers, merchants, grain brokers, and moneylenders. By virtue of their caste status, power, and wealth these elite or "forward" castes dominated the political and commercial life of the region.[20] The only exception to total upper-caste dominance in Uttar Pradesh was the Doab region (now the districts of Aligarh, Bulandshahr, and Meerut in Uttar Pradesh, and Rohtak in Haryana), where Muslim landlords and the "elite cultivating" peasant castes such as *jats* and *bhumihars* (technically of "upper *shudra*" status) were heavily concentrated, utilizing their skills to become prosperous farmers and even petty and substantial landlords.

In accordance with their high ritual status and social precedence brahmins, including the other high-caste landlords who accepted the brahmanical status culture, considered it beneath their dignity to "touch the plough" or engage in any form of direct manual cultivation. Indeed, many of the big Uttar Pradesh zamindars or *taluqdars* were either estate managers or urban-based absentee proprietors, who lived off rents and left the actual cultivation of the land to their shudra and other low-caste tenants and workers. Hence, the castes in the shudra varna, which represented the majority of the populace, also contained the "core agriculturalists." The ritual caste divisions between the "middle-caste" *jat* peasantry and the "lower shudras" legitimated under the brahmanical caste hierarchy were shrewdly manipulated by the upper castes to subordinate common economic interests within the cultivating peasantry. The jats and other middle peasant castes, who were regarded under the prevailing belief and value system as the most efficacious cultivators, were usually granted more favorable terms of tenure, such as lower land rents and secure occupancy rights to land. In contrast, the "backward" *yadavs* (also referred to as *ahirs*), *kurmis, koeris, gujars,* and *lodhs,* who provided the backbone to the agriculture of the gangetic plains along with their cognate caste members, were subjected to caste and ritual discrimination, as well as arbitrary rent increases and extraeconomic demands. However, the worst forms of caste discrimination and socioeconomic deprivation were faced by the "un-touchable" castes or *harijans: chamars* and the *jatavs* (carrion removers and leather workers), *dhobis* (washers), *musahars* (rat catchers), *doms* (latrine cleaners), *bhangis* (human waste removers), and *dusadhs* (pig herders), among others. In addition to their traditional occupations, they also constituted the bulk of the poor peasantry of sharecroppers, landless laborers, and menial and bonded servants. Finally, the Muslims, contrary to the tenets of Islam, were also divided into caste-like groupings. Muslim families who could trace their lineage to the Moghuls were big zamindars; the rest followed a variety of agricultural and urban occupations.

As discussed in Chapter 3, the postindependence land and tenure reform measures, despite all their limitations, reduced the sharp concentration of landownership, especially at the upper deciles of the pyramid. In rural Uttar Pradesh the absentee landlords, including some of the large resident taluqdars, lost varying portions (and some lost significant acreage) of their estates to zamindari abolition. The major beneficiaries were the "middle" and "small" or village-level zamindars (mostly drawn from among thakur, jat, and bhumihar castes groups) and the large "occupancy tenants" who constituted the rich and middle peasantry (also belonging to jats and bhumihars) in western Uttar Pradesh, including the top strata of the yadavs, kurmis, lodhs, and koeris, who became "owner-cultivators" after purchasing bhumidari or full proprietary title to the land. Since the mid-1960s, this emergent rural elite has become the "backbone of commercial agriculture" in the state, as well as the major beneficiary of the green revolution strategy (Hasan 1989a, 158). However, the vast majority of the poor shudras *(*or "backward castes") and the "scheduled caste" groups (i.e., smallholders, sharecroppers, and the landless) did not benefit from land reforms or the fruits of the green revolution strategy. To the contrary, the complex of changes introduced into rural society exposed the vulnerable and poor to more exigent forms of domination and exploitation. The following case study of Vikaspur, a typical village in western Uttar Pradesh illustrates these issues in greater detail.

Vikaspur: Caste, Class, and Power

From the vibrant, bustling town of Aligarh a single-lane road heads east across the vast expanse of the Ganges Valley. The surrounding landscape, despite the unusually poor rains, has lost only a little of its lushness—a testimony to the region's fertile soil and the intricate canal and dike irrigation systems feeding off the many tributaries of the Yamuna and Ganges Rivers, and the numerous water pumps and tubewells tapping the area's abundant underground water. It is easy to understand why Aligarh was selected as one of the original eight districts for the joint Ford Foundation and Government of India's Integrated Agricultural Development Program (IADP) in the 1960s. The district's rich agronomical endowment has allowed it to develop a productive agricultural base. The land is intensively worked growing wheat and millet throughout the year, while rice is cultivated mainly during the rainy season. The open fields are interspersed with orchards around which mangoes, pineapples, guavas, bananas, tamarinds, vegetables, pulses (especially *arhar, masur,* and *mung*), potatoes, sesame, mustard, oilseeds, and patches of fodder and sugarcane are grown. Work on the fields usually starts at dawn and ends at dusk as peasants prepare for the demanding *kharif* (monsoon harvest) season. Even under the gaze of the merciless sun, rows and rows of peasants—men and women and children as young as five—are hard at their tasks, their rhythmic movements visible as their sweat-covered bodies glisten in the unrelenting heat.

Following the narrow dusty road that meanders through the region, we pass clusters of villages, the wealthier sections made visible by their brightly painted *pucca* (brick-and-tile) structures and television antennas atop roofs. Several kilometers away from Aligarh the road is just as busy and congested. People and goods crammed precariously in buses, trucks, three-wheelers, tempo-cabs, tractor-trolleys, and scooters dart by. Even the slow-moving buffalo hauling large "buggis" piled high with fruits, vegetables, edible oils, condiments, and kerosene are impatiently prodded onward. The rickshaw drivers, some on bicycle and others on foot, pull their human load with practiced movement, sliding in and out of the mayhem. "It is like this four days a week" I was told, "on market day . . . the farmers have to get their goods to Aligarh and to the markets in Delhi."

Periodically we pass clusters of roadside settlements or "coolie colonies"—ramshackle contraptions of dirt and straw that are home to the poor, some of whom are migrants from as far away as Uttarkashi in northern Uttar Pradesh and from Bihar. Standing on the roadside, the wretchedness of their physiques matching their dwellings, the men and boys of the colonies clamor for attention, shouting and waving their arms to passersby and begging for money and work.

Finally the road passes through a dense patch of eucalyptus and mango groves sheltering a tiny tea stall, an untidy bicycle repair shop, and a hastily erected roadside market. Just beyond and a stone's throw from the main road lies Vikaspur. With a population of roughly 3,000 individuals and 416 households it is an average-sized north Indian village. And, although no one village can be truly representative, Vikaspur is a typical green revolution village in the process of transition.

The village settlement area reflects some of the visible changes that have taken place in recent years. Although high-tension power lines run along the main road, electricity is only available to the village for four to five hours a day, during the day for one week and the following week at night. At the entrance of the village courtyard lies a small *pucca*-constructed and brightly painted office of the *pradhan* (elected village headman), an educated rich thakur landholder, his B.A. degree from Aligarh University prominently displayed in his office.[21] The office is flanked by a modest-sized post office and a small medical dispensary and clinic (a doctor comes in once every two weeks). Nearby is a newly built branch of the State Cooperative Bank, a well-stocked *parchoon* shop (selling miscellaneous items such as sugar, salt, flour, spices, cooking oil, matches, soap, locally made cigarettes, and tinned goods), and a "large" *patschala* (village school) providing instruction in the vernacular up to grade six and serving two other adjoining villages. The school charges a quarterly fee, thereby limiting access to children from poor families.

The village residential area is divided into zones that run roughly along caste lines, corresponding to the local class and economic hierarchies.[22] Since the village is situated on a slight hill, the best "real estate" overlooking the village and surrounding area is occupied by several thakur households that trace their lineage to the Chauhan clan, the founders of the village and the wealthier of the two thakur clans residing in the village. The thakurs, who make up about 10 percent of the village households, are the traditional (and current) landlords in the village. Almost every thakur household has one or more male members engaged in wage employment in nearby towns, including three who serve as labor contractors for the Public Works Department and two who are *thandedars* (policeman) and reside in a nearby town. The houses in the thakur *tola* (residential quarter) are all *pucca* constructed, the narrow lanes between the houses paved with stone and bricks that make it easily passable during the monsoons. The house of the village's wealthiest landlord, Choudhuri Shiu Shankar Singh (the scion of the district's ex-taluqdar), is by the standards of the region a palatially constructed two-story *pucca* dwelling with a bricked courtyard boasting five rooms, a guest house, a small diesel-operated power generator, a *gobar chulla* (cow-dung biogas stove), a handpump for water, a garage for the family's two scooters, a radio, and, perhaps the most prized possession, a recently acquired color television, its antennas conspicuous from a distance.

Adjoining the thakur *tola* is the brahmin quarter. It is small, comprising only three households strategically located near the village temple. The head of one household is the village schoolteacher, another is the local *gram sevak* official (block-level, government-appointed administrator of Vikaspur and four adjoining villages), and the third works full time in a factory in Aligarh and also serves as the village (*purohit*) priest. None of the brahmin households takes an active part in agriculture, but as owners of two to five hectares of irrigated land they derive a reasonably good living from the rents. The jats also make up roughly 10 percent of the village households. About one-fourth of the wealthier jat households reside next to and among the thakur tola, with one wealthy jat household (the owners of the *parchoon* shop) residing right next to the Singhs. Another fourth reside beside and among the backward caste quarter. The jat tola itself is the most integrated residential quarter, with an odd mixture of jat, thakur, backward caste, and two harijan households. Almost every jat household has at least one male engaged in either regular or off-farm employment.

The most numerous of the backward castes in the village are the yadavs, followed by the *khatiks, kohars, kurmis,* and *dhimars.* The "backwards" make up roughly 36 percent of the village households and live mostly at the base of the village, some next to and among the scheduled castes. These dalit castes comprise traditional artisans and service providers; such farm laborers as the jatavs (the most numerous), *bhangis, balmikis,* and *chamars* make up about 40 percent of the households. Their dwellings, equally divided between *pucca* homes and sagging mud-and-straw hovels stand side by side, some housing both people and cattle. I also counted five households among the scheduled castes and four among the backwards as homeless squatters (after the previous monsoon rains destroyed their huts) living in crude contraptions around the village mango grove on the outskirts of the village. The few Moslem families are perceived as low-caste *julahas* (so-called criminal caste) who live at the outer edges of the village.

Vikaspur is characterized by extremely unequal land distribution and ownership. In my estimation, approximately 60 to 65 percent of the total households are landless families, the vast majority belonging to members of scheduled castes, followed by backward castes (especially the service and artisan castes within the OBCs). Also, three thakur households and, from what I could determine, all the Muslim households were either land poor or landless.[23] The landless households have grown consistently, both proportionately and in absolute numbers.[24] Some of the landless are former tenants who, lacking secure titles, were thrown off the land; a few others were small landholding peasants forced to sell their plots due to indebtedness and incapacity to derive minimal levels of subsistence from their marginal plots. About 20 to 25 percent of the households own marginal and smallholdings of between 0.4 and 2.0 hectares. This group, composed of members from the backward castes, including several jat and thakur households, as well as a sprinkling of scheduled castes, has through hard work and a multiplicity of mechanisms been able to maintain a tenacious hold on plots of land. Of the larger landowning households, 15 percent of the medium and big landlords own about 90 percent of the village land area of approximately 608 hectares, with the top 5 percent of the households owning about 30 percent, usually the best arable or *mitti* ("sweet") lands.[25] The "aristocratic" ancestors of Singh, the village's biggest landlord, who currently owns about 900 *bighas* (about 80 hectares of *mitti* lands divided among his extended family members), owned over 80 percent of the village lands as well as land in the neighboring districts prior to zamindari abolition.[26] The other big landlords and rich peasants in the village include some of the direct beneficiaries of zamindari abolition—several thakur, jat, and OBC households (the former hereditary "occupancy tenants") that each own anywhere from 12 to 20 hectares of land. I also estimated four jat and five backward caste households (three yadava and two lodh) each owning between 8 to 10 hectares of relatively good irrigated land. Hence, despite its many limitations, the changes ushered in by state land reform policies have tangibly diminished the huge sociocultural and economic distance that existed between the upper-caste landlords and their emergent jat and shudra "owner-cultivators" or rich peasants.

Although the green revolution technology was introduced in Vikaspur in the mid-1960s, the primary beneficiaries have been the landlord and rich peasant households, including some of the top strata of the small peasant households (owning land of 2 hectares or more). Through diligence in optimizing the use of land and capital, these beneficiaries have been able to achieve a modicum of consumption self-sufficiency and security. On the other hand, for the larger landowning households the improved varieties of wheat and paddy, the almost year-round availability of water (over 85 percent of the village's cultivated land is irrigated) via the use of electric tubewells and diesel pump sets have allowed for multiple cropping and high crop production and yield. In Vikaspur remunerative crops with guaranteed market prices have seen a marked increase in cultivation. Those crops that bring in the highest monetary returns are HYV wheat and rice,[27] as well as short-duration improved varieties of paddy and such pulses as the prized and expensive red and green gram that can be harvested as sixty-to-ninety-day crops. Also, during the last decade the cultivation of mangoes, pawpaws, bananas, guavas, oranges, and limes and a variety of produce such as potatoes, sugarcane, brinjal, pumpkins, bitter melons, cucumbers, peppers, carrots, tomatoes, beans, cabbage, eggplants, and okra have greatly increased. Some of these crops are not only less labor intensive but also fetch "good prices" in the surrounding rural towns and not so distant large urban centers like Aligarh and New Delhi.[28]

The profitability of commercial agriculture has released an entrepreneurial dynamism among the wealthy landowners and peasants alike. Two of the rich peasant households in the village each own a large diesel-operated wheat-threshing and -winnowing and rice-shelling machine that enables them (and other villagers at a moderate cost) to process and bag much of their grain in the village (thus eliminating the middlemen and transport cost to the mills), and then to sell it directly to grain merchants in Aligarh and Delhi for a much higher return. The several imposing brick *godwons* (grain storage barns), some with "guards" posted outside during harvesting, act not only as storage facilities but also allow the rich landowners periodically to withhold grain from the market until prices improve. Similarly sugarcane, which is a long-duration crop and makes for difficult intercropping, has in recent years become popular among the large land-owners in Vikaspur.[29] It is seen as a profitable "quick-return" cash crop that fetched Rs 34 per quintal in 1989, a dramatic increase from Rs 7 per quintal in 1967. In fact, four of the big landowners in the village each own an expensive motor-driven *kolhu* (cane crusher costing more than Rs 20,000) and vats for boiling cane juice. Some of the sugarcane is processed in the village to make *gur* (jaggery) and black molasses, an important ingredient of a heady locally made alcoholic beverage. Molasses also fetches a high price at the urban breweries.

Vikaspur's wealthiest landlord has recently branched out into dairying, which he views as a subsidiary economic activity. He owns forty-two milch cows and has increased the cultivated area under *berseem* (green fodder) and *cheri* (sorghum fodder) in his holdings, which he supplements with *agolas* (sugarcane tops). The landlord sells only a small portion as fluid milk, choosing to concentrate on such processed byproducts as *ghee* (clarified butter) and *mawa,* a thick rich cream that is the main ingredient in making ice-cream and sweets, and that fetches over ten times the price of fluid milk in the urban centers. During the time of fieldwork the land-lord was in the process of finalizing a lucrative business contract with Glaxo Diary, a joint foreign-Indian milk-processing plant operating on the outskirts of Aligarh. This enterprising landlord also uses the cattle dung for his household's *gobar chulla* and sells the surplus *bithaura* (dried dung cakes) to the poorer households to be used as cooking fuel—further limiting the availability of organic fertilizer. During my stay in the village one of the rich jat peasant households invested in a small power driven *atta-chakki* (a grain mill costing about Rs 18,000). This machine, besides reducing the drudgery of women and young girls, has added to the household's income, since others pay a small fee (Rs 4 per hour) for the services. This kind of economic portfolio diversification has tended to make the rural rich less susceptible to the vagaries of the market and fluctuations in agricultural production. Moreover, it has strengthened their urban-industrial and manufacturing economic and political connections.

Today farmers in Vikaspur and the surrounding region harvest three crops per year. One would assume that multiple cropping combined with high levels of agricultural production and productivity and profitable market returns would enable many of the small and marginal farmers to incrementally improve their incomes and living standards. While some small farmers in Vikaspur (those owning over 1.5 hectares of irrigated land) have indeed benefited, the vast majority are marginal farmers who own or operate plots of fragmented or "uneconomic holdings," and often do not have the resource base to purchase and invest in inputs such as chemical fertilizers, HYV seeds, herbicides, pesticides, or irrigation pump sets and tubewells on a sustained basis.[30] In fact, landlords-cum-"waterlords" (those who sunk their tubewells first) have not only monopolized ground-water use, they even claim ownership rights—selling groundwater to the poor and marginal peasants or demanding a share of their farm output. Overall, the vast majority of poor peasants, tenants, and landless peasant cultivators in Vikaspur have not benefited from agricultural modernization. However, they have adapted to the exigencies of modern agriculture in a variety of ways.

Faced with changing (and often deleterious) production conditions, the poor peasant households, when their size and composition allow, engage in strategies of risk minimization through the allocation of their resources and labor across economic sectors and geographical space to secure their basic subsistence needs. For example, even though I did not find much evidence of big landholders buying out small and marginal holdings in Vikaspur and the surrounding villages, there is, nevertheless, strong evidence of de facto concentration of land holdings via "reverse tenancy." Under this method, the small and marginal holders often engage in a number of sharecropping (or *bataai*) arrangements or lease out their plots to medium and large landholders on a crop-sharing basis, often hiring themselves out as workers to these landowners.[31] However, *bataai* relationship has not only further subordinated the land-poor and landless peasantry, it has hardly improved their subsistence needs or security, because in "lean times" such plots are the first to be let go by the big landowners.

About 30 percent of the small and marginal peasant households in Vikaspur that choose to cultivate their lands have invariably to take production, or *aadhai,* loans from the richer landowners-cum-moneylenders. The rural rich provide them with HYV seeds, credit, technological inputs, and access to tubewell irrigation and market facilities in exchange for 50 to 75 percent of the crop when harvested and a liter of milk daily per cow if the tenant owns milch cows. However, even if these households maintain some control over production decisions, most are heavily in debt, constantly intensifying cultivation and "hyperexploiting" their family labor to achieve a modicum of family subsistence security. Yet, each year the effort necessary to maintain the precarious equilibrium increases, and it seems to be a spiral that constantly demands more work and investments. As traditional farming methods and technologies such as fallowing, crop rotation, and intercropping give way to intensive and repetitive use of the land for single remunerative crops—a process that leaches and depletes soil fertility and productivity—the results are usually poor harvests and lower quality crops. This in turn has necessitated greater doses of inputs of fertilizers and improved seeds, the purchase of which invariably has led to even more indebtedness.

Several of the poor peasant households interviewed reported that since they purchase much of the HYV seeds and other modern inputs from large landowners, they were charged higher prices. Moreover, because the rental price of draft animals and machinery such as pump sets is much higher during the peak season, small proprietors often face pressing need for cash. It is not uncommon for small and marginal proprietors in Vikaspur to sell portions of their "reserve" crop, which were intended for family consumption, to landlords and urban-based commercial monopsonists for cash. Paradoxically, they would then have to buy back the same goods at much higher prices at a later date, increasing their indebtedness in order to do so.[32]

Households reluctant to place themselves in such vulnerable and exploitative relationships often cultivate "humbler" crops and hire "surplus" family members out as agricultural workers during the peak agricultural seasons. In a sense, these poor peasant families have adapted to the exigencies of agrarian capitalism by "retreating" from commercial agriculture and market relations, minimizing expenditures for productive inputs like fertilizer and HYV seeds and growing staple crops primarily for family subsistence, seeking the cash necessary for survival in casual wage employment, and selling some of their commodities on the market. However, it is important to note that only a few households in Vikaspur have adopted such a strategy. In a rapidly expanding capitalist agriculture where agro-industrial goods are fast replacing those formerly provided locally through cottage industries and traditional handicrafts, cash is fast becoming a necessity (indeed the dominant nexus of exchange) to meet minimal subsistence needs. Thus, the "exit option" or retreat into subsistence is not always a viable alternative for the rural poor.[33]

It is important to reemphasize that entrenched structural inequalities, coupled with inaccessibility to technological inputs and institutional credit, have been major obstacles to technological diffusion among the marginal and small farms. Since smallholders purchase the new inputs in smaller amounts, they are obliged to pay higher prices than the large landowners pay for bulk purchase. Therefore, the price and risk involved in technological improvements is too high for the "risk-minimizing" poor peasants. In other words, the scale neutrality of inputs in the narrow technical sense is often canceled by the social reality of rural inequalities that exclude poor peasants from the process of agricultural modernization. Also, credit loans in excess of Rs 5,000 not only require collateral (i.e., sufficient land, the norm being 1.5 hectares) but in some cases require two "big" landowners from the village to stand as guarantors for the borrower. The other option is to borrow from private sources (landlords-cum-moneylenders) at interest rates that vary anywhere from 60 to 80 percent per annum, as well as other obligations such dependence entails.[34] The form and voraciousness of the intermediaries' extractive and exploitative capacities vary, but the potential for small and marginal producers to retain a profit from their labors are small because their income is continuously siphoned off through debt and exploitation.

It is logical to assume that with multiple-cropping practices intensifying the need for timely labor for field preparation, planting, and harvest, the additional worker-days of farm employment generated would enhance the bargaining position and, therefore, the wage rates and the income levels of the poor and landless workers. However, this has not been the case in Vikaspur and the surrounding districts where on-farm employment has been offset by the increasing use of mechanization. One of the peculiarities of agrarian capitalism in this part of Uttar Pradesh has been that the vast majority of the poor and landless householders are not rural proletarians in the sense that they are mobile and "free" to sell their labor for set wages and benefits. In Vikaspur, about 40 percent of the landless households contain, in fact, semiproletarianzied sharecroppers engaged in various forms of sharecropping-tenancy arrangements with the rich landowners. There was virtual unanimity among the landless household members I interviewed that they preferred such a relationship with the *maliks* (landlords) because such a relationship at least provided them and their families with some security of subsistence, given the limited availability of off-farm employment, the growing mechanization in agriculture, and the abundant supply of cheap labor in the district (largely the result of incoming migrants from poorer regions during the peak seasons). One landless laborer aptly summed up the common sentiment: "Here the *malik* is *mai-baap* (mother and father) and the *sarkar* (government). . . . I am a poor man with a family to feed . . . I need to keep the *malik* happy with my work."

The traditional etiquette of cultural discourse and multiplicity of crosscutting traditional ties and norms of unequal, albeit reciprocal, rights and obligations that have long bound the tenant and the landlord in South Asia have not been entirely eroded in Vikaspur. The poor can still approach the landlords and richer peasants for small favors and "crisis-assistance," but most older peasants I interviewed agree that the current tenant-landlord contracts are qualitatively different from the earlier or traditional forms of patron-client or *jajmani* relationships. The exigencies of commercial agriculture have tended to blur the landlords' traditional obligations (in exchange for services rendered) to customary tenants and attached laborers. Similarly, in the hiring and firing of agricultural laborers formal, impersonal bargaining arrangements, overlaid with the customary caste-based patron-client relations, have increased the dependence and powerlessness of the rural poor and decreased their capacity for collective class-based strategies and actions. For example, in Vikaspur the practice of tenant rotation or tenant "switching" has become common. Since the federal law stipulates that if a sharecropper or any landless tenant cultivates the same plot of land for three consecutive years, he can claim ownership rights to that land, the landholders have developed an aversion to long-term tenancy. They are careful to constantly switch their tenants to prevent such an occurrence. Moreover, another important new trend has been the shortening of the lease periods. Nowadays contracts are made not on a more secure yearly arrangement but rather by crop, with the leases orally renewed at the beginning of each agricultural cycle. This adds to the landowning castes' and classes' already tremendous arbitrary powers. Since the lease contracts are always oral in nature, the landlords can terminate the lease and expel the tenant at any given moment, change the original terms of agreement (some tenants complained about being paid far less than what they had earlier agreed to), and also selectively move the laborers to different plots whenever they wish. While the landless share-cropper-tenants in Vikaspur are paid in both kind and cash, the precise percentages are subject to the *maliks'* costs and deductions. From the landowners point of view, tenancy that involves joint risk sharing between the two parties not only makes the tenants more "accountable and honest" but also makes for more "dedicated and sincere workers."

The majority of Vikaspur's inhabitants, the landless households or *majdoors* (laborers), though formally "free," nevertheless live under conditions of chronic poverty and destitution as agricultural labor has become overwhelmingly seasonal, temporary, and insecure. Moreover, given their poor skill endowments, and since the limited multiplier effects of agricultural growth have hardly trickled down to the poor landless *majdoors* of Vikaspur, only a few of the low-caste and illiterate poor families have found their way into nontraditional rural jobs or have benefited from the long-term, pull-type upwardly mobile migration from the rural to the urban areas. Also, within the highly skewed agrarian structure the process of agricultural modernization has failed to make any appreciable reduction in the chronic poverty of poor and landless households (which has increased both proportionately and absolutely) through the trickling down of agricultural or farm employment. Recent all-India data indicate that these findings are not exceptional (see Kurian 1990). Even in a good agricultural year the agricultural worker, on average, finds only 130 worker-days of employment in irrigated two-crop areas and hardly eighty worker-days of employment in dryer or "low-growth" areas (Kurian 1990, A-178). In my estimation (cross-checked with village laborers), the worker-days of employment in a high-growth village like Vikaspur in a good agricultural year would be roughly 160 to 180 a year. In other words, even under the best of conditions the poor and landless households have access to full-time rural employment only during peak periods totaling an intermittent six months of the year. The stagnant periods are marked with short-term, insecure casual work and prolonged periods of underemployment and unemployment.

In Vikaspur, the aggregate amount of wages currently paid to the poor has remained constant at the mid-1970s rate. The weak bargaining power of the laborers and the large influx of migrant labor from neighboring districts in eastern Uttar Pradesh and Bihar during the peak periods have meant that landowners can (and do) pay the laborers well below the minimum wage established by legislation. Migrant labor, usually working as cheap contract or "gang labor" (under a highly exploitative piece-rate system), is one major reason why wage rates have not increased much. Also, the growing influx of women and children into the ranks of the landless agricultural labor has meant a further depression in wage rates: if male laborers are paid below the minimum wage, then women and children receive even less. Moreover, the monetitization of wages, coupled with the recurrent seasonal deficit in the purchasing power of rural wages in terms of daily subsistence needs, and skyrocketing food prices have adversely encroached upon the poor households' precarious conditions of consumption security. Increases in food prices are not accompanied by comparable increases in wages for farm labor. Since the Agricultural Prices Commission each year sets what effectively are support purchase prices by the multiple criteria of production costs, trends in market prices, intercrop and input-output price parities, and (since the early 1980s) intersectoral price parity, the procurement prices of such staple food items as rice, wheat, and nontoxic varieties of grams and lentils have sharply increased at annual rates, with simultaneous increases in their wholesale market prices.[35] The food-buying poor, in particular those in the rural poor households, who have received almost no protection from these inflationary policies, have become further subordinated and impoverished.

The poor peasant household members I interviewed bitterly complained that during the drought of 1988, the enormously high food prices along with speculative hoarding of foodgrains and other essential commodities by traders and rich farmers had so severely exacerbated the poor peasants' existence that they had to fall below their already marginal levels of income and consumption security.[36] During such harsh times these poor subsisted on either poor-quality rice supplemented with large portions of very hot chilies (because it soothes chronic hunger) or *sattu* (paste made of coarse grain) supplemented with boiled onions and chilies. However, even in relatively good times the consumption patterns of poor households in Vikaspur are far below the ideal figure of 2,200 calories a day. In my observation, during the peak harvesting season a typical diet of a poor household consisted of barely two meals a day for adults and slightly more for children. The meals are basic, consisting of either low-grade rice and "brown chappatis" supplemented with watery *dal* (lentil soup), boiled mustard leaves, chilies, and, occasionally, vegetables and locally grown fruits. Indeed, the precarious and harsh conditions under which the poor in Vikaspur live are aggravated by insufficient caloric and protein requirements, lack of protective shelter, and inaccessibility to such basic needs as primary health services and safe drinking water, and are constantly reflected in frequent and chronic health problems, especially among the elderly, women, and children, whose low resistance makes them vulnerable to a host of infectious diseases. Life of the poor and marginalized is harsh and short in the Indian countryside.

Evidence from Vikaspur does vindicate Theodore Schultz (1964), who long ago questioned the notion that the cause of low agricultural productivity was the economic unresponsiveness of the "tradition-bound" peasant. Rather, like rational modern capitalists, farmers will respond to change if the result does not increase the risk of crop failure. The relatively low-risk green revolution technologies and the incentives for quick profits released an entrepreneurial dynamism in the Indian countryside. However, as John Mellor (1976) has long argued, if the fruits of the green revolution are to be equally shared, then they must be based on a broad-based agricultural strategy associated with technical diffusion at the level of the farmers of small- and medium-sized holdings. This did not occur on a large enough scale in the Indian countryside, and the green revolution ended up creating its own contradictions. That is, the green revolution technologies have helped increase agricultural production and productivity, but the major beneficiaries have been the wealthier sections of rural society. The vast majority of the rural populace have not benefited from agricultural modernization—indeed, for most there has been a deterioration in their living standards. The following further illustrates the political and structural constraints to growth with distribution.

Authority and Dominance in Rural Society: Case Studies from Vikaspur

Despite the often repeated universalizing claims that all residents of Vikaspur are kindred *ek basti ke log* (brothers of the same settlement), transcending the irrevocable class and caste fissures pervasive in village society has proven difficult. As noted earlier, even though the deepening of democracy and the expansion of capitalist production relations in the countryside has led to the erosion of the traditional or more "feudal" forms of authority and deference, newer forms of dominance and exploitation have taken its place. Today these forms govern the lives of the rural poor.

The standard narratives I heard repeatedly and the many incidents I witnessed during fieldwork made me realize that the village society was quite "uncivil"—faction ridden and divided sharply along caste lines. This has made collective action almost impossible. For example, an incident I witnessed, which represented a minor breach in the traditional and emergent patterns of authority and domination in Vikaspur, brought to the surface the latent tensions and animosities in the village. On one occasion a young landless backward-caste laborer was publicly "disciplined" by the village panchayat for stealing mangoes and cucumbers from a prosperous thakur farmer's field. The accused youth, surrounded by some of his "caste brothers," in open defiance admitted to the act and accused the thakur farmer of being "too stingy and a known cheat" and some members of the panchayat of being "against small people." For his "shameful" actions against the *basti* (settlement), the youth was harshly admonished by his father (also a landless laborer), who called his son "lazy . . . good for nothing" and apologized on his behalf to the panchayat. After some deliberation the panchayat punished the youth by requiring him to "do half-a-day labor to make up the thakur farmer's loss." After some grumbling the youth accepted the punishment and apologized for his "errors" and the matter was laid to rest.

In my numerous one-to-one private conversations with the thakur, jat, and backward caste panchayat members, including the ordinary villagers, it was hard to miss the distrust and enmity they have toward one other. Among the thakurs there was an unmistakable tone of bitterness toward central and state government policies perceived to be responsible for the erosion of their wealth, status, and power. They held the Congress responsible for "filling these simple-minded *shudrans* [OBCs and jats] and *chamars* [a pejorative term used to denote all scheduled castes] with wild ideas and spoiling them with easy loans, gifts, and *gaddi* [positions of power]." The brahmin priest and several influential thakur landowners concurred that "the Congress is now reaping the discord it planted. Once these *neech jatis* (inferior castes) tasted power they back-stabbed the Congress and formed their own parties starting with the BKD [Bharatiya Kranti Dal] and now the Samajwadi Party and the Bahujan Samaj and what have you. Now they control the power and this is what explains their growing belligerence and disrespectful behavior." To these upper castes, the *neech jatis* are prone to corruption and violence, and "absolutely untrustworthy." Not surprisingly, several of the upper-caste landowners, including the prosperous owner-cultivators, admitted that the main reason they "stay away from" (and indeed are hostile to) the explicitly pro-rich-farmer organizations, such as the Bharatiya Kisan Union, is because they see it as an expression of assertion by the low castes. This will be discussed in the next chapter.

Fully aware of these stereotypes, the jats and OBCs and the low castes, on the other hand, view members of the upper castes as lazy and untrustworthy, "who spent much of their time on liquor, gambling, and hosting lavish weddings rather than investing in farming." They also hold that these upper castes still "want to maintain their traditional ways and thereby prevent the village from prospering." Reflecting national and state-level political currents—since most of the thakur households in Vikaspur are supporters of the Hindu revivalist Bharatiya Janata Party (BJP)—the upper castes are seen by many of the jats, backwards, and the other lower castes as "communal" and elitist.

The next chapter will also illustrate that attempts by the forces of "new agrarianism" to forge multiclass and multicaste alliances among all the kisans (cultivators), especially among the jats, the OBCs, and the scheduled castes, have not been very successful. Indeed, during fieldwork I was constantly observing the disturbing reality of how the established and emergent hierarchies maintain their power and authority and secure compliance in the countryside. The methods varied from subtle pressure and harassment to outright violence against the poor, especially the scheduled castes. Interestingly, in such a productive, "high-growth," capitalist-oriented village such as Vikaspur there is some evidence of organized collective action by the owner-cultivators (the so-called emergent kulaks), but organized "class struggles" by the scheduled and backward caste land-poor peasants and landless rural proletariat are absent. To the contrary, the rural poor are unorganized and fairly acquiescent. And, while actions designed to uphold or protect threatened rights occur routinely in Vikaspur, these everyday forms of peasant recalcitrance and resistance are usually aimed at alleviating the immediate subsistence crises and removing specific disputes and grievances, and they rarely represent any sort of organized collective or class action.

The scheduled caste laborers and land-poor peasants related many instances of *zabbardasti* (heavy-handedness) imposed upon them by the thakurs, jats, and the OBCs, especially the new rural rich from among the yadavs.[37] They accused the jats and the yadavs of being "without any principles, cruel, treacherous, and blood-suckers." Their common complaints included never being paid the agreed to salary, or paid on time, despite the long thirteen-to-fourteen-hour workdays;[38] constantly being pressured to provide extra services such as sending their wives and children to do domestic work for the "uppity" OBCs and the upper castes; always being paid less than backward-caste laborers for performing the same tasks; and getting "roughed up" for even "slightly questioning their *zulum*" (i.e., injustice). Several jatav laborers painfully recounted much the same story: "By the grace of God I was granted a small plot of land that was declared *gair mazarua* or ceiling surplus, but the yadav and jat landowners who have no respect for law completely disregarded my rights and tore up my government-signed *parcha* [land ownership deed] right in my face, and then taunted us. They now lease the land that was granted me to their caste brothers." The Report of the Commissioner of the Scheduled Castes and Tribes noted this new form of oppression: "The backward castes have been surging forward to take control of positions of power and control in society. . . . In the process of marching forward, the backward castes tend to push back the Scheduled Castes and others who occupy the lowest rung in the social hierarchical order. There is greater tension between the structural neighbors in this hierarchy than between the top level and the bottom level."[39]

In their efforts to counter the perceived growing power of the jats and backwards, the thakur landowners have made attempts to woo the scheduled castes (the thakur *pradhan* was elected due to the scheduled-caste vote bank), but such "alliances" of expediency are not enduring. Several scheduled-caste households still shudder with fear when relating how during each election time, the jats and prosperous backwards make a point to "warn us that if we vote for the Congress or the Bahujan Samaj Party[40] then the whole of Uttar Pradesh will become even worse than Pipra and Arwal." Pipra is a one-time harijan tola in Bihar where low-caste landless laborers demanding better wages were brutally tortured, their wives raped and then "roasted alive" by the thakur landlords and prosperous kurmi owner-cultivators in 1980. Arwal in Gaya district in Bihar is where twenty-three harijans belonging to the Mazdoor Kisan Sangram Samiti, an organization of poor and landless peasants, were massacred by the yadav landlords and local police.[41] As one scheduled caste laborer put it: "We could only sleep when we knew that the jats and shudras had captured the polling booths. . . . They could now mark our ballots, or we could show them that we voted with them."

While Vikaspur and the surrounding villages have not experienced the kind of routine terror and brutal violence of Pipra and many other such villages, other parts of Uttar Pradesh have not been so immune. Districts in eastern Uttar Pradesh and in the neighboring state of Bihar have since the mid-1970s been caught in an escalating cycle of violence against the scheduled castes. It is important to note that although atrocities against the weaker in earlier periods were more in the nature of action against a specific individual for a specific contravention of a village custom, the recent trend has been organized group action against poor backwards and scheduled castes. While conducting research in the districts of Patna and Bhojpur in Bihar and Deoria, Gorakhpur, and Basti in eastern Uttar Pradesh, I was repeatedly warned by senior government officials that "poking your nose in these lawless parts is extremely dangerous." Indeed, I quickly found out that in these districts the government's presence and writ is limited, if not altogether nonexistent. The real power and authority lie in the hands of landlords and their private armies, or *senas,* made up of well-armed "caste gangs," including the local police and other "law and order" officials willing and ready to eliminate any real or perceived threats to the interests of the local hierarchies in "encounter killings." Professors Pradhan H. Prasad (1979; 1985; 1987), Arvind Das (1983), Ghanshyam Shah (1988), and investigative reporter Arun Sinha (1982; 1991) in their important contributions have carefully documented that in such areas the armies of landlords and rich peasants (whom Prasad calls "warlords") enjoy "unchallenged supremacy." Their *senas* often resort to prolonged "reign[s] of terror" to intimidate the rural poor. These writers point out that upper-caste landlords are used to "unquestioned feudal rights" (a behavior now also adopted by such backward shudra castes as the yadavs and kurmis) and "customary rights." Such "rights" include *beth begar,* or free exactions, and "rights over the wives and daughters of their laborers . . . taken as common property by the rich landlords, to be thrashed, toyed with, raped, offered to friends as a sign of hospitality" (Shah 1988, 280). And these landlords have reacted to the slightest questioning of their authority and power with unprecedented violence. According to Sinha (1982), members of the newly emergent elites among the backward castes, who did not traditionally enjoy such rights but are increasing demanding them, have provoked hostility among the poor scheduled castes, and have made common alliances between the poor backwards and the scheduled castes difficult.[42] Most important, the writers point out that the growing economic and political alliance between the landed upper and backward castes have had tragic consequences for the poor. According to *India Today* of 31 December 1986,

> [Bihar] has notched up one deadly milestone after another with sickening regularity. In Belchi, the *kurmi* raiders prepared a funeral pyre, lined up the *Harijans,* shot them and tossed the bodies in, one by one. In Pipra, raiders surrounded the *Harijan* hamlet, set fire to their houses and when men, women and children fled outside, it was only to be tossed right back into the inferno. . . . The root cause of almost all rural conflicts of course is land.

Arun Sinha's (1982, 150–151) chilling firsthand account documents the ugly side of rural society.

> In Buxara village . . . where laborers had organized an indefinite strike to secure the revised minimum wages, the landlords ransacked the *harijan* ghetto . . . and burnt them alive in a haystack. In Gopalpur, where also strikes had been called by the laborers, the landlords attacked the *harijan* ghetto with 50 armed men and wounded some half a dozen workers, humiliated their women, and looted a shop. . . . All these outrages were committed by big landlords [mostly of the bhumihar peasant caste], who hold near-absolute economic, social and political power in their respective areas. . . . In each case the big landlord [is] virtually the "raja" of his area. He possesses one-fourth or more of the total land in his village. He lives like an aristocrat in a large brick house. He employs large numbers of both slave and free laborers. . . . He maintains a small private army . . . he has captured the instruments of local government. . . . He now commands the *panchayat* and thus the various executive bodies; he has the services of an obsequious police force.

Again, in December 1997 sixty-three scheduled-caste landless laborers of Lakshmanpur-Bathe village in Jehanabad district in Bihar were murdered in cold blood by the Ranbir *sena,* a private militia of the powerful bhumihar (traditionally middle-peasant caste) landlords. According to Kalyan Chaudhuri (1997), the long-simmering dispute between local landlords and landless peasants over 60 acres of *gair mazarua,* or disputed ceiling surplus land, ended on the night of 1 December, when, in a well-planned operation, about 100 Ranbir *sena* activists carrying firearms descended on Lakshmanpur-Bathe. They forced their way into huts by breaking open the doors and fired on people who were asleep. The entire hamlet was virtually decimated in a bloody attack that lasted more than three hours.

The Attack on Rural Poverty:
Misguided Strategies and Failed Outcomes

As in other Indian villages, in Vikaspur the actual structures of authority and dominance closely, although imperfectly, parallel the distribution of landownership and wealth in the village economy. The propertied castes, given their control over land, their monopoly over production and distribution of its resources, and their control over credit and marketing networks, command significant discretionary powers and authority within the boundaries of the village and the surrounding region. Furthermore, the castes' expanding network of political and economic ties with the wider state and society, their close linkages and alliances with political authorities, and, indeed, their official positions as district members of the legislative assembly (MLAs), block development officers; district, block, and village panchayat members; and the village pradhan and *patwari* have tended to reinforce and perpetuate the strategic positions of the landowning interests.

In fact, during fieldwork it became apparent to me that viewed from the vantage point of the village and district, the state is quite indistinguishable from the local structures of power and dominance. In other words, the state as it spreads out from the political center tends to dissolve or taper off sharply at the levels below the district. As the reach of the state declines and its overarching structures and institutions become gradually intertwined with and embedded in the traditional, informal hierarchies of power and authority, there is a simultaneous diminution in the degree of its autonomous capacity, authority, and influence. In Vikaspur, then, the formal and informal structures of rule and governance have become woven into the same tapestry, a process that over time has further reduced central state authority and eroded its efficacy in the countryside. Under these conditions, local notables and seasoned political brokers (some located ambivalently between state and society) have been able to extend their powers, actively pursuing the interests of the societal hierarchies, as well as their own individual imperatives, by deflecting, delaying, or reducing certain central directives and demands made against them, in particular demands to implement reformist or distributive policies. Through stratagems of collaboration, patronage dispensation, and construction of supportive coalitions with clientele groups and classes, as well as opportunistically manipulating the formal apparatuses of the state (e.g., local courts, bureaucracy, police, the various political and administrative structures), they have legitimized their powers, authority, and mechanisms of economic extraction and accumulation. As noted earlier, beyond the pale of law are stratagems of control centering on the blatant manipulation of cleavages within the village society—ranging to outright violence against the poor. In such an inhospitable environment the poor and the dispossessed, who control very little of the material and institutional conditions under which they exist, have great difficulty in getting their voices heard and their interests advanced. With their range of options and strategies constantly circumscribed by the vicissitudes of political-economic change, the poor often find themselves subject to the decisions and imperatives of the dominant socioeconomic and political elites and under immense compulsion to comply.

Since independence, at the prodding of the central government, the various state governments have promulgated a panoply of legislation designed to improve the living conditions of the rural poor. The attack on rural poverty has been multipronged. Since the early 1970s, as the states' incapacity to deliver on land and tenure reforms became clear, the emphasis has shifted to "pro-poor" or basic needs strategies aimed at "directly" reaching the hitherto excluded social groups and classes. This is to be done through a variety of small-farmer programs: for instance, the Small Farmer Development Agency (SFDA), the Marginal Farmers and Agricultural Laborers Scheme, and various wage and employment schemes for the landless laborers such as the Food for Work Program (FWP). More recently (since the mid-1980s), there have been the Jawahar Rozgar Yojana (Jawahar Employment Scheme) and the Indira Aabas Yojana (Indira Housing Scheme).[43] These programs were politically attractive not only because they did not entail dealing with the touchy issues of landownership and land and tenure reforms, but also because they reaffirmed the policymakers' belief in the old dualistic trickle-down approaches to solving the problem of agricultural development and rural poverty.

In the summer of 1989, much to everyone's surprise, the former prime minister, Rajiv Gandhi, stated the obvious when he noted that "out of Rs. 1 billion [$69 million] allocated to an anti-poverty project, I know that only Rs. 150 million [$10 million] reaches the people. The remainder is gobbled up by middlemen, power-brokers, contractors and the corrupt."[44] To "fix this leaky bucket," Rajiv Gandhi proposed the creation of a uniform and democratic three-tiered *panchayat raj* structure at the district, block, and village levels. The prime minister's proposal made clear that all panchayat office bearers were to be elected to a five-year term, with proportional representation for the scheduled castes and tribes, a quota for women, and periodic auditing of accounts. He portrayed the creation of these institutions as a democratizing measure that would create thousands of grassroots representatives, reduce the distance between the people and the power brokers, and make "people-centered" rural development a reality. To put his proposal into practice, he further proposed the creation of a new program, Jawahar Employment Scheme, under which all government funds for development were to be managed by the panchayats.

In September 1991, the Congress government introduced a new constitutional amendment (the 72d Amendment Bill), which was passed with near unanimity in both the Lok Sahba and the Rajya Sabha in December 1992. In the following four months the bill was ratified by seventeen state governments, and, after the president gave his assent to the bill, the 73d Constitutional (Amendment) Act came into effect on 24 April 1993. Raghav Gaiha (1996, 28) notes that "in its comprehensiveness, the 73rd (amendment) Act is a landmark." True to the former prime minister's goals, it provides a uniform three-tiered structure of the panchayats—with clear demarcation of areas of responsibility at different levels and mandatory elections every five years at the district, block, and village level.[45] It guarantees the scheduled castes and scheduled tribes ("the poorest of the poor"), and women via proportional representation and quotas, membership, participation in decisionmaking, and the right to hold office at all levels of the panchayats. Moreover, the panchayats at all levels are to be subjected to regular financial audits and meet the transparency and accountability requirements to both their community and official agencies. The governments, on their part, are required to provide adequate financial and administrative support.

However, as Gaiha (1996, 30) notes, "the claim, however, that the 73rd (amendment) Act" signifies "power to the people is exaggerated, if not largely mistaken." Evidence indicates that the panchayats have failed to enhance the participation or empowerment of the rural poor, especially the scheduled castes. The inadequacy of funds to meet the expanded responsibilities of the panchayats and bureaucratic delays and corruption, coupled with the collusion among rural elites, bureaucrats, politicians, and panchayat members, have made a mockery of this program. For example, a major study conducted by the National Institute of Rural Development (NIRD, 1995) of several villages in the states of Uttar Pradesh and Karnataka found that in most villages no panchayat elections had been held as late as 1995—largely because of the social resistance to quotas. In villages where elections had taken place, the chairpersons and deputy chairpersons at all three levels belonged either to members of the landed upper or prosperous backward castes.[46] My research in Vikaspur and other villages concurs with these findings. The following case studies show that despite the rhetoric and lofty goals, "pro-poor" programs have failed to stimulate technological diffusion or alleviate the conditions of rural disparities and poverty in Vikaspur. As such, these programs are more a politically attractive palliative than a solution to the problems of rural poverty and underdevelopment.

The Small-Farmer Programs

Although such small-farmer schemes as SFDA were widely touted as a solution to agricultural stagnation and rural poverty in Uttar Pradesh, the small amount of capital/resources allocated to it, and excess bureaucratization combined to doom the schemes from the beginning.[47] In Vikaspur the thrust of the SFDA schemes has been to provide the small and marginal farmers with subsidized credit to enable them to purchase technological inputs and animals (e.g., bullocks, cows, goats, poultry) to help raise farm productivity and household incomes via technological diffusion and animal husbandry. However, because these schemes are "implemented" through the local bureaucracy, which is deeply entrenched in the corruption-patronage network linking propertied interests, local notables, and political authorities, the schemes' results have been at best piecemeal and superficial. The complexity of this process is best exemplified by some of the actual cases I encountered during fieldwork. Suffice it to note that the stories as recounted to me were to the best of my ability cross-checked for accuracy in conversations and interviews with other villagers who had applied for loans, as well as a host of individuals such as the village pradhan and patwari. The stories reveal a complex relationship based on complicity and compliance as the rural poor try to make the best of the circumstances. The original interviews were in Hindi, the translations are mine.

Case study 1. My name is Gopal Ram, I am an *ahir* [backward caste] and own 3 bighas (.3 hectares) of land in Vikaspur. In 1986 I came to know from the pradhan that the government had created some scheme for the poor in which some business could be done by borrowing, because aside from the loan one could also get a grant. With the help of the pradhan I immediately applied for a loan of Rs 4,500 [about US$300] for the purpose of buying a male buffalo [to rent out] and some chickens. I filed the application through the *gram sevak* and had to pay him Rs100 in *rishwat* (bribe) with the understanding that a further Rs 200 would be deducted if I received the loan. After six months my loan was approved . . . but I had to do a lot of running around to get it done. I had to visit the office of the *gram sevak* and the secretary [another government functionary] several times, taking them gifts, and at one time a rooster. I wasted a lot of time and money in transportation. However, even after my loan arrived the *gram sevak* sat on it for two weeks. Finally, he made me sign the form that I had received the loan of Rs 4,500 even though I had not gotten anything. He told me that the pradhan and the circle and block development officers[48] were very helpful in speeding my application and needed to be rewarded. Similarly, the cooperative bank manager needed to be rewarded. The *gram sevak* then told me that he had already spoken to the veterinarian in Aligarh and that the veterinarian had already picked a bull for me [a veterinarian's certificate of approval is necessary if the animals are purchased with SFDA money]. I went with the pradhan and the *gram sevak,* and we purchased a bull and two chickens. After everything was done I was given Rs 237. In October of 1988 the bull died. . . . I think it was an old animal and we ate the chickens. To this day I am paying back the loan of Rs 4,000 to the bank of which I received only Rs 237. You can say that instead of gaining from the scheme, I actually came out the loser. But that is fate in this era of *kul-yug* (dark age). What can I do?

Case study 2. My name is Kisan Lal, and my jati is *balmiki* [scheduled caste]. I own 3 bighas of land and also sharecrop some. Since I am newly married and have no children I felt that I and my wife could do some business in dairying. With the help of the pradhan I applied for a loan of Rs 4,000 with the aim of purchasing a milch cow and two goats. After several months the loan was approved, but I only received Rs 1,800 because of the cost deducted by the circle officer, the *gram sevak,* and the vet. With the money I got I could only purchase three goats. Some months later one of the goats became sick and does not produce much milk. The other two are really pigs, they eat all day but do not give much milk. This has been a bad investment for me. . . . I am losing money and I have to pay back the loan. . . . I am planning to sell the goats.

Several other individuals and families who had applied for such loans recounted similar experiences. In my mind, this leaves little doubt that the illiterate and poor peasant families unable to read records and receipts were routinely cheated, overcharged, and left to pay back more than they had borrowed. Not surprisingly, many felt victimized and the experiences have left a bitter sense of cynicism and deterred others from applying for such loans.

The schemes aiming to make the small and marginal farms economically viable by channeling state-subsidized scientific agricultural inputs and working capital to them have been failures in Vikaspur and the surrounding villages. That is, the benefits have gone disproportionately to the large landowners, and the trickle-down to the poor, small, and marginal farmers has been minuscule. Aside from being ineligible for loans due to lack of sufficient collateral, small and marginal farmers found that critical inputs like "DAP" (diammonium phosphate) hardly ever arrived on time (and timing is essential to HYV use). The farmers complained that what was available was often inappropriate and expensive and that the program planning, coordination, monitoring, and evaluation, which are the responsibility of government experts, were hardly ever carried out. Several of the small farmers interviewed blamed the rich landowners for "drinking up" the technological inputs allocated for the former. For example, large landowners through their allies manipulated the definition of the "small farmer" to appropriate a lion's share of the funds and inputs intended explicitly for the small and marginal farmers. Indeed, the district MLA—who incidentally is a close relative of Vikaspur's big landlord and has been a member of the Uttar Pradesh Vidhan Sabha for the past seventeen years— was known to operate a lucrative business selling publicly funded resources earmarked for small and marginal farmers on the black market.[49] This particular MLA, along with his "personal friend," the then chief minister of Uttar Pradesh, Bir Bahadur Singh (1985–1988), was implicated in a wide-ranging and much publicized fraud and corruption charge regarding the misuse and embezzlement of public funds; the allegations against the MLA were never proved for lack of "credible" witnesses. The adroit MLA, who has since "retired from politics" (and now is a district chief magistrate), is a quintessential example of what Yogendra Malik and Joseph Marquette (1990, 75) have described as "political mercenaries" who "exercise total control over an enormous amount of money without any democratic accountability."

Programs for the Landless

The demand for rural employment far outstrips the state's capacity to create gainful employment opportunities for all the rural poor, but it should be noted that the various governments in Uttar Pradesh have consistently failed to make the necessary financial allocations for employment schemes or to reform the corrupt "top-down" bodies responsible for the management and implementation of such programs. The minimum-wage legislation and social welfare programs, while impressive on paper, are seldom if ever successfully implemented on the ground. Instead, over the years the employment generation programs and schemes have provided a convenient mechanism, a conduit through which a hierarchy of notoriously self-serving political and economic elites appropriate public funds for private and sectional benefits. Hence, wage and employment schemes, although ostensibly directed to the poor and the landless, have hardly benefited these classes. In fact, in the cases I scrutinized the major recipients of the benefits were anyone but the landless.

For example, the Indira Aabas Yojana and the Jawahar Rozgar Yojana, initiated and sponsored by the central government with much fanfare, offered considerable opportunities to the hierarchies to divert public funds for private benefits. There was one illustrative case during my stay in the village. A truckload of bricks and other building materials was delivered to the pradhan's office under the housing scheme to "uplift" the homes of the landless poor and repair the village school building. It was also explicitly stated that poor households, especially the scheduled castes, were to be hired to do the work. However, a week later the materials mysteriously disappeared. The pradhan told me that the materials had been stolen one night by "criminal gangs" operating in the area. In any case, no official investigation was undertaken, except for the block development officer's and the local police inspector's noting several "eyewitness accounts," which identified the thieves as belonging to "troublemakers" from outside the village. Later some of the villagers in muffled voices told me that "things" commonly disappeared from the pradhan's office.

Similarly, the Jawahar Employment Scheme operated under the panchayati raj has not helped the poor. Vikaspur was allocated a paltry Rs 50,000 to create employment opportunities for the landless and the "near landless." The administrative authority as well as the decisionmaking powers regarding the selection and location of projects, the choice of employees, and the administration of funds were given to a six-person committee made up of the district, block, and gram panchayat chairpersons and their deputies. This was in complete violation of the central government's *Jawahar Rozgar Yojana: Manual* (GoI 1994, 25–26) which stipulates that

> the plans for development of villages . . . should be discussed throughly in the meetings of the Village Panchayat and the final decisions arrived at should determine the plan of works to be taken up during a particular year. While preparing the plan of works . . . highest priority should be given to works benefitting the SCs, STs, women and the other weaker sections of the village society. The Gram Sabha [village assembly] should be apprised of the progress of implementation of the program at least twice a year.

Although the funds were deposited in the village cooperative bank in a joint account in the name of six committee members, in order to promote greater accountability and to minimize waste and corruption, in practice the village panchayat allowed considerable latitude in determining who actually received the funds and the amounts that they were given. It is enough to note that the "committee," as part of the complex web of the local patronage-corruption network, used the public largess for both individual and sectional social interests. While (for obvious reasons) I did not find any evidence of outright appropriation of public funds, there was ample evidence to indicate that the use of the funds and the selection of the projects did not reflect the needs of the poor, but the narrow, private preferences of the local hierarchies of power and dominance. For example, several of the landless who supposedly were working under the schemes mentioned that they were only vaguely aware of the government programs. In any case, most had spent time working in the fields of the large landowners, clearing irrigation ditches, building dikes, and pruning the orchards. Six laborers, who according to the pradhan were "directly working under Rozgar Yojana," were in fact "employees" of the rich peasants, working on the wheat-threshing and rice-shelling machines for a mere pittance.

Four others who worked as *kohlu* and vat operators did not even know about the programs; one actually said that he was working to pay off an earlier debt. Two other laborers hired under the scheme were like personal servants (according to some, "spies" of the maliks) who, aside from "serving tea," were employed as casual workers, painting and doing minor repairs to the pradhan's office and house and the homes of other clientele groups. These landless poor could be considered "lucky" in the sense that they had gained some employment and income from the schemes (all, however, being paid below the statutory fixed minimum wage as outlined by the programs), but it clearly will be a very long time before "pro-poor" programs make a significant dent in the problem of rural poverty and inequality in Uttar Pradesh.

In summary, this chapter has attempted to provide a picture of rural poverty in India by showing how socioeconomic and political structures at the macro and microlevel perpetuate inequalities and limit reformist and distributive change. Moreover, the chapter has argued that state expansion, whether through its administrative infrastructure or through laws, decrees, and regulations, does not necessarily give the state greater authority or autonomy. In India, where state expansion has been paralleled by the growing power of agrarian capitalism, state policies have helped to create and reinforce the powers of economic elites whose growing influence has sapped the state's already limited capacities, and limited the range of options available to the state elites for improving the living conditions of the growing pool of rural poor. The changing patterns of the sometimes implicit and sometimes explicit alliance, and, increasingly, the strains between the forces of agrarian capitalism and the state (both at the national and provincial levels), are the subjects of the next chapter. It examines the broad political dynamics of development and poverty reform in the countryside, arguing that the emergence of what Rudolph and Rudolph (1987) call the "new agrarianism" does not bode well for the rural poor.

Notes

1. It should be noted that foodgrain output increased by 46 percent, from 61 million to 89 million tons, during the period 1949/50–1964/65, with an average annual compound growth rate of 2.9 percent. Although this growth barely exceeded the population growth rate, it represented a considerable advance over the negligible rate of growth of 0.1 percent achieved during the pre-independence decades (Balasubramanyam 1984, 82).

2. All data up to 1981/82 are cited in Mellor (1988, 66). The data for 1989/90 are from *India Today*, 31 July 1991.

3. Fertilizer use per hectare has increased from 1 kilogram (kg) in the mid-1950s to 5 kg in the mid-1960s, then to 32 kg by the late 1980s. The irrigated proportion of the crop area has also increased from 17 to 20 to 32 percent over the same period (Bardhan 1984, 11).

4. Over 75 percent of the cropped area in this region is currently under irrigation.

5. The literature on this subject is vast. Authors have emphasized variables ranging from geographic, ecological, and demographic to institutional, political, and sociocultural constraints. For a sample of the literature see Bhalla and Alagh (1979); Bhalla and Tyagi (1989); Byres (1972; 1981); Dasgupta (1977); Farmer (1986); Frankel (1971; 1978); Griffin (1974; 1976); Krishnaji (1975); Lipton (1977); Lipton and Longhurst (1989); Mellor (1976); Pearce (1980); Rao (1975); Staub and Blase (1974); and Subbarao (1985).

6. The literature on this topic is vast. For comprehensive analysis see Abel (1970); Bardhan (1970; 1985); Byres (1972; 1981; 1988a); Dasgupta (1977); Dhanagre (1987); Farmer (1986); Frankel (1971; 1978); Harriss (1988); Kohli (1987); Lipton (1977); Rudra (1971); and Subbarao (1985); among others.

7. See Dasgupta (1977); Jannuzi (1974, 164–165); Byres (1988); and Frankel (1978, 335–336).

8. See Frankel (1978, 336).

9. Even today, after decades of credit reform, allocation of institutional credit is still heavily dependent on the value of assets owned.

10. See Byres (1988); Joshi (1982); Thorner (1982); also Kohli (1987).

11. These articles have been reprinted in Thorner (1980).

12. A brief sample of these studies would include Zoya Hasan's (1989) macrostudy of western Uttar Pradesh from 1930 to 1980 and Ashwani Saith's and Ajay Thankha's (1972) detailed village study; John Harriss's (1982; 1988), C. T. Kurien's (1979), G. Djurfeldt's and S. Lindberg's (1975), and Joan Mencher's (1978) studies of Tamil Nadu; Joesph Tharamangalam's (1981) and Kathleen Gough's (1989) macro-microanalyses of southeast India; Jan Breman's (1974; 1985) detailed studies of western India, with particular reference to Gujarat; Krishna Y. V. Rao's (1984), V. V. N. Somayajulu's (1982), and K. S. Upadhyay's (1982) studies of Andhra Pradesh; Shahid Ahmad's (1977) and G. K. Chadha's (1986) studies of the Punjab; Sheila Bhalla's (1976) and Utsa Patnaik's (1987) studies of Haryana; Arvind Das's (1983), Harry Blair's (1980; 1984), and Abdul Matin's (1989) studies of Bihar; A. Ghosh's and K. Dutt's (1977) study of West Bengal; Pranab Bardhan's and Ashok Rudra's (1984a) intensive large-scale survey of 334 randomly selected villages in West Bengal, Bihar, Uttar Pradesh, and Orissa; and all-India surveys (based largely on analysis of aggregate *NSS* data) by Indradeep Sinha (1980), Gail Omvedt (1983), Terry Byres (1981; 1988a), Pranab Bardhan and Ashok Rudra (1984; 1984a), and Krishna Raj (1976), among others.

13. These figures are cited in Omvedt (1983, 35).

14. Cited in K. Bardhan (1989, 13).

15. See Bhalla and Alagh (1979); also Booth and Sundrum (1985) and K. Bardhan (1989).

16. John Roemer (1982) provides a fascinating empirical understanding of how rural classes emerge from unequal endowments of means of production. He argues that with the "objective of minimizing labor time spent to produce given subsistence requirements," individual peasants with differential endowments of means of production will sort themselves out into an equilibrium of five classes characterized by the following:

1. SE = O ; HI > O ; HO = O
2. SE > O ; HI > O ; HO = O
3. SE > O ; HI = O ; HO = O

4. SE > O ; HI = O ; HO > O
5. SE = O ; HI = O ; HO > O

SE represents self-employment, HI hiring in others' labor power, and HO hiring oneself out. How an individual relates to the buying and selling of labor power defines an individual's class position. In an agrarian economy class 1 above may be described as that of a capitalist landlord, class 2 that of a rich farmer, class 3 that of a family farmer, class 4 that of a poor peasant, and class 5 that of a landless laborer. Roemer also claims a one-to-one correspondence between this hierarchy of class positions and wealth distribution of individuals (the richest in class 1 and the poorest in class 5) and exploitation status (labor-hiring classes 1 and 2 as exploiters and labor-selling classes 4 or 5 as exploited, defining an individual as exploited if at the equilibrium he works more time than is socially necessary and as exploiter if he works less). The results are generalizable to an accumulation economy in which producers maximize revenues and one adopts a more general definition of exploitation. An individual is exploited if he works more hours than what is embodied in any commodity bundle he could have bought with his income; similarly, he is an exploiter if any commodity bundle he could have bought embodies more labor than he performs.

17. To my knowledge only one researcher, namely Ashok Rudra (1988), has described the emerging class structure in the Indian countryside in such stark class terms. For an excellent review and criticism of the "polarization thesis," see Rudolph and Rudolph (1987, 346–354) and Thorner (1982).

18. Following the usual social science practice, "Vikaspur" is a pseudonym.

19. This census was conducted by the Samajwadi-Bahujan Samaj Party government in 1994 to determine the population of the OBCs in order to provide reservations for them. For details see Government of Uttar Pradesh, 1994. *Rapid Census.*

20. For example, the majority of the "800 biggest zamindars" in the state prior to zamindari abolition were upper-caste Hindus, with a sprinkling of elite Muslim castes. They constituted about 0.001 percent of the rural population, but controlled one-third of the total agricultural land. See Singh and Mishra (1965, 13); also Trivedi (1975).

21. This particular pradhan was elected to office just two weeks before my arrival in the village. In a bitterly fought contest he had replaced a rival yadav candidate.

22. The residential separation between castes persists, and is the norm in most Uttar Pradesh villages. Thus, although the village appears as a unit from the outside, there are deep-rooted and clear physical divisions within.

23. I later learned that the thakur families became landless after family disputes regarding inheritance. It should be noted that estimating the distribution of landownership was a difficult and time-consuming task. I found government records in Aligarh to be incomplete and quite unreliable. However, by cross-checking the patwari (village record keeper) accounts, some of which he made available to me for a fee, with my own independent survey (which often meant walking to the various plots and asking the villagers about their ownership), and carefully interviewing the various households, we were able to get a rough estimate. Needless to say, all the big landholdings were conveniently broken up by the patwari (himself a landowner) to conform with the government's requirements. I should state that to my surprise Singh, the largest landlord, flatly told me that even though his family had lost a good part of their land under zamindari abolition, he still "owned a large area," which he considered to be his "inherited birthright" and which "none of these gaddari (corrupt) and immoral government officials will ever take."

24. Similar patterns of growing landlessness and a "dramatic increase in agricultural laborers as a proportion of all workers for UP as a whole" is noted by Hasan (1989a, 167).

25. Initially, I was surprised to find such a high level of land concentration. However, other village surveys have shown that such extreme concentration is common place in rural Uttar Pradesh. See Baig (1990, 77); also Kohli (1987, 214–217), Hasan (1989), and Metcalf (1967).

26. During our interview, Choudhuri Singh stated with much bitterness that his family's estate and possession were "looted after independence by unscrupulous sycophants who took advantage of my grandfather's honest and trusting nature." His anger was directed at the lesser landed thakurs, jats, and backwards, and the government of Nehru.

27. Recently I have noticed a movement away from wheat, the relative price of which has been declining for some time.

28. In their detailed survey of a village in western Uttar Pradesh, Saith and Ajay Tankha (1992) note a marked shift in cultivation patterns toward high-value crops such as vegetables sold for the market.

29. There has been a substantial increase in sugarcane acreage in Uttar Pradesh from 12 *lakh* hectares in 1980/81 to 17.3 *lakh* hectares in 1982/83 (Hasan 1989a, 166).

30. Peasants in Vikaspur told me that a family of five (i.e., two adults and three children) can expect to earn a satisfactory subsistence by cultivating 1.5 hectares of irrigated land.

31. Saith and Tankha (1992) and Hasan (1989) also documents similar trends.

32. Ashok Mitra (1977, 210) has shown the growing market dependence of rural households for foodgrains, arguing that for poor peasants (i.e., the landless and those with less than 2.5 acres of land) the dependence varies between 74 to 100 percent.

33. Writing in the context of Sub-Saharan Africa, Goran Hyden (1983) has provocatively argued that African peasants have the capacity to retreat from market relations into the traditional "economy of affection." In my judgement, Hyden overemphasizes the "exit option" the African peasantry has. He not only underestimates the extent to which rural communities have been integrated to the market system, but also forgets Hirschman's (1970) maxim: that as the political and economic system becomes monopolistic the prospect for exit declines. Second, exit and disengagement are not always a voluntary choice nor an optimal alternative. The spaces of survival into which the peasantry retreat are not autonomous systems of production, thus the spaces are never completely free from state intrusion and intervention. Robert Bates (1981, 87) argues that "[withdrawal] should not be heralded as a triumph for the peasantry. The fact is that the peasants avoid the state by taking refuge in alternatives that are clearly second best." Indeed, for the peasantry to retreat into the subsistence-based "economy of affection" is not only costly but risky—it means facing a harsh and unpredictable environment and a more unforgiving and brutal state apparatus determined to "capture" and transform rural life.

34. It is useful to note that state agencies in Kerala and the Grameen Bank in Bangladesh have encouraged, with some success, cooperation among marginal and poor households to pool their resources to purchase necessary inputs. However, such arrangements are absent in Vikaspur.

35. For a good discussion of these issues see Srinivasan (1985) and K. Bardhan (1989).

36. John Mellor (1968, 25–26) notes that "for a low income consumer (rural or urban) who spends 70 percent of his income on food, a 10 percent increase in

food prices will represent a 7 percent decline in real income. For a high income urban consumer, spending only 20 percent of his income on food, a 10 percent rise in food prices provides only 2 percent decline in income."

37. The characteristic attitude of the jats and the landed OBCs toward the scheduled castes was that "*chamars* are lazy and untrustworthy by nature, and like wayward children they need to be occasionally punished to teach them proper manners and how to behave in front of superiors."

38. Since farm laborers are usually paid under a piece-rate system, it provides many opportunities for salary manipulation. And although it is stipulated that wages must be paid once a week, it is not uncommon for wages to be delayed for several weeks.

39. See Government of India (1981).

40. As noted earlier, the BSP is a relatively new arrival in Uttar Pradesh party politics. Launched in 1984, and drawing inspiration from the legacy of harijan leader B. R. Ambedkar, it represents the most recent organizational expression of the scheduled castes. The arrival of the BSP as a significant political force in Uttar Pradesh politics was confirmed by the advances it made in state assembly elections. In the 1985 elections it took only 2.5 percent of the vote, but in a series of by-elections held in March 1987 it polled some 25 percent of the vote. By the time of the 1989 elections, the BSP had built an organization across the state and stood in contest in all but thirteen Lok Sabha seats.

41. For details of the Pipra massacre and similar incidents see Arun Sinha (1982; 1991).

42. The authors agree that manipulation of caste identities by the rich have prevented political mobilization by the lower classes.

43. At the national level, the Food for Work Program was introduced in 1977 and was replaced by the National Rural Employment Program (NREP) in 1980. To this was added the Rural Landless Employment Guarantee Program (RLEGP) in 1983. The NREP and RLEGP were very similar rural employment schemes, differing mainly in the arrangements for sharing the cost between the center and the states. In 1989 these two programs were merged into a single and expanded new program called the Jawahar Rozgar Yojana, named after the first prime minister.

44. Cited in *India Today,* 30 November 1989, p. 16.

45. The rules mandate elections every five years, but in the event of a dissolution earlier they mandate elections within six months of the dissolution.

46. Also see Gaiha (1996) and Rao and Linnemann (1996).

47. Kohli (1987, 217) points out that about Rs 8 million were allocated to SFDA in Uttar Pradesh in 1979/80, constituting less than 0.3 percent of the state-level public investment in agriculture.

48. The circle and block development officers are state government officials above the gram sevak but below the district officer. The circle officer normally oversees a circle (made up of about ten to fifteen panchayats or villages), while the block officer oversees twenty to twenty-five circles.

49. Several of the farmers in Vikaspur and the neighboring villages mentioned during interviews that they had purchased inputs such as HYV seeds and fertilizers from this MLA. Most of the inputs were stored in a large warehouse not far from the MLA's residence in Aligarh.

6

The New Agrarianism and Rural Development

Critics of organizations like Mahendra Singh Tikait's Bharatiya Kisan Union (BKU) and Sharad Joshi's Shetkari Sanghatana will charge that they are only the new voice of the kulak lobby. Perhaps there is a grain of truth in this. In Gujarat, for instance, one of the demands put forward by the Bharatiya Kisan Samiti was the abolition of minimum agricultural wages. And several economists have pointed out that the demand for higher farm prices is one that will only benefit the relatively richer farmers, while adversely affecting millions of marginal farmers and others in the countryside.

—Editorial, *Times of India,* 29 February 1988

Robert Bates (1981) argued that governments in Sub-Saharan Africa get away with "urban-biased policies" because the voices of the smallholder peasantry are weakly articulated in the state's policymaking institutions. Implicit in the argument is the assumption that an agrarian elite with political and economic connections would more effectively check the abuses of the state and advance the interests of rural society as a whole. However, betting on the strong can also have undesirable consequences. The Indian case is instructive in highlighting that despite the increasing economic and political influence of the rural propertied classes and castes, the weaker sections of society have benefited little, if at all, from the patterns of development generated by the institutionalized system of state-dominant class-caste alliance.

Yet, despite all its internal contradictions, the Indian countryside in recent years has experienced the rise of a rather novel phenomenon: the so-called politics of new agrarianism. The leaders and ideologues of the new agrarianism admittedly view all rural dwellers, regardless of their class or caste status, as archetypal toiling kisans (peasants), discriminated and exploited by the corrupt pro-urban state. The new agrarianism's stated goal has been to mobilize and empower the countryside through a broad-based, horizontally organized farmers' movement. The rise of the new agrarianism has opened a "fresh cleavage in national politics between the countryside and the city" (Rudolph and Rudolph 1987, 354) and has forced the Indian state to modify its earlier "urban-biased" policies with more favorable terms toward the rural sector. But it is important to note that pro-rural policies are not necessarily pro-poor, nor do organized sectoral interests as exemplified by the emergence of kisan movements necessarily advance the interests of small producers, the land-poor, and the landless. Rather, the rise of the new agrarianism has paralleled the concurrent rise in the political and economic power of agrarian capitalism. Hence, despite its populist posturing and rhetorical claims as the champion of all peasants, the new agrarianism in practice articulates, promotes, and defends the interests of the landowning interests—though in the "Hindi belt" the jats and the OBC are its main supporters, while the upper-caste interests tend to discretely "sit on the sidelines." The new agrarianism clearly does not represent the interests of the poor tenants, small and marginal farmers, sharecroppers, and the landless laborers. Nor does it augur well for reform and redistribution. But, first here is a survey documenting the reasons behind the rise of the new agrarianism.

The Politicization of Agrarian Interests in Uttar Pradesh[1]

If until the late 1960s the landowning classes and castes could exercise political power largely within the confines of state politics, by the end of the 1970s they had emerged as significant players in national politics. The interests of the emergent jat and OBC landowners were represented most forcefully by the iconoclastic Chaudhuri Charan Singh, who became one of the most powerful rural leaders in postindependence India by mobilizing the countryside and providing the dominant rural interests a greater voice in the state's ruling coalition. The growing influence of the new agrarianism has meant that policies and programs favored by the landowning interests have become synonymous with rural development. Demands for higher remunerative prices, lower input prices, and more government subsidies and loans have replaced earlier calls for land and tenure reforms, cooperative farming, and poverty alleviation programs for the rural poor. In fact, all political parties, regardless of whether they are urban or rural based, left or right ideologically, regional, national, or ethnically based, now support the demands put forth by the forces belonging to the new agrarianism.

The political influence of the emergent jat and OBC landowning peasantry first became visible in India when Charan Singh, a long-time Congressmen and a minister in the Uttar Pradesh state cabinet from 1951 to 1967, precipitated the collapse in Uttar Pradesh of the Congress ministry of C. B. Gupta in April 1967 by defecting (with 17 followers) to form the Jan Congress.[2] Days later Singh became the chief minister and leader of the successor Samyukta Vidhayak Dal (SVD) government—a coalition that included the pro-Hindu Jan Sangh, the rightist Swatantra Party,[3] and various socialist parties. Charan Singh, a member of the "cultivating jat" peasantry with a firm political base in western Uttar Pradesh, especially among the jats and "cultivating" backward castes, was the first member of the non-elite caste to hold the highest political office in the state.

Charan Singh's government survived less than a year. Infighting among the improbable allies and disagreements over the assignment of key ministerial positions and distribution of patronage led the Jan Sangh to withdraw its support, culminating in the downfall of the SVD government and the imposition of president's rule from the center that lasted for about a year.[4] This interregnum allowed Charan Singh to further consolidate his newly formed party, the Bharatiya Kranti Dal (BKD).

The BKD was the first organized political party to articulate the interests of the landowning interests. Its "partisan rural stance" and ideology that Charan Singh had earlier articulated in two publications, one in 1947 and the other (which was controversial) in 1964,[5] advocated strong opposition to the implementation of land ceilings and cooperative farming, "demanding low land revenue rates, low agricultural taxation and good prices for agricultural produce within the procurement schemes." All of these appealed specifically to "mainly the well-established middle and rich peasant proprietors" (Hasan 1989, 125–127). Charan Singh's peasant background, his conscious identification of his numerically small and spatially concentrated jat peasant community with the majority backward castes[6] and his unrelenting barbs against upper-caste, especially brahmin-*bania,* privileges and socioeconomic political domination and "exploitation" won him support among the poor and lower peasant caste cultivators. Also, his sharp criticism of the Nehruvian developmental strategy's overemphasis on urban and industrial development, and the illegal extraction of rural surplus by corrupt urban elites, struck a responsive chord with the broad spectrum of the rural populace, earning him a reputation as "true defender of the kisans" and "son of the soil."[7]

Charan Singh's BKD, by portraying a progressive pro-rural image and effectively aggregating its expanding support from the peasantry, in particular the jats and backward castes (who were given the majority of BKD's state assembly tickets), was able to rapidly consolidate itself. The BKD had the ability to attract, if not "buy," sections of upper-caste members (indeed, it had a relatively good representation of small and middle upper-caste thakur peasants in its support base), and it emerged as the second largest party after the Congress in its first electoral contest in the 1969 midterm legislative assembly elections in Uttar Pradesh. However, even as the Congress Party returned to power, deep intraparty conflict between the

C. B. Gupta faction and the (pro-Indira Gandhi) Kamalapati Tripati faction severely weakened the Uttar Pradesh Congress's ability to command majority support and to govern effectively. As a result the government was dissolved after only eleven months. In this unstable and fractious political environment Charan Singh once again emerged as the political kingmaker, demanding the position of chief minister of Uttar Pradesh for his and the BKD's political support. The Tripathi faction of the Uttar Pradesh Congress acquiesced, and Charan Singh emerged as the chief minister for the second time. However, once again, the fragile political accommodation was short lived (lasting only eight months), largely because of political infighting and the BKD members of parliament in the Rajya Sabha refusing to support Mrs. Gandhi's attempt to abolish the privy purses and privileges of the big feudal zamindars and princes. As a consequence, the central government failed by three votes to acquire the two-thirds majority necessary for the passage of the abolition bill. But even as the Congress withdrew its support, Charan Singh in a sharp about-face once again joined forces with the Jan Sangh, the Swatantra, and the various socialist parties, including the newly formed Congress (O) faction to keep himself, his party, and supporters in power.

In the roller-coaster, unstable politics of the time, amid the virulent accusations and counteraccusations between the Congress and the BKD about which group was promoting "casteism," the BKD continued to expand its base in rural Uttar Pradesh. In 1974 the increasingly moribund Swatantra Party and the various factions of the Socialist Party in both Uttar Pradesh and Bihar, consisting primarily of those leaders whose support came from the backward castes, including the small and middle upper-caste peasants in these states, merged with the BKD, which was now called the Bharatiya Lok Dal (BLD).[8] In effect, the merger provided Charan Singh with a wider constituency among the cultivating rich and middle peasantry, in particular, the "well-off" cultivating backward castes that included rich and middle upper-caste peasants from across the state.

The political and electoral success of the BLD in Uttar Pradesh and its growing influence in the other parts of the Hindi belt had reverberations in other regions of the country. The commercially oriented farmers in Punjab, Maharashtra, Haryana, Tamil Nadu, Karnataka, and Gujarat also began to mobilize and demand more favorable terms for the countryside. Charan Singh, as the undisputed leader of the kisans, once again mounted an aggressive campaign accusing the "nontoiling" ruling brahmin-*bania* urban alliance (i.e., the Congress Party) of deliberately neglecting the interests of the countryside, and the interests of the "toiling kisans" in particular. He demanded larger government investments and subsidies for agriculture and higher procurement prices for agricultural commodities. Despite its agrarian populism, however, the BLD's stance reflected a clear bias for the rich farmers. Specifically, even as Charan Singh defended kisan interests, he simultaneously argued "that reducing land ceilings and distributing surplus land was an inadequate substitute for a policy of promoting rural industries that would provide employment for the poor because there was not sufficient land to distribute" (Brass 1984, 41). Similarly, he ridiculed the Congress strategy to end rural poverty by giving every landless and poor scheduled caste person a milch cow as "based upon pure ignorance," arguing that other so-called ameliorative measures (such as the Integrated Rural Development Program) had only benefited the urban-based bureaucrats and Congress Party officials.

The emotionally charged and polarized political atmosphere of the mid-1970s was exacerbated further by food shortages, spiraling food prices, and the rise in the tempo of food riots and violence, especially in the major urban areas. The electoral defeats of Congress-led governments in several state elections was the last straw, and Mrs. Gandhi's Congress government imposed emergency rule in June 1975, thereby suspending the democratic process. Under the new "emergency measures" her major political opponents, namely Charan Singh, Jayaprakash Narayan, and Morariji Desai, were the first to be arrested and thrown in jail for causing "internal disturbances." However, the emergency rule and the arrests only enhanced the political legitimacy, stature, and prestige of the opposition leaders. And, at the end of emergency rule in March 1977, and in the subsequent national parliamentary elections, the BLD, the Jan Sangh, the Socialist Party, and the Congress (O) became amalgamated as the Janata Party.[9]

The Janata coalition won a landslide electoral victory in the 1977 national elections, catapulting Charan Singh from state to national politics. During the next three years of Janata rule, Charan Singh presided over some of the most important national ministries: first the Home Ministry, the number two position in the twenty-member cabinet, then the powerful Finance Ministry, and upon the breakdown of the Janata coalition in mid-1979, also the prime ministership of the country, albeit only for a few months.[10] In Uttar Pradesh where the Janata Party (in particular, the BLD) won the largest number of the 383 seats captured by the coalition, Charan Singh once again emerged as a key political broker. Indeed, during the three years of Janata rule in Uttar Pradesh both the chief ministers, Ram Naresh Yadav and Banarsi Das, belonged to the erstwhile BLD and, as the nominees of Charan Singh, depended entirely upon his political support.

Congress Decline and the Politicization of Agrarian Interests

Before proceeding to examine the content and implications of the Janata Party's agrarian policies for the rural political economy, a few caveats need to be stated. First, what accounts for the decline of the Congress system in the Hindi heartland?[11] Why did influential leaders like Charan Singh who occupied prominent positions within the Congress system leave the party? Why did large sections of the emergent commercially oriented rich and middle landowners abandon the Congress to support Charan Singh and parties like the BLD and the Janata? To pose the question differently, how and why did the Congress political machine with its elaborate structures of patronage distribution and intricate transactional linkages with the dominant rural propertied classes and castes fail to co-opt and incorporate these emergent groups into its political networks and institutions? After all (as discussed in Chapter 4) it was the Congress regime under Prime Ministers Shastri and Mrs. Gandhi who were the chief architects of the market-oriented, technological strategy for the countryside. In fact, from the mid-1960s Congress agrarian policies can hardly be criticized for neglecting the interests of the emergent agrarian elite. Congress policies not only created the class of prosperous capitalist farmers, but, with the introduction of the green revolution strategy, both the central and state governments (which were all Congress up to 1967) had further invigorated their support for agrarian capitalism.[12]

Scholars have provided various explanations to account for the decline of the Congress or the "one-party dominant system" in India.[13] Radical analysts have argued that the emergent class of "kulaks" wanted their own political organization to advance the particularistic interests of agrarian capitalism, and to expand their political power commensurate with their enhanced economic standing.[14] However, they all fail to provide adequate explanations of why this occurred outside the Congress system. Other analysts have blamed the Congress decline and eventual split on the interpersonal conflicts among the central "high command" and, in the case of the Uttar Pradesh Congress, on bitter factional infighting between "egoistical, opportunistic and power-hungry" leaders like Charan Singh, whose admittedly "cantankerous nature" and arbitrary leadership style broke the ruling political alliance assiduously built by an earlier generation of Congress leaders (Kashyap 1974). Still others view the decline of the Congress Party as the inevitable result of competitive electoral politics in a polarized, hierarchical society—in particular, the growing politicization and mobilization of the middle and backward peasant castes that allowed non-upper-caste leaders like Charan Singh to challenge the top-down patterns of vertical mobilization and weaken the traditional dominance of upper-caste Congress leadership in the Hindi heartland (Brass 1984; 1985; Frankel 1988; Hasan 1989).

All these explanations provide valuable insights, but they need to be elaborated within the context of a broad state-society conceptual framework. Specifically, as the competing explanations illustrate, the endemic pressures emanating from within both the state and society severely tested the subtle and resilient Congress systems' proverbial capacity to absorb dissent, making compromise and accommodation difficult within the dominant coalition. Stanley Kochanek (1976, 110) has argued that "during the period from 1963 to 1969, the passing of the old nationalist leadership eroded the effective power of the high command, and power in the Congress became more decentralized." As a result, district and state levels of the party operated with a considerable degree of independence, and there was a general dilution of power throughout the party structure. At the national level, the authority vacuum (following the death of Nehru in 1964 and Shastri in 1966) and the precipitous defeats sustained by the Congress in the 1967 elections[15] intensified the contests for party leadership and control of the government. The growing schisms among the Congress "high command" (i.e., between factions loyal to Mrs. Gandhi and those allied to the party bosses, or the "syndicate"), combined with the aggressive, if not autocratic temperament and confrontational style of politics of the new Prime Minister, Mrs. Gandhi, greatly weakened the Congress system, ultimately resulting in the permanent "split" of the venerable party in 1969.

Although the split was in Mrs. Gandhi's favor (with the Congress members of Parliament reaffirming their support for her by a vote of 226 to 65), the Congress no longer commanded an absolute majority in the Lok Sabha. For the next nineteen months, she headed a minority government with a temporary and implicit alliance with the pro-Soviet wing of the Communist Party of India and the Tamil nationalist DMK. During this period, understandably, the Congress turned sharply left (if not populist) in its policies and programs, and Mrs. Gandhi in her efforts to better control the regional party bosses, including the party intermediaries, began more and more to bypass the party organization in favor of populist appeal, demagoguery, and personal charisma. In the 1971 elections it was the "Indira wave," rather than machine politics, that swept Mrs. Gandhi to power.

Analysts such as Kohli (1990) and Rudolph and Rudolph (1987), among others, blame the "personalization of power" under Mrs Gandhi, including her intransigency and the "criminalization of politics" under her son and putative heir Sanjay (who died in a 1980 plane crash), as the major reason for the Congress's organizational decline. They note that as prime minister and later as Congress Party president, Mrs. Gandhi repeatedly demonstrated cavalier disregard for both constitutional and legal constraints, winking at the violations and transgressions of her coterie and using her position to centralize power to perpetuate her cult of personality and further dynastic ambitions. The Rudolphs (1987, 134–135) see Mrs. Gandhi's "imperious, self-righteous and inquisitorial"governing style, in particular her reliance on "populist waves" to secure electoral majorities and her habit of reconstituting party committees through ad hoc appointments of the presidents of the leading bodies of the Congress, as resulting in the erosion of intraparty democracy and accelerating the trend toward political-institutional decline.[16] Under this arbitrary system, Congress members no longer entered the state or national politics by getting elected to local party committees and then moving up through the party ranks by distinguishing themselves in *sarvodaya* (community work) or by building and eliciting the confidence and support of their colleagues, rank-and-file members, and their constituencies, but by demonstrating their allegiance and deference to the prime minister. Consequently, almost any MLA could aspire to consideration for a ministerial position provided that he or she satisfied the requirement of loyalty to Indira Gandhi. Similarly, the process of selecting candidates to run on party tickets for election to the district and state legislative assemblies and to the Lok Sabha became centralized in New Delhi and stage-managed under the directorship of the prime minister and her coterie. In many instances individuals chosen to run on the Congress Party tickets had no grass-roots base and only a pro forma affiliation with the party, yet they were selected because they could collect large sums of money (usually by dubious means) for the party and campaign coffers and were Mrs. Gandhi loyalists. In fact, nepotism, corruption, and venal personal conduct became such a pervasive part of the political culture that the "new breed of Congress politicians" engaged in an orgy of self-aggrandizement and manipulation of the political process. They used their offices to enrich family members—thwarting the democratic process by enrolling bogus members to produce fictitious majorities, arming gangsters and criminals, and colluding with the police to capture polling booths during elections. They also protected businessmen and even known criminals from prosecution for possession of "black money," as well as colluding with them in elaborate kickback schemes. Indeed, as a centralized, autocratic, and confrontational style of personal rule became the norm during Mrs. Gandhi's sixteen-year tenure, the decisionmaking institutions and procedures of governance such as the cabinet, the parliament, the judiciary, and the civil service were consistently bypassed and their capacity to amplify their authority and legitimacy was greatly weakened. As the bulk of the strategic positions in these institutions became rewards for obsequiously "loyal" flunkies and palace courtiers, the consequence was predictable: these institutions and their managers not only lost their legitimacy (and earned the enmity of many) but also were emasculated, losing their professionalism and élan. And so, as it was dispossessed of its ideological and moral suasion the Indian state and its interlocutors, once seen by society as the mediators of conflict, soon became the source of conflict. The thoroughness of the Congress's degeneration was made vividly manifest with the imposition of an authoritarian "emergency" regime in 1975, and in 1978 when its name was changed to Congress (I)— for Indira Gandhi.[17]

The exigencies of competitive electoral politics further compounded these problems of political-institutional decline. Given their party's decidedly populist swing, the upper-caste Congress elites were forced to form political alliances with the disadvantaged backward and scheduled castes against rival leaders and parties whose bases were among the rich and middle income farmers, but such a strategy only served to fragment and weaken the vote banks and the old top-down transactional linkages and alliances between the Congress Party and the dominant landowning castes and classes. Even though the subsequent deinstitutionalization of the Congress Party and its replacement by populist and plebiscitary politics won national elections for Mrs. Gandhi and her party, it also produced unintended consequences. In effect, by the mid-1970s the Congress had come to resemble a lame Leviathan, a party omnipresent but hardly omnipotent, that reacted but could not effectively govern or promote economic development. In these circumstances Mrs. Gandhi, even as she was returned to office, had to rely ever more on populist-cum-plebiscitary appeals and demagogic manipulation to consolidate her political base and to keep the opposition at bay. But in the absence of structured and dependable institutions operating within accepted rules of political conduct and established legal-judicial procedures, populist "waves" were too ephemeral and superficial to respond to the demands and needs of a complex, variegated society. Under such conditions politics became even more personalized and erratic, with provocative slogans and hard-to-fulfill promises substituting for performance. By the mid-1970s the Congress Party (both at the national and state level) had lost its political-institutional coherence and élan. The result was an intensification of factional disputes, political intrigues, and instability, allowing erstwhile Congress opponents to absorb the political and societal dissent and to co-opt individuals, groups, and classes alienated from the Congress system.

The Congress Party's populist economic policies greatly weakened the alliance between the state and sections of the dominant economic interests. For example, flush with the landslide victory after the 1971 "khaki elections" (her reward for the military victory over Pakistan), Mrs. Gandhi tried to reassert the authority of the Indian state to tame the dominant economic classes and their representatives (the "party bosses" in the Congress) and to consolidate and expand her political base among the poor, who had thrown their political weight behind her during the election because of her promise to *garibi hatao* or eradicate poverty. Seeing her victory as "only the beginning of a bitter struggle between the common people and the vested interests" (Hardgrave and Kochanek 1986, 206), Mrs. Gandhi announced further nationalization of industries (fourteen of the major banks were nationalized in 1969) and a concerted effort to implement her "radical" poverty alleviation plans. Indeed, the Planning Commission's May 1972 approach paper to the Fifth Five Year Plan (1974–1979) sounded like a throwback to the Nehruvian era. It envisaged a renewed commitment by the center to land and tenure reforms and assistance to small and marginal farmers, agricultural laborers, and artisans by proposing to extend to them subsidized credit in loans and grants and establishing price stability and easier access to foodgrains by nationalizing the grain trade and creating more government-subsidized fair-price shops.

These proposals perceived as Nehruvian socialism in a new guise alienated many in the ranks of the dominant propertied classes and castes, in particular, the forces representing agrarian capitalism. Specifically, the Planning Commission, realizing a shortfall in its Fifth Plan investment outlays (given the central government's "ambitious poverty-alleviation programs"), suggested that agricultural taxation was a fair and viable solution (to make up the shortfall) since agricultural income accounted for 45 percent of the national income at the end of the Fourth Plan, while direct agricultural taxes contributed only 1 percent of the total tax revenue (GoI 1978). Needless to say, the proposals were strongly opposed by the hierarchies of dominance in the countryside, namely the forces of agrarian capitalism. As discussed earlier, the negative reverberations were quickly felt within the Congress Party in Uttar Pradesh and other state governments as individuals and factions representing vested interests engaged in mass defections and floor crossings from one coalition to another, ultimately eroding the vote banks and the machine politics that sustained the Congress Party in the countryside.

Under intense political pressure the central government backed off from its proposed taxation plans. Mrs. Gandhi candidly noted "that agriculture could not be taxed for political reasons and so alternative ways of financing the plan had to be found."[18] However, the additional funds were not found; obviously, the central government's much touted poverty alleviation programs did not amount to much. The state governments (some like the Uttar Pradesh government were no longer Congress) adopted the time-honored strategy of mutely accepting the proposals of the center and doing little by way of implementation.

What angered and alienated vested agrarian interests even further were the central government's proposals via the Agricultural Prices Commission (APC) regarding agricultural prices and foodgrain nationalization.[19] Paradoxically, the need for such policies stemmed from the success of the green revolution. In 1971/72 India's food output stood at 108.4 million tons—a significant increase from 73 million tons during the pre–Green Revolution of 1965/66. Wheat imports from the United States dropped from 10 million tons in 1965/66 to 2 million tons in 1970/71, and domestic procurement in the same period went up from 3.4 million to 8.1 million tons. The central government's APC, under the leadership of respected agricultural economist Dharam Narain, concluded that given the relatively plentiful supplies and availability of wheat, the government's procurement price should be lowered. In its 1972/73 report (GoI 1972a), the APC argued that the cost of production of wheat in Punjab and Haryana in 1970/71 and in western Uttar Pradesh in 1971/72 was Rs 61.0, Rs 48.1, and Rs 49.7 per quintal, while the government's procurement price had been kept at Rs 76 since 1968—a level that was unreasonable, "market distorting and limiting consumer accessibility," especially to the poor. The report stated: "that the producers have benefitted from the wheat revolution is only as it should have been. But there must come a stage when the benefit starts percolating to the consumers too" (GoI 1972a, 3; also Krishna 1980).

Predictably, the APC's recommendations were attacked immediately in the Lok Sabha and the state legislatures by the powerful agrarian lobby. Leaders like Charan Singh and other chief ministers accused the Congress government and its handpicked urban-based technocrats in the APC of gross incompetence and of deliberately undermining agricultural growth on the grounds that the proposed reductions in producer prices would only serve as a disincentive to the farmers and adversely affect food production over the long term. Under relentless political pressure the central government once again had to back off. Despite the fact that it had publicly rejected all of the APC's recommendations between 1971 and 1973, and refused to lower the wheat procurement price, the political damage to the Congress could not be easily reversed as it became even more identified as an "antirural" and anti-kisan party.[20]

The growing power (and anger) of the dominant agrarian interests was felt yet again during the central government's attempt to nationalize the grain trade (in particular the wheat trade) during 1973/74.[21] In early 1973 the central government banned all private grain retailers and wholesalers and authorized the Food Corporation of India to act as the sole purchaser of grain in the market. The government made it clear that nationalization was against traders and not farmers. The policymakers argued that banning wholesalers and other middlemen would end foodgrain speculation and price distortions, provide farmers with ensured (indeed higher) prices, make available to consumers (especially the poor) staple food grains at reasonable prices, and allow the country to build adequate reserves of foodgrain.

However, even if the central government's arguments made sense on economic and distributional grounds, politically it was a hard sell. Spokesmen for the vested agrarian interests, including the opposition parties from the right to the left, started mobilizing the countryside against the nationalization plan. Charan Singh and other leaders denounced the plan as an example of yet another attempt by the myopic urban-based technocrats in the Congress Party and central bureaucracy to dominate and exploit the countryside.[22] They castigated the government for offering farmers lower prices than the private retailers and urged the farmers not to sell their wheat to the government. The farmers heeded the advice and responded favorably. By 1974 the central government's stocks were far below the target 8.1 million tons set for procurement. Wolf Ladejinsky (1977, 108) documents the unanticipated consequences of the nationalization plan:

> Farmers sold or did not as suited them; wholesalers didn't sit idle; retailers indulged consumer-hoarders; and smugglers had a field day . . . the immobilization of customary wholesale trade channels caused a large quantity of wheat to disappear underground . . . finding its way into the thriving black market. The consequences were all too obvious: millions who depended on the distribution system for their food had to make do with their short rations and not infrequently the fair price shops had no ration to dispense.

The declining grain supplies to the government's food distribution centers and rising inflation led to food riots in major cities and towns throughout India—with the angry mobs often attacking warehouses, homes, and offices of the Congress politicians. Yet again, under the growing political pressures the central government made a quick retreat, hastily lifting its "ill-fated" takeover of the wheat trade and restoring private wholesale trade. Further, it abandoned all of its proposed nationalizations of the foodgrain trade, and significantly increased the procurement price of wheat from Rs 76 in 1972/73 to Rs 105 per quintal in 1974 to placate the farmers and quell discontent. Yet, the political damage to the central government and the Congress Party could not be easily checked or reversed. The Rudolphs (1987, 137) note that "by 1974, Congress governments at the center and in the states had squandered their electoral mandates." Alienated from the Congress system the erstwhile Congress notables (many with organizational muscle and a support base among the rural rich) lent their support to leaders and political organizations, promising to defend the interests and imperatives of the agrarian elite.[23]

In Uttar Pradesh (and India) the ideologue and stout champion of the kisans was Charan Singh and parties like the BKD and, later, the BLD. Yet, defending policies and programs that were often—and at times explicitly—in the interests of the landowning proprietors could be politically limiting in an environment where the vast majority of the rural populace was made up of small or marginal farmers, poor tenants, sharecroppers, and landless laborers. However, the underlying caste/class dynamics in rural Uttar Pradesh offered new opportunities (and some limitations) to the forces of agrarian capitalism. First, the often bitter intraparty conflict among the "political elite" upper-caste brahmins, banias, and thakurs in the Uttar Pradesh Congress, and the introduction of electoral politics under the existing caste configurations, created new opportunities for the numerically larger cultivating backward castes to assert their political weight against the ruling upper-caste "dominant coalition." As primary beneficiaries of land reforms and the green revolution strategy, the middle-caste jats and the "cultivating backwards" (i.e., yadavs, kurmis, ahirs, and lodhs) constituted a significant core of the rich and middle commercial peasantry in many districts in Uttar Pradesh and Bihar.[24] As a result they, as beneficiaries, were less dependent economically on the traditional upper-caste elites, and less likely to be diffident or to act as passive vote banks for them. Zoya Hasan (1989a, 175–176) notes that "Charan Singh was the first Congress politician [before the Congress split] to recognize the political potential of mobilizing the discontent of the Backward castes."

Specifically, the BKD's (and later the BLD's) political strategy of simultaneously emphasizing populist themes that cut across the caste/class divide and defining the kisans broadly and loosely allowed the party to build vote-winning multicaste-class alliances, appealing to the common interests of the jats, backwards, and other low-caste peasants. In the end, the new forms of political alignments and alliances allowed Charan Singh and his BLD to erode the political monopoly of the upper-caste urban and landowning elites associated with the Uttar Pradesh Congress. However, in the process, Charan Singh's invectives against brahmanical or upper-caste socioeconomic and political "privileges and dominance," and his demands that reservations in educational institutions, government posts, and high-prestige occupations (i.e., medicine and law) be set aside for the backward and other low-caste groups, alienated many of the upper-caste elites. Hence, even as the BLD emerged as the most popular party in the Uttar Pradesh countryside, a core of upper-caste brahmin and thakur landowners (in particular, those well placed in the Congress system) continued to lend support to the Congress Party.[25] The split along "caste lines" within the ranks of the new agrarianism, while divisive, nevertheless provided the dominant rural interests with representation and voice in India's major political organization. And, as is illustrated below, despite the divisions, the influence and power of the new agrarianism have not diminished. To the contrary, the new agrarianism has continued to expand as the common economic interests of the rural propertied classes and castes (especially the forces of agrarian capitalism) encourage and necessitate tacit political cooperation. The significance of the new agrarianism in both state and national politics became very clear with the electoral victory of the Janata Party in 1977.

The Janata Regime: Consolidating the New Agrarianism

The rise to national power by dominant agricultural interests is evidenced by the growing representation of the "agriculturalists" in the Lok Sabha. Although the ratio of representation of agricultural interests to business and industrial interests was 2:1 in favor of agriculturalists in the first Lok Sabha in 1951, it increased steadily to 3:1 in the second (1957), 4:1 in

1967 as the green revolution was gaining momentum, 5:1 in 1971, and to 9:1 in 1977 under the Janata coalition. Lloyd and Susanne Rudolph (1987, 355) note that

> with the formation and victory of the Janata party, agrarian politics were for the first time transposed from the state to the national level. From being junior partners in the Congress governments, agrarian interests and classes became senior partners in Janata's ruling coalition. The new configuration put agrarian ideology and policy at the forefront of national attention and concern and was reflected in policies and reoriented investment patterns.

In other words, the move from the arena of state to national politics was a significant development for the dominant agrarian interests and their political allies. Control of the district and state-level political structures and institutions allowed these interests to block or dilute unfavorable central policies and directives, and control of national politics offered new opportunities for directly changing the country's development policy and resource allocation in favor of the countryside. The Janata Party's "agrarian program" (see *Janata Party: Election Manifesto* 1977), drafted by its major constituent, the BLD, vividly reflected the new "rural tilt" as well as the power of the agrarian bloc within the Janata:

> The relative neglect of the rural sector has created a dangerous imbalance in the economy. The farmer has been consistently denied reasonable and fair prices for what he produces. Allocations for agriculture and related development have been grossly inadequate. . . . The farmer must get remunerative prices based on the principle of parity that balances the prices at which he sells his produce and the price he pays for the goods he buys. If the rural sector is to grow and flourish, it must be accorded favorable terms of trade as a matter of overall national policy.

The Janata's "pro-agrarian" (if not pro-rural-rich) programs were swiftly implemented. The planned investment for the agricultural sector increased to 26 percent, and duty on chemical fertilizers was cut by half. Also, generous subsidies for fertilizers, pesticides, rural electrification, irrigation, and modern green revolution inputs were made available to the "enterprising farmers." Moreover, the APC, long considered by vested agrarian interests to be an "anti-rural body" was "captured" when Professor A. S. Kahlon—according to Byres (1981, 447) "a notable spokesman for the rich peasantry"—was chosen to succeed Professor Dharam Narain. During Kahlon's tenure, the procurement price of wheat increased sharply from Rs 105 per quintal in 1976/77 to Rs 130 per quintal in 1981/82 and Rs 142 per quintal in 1982/83. The price of rice also increased from Rs 74 to Rs 115 between 1976/77 and 1981/82.[26]

The growing influence of the BLD in the Janata Party coalition alarmed the other two main constituents, the Congress (O) led by then Prime Minister Desai and the Jan Sangh. This alarm, combined with the personal animosity between Desai and Charan Singh, and the growing rift over policy and resource allocation between the BLD and other Janata factions led the BLD leadership to attack the other constituents as "ganging up" on Charan Singh and the BLD (Hardgrave and Kochanek 1986, 236–247). Charan Singh, well known for using any chance to score political points over opponents (even if they were coalition partners), utilized the internal dissension to flex and consolidate his political muscle by organizing farmer rallies in New Delhi—in Singh's own words, the "hub of urban-industrial power" (Singh 1981). During one such mass rally, organized in conjunction with Singh's seventy-seventh birthday in December 1978, an unprecedented one million peasants (mostly from North India, but from other regions as well) descended upon New Delhi to heed Singh's call. Marcus Franda (1980, 23) vividly captures the charged atmosphere and the growing organizational strength of the new agrarianism:

> For two days, the traffic in and around Delhi was completely disrupted, as row on rows of tractors, trucks, buses and bullock carts poured into the city. Most of the Ring Road, the beltway that surrounds New Delhi was used as a parking lot on the day before and during the rally. The largest open spaces in the city, the Red Fort grounds, the Ferozeshah Kotla grounds all became kisan grounds for two days.

Pledging their loyalty and support to Charan Singh, the farmers criticized the other Janata factions of betraying the toiling kisans and presented a twenty-point charter of "kisan demands" to the government for "immediate action." In so doing, the vested agrarian interests made their point. Indeed, soon after the massive rally, Charan Singh was given charge of the Finance Ministry and literally a complete carte blanche over the national budget.

Not surprisingly, the subsequent budget tabled by Finance Minister Singh (dubbed by some observers the "kulak budget"—see Byres 1981; Omvedt 1983; Vanaik 1990) made significant concessions to the rural propertied interests.[27] For example, duties and indirect taxes on agricultural inputs such as chemical fertilizers were reduced by 50 percent; taxation was either reduced or altogether abolished for mechanical tillers, light diesel oil (for electric water pumps), diesel pump sets, irrigation pipes, and power-generation machinery. Substantial financial allocations were made for rural electrification and irrigation, and procurement prices were guaranteed for selected crops. The Agricultural Refinance and Development Corporation was exempted from income tax so that the savings could be passed on to farmers in the form of subsidies and grants. As well, the institutional and commercial banks were asked to provide farmers loans at lower interest rates and extend capital outlays for "minor irrigation to large farms" and to "enterprising farmers" starting or upgrading dairy farms and farm infrastructure and grain storage facilities (Byres 1981, 447–449). Further, the procurement price of some agricultural commodities was further increased, and the excise duty on tobacco was transferred from the grower to the manufacturer in order to provide help to the farmers in the southern states. Finally, the government also promised to seek foreign markets for agricultural and agriculture-based commodities.

No doubt, the primary beneficiaries of the "kulak budget" were the dominant rural classes and castes whose economic and political powers allowed them to appropriate a disproportionate share of the gains from public investment, higher commodity prices, and capital from the proliferation of subsidies and grants. Finally, Charan Singh's "pro-rich-farmer" programs and policies were acted upon: the chief ministers he selected, such as Devi Lal, a jat in Haryana, Ram Naresh Yadav, an ahir in Uttar Pradesh, and Karpoori Thakur, from a caste of *nais* (barbers) in Bihar, made certain that "state governments in turn took measures on behalf of agricultural development . . . that ensured continued support for Charan Singh and his allies" (Brass 1985, 173).

However, in spite of the Janata's much publicized "rural tilt" and its rhetorical claim as the defender of all kisans, in reality it offered little more than broad platitudes to the poor. The ideology, political-organizational structure, and class-caste alliances that undergirded the Janata regime made the prospects of state intervention in implementing reformist measures or mitigating poverty under Janata rule highly unlikely. In fact, Charan Singh's "kulak budget" was matched by his almost total neglect of distributional and distributive programs. Not only did it fail to initiate any autonomous redistributive and reformist programs, but the pro-poor programs already on the books were assigned low priority and remained ineffective. In fact, the Janata's taxation system was regressive because the tax burden fell heaviest on the lower classes.[28]

The Janata government in Uttar Pradesh also neglected poverty reforms. For example, the question of land and/or tenure reforms were systematically excluded from political discussions and the demands of the rural poor simply referred to courts to be mediated by costly, time-consuming, and inefficacious bureaucratic procedures. Kohli (1987, 215) aptly notes that "the ascension of the Janata regime to power in U.P. put a stop to even mild renewal of the reformist thrust within the state. This shift is clear in the U.P. *Five Year Plan* (1978–83), designed under the Janata regime . . . [while it] paid lip-service to the cause of the poor . . . land reforms as a means of poverty alleviation were downgraded to a point of being totally insignificant." Further, the Janata regime, representing a coalitional alliance of dominant classes, frequently turned a deaf ear to the voices of the poor and the growing "caste wars" (a euphemism for the brutal repression of poor scheduled caste peasantry and landless laborers by organized proprietary interests). As it turned out, the coercive powers of the state in alliance with landed interests and their henchman were, all too often, let loose against the rural poor to reinforce the hegemonic political and economic powers of the dominant propertied classes.[29] Thus, the rise of the new agrarianism as manifest in the Janata regime had negative consequences for the rural poor.

The New Agrarianism in the 1980s

Even though the Janata regime disintegrated before it could complete its mandate,[30] the agrarian consciousness and the politics and policies that leaders like Charan Singh fashioned and defended continue to have an impact on state and national politics. Naturally, the political clout of the agrarian interests did not escape the attention of parties and leaders hoping to get a share of the rural vote. Most observers agree that after Charan Singh all political parties, regardless of whether they are urban or rural based, left or right, nationally or regionally based, have had to accommodate themselves to the interests and demands of the new agrarianism in their political programs, ideologies, and strategies.

As a notable example, in the 1980 national elections Mrs. Gandhi's Congress realized the electoral importance of the rural hierarchies and the vote banks they commanded, and so it jumped on the "protect the kisan bandwagon." Ironically, here, the Congress accused the Janata of incompetence and betrayal of the kisans, and in its election platform boldly claimed that "the working of the Agricultural Prices Commission and the Food Corporation of India needs vast improvement and reorientation" and that in the future "greater attention will be paid to the farmers cost structure," namely that "the input cost indexation of support prices will be instituted so as to safeguard the farmers income from inflationary trends."[31] Conspicuously less prominent in the election manifesto were the populist slogans of *garibi hatao* and other such promises to the rural poor. Indeed, on returning to power in 1980, Mrs. Gandhi's government immediately acceded to many of the farmers demands. The new agriculture minister, Rao Birendra Singh (with strong rural connections), quickly approved higher procurement prices for agricultural commodities, increased subsidies for modern inputs, and lowered input prices. This led the highly respected *Economic and Political Weekly* to editorialize that the new Congress government, like the previous Janata regime, was simply "appeasing the Rich Farmer Lobby."[32]

As the 1980s unfolded, the forces of new agrarianism not only became better organized, forging closer link with each other, but also experimented with new political strategies and tactics. The concurrent rise of organized militant "autonomous farmers' movements"[33] in various parts of the country testified to the creativity and power of the rural capitalists. The new agrarianism's strategy of multi-class/caste agrarian alliances, undergirded by populist ideology propagated in the regional and local idioms as *Bharat* (or India of the toiling, yet poor rural dwellers) versus *India* (the privileged world of the urban frivolous and arrogant), captured the imagination of broad sections of the rural populace and enabled farmers' movements to substantially expand their social base in the countryside (see Nadkarni 1987; Sahasrabudhey 1989). However, unlike the earlier phase in which the interests and imperatives of the new agrarianism were mediated largely by political parties and their representatives in the cloistered world of government legislatures, the rise of farmers' movements meant the expansion of the new agrarianism in the arena of noisy and militant agitational politics, or what the Rudolphs (1987, 360) have termed the "unmediated politics of *rasta rokos* (road-blocks), *gheraos* (sit-ins) and long marches." However, as the following will show, the strategy of maintaining an arms-length distance from "mediated politics" has paid dividends. It has allowed the farmers' movements to not only harness and mobilize broad local and regional support, but to put additional pressure on all political parties and governments (at all levels) to pay attention to the interests of the rich farmers.

Although the tactics and strategies of the farmers' movements and pro-rural parties may differ, the primary objective of both is to support and advance the interests and demands of the rich, commercially oriented propertied classes in the countryside. It is no coincidence that farmers' movements have attracted their largest support in regions and in states with a relatively high degree of agricultural commercialization: the Punjab, Haryana, western Uttar Pradesh, Gujarat, Tamil Nadu, Karnataka, and Maharashtra.

The most articulate spokesman and ideologue of the new agrarianism since Charan Singh has been Sharad Joshi. Joshi, an affluent farmer and the founder of the Maharashtra-based Shetkari Sanghatana (Farmers Association), first rose to national prominence in 1980 when he organized a large and militant *rasta-roko* agitation in Nasik district in support of higher prices for sugarcane, cotton, and onions; lower input prices; greater subsidies for fertilizer; and an overall rectification of the terms of trade between the agricultural and industrial sectors. For three weeks in November the Shetkari Sanghatana mobilized several thousands of peasants and blocked the main railway lines and roads north of Bombay with tractors, buses, and trucks and surrounded officials to press their demands. As the agitation gained momentum a wide spectrum of political parties—the Congress-U, BLD, Janata, and even the two communist parties—joined the "farmers struggle," hoping to capitalize on or control the new force. The demonstration was called off only after the movement won important concessions from the state government, as well as the government's promise to consider the broader issue of terms of trade raised by the farmers.[34] Since the 1980s, the Shetkari Sanghatana has led several successful agitations attracting broad rural support (anywhere from 100,000 to 500,000 organized peasants on any one occasion) and spreading to other districts in Maharashtra and the neighboring state of Karnataka.

However, despite the Manichaean slogans of the Bharat-India divide, the Shetkari Sanghatana (and pro-rich-farmer organizations and parties) articulates and represents the interests of the rural capitalists.[35] The class bias of the movement can be gleaned from Sharad Joshi's writings (1986; 1986a).[36] He argues, in a way evocative of Charan Singh, that the root cause of "widespread misery" and the "vicious cycle of poverty" in rural India is the direct result of "internal [urban] colonialism" that has "now replaced earlier transcontinental [British] imperialism." Specifically, "savings in agriculture [are] expropriated through a policy of cheap raw materials and artificially depressed prices" by "urban-based exploiters" to fuel the "urban-industrial revolution." Hence the only way the countryside can break this stranglehold is to end the "coercive extraction" of agricultural surplus. According to Joshi, one immediate way to achieve a more equitable balance is to provide the farmers with remunerative agricultural prices, waive repayment of all agricultural loans (on the grounds that unfavorable farm prices have yielded grossly inadequate incomes for loan repayment), abolish taxes and duties on agricultural implements and green-revolution inputs, and provide crop and farm insurance to farmers.

Although Joshi's program calls for larger allocation of public resources for "rural uplift" programs, reservation of seats in educational institutions and quotas in government employment for farmers' sons, questions regarding land and tenure reforms, or the payment of higher minimum wages to the poor and landless laborers have not been on the movement's agenda. Also, while the farmers' movements champion price increases for all crops, demands for remunerative prices for commercial crops (sugarcane, tobacco, and cotton) and marketable staple foodgrains (wheat and rice) have been at the forefront of the agitations. The crops (i.e., coarse grains) grown mostly by the poor and marginal peasants have not attracted the attention of the farmers' movement.

The success of Shetkari Sanghatana has spawned similar farmers' movements in other parts of the country. For example, taking their lead from Joshi, the Karnataka Rajya Ryota Sangha led by Dr. Nanjundaswamy and the Tamil Nadu Agriculturalist Association headed by G. Narayanaswami Naidu started large-scale protests demanding higher prices for paddy, writing off of agricultural loans and debts owed by farmers, and immediate moratoriums on electricity and irrigation payments. Even when many of their demands were met by the state governments, the movements staged a violent demonstration that left eight dead and 8,000 arrested

(Nadkarni 1987, 60–66). Similarly, in Karnataka, demands by the mobilized farmers for higher prices for tobacco, lower power rates for tubewells, and the abolition of the diesel tax were quickly met. In fact, in early 1983 "organized farm interests" played a decisive role in defeating Karnataka's Congress government and replacing it with a more pro-rural Janata-led coalition even though the state Congress government had been generally responsive to the farmers' demands. Also, in March 1987 the Gujarat Krishi Rakshak Sangh, representing rich and middle farmers, mobilized about a million peasants and *gheraoed* the state assembly buildings to enforce its demands for lower input prices, higher output prices, waivers of past agricultural loans, and subsidized credit to farmers. When the talks broke down massive violence resulted: over seventy-five government vehicles were set on fire, the surrounding government offices were ransacked, and the former chief minister (and a supporter of the farmers) was beaten up for "not doing enough" for the farmers while in office.[37]

In Uttar Pradesh the political vacuum left by the illness and death (in May 1987) of Charan Singh was filled by Mahendra Singh Tikait, a well-off jat farmer from the prosperous Muzaffarnagar district.[38] An admirer of Charan Singh and Sharad Joshi, Tikait opted to defend the interests of his influential constituency through militant agitation, even though dominant agrarian interests were well represented in the Uttar Pradesh state legislature. In 1987 Tikait formed the Bharatiya Kisan Union (BKU), stoutly announcing that while the BKU would not have affiliation with any political party, it would nevertheless support those most committed to the interests of the kisans.[39] Since its inception the BKU has flexed its political muscle on several occasions by staging mass rallies and often violent *rasta-rokos* and *gheraos*. It has not only won some important concessions from the state and central governments, but its "charter demands" (as reiterated to me by a key member) have increased from the initial ten to thirty-five points by early 1990. These include the following:

- *Karjmukti* (debt liberation), or the immediate writing off of all agricultural loans owed by farmers
- Regular supply of affordable power, reforms in the Uttar Pradesh State Electricity Board, and the abolition of electricity dues[40]
- Lower input prices and greater subsidies for such farm machinery as tractors and sugarcane crushers
- Increase of sugarcane procurement price from Rs 27 per quintal to Rs 40 and nationlization of sugar mills in Uttar Pradesh
- Higher, and guaranteed, procurement prices for wheat and other foodgrains
- Reservation for farmers' wards in government jobs and guaranteed pensions for farmers

- Greater representation of farmers in the APC and other government bodies
- Waiver of criminal charges against farmers during demonstrations

In interviews, senior officials in the Uttar Pradesh government told me that Tikait is misleading farmers by promising them impossible things. They reject the charge that the government is "antifarmer." To the contrary, they argue that rural electricity charges are still below the pre-1985 level and the procurement prices offered by the Uttar Pradesh government are higher that those set by the central APC.[41] They admit that they would like to do more for farmers, but severe budgetary limitations prevent them from meeting all of the farmers' demands. As one official noted, "If we waive electricity bills it will cost about Rs. 900 crore. The increase in sugarcane prices will mean Rs. 200 crore" (Pachauri 1988, 37). Yet, the BKU leadership never misses the opportunity to note that in the neighboring state of Haryana, former BLD Chief Minister Devi Lal promised to write off all agricultural loans of up to Rs 20,000 during the 1987 election campaigns. Indeed, immediately after assuming office the popular Devi Lal did precisely that, costing the Haryana state treasury a whopping Rs 150 crores (Rs 1,500 million). As one BKU activist said to me, "The UP government will listen to us yet. . . . We will not rest until our just and legitimate demands are met."

Before proceeding, however, a point of clarification is necessary. Some observers have argued that the emergence of an organized farmers' movement is evidence that state and central governments are not really responsive to the needs and demands of farmers, and that farmers have to agitate to get their voices heard and interests protected.[42] There is no doubt that not all of the farmers' demands are unreasonable, but to suggest that the economic and political interests of the dominant landowning interests are poorly represented is misleading. The fact is that the central and provincial governments have gone to great lengths to meet and cater to the growing demands of this influential group. Not only is "there hardly any significant taxation of agricultural income and wealth" (Bardhan 1984, 46), but the governments have continued to subsidize electricity, irrigation, and fertilizers far beyond the cost of production, as well as to provide remunerative prices and forgive unpaid loans. For example, in 1987/88, the agriculture-related subsidies "bloated to a level (over 5,000 *crores*) where they are burning a huge hole in the government's coffers."[43] Also, if the return on public-sector investment—especially in the states—is so low, it is partly because of the massive subsidies built into the power tariffs that the state electricity boards charge farmers. Similarly, the irrigation charges in most states are so low as to not even recover operational costs, let alone the cost of the initial investment.[44] In terms of treasury costs, fertilizer subsidies accounted for the massive amount of Rs 9 billion in 1983/4. This amount consisted of the difference between the domestic cost of fertilizer and the actual (subsidized) price at which it was supplied to the farmer.[45] Hence, the problem is not that the interests and imperatives of the rural propertied classes are not protected or advanced by the state, rather that the "patronage-dispensing state," to use Pranab Bardhan's phrase, with dwindling resources at its disposal, has great difficulty in satisfying the insatiable appetite the dominant propertied classes have for state largess. In other words, even the milch cow that is the Indian state cannot meet the growing (and "unrealistic") demands of the dominant classes.

Implications for Reform and Redistribution

A few observers have argued that broad-based rural support for the politics and programs of the new agrarianism, in particular, the farmers' movement, is evidence that all groups and classes in rural society benefit from the gains won by the forces of the new agrarianism. No doubt the landowning, commercially oriented farmers have appropriated and will continue to appropriate a disproportionate share of the gains from public investments, higher commodity prices, input subsidies, and loan waivers, but there has been some trickle-down of benefits to the middle peasantry and sections of the small peasantry. However, as the Vikaspur case study has illustrated, there are formidable limits to trickling down in rural India; it is a gross exaggeration to suggest that all rural classes have benefited. The vast majority of small and marginal peasants and the landless laborers has won little, if at all, from the gains associated with the new agrarianism. Now, before I elaborate upon these issues, an important caveat should be noted.

It is valid to ask: If the new agrarianism advances the interests of the landowning jats and OBCs, then why does a broad spectrum of the rural populace often acts collectively to support the farmers' movement?

As discussed in Chapter 1, the ways rural society with its crosscutting ties and linkages defines and pursues its interests are complex. The preceding discussion has shown that such populist ideologies as the Bharat versus India, as well as traditional forms of legitimizing ideologies and domination rooted in the power asymmetries of local hierarchies, powerfully shape and condition peasant interests and actions. But it should also be noted that the farmers' movements have not always been able to sustain their support base or build a progressive multiclass and multicaste alliance. For example, because of the charismatic leadership of Sharad Joshi the Shetkari Sanghatana has relatively broad rural support, but in Uttar Pradesh pervasive class and caste divisions have not allowed the jat and backward-caste-dominated BKU or the BLD to harness broad multicaste support in the countryside.

In Vikaspur, for example, upper-caste members, especially the upper-caste landowners, are generally selective in their support. They tended to view the Bharatiya Kisan Union as an expression of jat and backward-caste assertion. They would attend meetings and rallies organized by the BKU, and many claimed to be members of the union, but they were also long-time members of the Congress, and now of the BJP. Indeed, several of the upper-caste landowners admitted that they had become supporters of the BJP because of their opposition to jat, backward-caste, and dalit de-mands for employment quotas and educational reservations. The scheduled castes, including some poor backward-caste families, were less sanguine about politics in general and the farmers' movement in particular. Many complained that Tikait and the BKU activists have shown little concern for specific issues concerning the *mazdoors,* such as minimum wages for agri-cultural laborers, employment opportunities, and the ending of *begar* (corvée labor).They also complained about the heavy-handed tactics used by Tikait's men against the BSP's efforts to organize the dalits. Most often, the scheduled-caste poor and landless were simply herded into buses and trucks and taken to the farmers' rallies. As one low-caste landless laborer remarked to the author, "We go because the malik told us to. . . . It is not a bad thing, sometimes we are given meals, and during the last rally the organizers in Meerut even provided us with *shirra* [a sweet dish made of wheat]."

Returning now to the complex question of how the gains of the new agrarianism had an impact on the rural poor: there is general agreement in the development literature that the high levels of production subsidies and price support programs for agricultural commodities (i.e., food staples) and the resultant increases in food prices disproportionately hurt the poor because, as net buyers of food, their declining real incomes severely limit their purchasing (and consumption) abilities.[46] On the other hand, the landlords, rich peasants, and sections of the surplus-producing middle peasantry who produce or control the bulk of the marketed surplus benefit from remunerative prices and subsidies. Indeed, most elasticity estimates support the view that the rural poor, on average, depend on the market for food, and that they have little choice but to cut their consumption in-take as food prices increase. Specifically, in India, the few subsidized pub-lic food-distribution systems notwithstanding, the poor, especially the landless, pay higher prices for staple foodgrains and other necessities. This is not only because they are forced to make frequent small purchases in the seasonally fluctuating market, but also because they are constrained to take expensive consumption loans in the slack season before the harvest, when both unemployment and food prices go up. Analysts, including the late Paul Streeten (1987), Alain DeJanvry and K. Subbarao (1987), and Amartya Sen (1981), have cogently argued that sharp increases in food prices—the result of either high price-support programs to satisfy the pro-ducer class or International Monetary Fund and World Bank adjustment policies—are extremely regressive for the rural poor, who constitute the vast majority of the poor in developing countries. These authors note that the poor already subsist at extremely low nutritional levels, and therefore even small increases in food prices can be, and often are, catastrophic. In India the practice of increasing producer prices and then passing the increased food costs on to the consumers, most of whom are not able to purchase it and are not covered by the few subsidized public distribution systems,[47] has resulted in the paradoxical outcome of accumulating food surpluses (public stocks of foodgrains soaring to 30 to 35 million tons) in a country where the vast majority of its citizens remain underfed and hungry.

As noted earlier, the leadership of the new agrarianism has pressed for remunerative agricultural prices, loan waivers, concessions in electricity dues, and higher levels of subsidies for green revolution inputs, but it has hardly pressed for the implementation of minimum wages and pro-poor programs with the same vigor. In fact, the farmers' movement has never made the implementation of minimum wages for agricultural workers a priority: the leadership of the BKU and other farmers' organizations has altogether ignored this issue. For such leaders as Sharad Joshi, Mahendra Tikait, and the late Charan Singh, the "solution" to the problem of low rural wages is simple: once procurement prices increase, rural wages will automatically rise.

Comparative evidence from India, however, does not support such claims (K. Bardhan 1989; Nadkarni 1987; Joshi 1986). For example, in Vikaspur the prices of foodgrains (especially wheat and rice) and commercial crops more than tripled in the preceding decade, but the actual wages have remained practically constant, at the mid-1970s rate. Moreover, neither the district, the local Congress, the Lok Dal, nor the BKU have pushed for the implementation of government minimum wage laws. To the contrary, throughout the north Indian countryside I repeatedly heard complaints from agricultural laborers about how on the one hand the landlords and the BKU activists mobilize them to rally against the government for concessions in input prices, electricity dues, and loan repayments, and on the other hand refuse to pay them fair wages and threaten and physically abuse those who demand fair wages. In fact, several villages I surveyed in Aligarh, Meerut, and surrounding districts were "out of bounds" to the Mazdoor Kisan Sangram Samiti, an organization aimed at helping the low-caste poor and the landless, and to the BSP. I was told that the order was issued by "overly enthusiastic Tikait's men," who were armed with *lathis* and knives and had viciously beaten several people they suspected of organizing low-caste landless laborers. However, such bullying tactics are not restricted to Uttar Pradesh. Even in prosperous, high-growth states like Haryana and the Punjab agricultural laborers do not receive the prescribed minimum wages. According to Gill and Singhal (1984, 1732),

"In 1979, when agricultural workers launched their struggle in Gurudipura village (in Ludhiana district) on the wage issue, the BKU president [a wealthy landowner] threatened to teach them a lesson in the same way as in Muskbad village [where farm laborers were brutally beaten] . . . in Ludhiana where they were forced to take shelter in the sugarcane fields against the farmers' fury."

Also, contrary to conventional wisdom, the demand for loan/debt waivers as formulated by the farmers' movement does not necessarily help the sharecroppers, small or marginal peasants, or the landless agricultural laborers. It is important to note that the major borrowers, or those who typically qualify for credit and loans from commercial and cooperative banks, are the rural rich and the relatively well-off landowning middle peasants. The vast majority of land-poor rural households, given their insufficient collateral, have to borrow from the local informal credit channels controlled by the local landlords-cum-moneylenders. The champions of the new agrarianism have been very specific in their demands for loan waivers: they have asked for the waiver of only institutional loans and not the loans the poor owe to local lenders, most of whom charge exorbitant rates of interest. Similarly, while the champions of the new agrarianism have demanded higher levels of subsidies for inputs and rural credit, they have failed to demand the extension of subsidized institutional credit to the small and marginal peasants and the landless. When I raised this issue with a key BKU strategist, his response was blunt:

> These chamar coolies [generic for the scheduled castes] are like pampered children. . . . The government has been giving them money and grants of all kinds to buy their votes . . . but giving credit to the coolies is useless. The minute they get the money they spend it on liquor and loose women, and then they are too lazy to work. . . . Subsidies should first help the honest farmers . . . that is what Chaudhuriji in UP and Haryana [Tikait and Devi Lal] have been fighting for.

A strategist with the Karnataka Farmers Association gave a similar reason why his association has only demanded a waiver of institutional loans (albeit, he adds one important point): "If laborers get monetary or material benefits or loans from the government, they cannot repay them since they spend [them] on liquor; or, they would develop their own activities and *would not come for agricultural coolie work.* Agriculture would then suffer without coolies" (Nadkarni 1987, 153, emphasis mine).

To summarize, the politics and policies of the new agrarianism do not bode well for the rural poor. In spite of its claims as the defender of all kisans, the new agrarianism's priorities and actions have been anything but for the poor. The ideology, organization, and the pattern of class-caste alliance underlying the various manifestations of the new agrarianism have been aimed primarily at satisfying the interests and imperatives of agrarian capitalism rather than promoting distributive reforms in the countryside. In the process, leaders such as Sharad Joshi, Mahendra Singh Tikait, and the late Charan Singh have acted as vigorous and skilled political entrepreneurs between the forces of agrarian capitalism and the state. What has emerged from this is an implicit alliance between rural capitalists and the state to continue and invigorate support for capitalist expansion in the countryside. Concurrently, the formal and informal political and economic muscle of the new agrarianism has further limited the reformist-oriented state elites' maneuverability, forcing them to operate within an ever narrowing range of choices.

As India approached the 1990s, the long established top-down patterns of mobilization by which the propertied upper castes once dominated lower castes and disadvantaged groups in the countryside have come to an end. The Congress's loss of its traditional vote banks among peasant castes, the dalits, and Muslims undercut its ability to perpetuate its political dominance. In November 1989, following the Congress's precipitous defeat, the Janata Dal, a coalition of several parties and groups representing the core MAJGAR (a social grouping of Muslims, ahirs, jats, gujars, and rajputs) formed the central government.[48] It was a historic event in that it brought, in a dramatic way, the socially unprivileged lower castes and the cultivating peasantry to the highest positions of government. In his first act, Devi Lal (the self-described jat farmer), who became deputy prime minister and minister of agriculture in the new V. P. Singh government, with much fanfare announced the Agricultural Debt Relief Scheme that immediately waived agricultural loans of up to Rs 10,000 per person. Devi Lal had strong support in the government—the 323 members of the newly elected parliament were representatives of farmers, and farmers' sons were also chief ministers in Uttar Pradesh, Bihar, Madhya Pradesh, Haryana, Gujarat, and Rajasthan.

However, the political center cobbled around precarious coalitions could not be easily sustained, nor could it always provide effective governance. Since the 1990s the BKU, caught between rival Janata Dal factions and increasingly divided by the caste tensions around it, has lost some of its steam. Tikait and the jat BKU activists have found themselves arrayed against Mulayam Singh Yadav, the powerful OBC leader and former Uttar Pradesh chief minister. But both these rivals are also engaged in bitter confrontation with its "new enemy"—the dalit-led BSP. The frequent jat, OBC, and dalit conflicts has even pushed the BKU to cast its lot with the allegedly upper-caste Hindu nationalist BJP.

Notes

1. This background section draws much from the important contributions of Paul Brass (1980; 1983; 1984; 1985; 1990), Craig Baxter (1975), Atul Kohli (1987,

chap. 5), and Zoya Hasan (1989; 1989a).

2. Charan Singh joined the Congress Party in the 1930s, and despite disagreeing fundamentally with the policies of the Congress remained in the party so long as the Congress was strong in Uttar Pradesh—from 1930 to 1967.

3. The Swatantra Party was largely "a coalition of urban big business and rural aristocratic and landlord elements in which the latter were dominant" (Brass 1990, 76).

4. Under the Indian Constitution, the president may declare a constitutional emergency in a state if, on receipt of a report from the governor, a situation has arisen in which the government of the state cannot be carried on in accordance with the constitution. The president may then (1) assume any or all of the state functions or vest these functions in the governor, or (2) declare that the powers of the state assembly shall be exercised by the Parliament.

5. In addition to *Abolition of Zamindari: Two Alternatives* (1947) and *India's Poverty and Its Solution* (1964), Charan Singh's ideas are further elaborated in his many other writings, namely *Joint Farming X-Rayed: The Problem and Its Solution* (1959), *India's Economic Policy: The Gandhian Blueprint* (1978), and *Economic Nightmare of India: Its Causes and Cure* (1981).

6. Charan Singh often refereed to himself as the "old yadav," and during his stint as chief minister appointed many members of the backward castes to key ministerial positions.

7. It is useful to note that Charan Singh had been writing about urban bias in Indian development since the mid-1950s, almost a decade before the concept was made fashionable by Michael Lipton. Singh (1981, 205–208) argued that the persistence of poverty in rural India was due to the fact that "political power lies in the hands of the urbanites to whom urban interests naturally come first" and that "the farmer was a mere grist in the mill of economic progress on whose bones the structure of heavy industry was to be reared."

8. Most notably, the dismantling of the Socialist Movement by Raj Narain and the decision to merge its most important segment, the Samyukta Socialist Party, with the BKD gave the BKD a more balanced support base in Uttar Pradesh.

9. The Janata coalition was hastily put together in response to Mrs. Gandhi's surprising call for elections after the emergency. The leaders instrumental in the creation of the Janata were Charan Singh, Jayaprakash Narayan, and Morariji Desai.

10. Indira Gandhi was returned to power in 1980. For an excellent discussion of the personal and factional infighting leading to the demise of the Janata Party, see Weiner (1983) and Rudolph and Rudolph (1987).

11. It is important to note that the Congress decline was not simply an Uttar Pradesh phenomenon. In the fourth general election of 1967 the Congress lost power in eight large states, and almost did so nationally. Two years later it split for the first time. In a sense, the 1967 general elections marked the beginning of a transformation of the Indian political system from a dominant one-party system to a multiparty system.

12. Also, Ashok Mitra (1977) cites data to show that over the period 1963/64–1973/74, the weighted terms of trade between agriculture and industry had moved by almost 50 percent in favor of agriculture. The primary reason for this steep increase in the relative price of agricultural products, according to Mitra, was the government's favorable agricultural pricing policies.

13. For a good overview see Kohli (1988); Kothari (1967; 1988); Brass (1984; 1990); Manor (1982); and Rudolph and Rudolph (1987).

14. See Byres (1981; 1988a); Omvedt (1983); and Vanaik (1990).

15. The results of the 1967 elections revealed the extent of the Congress's de-

214   *Development and Democracy in India*

clining authority. The Congress failed to secure majorities in eight states, and its majority at the center was reduced to a narrow margin of 54 percent of the seats. In other words, it came within ten seats of losing its majority in the national parliament. Prominent Congress leaders, including party president Kamaraj, nine union ministers, and four state chief ministers were also defeated at the polls.

16. The Rudolphs (1987, 84) lucidly sum up the two contrasting political eras since independence, one associated with Nehru and the other with his daughter, Indira Ghandi: "Unlike her father, Mrs. Gandhi depleted India's political capital by eroding the autonomy, professional standards, and procedural norms of political institutions and state agencies. She tried to make those responsible for Parliament, the courts, the civil services, and the federal system answerable to her. The effort succeeded, to varying degrees, in orienting their conduct to her personal will. A paradoxical consequence was to diminish the legitimacy and effectiveness of the state. Centralization based on personal loyalty and obedience to a monocratic executive lessened the state's capacity to amplify itself through multiple agencies extending beyond the limited control and attention of one person. Jawaharlal Nehru was the schoolmaster of parliamentary government, Indira Gandhi its truant."

17. Not surprisingly, from 1969 to 1977 the Congress had five presidents—a turnover, no doubt, aimed at preventing institutional consolidation of power by any potential challenger.

18. This is cited in an article by B. M. (1974) in *Economic and Political Weekly,* vol. ix, no. 21, p. 814.

19. The establishment of the APC and the Food Corporation of India (both in 1965) marked a new phase in the government's food price policy. The APC formalized the process of setting procurement prices by more systematically taking into account costs of production and the past and current trends in prices. The APC (renamed the Commission on Agricultural Costs and Prices in 1985) is an advisory body determining procurement prices, but in practice the government's actual prices have historically been close to (if not slightly higher) than those recommended. The Food Corporation of India became the government's principal agency for domestic procurement, storage, and public distribution of and foreign trade in foodgrains.

20. The central government defended its level of support and procurement prices, arguing that although its prices were slightly lower than those prevailing in the open market, every increase in the procurement prices signaled a rise in the open market prices by the same proportion. In other words, the system of procurement prices imparted a bullishness to the market (Balasubramanyam 1984, 98). A good overview of the heated nature of the debates in the Lok Sabha and state legislatures during this period can be found in several issues of *Economic and Political Weekly* from 1971 to 1973.

21. This was a policy initiative taken by the central government, not a recommendation of the APC.

22. Again, a good flavor of the debates and rhetoric of the times can be found in the various issues of *Economic and Political Weekly* from April to June 1973.

23. Stanley Kochanek (1975, 85) notes that "despite the commanding position Mrs. Gandhi occupies in both party and government and despite her decisive role in selecting Congress chief ministers, she has not been able to reverse the pattern of center-state relations which emerged toward the end of the Nehru era. At the same time, however, some of the most important new programs which are part of her promise to abolish poverty require action by the state governments. The lowering of ceilings on land and the introduction of an agricultural income tax both fall under the jurisdiction of the states."

24. Francine Frankel (1988, 255) refers to the jats and backwards as forming the

"backbone of commercial agriculture in the state [i.e., Uttar Pradesh and Bihar]."

25. However, it should be noted that the BLD's alliance with the Jan Sangh, the party of militant Hindu nationalism, which like the Congress drew its main support from the elite castes of brahmans, rajputs, and kayasthas, allowed Charan Singh to split the upper-caste support base of the Congress.

26. See Balasubramanyam (1984, 99). For an overview of the "political reasons" behind the increase see Kahlon and Tyagi (1983) and Tyagi (1979).

27. It should be noted that although agriculture received a big boost, it was not at the expense of industry (Kohli 1987, 90).

28. Kohli (1987, 90) points out that because both the agricultural and industrial producers received considerable state support, the resulting budgetary gap was filled in part by a wide range of indirect taxes that were underscored by the lack of emphasis on equality.

29. Zoya Hasan (1989a, 190) notes that during the Janata period "the extent of terror unleashed by landowners can be gauged from the fact that the Janata government was compelled to set up a monitoring cell in Meerut to deal with complaints of brutalities against Harijan rural labor . . . the apparent middle and Backward caste bias of the Janata government exacerbated the insecurity of the Harijans; their leaders complained of inadequate protection and representation given to Harijans in U.P. and Bihar." Atul Kohli (1987, 220) comes to a similar conclusion, arguing that "in the absence of a political force to tilt the power balance towards the landless, a tacit alliance of domination involving the state, the landowners, and local thugs continued to reinforce the socio-economic misery of U.P.'s lower rural classes."

30. After the disintegration of the Janata coalition, the political parties that initially joined it either re-formed themselves with new names or ceased to exist. After Charan Singh resigned from the Janata Party in April 1979, he revived the BLD under the name of Lok Dal. Further divided during the illness and death of Charan Singh in 1987, the Lok Dal (A) and the Lok Dal (B) have further split. For an excellent discussion of the reasons behind the Janata split see Hardgrave and Kochanek (1986, 236–247).

31. The quote taken from Indian National Congress [I] *Election Manifesto* 1980, p. 22.

32. See B. M. (1980), pp. 459–461.

33. I use the term "autonomous" in the sense that the farmers' movements maintained institutional autonomy from all political parties, even the pro-rural Lok Dal.

34. For example, the price of onions was increased by 25 to 30 percent, and sugarcane prices from Rs 150 to Rs 180 per ton (Nadkarni 1987, 72). Also, cash concessions were paid to farmers of cotton and paddy.

35. Gail Omvedt (1980, 2042) says this about Shetkari Sanghatana: "It is safe to say that not only is the movement being led by rich peasants, but it is also a movement basically of the rural rich which is in contradiction to the interests of the majority of rural poor families. . . . Even middle peasants, who buy on the market as much as they sell, have little to gain." For similar arguments see Bardhan (1984) and Hardgrave (1984, 47–48).

36. Many of the ideas presented in this book were published earlier in Hindi. See Joshi (1983).

37. For details see the report in *India Today,* 15 April 1987, p. 22–23.

38. See Pachauri (1988, 36–37) for details.

39. This point was repeatedly stressed to me during interviews I had with BKU activists and supporters. Also see Pachauri (1988, 36–37).

40. Under Tikait's orders the BKU activists mounted an effective nonpayment

campaign, persuading farmers not to pay electricity dues.

41. Their claims regarding electricity charges are misleading since in August 1986 power rates were raised from Rs 22.50 to Rs 30.

42. See Sahasrabudhey (1986; 1989).

43 Cited in *India Today,* 29 February 1988, p. 5.

44. The subsidies for irrigation consist of the difference between the revenue from the expenditures (including a nominal return on capital invested) on the publicly operated major, medium-sized, and minor irrigation systems. A substantial part of the subsidies is for the canal irrigation system.

45. Subbarao (1985, 544) points out "that these subsidies are in addition to the subsidies given to the fertilizer industry for the naphtha which goes into producing fertilizer. During 1981–82, naphtha was imported at the rate of Rs. 2,900 per ton but supplied to the fertilizer plants at the administered price of Rs. 1,723." Further, the electricity supplied to fertilizer plants is subsidized, and the freighting of both inputs by rail to fertilizer plants and the movement of fertilizer from plants to the farmers are also heavily subsidized.

46. See Byres (1988a); DeJanvry and Subbarao (1987); Mellor (1985); Mitra (1977); Nadkarni (1987); and Omvedt (1980).

47. Balraj Mehta (1978, 5) notes that "those, generally speaking, living in slums, the migrant laborer, the destitute or the people without any settled living or regular incomes in the cities and the landless and the underemployed in the rural areas . . . have no access to the benefits of subsidized production and distribution by public agencies. Those with small incomes or purchasing power are, in any case, in no position to command the consumption of goods and services which have price tags on them."

48. The Janata Dal was cobbled together from the political fragments of the defunct Janata Party, including its core socialist constituency headed by Chandra Shekhar, and the BLD, whose support is rooted in the lower-caste cultivating peasantry of the Hindi belt. The driving force behind the Janata Dal was the Jan Morcha, spearheaded by a group of ex-Congressmen led by V. P. Singh who defected from the party in the late 1980s.

7

Democracy, Neoliberalism, and Development with Equity: India in Comparative Perspective

In my lifetime, I want to see India grow at 8 to 8.5 percent per annum, year after year, and so eliminate the poverty that we have known for five thousand years. In my estimate, that requires a per capita income of US$1,500. If we grow at 8 percent per year, we can reach this target in 18 or 20 years. Look, I am not talking of $5,000 or $10,000. Just a per capita income of US$1,500, which will remove poverty from this country.

—Finance Minister Palaniappan Chidambaram,
address to Indian Parliament, 28 February 1997[1]

This concluding chapter examines the nature and changes in India's political economy in the 1990s, the era of economic liberalization. The chapter questions the conventional view that democratic regimes are ill suited to reconciling growth with distribution. Drawing on the experiences of post-liberalization India (1991–1998) and post-authoritarian Chile (1990–1997), it posits the question differently: what explains why Chile's new center-left coalition democracy (the Concertación) has been able to judiciously combine market-guided or neoliberal economic policies with reformist and redistributive programs, while India, the developing world's largest democracy, has failed to combine its ambitious "economic liberalization with a human face." Moving beyond worn-out arguments stressing the merits of authoritarian systems over democracies, the following comparative study illustrates that it is the *state's institutional capacities* that really matter. For countries engaged in economic restructuring, the message is unambiguous: building and reinvigorating the state's administrative and institutional capacities are critical.

The Background

By the latter part of the 1980s the combination of poor fiscal management, excessive protectionism, a restrictive investment regime, and adverse external shocks was beginning to have serious negative impact on the Indian economy. By early 1991 India was caught in an economic crisis of exceptional severity. Battered by rising oil prices as the result of the Persian Gulf crisis, the already floundering economy suffered a precipitous decline. As the external balance on current account worsened,[2] the central government's fiscal deficit rose to an unprecedented 9.5 percent of GDP, the inflation rate that had fluctuated within single digits throughout the 1970s and 1980s soared to an unprecedented 17 percent.[3] Moreover, the external debt mushroomed from $20.6 billion in 1980/81 to over $70 billion, and the debt-service ratio increased to a debilitating 32 percent of GDP. By the second quarter of 1991 the rapidly deteriorating fiscal situation resulted in the downgrading of India's credit rating in the international financial markets. This further eroded the confidence of external creditors, including the nonresident Indians with sizable deposits in Indian banks—triggering a panic run on the foreign exchange reserves that left India with a paltry $1.1 billion, an amount barely sufficient to pay for two weeks of imports (World Bank 1996a). In mid-June, on the verge of defaulting on its foreign debt, India was given an unexpected reprieve by external creditors and was in fact saved by emergency loans from the International Monetary Fund from the humiliation of default. In July 1991, keeping with the structural reform conditionality, and to maintain minimal external financial liquidity and debt-servicing obligations, the Reserve Bank of India temporarily transferred to the Bank of England a part of the nation's gold stock, something it had never done before despite serious macroeconomic difficulties in the 1950s and mid-1960s.

In the summer of 1991 a deep sense of pessimism pervaded the country. Many seasoned "India watchers" were already writing the country's obituary. If some feared the "Latin Americanization of India," others concluded that the subcontinent was fated to be a perennial economic basket case, a region so intractably mired in "a million mutinies" that it was doomed to be a "caged tiger"—while India's erstwhile Asian counterparts, particularly China and the high-performing East Asian newly industrializing countries (NICs), marched triumphantly into the new millennium.

Amid the "growing crisis of governability," fueled in part by the sharp economic downturn, the besieged and precariously positioned minority Congress-led government under Prime Minister P. V. Narasima Rao[4] finally embraced the global consensus on "neoliberalism," a modernist project that rejects Keynesian and statist interventionist assumptions and argues that economic prosperity can only be generated by subjecting the economy to the competitive logic and discipline of the marketplace.[5] In practice, this meant a dramatic break from past policies, ending decades of pervasive regulatory intervention and arbitrary bureaucratic meddling in markets. It also meant "opening" the "closed" Indian economy and integrating it with the global economic system, including improvement of the efficiency and competitiveness of the national economy through deregulation of financial and labor markets, price liberalization, trade and exchange rate reforms, reduction and unification of tariffs, privatization of public enterprises, tax reforms, transparency in fiscal or resource allocation, and the reliance on technocratic or "expert" decisionmaking in the economic arena.

In June 1991 the central government unveiled its ambitious market-friendly economic reform program, unpretentiously dubbed "economic liberalization" by its architects. At that time the program was widely viewed as a nonstarter because earlier attempts had been failures. Cynics argued that, as in the past, the vagaries of democratic competition would make it impossible for the would be reformers to resist the "demagogic populist temptation" of engaging in politically expedient but fiscally irresponsible behavior, thereby gutting the neoliberal project even before it started. Indeed, the prevailing scholarly wisdom held that "developmental authoritarian states" of the East Asian variety, not competitive and adversarial democratic regimes, were a *sine qua non* for the implementation and the sustainability of the often painful macroeconomic reforms associated with the neoliberal project.

However, less than a year after its implementation, India's economic liberalization program dumbfounded the critics, accomplishing what has been widely regarded as a convincing macroeconomic recovery. To the state elites liberalization quickly became a developmental panacea for growth-depressing statism, fiscal profligacy, and the problems of economic stagnation and poverty.[6] Indeed, the overall success of the reform program in irrevocably dismantling the ubiquitous command economic structure and abandoning some five decades of commitment to economic nationalism and statism has made "liberalization" an indelible part of contemporary India's developmental idiom.

Yet, as with earlier developmental strategies (such as import-substituting industrializing, land reforms, and the green revolution), the available evidence confirms that the primary beneficiaries of economic liberalization in India have been the upper two deciles of the population, with that all too familiar cruel ironic twist: the widening of income disparities and the accentuation of poverty and destitution.

Neoliberalism, Democracy, and Growth with Equity:
Conceptual Issues

Why is this the case with economic liberalization? Is it because orthodox market-oriented development strategies and the "deepening" global economic integration are intrinsically incompatible with reconciling growth with redistribution? If this is the case how do we account for East Asian

NICs that have combined market-guided, outward-oriented, export-led development strategies with rising incomes and substantial reductions in mass poverty? It is clear that market-guided economic growth need not be inconsistent with redistribution and poverty alleviation.

Moreover, the distributive failure cannot be attributed to sloppy implementation or to some sort of calculated emasculation of the neoliberal project by discontented actors. While eschewing Russian-style "shock therapy" in favor of "gradualism," India's reformers have remained fundamentally true to the neoliberal project, systematically (and at times dramatically) reorienting the country's macroeconomic structure to be commensurate with market principles. However, neoliberalism's painful austerity measures, such as the slashing of wages and reductions in social expenditures, public employment, and consumer subsidies (measures that many felt would result in a backlash from the "losers" and the disillusioned constituencies and eventually dilute, if not altogether derail, the neoliberal project), have been complemented by sustained economic growth generated by reforms, increases in government spending, and creation of targeted programs to ameliorate the social costs of market reforms. Hence, the market insecurities and the regressive distributive impact attendant on neoliberalism is inadequate in explaining the growing inequalities.

According to the large corpus of literature on the political economy of "regime types and economic development," neoliberalism and democratic rule are generally viewed as antinomies that represent fundamentally divergent, if not irreconcilable, projects. The widespread presumption is that authoritarian regimes are simply better able to implement the neoliberal programs than democratic ones.[7] The proponents of this view allege that an "elective affinity" exists between authoritarianism and the effective implementation of neoliberal macroeconomic policies because authoritarian regimes, given their "bureaucratic insulation"or autonomy, have greater capacity for efficacious intervention in the economy, including imposing unpopular structural adjustment and other austerity programs. In other words, unlike democracies, where pork barrel politics and partisan interests often prevail above the public good, and where mobilized political coalitions at critical junctures may have the capacity to exercise a veto over critical policy issues and "reverse the reforms," authoritarian regimes by limiting the avenues for popular opposition, not to mention a greater ability to use coercion, find it easier to "stay the course." However, cross-national evidence indicates that such assumptions cannot be generalized.[8] In the Indian case such claims are simply not tenable. India's far-reaching neoliberal project was articulated and implemented by not only a deeply fragmented and weak Congress-led government, it was continued by successor governments following the Congress defeat in 1996 that have been even weaker and more precarious coalition arrangements. Yet, even these governments went on with the liberalization program and in some instances have been responsible for "deepening" macroeconomic reforms. Given the uncertain political circumstances, India's sustained adherence to neoliberalism (and indeed its comprehensiveness and depth) is remarkable.

Similarly, there is the related claim that exclusionary authoritarian regimes have a greater capacity to combine economic growth with redistribution. However, claims that such regimes can ameliorate the social costs of reforms with targeted social safety nets and by delivering basic welfare entitlements to those hurt by neoliberal reforms because of the regimes' "relative autonomy" and ability to eclipse the pervasive rent-seeking proclivities of narrow interest groups and "distributional coalitions" is problematic. While casual empiricism may suggest that bouts of hard and soft authoritarianism are *sui generis* capable of removing the seemingly intractable impediments to policy reform and implementation and in promoting sustained economic growth with equity in the high-performing East Asian economies like South Korea and Taiwan, the reality is more complex. Rigorous empirical studies by Remmer (1990; 1995), Przeworski (1991; 1996), Haggard and Kaufman (1995), and Bates and Krueger (1993) have noted a "selection bias"[9] in such claims, and that the apparent correlation between authoritarianism, market reforms, and growth with equity may actually be spurious and an artifact of the high proportion of authoritarian regimes in the 1960s and 1970s, when such claims were first articulated. Moreover, critics have compellingly argued that regime type by itself has little to do with aggregate economic performance. Hence, authoritarian regimes have no clear advantage over democracies when it comes to economic performance measured in terms of per capita economic growth, nor do democracies appear to perform any better than their authoritarian counterparts in implementing reformist and distributive policies.

To the more radical critics, neoliberalism's excessive reliance on the discretionary proclivities of a handful of elitist and ideologically motivated "technopols"[10] (Western-educated, technocratic policy formulators and decisionmakers), dogmatic faith in the "magic of the market," and a minimalist government (which allows the state to conveniently retreat from welfare and distributive functions) makes the neoliberal project antithetical to the distributive and collective interests of the popular sector. Therefore, although neoliberalism is seen as having a natural inclination toward autocratic and technocratic forms of rule (given its urgency to check and suppress the opposition of organized interests that would be hurt by its draconian programs),[11] it can thrive just as well under conditions that Guillermo O'Donnell (1994) has provocatively described as "delegative democracy,"—where governance is patrimonial and arbitrary and untempered by either legal constraints or representative institutions.[12] No doubt, such explanations may have salience in the context of Yeltsin's Russia or Fujimori's Peru, and albeit India's liberalization program has the imprint of archetypal technocrats, but India's democracy is not "delegative"—and the failures of its liberalization program cannot be adequately explained through such variables.

This study maintains that democracies are not inherently incapable of mitigating or modifying neoliberalism's strict market logic in order to ensure that the fruits of the marketplace are more equitably shared. So, what explains why economic liberalization in India has been accompanied by growing economic inequalities, social dislocation, and heightened poverty levels? To pose the question somewhat differently, what explains the Indian government's inability (if not failure) to effectively implement measures that would promote the reformers own often stated goal of "economic liberalization with a human face"? This study argues that it is not democratic governance per se; rather, the failure to ameliorate the social costs of reform in India lies in the weak and fragmented administrative and institutional capacities of the country's democratic regime. India's weakness is vividly obvious when compared with the "embedded autonomy"[13] or the remarkable institutional capacities and the developmental resolve of Chile's new democracy or the Concertación under Patricio Aylwin (1990–1994) and Eduardo Frei (1994–2000).[14] In fact, the empirical evidence from postauthoritarian Chile (1990–1997) not only compellingly illustrates that democracies can complement neoliberalism with meaningful reformist and distributive programs, but also that *politics matter.* For India and a host of new and transitional democracies the message is clear: building and reinvigorating the state's administrative and institutional capacities are fundamental to resolving the economic challenges.

The following section examines the nature, impact, and implications of India's economic liberalization program. The aim is to show that while the Indian state has been successful in implementing major structural reforms and generating respectable economic growth rates, this should not obscure the fact that it has failed miserably to reconcile growth with redistribution. The next section outlines the core content of Chile's broadbased democratic coalition—the Concertación developmental and reformist programs, and the reasons behind their successful implementation. The concluding section compares the Chilean and Indian experiences to draw some broad conceptual and comparative insights on the complex relationship between neoliberalism and democratic governance.

India's Reforms: From State to Market

Immediately after taking office in mid-1991, the Rao administration implemented a package of structural reform measures designed to stabilize the economy and lay the bases for sustained economic growth. Guided by neoclassical assumptions of "market superiority," the liberalization program aimed to limit government intervention in domestic markets, trim the bloated and profligate public sector, end protectionism and the restrictive investment regimes, and reform the cumbersome and discretionary administrative-bureaucratic regulations that stifled trade and investment. Audaciously discarding more moderate alternatives, the "austerity budget" made deep cuts to government expenditures through reductions in subsidies on exports and on non-plan expenditures such as defense spending. The rupee was devalued by 22 percent against the U.S. dollar; new monetary policies were begun to allow production, prices, interest rates, and wages to find their "natural equilibrium" through the interaction of supply and demand; and the government outlined a strict timetable to deregulate the financial markets and phase out all forms of quasi-autarkic regulations and bureaucratic controls. In fact, so far-reaching was the government's reform package that the World Bank (which just weeks earlier had been highly critical of the Indian government's economic policies) gave its "seal of approval," making available substantial amounts of quick-disbursing assistance, including a $500 million structural adjustment loan. The International Monetary Fund (IMF) Executive Board followed soon by approving an additional special drawing rights $1.7 billion for India (World Bank 1996a).

Over the past seven years the Indian economy has undergone significant changes. The New Industrial Policy (NIP) in a broad sweep has effectively dismantled the ubiquitous industrial-licensing regime, thereby abolishing compulsory licensing of private-sector industries and government control over businesses' investment and production decisions, including ownership, location, local content, technology fees, and royalties. In addition, with the exception of a small list of "strategic industries" (declared by Parliament to be in the national interest),[15] all sectors previously reserved for public enterprises are now open to private investment. For example, civil aviation, mining, power, and energy, for long public-sector monopolies, are now open to private domestic and foreign investors. In 1995, with the liberalization of telecommunications and pharmaceuticals, followed by "further liberalization" of the coal industry, the only investment "restrictions" remaining are for railways—albeit foreign direct investment is encouraged in infrastructural development.

To attract foreign investment in "high-priority industries" that require advanced technological inputs, the NIP has rationalized foreign direct investments by providing "automatic approval" registration with the Reserve Bank of India of all foreign investments up to 51 percent of equity, and pragmatic provisions for expeditious clearances for investors seeking equity share exceeding 51 percent are already in place. Today, foreign investors incorporated in India are treated on par with domestic investors. They can invest up to 100 percent equity in any sector of the high-priority industries and remit dividends abroad without any restrictions, while flexible regulations are in place to allow the entry of foreign institutional investment to the stock markets, gilt-edged government securities, India country funds, and a wide range of nonbanking financial services. Moreover, as a member of the World Trade Organization (WTO) and the Multilateral Investment Guarantee Agency, India has demonstrated its commitment to free trade by removing quantitative restrictions on 542 items in a first installment as a WTO member.[16] No doubt, membership in such multilateral trade organizations ensures for foreign investors the country's commitment to fair treatment, especially legal security to monetary transactions and safeguards to investments, including financial and intellectual property rights.

As noted earlier, in India the role of public enterprises in the economy has been important since independence. The share of the public sector in gross value added rose from about 10 percent of GDP in 1960/61 to over 26 percent during the 1980s. The share of gross investment in the public sector rose from 40 percent in 1970–1975 to 46 percent in 1989–1990, and its share in the total capital stock rose from 37 percent to 45 percent during the same period. The public sector accounted for seven million jobs in 1961 and 19 million in 1989/90. However, India's public enterprises have suffered from low capacity utilization, low rates of return on capital, and low contribution to national savings.[17] Not surprisingly, complementing the NIP is an aggressive program to tame the "white elephants"—some 225 inefficient and failing public-sector enterprises. Unlike the former Soviet Union, the Indian government has been pursuing a more judicious multipronged gradualist strategy that includes (1) privatization of state-owned enterprises (SOEs) or the liquidation of chronically "sick" or unviable enterprises, (2) reduction of budgetary support (e.g., subsidies, tax breaks) and monopoly privileges to all public-sector enterprises, (3) partial divestiture to significant dilute SOE equities through market sales, (4) subjection of the lethargic public-sector firms to market discipline and accountability by creating a competitive environment for private and public enterprises, and (5) establishment of the National Renewal Fund (financed in part by the World Bank), to prevent the most vulnerable workers in SOEs from bearing a disproportionate share of the necessary adjustment costs (World Bank 1996a).

Equally significant, the government has gradually but systematically liberalized the trade and exchange regime. The rupee was made fully convertible in March 1993 on trade accounts, and in August 1994 the rupee was made fully convertible for current account transactions, and India achieved Article VIII status with the IMF. The rupee at a stable 31 to the U.S. dollar has made Indian exports more competitive and imports costlier. On trade liberalization, with the exception of a short list of "final consumer goods," licensing requirements for all other imports have been eliminated, and it is expected that even this list will be reduced progressively. Moreover, the government has already abolished all export subsidies but granted to exporters tradable entitlements (known as EXIM-scrips) for importing any restricted items needed to keep up export performance, including such consumer goods as computer systems, television tubes, commercial refrigeration equipment, batteries, and electrically operated vehicles. The government has also reached agreements on market access in textiles with the European Union and the United States, which consume about two-thirds of India's textile exports. The agreements *inter alia* involve the phased liberalization of India's tariffs on certain items and a phased opening of India's market for imported textile products. Indian policymakers see this as a welcome step toward eliminating nontariff barriers to consumer goods imports. To create a more favorable environment for export-oriented production the government has already slashed customs duties and greatly streamlined customs procedures, abolishing what it views as unnecessary regulations, to expedite export shipments.

Similarly, a more liberal trade policy characterized by rationalized tariff levels and reduced quantitative restrictions has been adopted. In the area of trade reform the maximum import tariff has been reduced from 85 to 65 percent at the beginning of 1994 to about 40 percent in 1996—it had been over 350 percent in June 1991. The 1995 budget introduced further tariff reforms that reduced the average tariff to about 27 percent, and under the 1996/97 budget imports of capital goods, either new or used, are permitted a concessional flat customs duty of 10 percent under the Export Promotion Capital Goods Scheme. The rates are lower for equipment imported for projects in specific sectors like infrastructure and agriculture and allied sectors.[18] The highest import duty has been cut from 65 to 50 percent, with wide-ranging reductions of tariffs on inputs and outputs in key sectors such as electronics, textiles, chemicals, and metal-based industries. Import duties on general machinery, machine tools, and instruments have been unified at 25 percent (World Bank 1996a). Fully aware that these rates are still high compared with international standards, the finance ministry, in keeping with the recommendations of the 1992 Chelliah Committee Report on Tax Reforms, has announced the government's commitment to free trade and promised reduction in tariffs and customs duties to levels comparable to the countries of the Association of Southeast Asian Nations (ASEAN) by fiscal 1997/98.

Recognizing that an efficient banking system and well-functioning capital markets are essential for the success of liberalization, the government has introduced far-reaching financial sector reforms. India's heavily regulated banking system, dominated by several large public-sector banks that control some 85 to 90 percent of all deposits, are currently undergoing a phased process of modernization—from rationalization of interest rate structure; through introduction of internationally accepted norms for bank asset classification and standardized formats of financial reporting to increase transparency; to deregulation and increased competition with the entry of new foreign and private banks into the market place. For example, to further improve competition the government has since 1994 licensed ten new banks, including three foreign institutions, and introduced measures that allow reputable Indian corporations to tap Euromarkets.

Similarly, major changes are being made to the capital markets with an array of reforms encompassing primary and secondary markets for equity and debt, foreign institutional investment, and market transparency, including disclosure norms. The Securities and Exchange Board of India (SEBI), established as a statutory body in February 1992 to modernize the capital and securities markets, has gradually introduced the basic framework of regulations, including monitoring and surveillance mechanisms within which a expanding stock market should operate. For example, in the aftermath of the Mumbai stock market scam of the early 1990s, new laws defining permissible and impermissible activities and allowing for on-site monitoring and off-site surveillance will help prevent fraud and mismanagement, especially insider trading and stock price manipulations.[19] A new National Stock Exchange was inaugurated formally in July 1994 in line with international standards; with computerized screen-based trading it will make India's currently cumbersome money markets operate more effectively.

Since 1991 India's tax regime has been gradually "reformed," that is, made more "fair" and transparent, with a more predictable regulatory framework. The aim has been to transform India's tax system from one with high (and highly differentiated) tax rates falling on a narrow base into one with tax rates at moderate levels falling on a broad base.[20] While this goal has yet to be achieved, tax reforms have nevertheless reduced customs and excise duties and significantly lowered corporate and capital gains taxes. For example, investing companies today enjoy full exemption for the first five years, and concessional taxation for an additional five, for locating industries in backward areas and a deduction of 100 percent on export profits from the gross total income. Moreover, export profits are exempt from income tax, as are export commissions, and expenses incurred for business purposes are generally deductible, including depreciation on fixed assets and interest paid on borrowing. In 1995 a major reform of excises was recommended to make the system more closely resemble a value-added tax, and the government has extended the coverage of MODVAT (a modified value-added tax) to include manufacturing and some service sectors thus far excluded. Although these reforms still lag behind international standards, they have nevertheless helped to simplify and modernize India's taxation system and make the country's industrial/business houses more globally competitive. For example, the 1997/98 budget (dubbed the "dream budget" by India's corporate leaders) slashed the top personal income tax rate to 30 percent (from 40 percent), and on foreign firms to 48 percent (from 55 percent); lowered to 20 percent (from 30 percent) the tax rate on royalty and technical services fees payable to foreign companies; exempted export profits from the minimum alternate tax (MAT);[21] and converted payment of MAT into a tax credit carried forward for five assessment years and abolished tax on dividends.

Finally, the reforms also proposed guidelines to "significantly reduce" government intervention in these areas of the agricultural sector:

- Product markets and domestic and external trade, which enables the Food Corporation of India to regulate and procure (at the official price) wheat, rice, sugar, cotton, and edible oils, as well as purchase via "compulsory acquisition" such commodities as sugar, molasses, and millet rice below market prices
- Input markets, which allows inputs such as machinery, seeds, electricity, and irrigation water to be produced and distributed by public-sector agencies and government-owned banks to farmers at highly subsidized rates
- Government control over the import, pricing, and distribution of fertilizers (again at subsidized rates), which has resulted in the proliferation of "agricultural subsidies" equal to $4.7 billion in 1990/91, or 1.5 percent of GDP[22]

This extensive state intervention has long being viewed as an unnecessary drag on agricultural growth and a heavy burden on government budgets.

Despite the ambitious reform guidelines, the agricultural sector, which accounts for two-thirds of the employed population and about 30 percent of GDP, has witnessed only limited (if not selective) liberalization. As discussed in the previous chapters, this is in large part due to the political and economic clout and organized opposition by the rich farmers' lobby to cuts in subsidies—but also to the realization that a "shock therapy"in the countryside may adversely affect agricultural production. Nevertheless, the central government has reduced (slightly in some cases) input subsidies on fertilizers, irrigation, and electricity.[23] The gradual removal of trade restrictions on agricultural commodities also has made domestic prices more in tune with world prices. In 1993 the union government decontrolled the price of phosphatic and potassic fertilizers and abolished the retention pricing system for phosphatic fertilizer producers.[24] Moreover, the inflows of private foreign and domestic capital investment in high-technology agriculture (biotechnology) and allied activities such as horticulture, floriculture, and agro-processing have forced inefficient high-cost government and rich-farmer cooperatives (subsidized by the state) and trading and processing "development boards" to become more competitive, if not go out of business. It has also increased the volume of agricultural exports.[25]

Macroeconomic Reforms and Economic Growth

India's postliberalization economic growth rates have not been as spectacular as those of China, the pre–1997 crisis East Asian NICs, or the NICs of
ASEAN, but the rates have been respectable, enabling the country to
achieve sustained economic growth and macroeconomic stability. During
the first five years of reform the Indian economy broke through the stagnant "Hindu rate of growth" syndrome, expanding by an average of 6 percent during the 1991–1996 period. Also, growth of the real GDP at factor
cost, which had fallen to 0.8 percent in 1991/92, recovered within a year
to reach 5.1 percent in 1992/93, 5.0 percent in 1993/94, 6.3 percent in
1994/95, and 6.5 percent in 1995/96.[26] In fact, it can be persuasively argued that the Indian economy was undergoing reforms on more stable
foundations than some countries of East Asia and ASEAN.[27]

In 1995 India was designated by the Clinton administration as one of
the world's ten emerging markets, a position it occupies with only three
other Asian nations—China, Indonesia, and South Korea.[28] Equally impressive, the rate of growth of the GDP has risen from 1.2 percent in
1991/92 to around 6.5 percent in 1996/97, and the projected growth of 7.0
percent in fiscal 1997/98 is not unrealistic. Second, the budget deficit has
been reduced to a manageable 5 percent of GDP. Third, inflation is down
to a modest 7 percent, and interest rates (while still high) have declined
from 22 to 17 percent, with further reductions forecast for fiscal 1997/98.
Fourth, foreign exchange reserves were up to a healthy $22 billion in mid-
1996 (up from $1 billion in July 1991), and the vigorous growth in ex-
ports, reaching $26.2 billion in 1994/95 (a 21 percent growth), has greatly
reduced vulnerability to external shocks. Similarly, capital flows have undergone significant compositional changes after 1990/91, with the non-
debt-creating inflows of foreign investment (direct and portfolio) emerging
as the dominant components. Total foreign investment has surged from a
measly $30 million in 1990, to around $4.3 billion in 1995/96, and then
to around $6.7 billion in fiscal 1996/97.[29]

Blue-chip corporations, including General Electric, American Express,
Black and Decker, Siemens, Proctor and Gamble, Mercedes-Benz, General
Motors, Ford, Kellog's, Pepsico, Nestlé, Honda, and Suzuki, are either establishing or expanding their Indian operations by increasing capital investments and acquiring majority stakes in their Indian joint ventures. For
example, Coca-Cola, which was ignominiously forced out in 1977 by Indira Gandhi, has bought its entry back into the lucrative Indian market by
taking over the three most popular local soft-drink brands. The pace of
change has been so dizzying in some areas that the once sleepy town of
Bangalore has been transformed into a noisy high-technology mecca, a
veritable "Indian Silicon Valley" as heavyweights like IBM, AT&T, Micro-
soft, Intel, Sun Microsystems, Texas Instruments, Digital Corporation,

Motorola, Hewlett Packard, Philips, and Polaroid have set up shop to cash in on India's abundant engineering talent. In addition, the sustained diversification and expansion of financial services, especially banking and stock market portfolios, clearly indicate that both domestic and foreign investors are no longer jittery about India. Indian businesses and commercial interests, despite a securities scam in the Bombay Stock Exchange in 1992, have been able to raise some $6 billion from new issues in the Indian capital markets compared with only $2 billion in 1991. In addition, India's stock market, with over 7,000 listed companies, has become one of the most active in Asia in terms of daily trading volume. Foreign financial investors representing banks, brokerage houses, trust and insurance companies, and pension and mutual funds have poured over $1 billion into Indian stock markets—and this may be just the tip of the iceberg as more and more Wall Street firms flock to the bustling and "hot" Indian market. For example, J.P. Morgan has already taken a 40 percent stake in one of India's largest investment banks, ICICI Securities, and Merrill Lynch, the largest securities house in the United States, has acquired shares in DSP Financial Consultants Ltd., another leading Indian investment bank. Perhaps the most often cited case is that of the investment firm of Morgan Stanley. In early 1994 Morgan Stanley launched its first Indian mutual fund, hoping for $100 million; it pulled in $300 million within three days. Similarly, another financial giant, GE Capital, has just incorporated an Indian company with capital assets of $100 million, and other such mergers and acquisitions are in the works (World Bank 1996a).

Neoliberal Reforms:
Growth, Redistribution, and "Safety Nets"

Even though the economic liberalization measures have produced unprecedented rates of sustained aggregate economic growth, reconciling growth with equity has remained as elusive as ever. A 1994/95 *National Sample Survey* (*NSS*) report of Indian market demographics in urban and rural areas indicates that the major beneficiaries of economic reforms have been the "upper two deciles" of the populace (i.e., the consuming middle and upper classes), which constitute some 28 million households, or about 150 million persons. This group has seen a rapid increase in disposable incomes as reflected in the booming sales of such consumer and luxury items as kitchen appliances, cellular phones, televisions, VCRs, computers, and both domestically assembled and imported automobiles. The *NSS* also notes some trickle-down to members of the country's low-income households—who are entering the market to buy some inexpensive consumer durables, especially bicycles and transistor radios, as well as low-priced consumables like detergents, toothpaste, soap, cooking oil, and tea.

However, overall the *NSS* data show "that in urban and rural areas there has been a marked deterioration in the consumption shares of individuals in the lowest three and the middle four deciles."[30]

The more methodologically sound and rigorous macroeconomic surveys indicate similar trends: namely that many people below the poverty line (an increase from 305.87 million in 1987/88 to 314.66 million in 1993/94) have been adversely affected by economic liberalization.[31] A comprehensive all-India study by the highly respected National Council for Applied Economic Research[32] and other reputable think tanks[33] documents the many negative impacts of economic restructuring on the majority poor households. Specifically, the reduction in government expenditure necessitated by the objective of containing the fiscal deficit has meant a decline in central government budget amounts earmarked for "human resource development" from 17.2 percent between 1984/85 and 1989/90 to 15.2 percent between 1989/90 and 1993/94. A simultaneous decline in state government budgets from 16.2 percent to 12.4 percent during the same period has "gravely hurt the poor." For example, the sharp reductions in central government outlay on medical care and public health, which has resulted in sharp cuts in expenditure in preventive disease control programs (against, for instance, malaria, tuberculosis, and leprosy), have hurt the poor, who rely most on the public health care programs (Gupta 1996, 141–143).

Moreover, (1) the sharp fiscal devaluation and partial rupee convertibility (wherein foodgrain exports and imports are priced at market rates) have made food prices higher in rupee terms; (2) the high rate of inflation, particularly in staple foodgrain prices, has resulted in higher procurement prices of foodgrains; (3) inflationary pressure has lowered real wages because nominal agricultural wages are slow to adjust to inflation; and (4) the output contraction in both farm and nonfarm sectors has pushed many more households into poverty. According to one study, based on the Planning Commission's nutritional norm of 2,400 calories per person per day in rural areas, "an extra 9.4 million rural households fell below the poverty line in 1992" (Datt and Ravallion 1996, 5). Indeed, one year after the implementation of the NIP, the prices of essential food commodities such as staple grains increased by 97 percent and the prices of coarse cereals by over 50 percent.[34] Also, between 1991 and 1994 the issue price of the common variety of rice increased by 85.0 percent and the price of wheat by 71.8 percent, while the wholesale price index increased 44.4 percent.[35] The poor, who are the most vulnerable to changes in relative prices, have witnessed sharp deteriorations in their already marginal standards of living, with their consumption of foodgrains "declining over the last three years [1991–1994] from 510.0g to 465.6g per capita per day" (Nayyar 1996, 174). Moreover, deep cuts in such social spending as education and health care, steep increases in public transport fares, and hikes in food prices have negatively affected the poor, who were before the reform period spending as much as 75 percent of their income on essential foodgrains. Cognizant of the fact that economic restructuring and the associated austerity measures (largely the result of cuts in budgetary subsidies) have meant "adjustment with pain for the weaker sections of society,"[36] the Indian government, with financial assistance provided under the World Bank's Structural Adjustment Loans (SAL) and the IMF's Structural Adjustment Facility (SAF), has established a number of "safety nets" to introduce "reforms with a human face." The purpose of these safety nets is mitigate the short-term "social and human" costs of economic adjustment and stabilization.[37] Several new programs, including some expanding on such earlier "pro-poor" and "poverty alleviation" programs as the Jawahar Rozgar Yojana, the Indira Awas Yojana, the Integrated Rural Development Program, and the Training of Rural Youth for Self-Employment, as well as "newer" (post-1991 period) "employment generation" programs (usually in labor-intensive public works), have also been adopted. Also, programs aimed at providing concessional loan schemes for on- and off-farm employment and subsidized food supplies through the Public Distribution System (PDS) have been revamped for "better targeting." In 1992 the central and state governments, on the basis of 80:20 financing, introduced the National Renewal Fund (NRF) to provide assistance to workers (especially in SOEs) made redundant as the result of industrial adjustment, including plant closure. In 1993 a "new" panchayati raj was introduced by the central government to decentralize to the grassroots level the planning and implementation of rural developmental and poverty alleviation programs.

Evidence indicates that the government has failed to implement these programs effectively. For example, the much touted NRF was expected to finance the retraining and redeployment of redundant workers via its "three windows": the National Renewal Grant Fund, which is designed to compensate workers through voluntary retirement schemes; the Employment Generation Fund, set up to provide job retraining (especially technological upgrading); and a short-term insurance scheme. However, the government's own economic survey points out the limited impact of these programs, in part because of the "jobless growth" under liberalization.[38] Similarly, the Indira Awas Yojana launched to build houses for the poor in rural areas has yet to materialize. The so-called housing project to be built on freehold land at normal rates of interest (subject to the borrower's putting in one-third of the value of the house) is obviously beyond the reach of the vast majority of rural households. The real beneficiaries of the project will be the rural rich.

The extensive PDS program, working alongside a free market, is designed to ensure food security to millions of needy consumers across the country by subsidizing rations of rice, wheat, sugar, and edible oil, as well as kerosene, soft coke, and standard cloth, through the approximately

350,000 retail outlets (the "fair price shops") spread across the country. Out of the total national buffer foodgrain stocks of 30.3 million tons (1995 figures), the PDS currently distributes some 20 percent of rice and wheat in the country, 23 percent of net availability of edible oil, and 43 percent of the total sugar consumed. However, a mounting body of evidence indicates that the much touted safety nets, such as the PDS, have failed to provide food security to the poor.[39] There are several reasons for this. The imperative to contain and reduce "food subsidies" simultaneously has greatly increased the issue prices of rice and wheat supplied under the PDS. In fact, between 1991 and 1996 the price of rice has increased by over 100 percent and wheat by 70 percent—hence "there is very little differential between market and PDS prices, both for wheat and rice" (Nayyar 1996, 175). Furthermore, inflationary pressures have not only reduced the purchasing power of the bottom 50 percent of the population, but data show that only 2 percent of the poor population in rural Bihar, Uttar Pradesh, Orissa, and Punjab are able to obtain supplies.[40] In the urban areas of eight states, less than 10 percent of the people are able to buy from the shops despite the fact that about 80 percent of these government's "fair price shops" are located in urban areas—but about the same percentage of India's poor live in rural areas. In other words, the PDS has not segmented the market into "low-" and "high-income" consumers, but instead rural and urban consumers. Hence, the rural poor, who are by far the largest group of poor people, have generally less access to the PDS than do the urban poor. Finally, given the widespread leakages of commodities (meant for distribution through the PDS) to those who are not poor[41] and into the more lucrative free market, it is not surprising that over 88 percent of those surveyed in the urban centers of eight states reported that they almost never receive the supplies when they need it most.[42]

Since the implementation of major antipoverty programs, such as the Jawahar Rozgar Yojana, is assigned almost exclusively to local or village panchayats (or gram panchayats), under the overall supervision of an official agency such as the District Rural Development Agency, the central government decided to finally act upon the recommendations of the 1977 Asoka Mehta Committee[43] to revitalize and "democratize" the panchayats by "empowering" the poor. Specifically, it was hoped that giving a "voice" to the poor would induce them to get involved in local self-governing institutions and in the common management of local public goods. As noted earlier, in September 1991 the Congress government introduced a new constitutional amendment (the 72d Amendment) bill, which was passed with a near unanimity in both the Lok Sahba and the Rajya Sabha in December 1992. In the following four months the bill was ratified by seventeen state governments, and after the president gave his assent to the bill, the 73d Constitutional Act came into effect on 24 April 1993. "In its comprehensiveness, the 73rd (amendment) Act is a landmark" (Gaiha 1996,

28). It provides a uniform three-tiered structure of the panchayats, with clear demarcation of areas of responsibility at different levels and mandatory elections every five years at the district, block, and village level.[44] It guarantees the scheduled castes and scheduled tribes ("the poorest of the poor") and women, via proportional representation and quotas, membership and participation in decisionmaking and the right to hold office at all levels of the panchayats. Moreover, the panchayats at all levels are to be subject to regular financial audits and meet the transparency and accountability requirements to both their community and official agencies. The governments, on their part, are required to provide adequate financial and administrative support.

However, as Raghav Gaiha (1996, 30) notes, "the claim, however, that the 73rd (amendment) Act signifies 'power to the people' is exaggerated, if not largely mistaken." Evidence indicates that the panchayats have failed to enhance the "participation or empowerment of the rural poor." The inadequacy of funds to meet the expanded responsibilities of the panchayats, bureaucratic delays, and corruption, coupled with the collusion among rural elites, bureaucrats, politicians, and panchayat members, have made a mockery of this program.

Chile's New Democracy: Reconciling Growth with Equity[45]

Chile is seen to be the quintessential model of neoliberal restructuring in Latin America in the late twentieth century. After the overthrow of the socialist regime of Salvador Allende in 1973, Chile's military government under Augusto Pinochet (1973–1990) implemented an orthodox neoclassical economic restructuring program that replaced state intervention with market incentives and opened Chile to the global economy—rapidly transforming it from a highly protected industrializing economy to a open, free-market economy based largely on agro-extractive exports. At the heart of the program was a draconian economic stabilization strategy aptly termed "shock therapy." This included the rapid and thorough liberalization of capital markets and prices and the elimination of quantitative restrictions on trade. Tariffs were cut to a uniform 10 percent, and a multiple exchange rate system was consolidated. The government also instituted a "crash privatization" program under which more than 300 firms with a total book value of about $1 billion were returned to private ownership by the end of 1974 (Bosworth et al. 1994, 5). Moreover, the budget deficit was cut sharply from 25 percent of GDP in 1973 to 1 percent by 1975, and labor-market relations were restructured through the harsh suppression of labor unions. The unions were first severely weakened by executive decree and then allowed to operate under a repressive new labor law (the infamous *plan laboral*) that precluded nationwide and sectoral negotiation over wages, collective bargaining, and other issues regarding working conditions. In fact, between 1973 and 1976 real wages were cut in half, wage indexation was abolished, and public spending in preventive health care, primary education, and public housing was drastically slashed.[46] And unemployment soared to an average of 17.6 percent of the workforce, and the postliberalization price hyperinflation averaged 350 percent (Sheahan 1997, 12).

While Chile's shock therapy stabilized the economy and produced sustained macroeconomic growth (at least until 1982), it also exacted a tremendous toll from Chilean workers, peasants, and sections of the middle class, worsening poverty and inequality.[47] Sheahan (1997, 12–13) notes that "Chilean households living in poverty almost doubled over the 1970s . . . with the proportion of Chilean households living in poverty increasing to 32 percent by 1980." These inequities were further compounded in 1982 when Chile faced a severe economic crisis that saw the GDP fall by 14.1 percent. However, by 1986 the economy began a process of sustained recovery under a "much more flexible approach to the construction of a liberal economy, one that Chileans dubbed *pragmatic neoliberalism*" (Silva 1997, 165). The new policy orientation[48] proved successful in terms of generating the "Chilean miracle"—an average annual growth rate of 7.4 percent during the period 1986–1990, with a reducion in external deficits. However, while the growth generated by sustained increases in exports helped to reduce unemployment (albeit most jobs created paid the basic minimum wage), "the miracle" failed to reduce socioeconomic inequalities and poverty. For example, from 1970 to 1988, total social expenditure per capita fell 8.8 percent, and health expenditures alone fell by nearly 30 percent (Scully 1996, 401). By 1987 as many as 2.1 million workers (more than half of Chile's labor force) lacked access to social security and other basic benefits (Graham 1994, 26). Not surprisingly, the percentage of Chilean households below the poverty line had jumped to 44.7 percent by 1987, and 16.8 percent were indigent *pobladores*—or shantytown dwellers (Weyland 1997; Collins and Lear 1995). On the other hand, the share of national income going to the highest 20 percent of households increased from 55 percent (in the Allende period, 1971–1973) to 62 percent under Pinochet, while the share for the lowest 40 percent of households decreased from 7.5 to 6.6 percent over the same period—or an average of 1.5 percentage decline compared with the 1960–1973 period (Marcel and Solimano 1994, 218–220). In sum, the seventeen years of orthodox neoliberalism under the autocratic Pinochet regime (which combined severe fiscal restraint with an iron-fisted economic austerity), even as the policies evoked images of probity, efficiency, and technocratic modernization, failed gravely in the task of reconciling economic growth with redistribution. In fact, the authoritarian military regime exacerbated socioeconomic inequalities to such an extent that by the end of the military regime, Chile had become a dual society, wherein a large percentage of the population was left without any tangible benefits of the "miracle."

The center-left democratic opposition bloc made up of seventeen parties, the Concertación de Partidos por la Democracia (the Concert of Parties for Democracy)[49] headed by Patricio Aylwin of the Partido Democratico Cristiano (PDC) defeated the Pinochet regime (first in the referendum of 1988 and again in the elections of 1989) and "normalized Chilean politics," forming the democratic coalition government in March 1990. Aylwin assumed office with the stated intention of being "president of all Chileans" and fostering a "culture of cooperation" after nearly three decades of political polarization that had turned Chile into a "nation of enemies." The members of the Aylwin administration recognized that mitigating the entrenched problem of inequality and poverty and advancing the long repressed needs of the popular sector were top priorities, as reflected in its campaign slogans *"crecimiento con equidad"* (growth with equity) and *"incorporar el mundo de trabajo"* (including the workers). Indeed, they were critical for the consolidation of Chilean democracy as well as strengthening the Concertación's base of support.

Keeping the promise it had made to its broad constituents, Chile's new democratic government, immediately following its inauguration, embarked on an ambitious plan to resolve the accumulated "social deficit" or the pressing socioeconomic needs the Pinochet regime had left unfulfilled. This was in spite of the immediate need for contractionary policies to cool an overheated economy. Contrary to conventional wisdom, the new democratic administrations of Aylwin and his successor, Eduardo Frei, in six short years (1990–1996) enacted and implemented a wide range of "equity-enhancing reforms" without breaking with the neoliberal economic model instituted by their predecessor.[50] As the following section illustrates, Chile's new democratic regimes have made up for much of the ground lost during authoritarian rule.

Despite dire warnings from the conservative Renovación Nacional Party (RN) and the military-bureaucratic establishment (including Pinochet) that tax increases would undermine investment and growth, and that the robust economic growth of 7 percent would cover social spending, the democratic government went ahead with its tax plans. Claiming that high growth rates by themselves would not cover the badly needed increases in social spending, the government introduced a progressive direct taxation (which was complemented by the "value-added tax"), which placed a higher personal income tax burden on the upper middle class, eliminated tax privileges and/or loopholes for the rich, and raised corporate profit tax from 10 to 15 percent. Carol Graham (1994, 41) notes that this move had immediate positive distributional effects:

During the Pinochet period the income share of the bottom 40 percent declined, on average, by 1.5 percentage points in relation to the 1960–73 period, a drop of nearly 14 percent in the income share of that group. During its first two years the Alywin government has reversed that trend: the share of the bottom 40 percent has increased by 1 percentage point in comparison with the Pinochet period.

This is, of course, in sharp contrast to India's postliberalization tax reforms, which only assesses 12 million people and, as noted earlier, is largely geared toward providing incentives to the business and corporate sector. On the other hand, the Aylwin government's tax reforms increased tax revenues to the state coffers by about 15 percent (or $600 million), and enabled it to increase fiscal spending on social and welfare programs to approximately 11.7 percent of the GDP by 1993 (Herrera and Graham 1994, 276–277). The primary beneficiaries or "the two poorest quintiles [40 percent of the population] received 65 percent of the new social expenditure benefits in 1990" (Graham 1994, 41). Specifically, the government raised family allowances for the poor by 50 percent and introduced subsidies to support nutrition supplements for the lowest income households through targeted school feeding and mother-and-child nutrition programs. In addition, under the government's core poverty alleviation program, FOSIS (Social Investment and Solidarity Fund), an array of programs designed to build the human capital of the poor, including a drive to improve the quality of public education and vocational training for unemployed youth and funds to start microenterprises, have been introduced. The public health system, long neglected by the Pinochet regime, saw its budget increased by 70 percent in real terms between 1990 and 1994. This has translated into greater accessibility of curative health care by the poor through the expansion of preventive health care facilities in the rural and poor urban districts (Herrera and Graham 1994, 278–279).

As the bulwark of protest during the long years of authoritarian rule, Chile's labor movement expected and demanded much more power and economic benefits than the democratic regime could deliver—at least in the immediate term. Nevertheless, the new labor laws passed by the Aylwin administration in 1991 have provided some important gains to labor— for example, the elimination of the clause that allowed arbitrary dismissal of workers; reestablishment of the right to strike and an end to time limits on strikes; the creation of an indemnification system for all levels of workers; and the right to organize and conduct collective bargaining. Labor has also benefited from legislation enhancing pension funds, longer periods of coverage for severance payments, unemployment and health insurance plans, and increases in minimum wage—by 15 percent above the consumer price index in 1990 and 6 percent in 1991. The percentage of the total work force affiliated with unions reached 16 percent or 700,000 workers by the end of 1991, an increase of 35 percent since the end of authoritarian rule (Herrera and Graham 1994, 274–275). These equity-enhancing and safety net programs of Chile's new democratic governments (the Eduardo Frei administration further deepened these programs) helped to greatly reduce the number of Chileans living below the poverty line: from 5.2 million in 1990 to under 800,000 by 1995. That is, between 1989 and 1995, the incidence of poverty in Chile was reduced by nearly 50 percent, from 44.7 in 1989, to 33 percent in 1992, and to 24 percent in 1996, while absolute poverty declined by half, from 14 percent in 1989 to 7 percent in 1995 (Vergara 1996, 39). By any measure these are remarkable achievements for the new democracy.

Explaining Divergence in the Two Democracies

Based on the rule of law, commitment to free and fair elections, and institutional checks on the abuse of political power by allowing the exercise of popular sovereignty, democracies allow the disadvantaged to influence and benefit from public policy. If this is the case, why has the developing world's longest functioning democracy performed so poorly in balancing economic growth with redistribution and ameliorating the social costs of neoliberalism, while Chile's upstart Concertación has performed so well?

John Sheahan (1997) attributes the Aylwin and Frei administrations' success to their pragmatism and remarkable ability to foster a culture of cooperation and determination to construct a "competitive market-plus-social model" of development. That is, the organizational, administrative, and political skills of the new democratic leadership and its ability to forge coherent multiparty coalitions enabled the new democratic governments to efficaciously combine free-market economic neoliberalism with balanced and equitable development. Kurt Weyland (1997, 64–65) also stresses (if more explicitly) the political variables. He argues that compromise and consensual politics, "especially political learning and encompassing organization, have played a decisive role" in making reform and redistribution a reality in postauthoritarian Chile.

No doubt, the Concertación's ability to develop and strengthen itself by developing an underlying political culture of cooperation was its great asset. To its credit, the leadership of the new democratic opposition "learned" early that party fragmentation and political polarization, coupled with incessant political-ideological confrontation, not only undermined democratic consolidation but also invited authoritarian intervention. Therefore, the democratic leadership has made every effort to seek consensus on economic policy, build cohesive "encompassing organizations" based on broad party coalitions with clear rules regarding the nature of interparty competition (via party-mediated electoral participation), and institutionalize linkages with society. The Concertación political-organizational linkages and carefully crafted tacit agreements with labor, peasant, the middle-class constituencies, and business classes (including other organs of civil society) helped develop the "social capital" and provided the new democratic regime power against the military oligarchy. It also gave it critical breathing space and greater room to maneuver in its efforts to reconcile economic growth with redistribution and to consolidate the new democracy. Moreover, it is important to recognize that the Concertación remained convinced that democracy and development were compatible, and did not compromise in its view that growth with redistribution was both necessary and attainable. Hence, rather than submit to the orthodox neoclassical view that dismantling the state was necessary, the democratic leadership went on to restructure, if not redesign, the state—giving it a place not only in guiding macroeconomic development, but also in promoting human development via investment in human capital, infrastructural development, and management of social programs. Chile's new democracy unequivocally stresses that responsive and relatively well-institutionalized political parties with strong links to autonomous civil organizations are essential to efficaciously building the elusive "developmental state." Indeed, other such democratizing Latin American countries as Brazil, Peru, Venezuela, or Argentina, with weakly institutionalized or inchoate party systems (popularly elected presidents have come to enjoy broad executive, if not quasi-authoritarian, powers), have demonstrated only limited capacity to implement neoliberal reforms with a human face.[51]

In India today a rich and vibrant associational life exists alongside fragile state structures. This has produced "polarized pluralism" and has greatly hampered the state's ability to aggregate interests, link functional groups, and build stable units of political affiliation and representation. This disjunction was most vividly reflected in India's twelfth general elections held from February to March 1998. The new government, the seventh since 1989, was once again a precarious coalition of disparate parties that together command a parliamentary plurality, but not a majority. The elections failed to end the political uncertainty that has plagued India over the past decade. Rather, the extreme fragmentation of the electoral verdict, reflected in the record number of parties (41 to be precise) represented in the Lok Sabha, confirmed that the country faces an indefinite period of coalition governments. However, unlike the broad-based and consensual Concertación, political alliances or "coalition building" in India have been opportunistic, dictated by the political arithmetic and expediency of the moment rather than consensus on economic or political programs. Under these circumstances, cobbling together a parliamentary majority that can provide stable and effective governance and implement a set of coherent development policies has proven extremely difficult.

In India party fragmentation and political deinstitutionalization that began imperceptibly in the mid-1960s have taken their toll, resulting in a "crisis of governability." The absence of institutionalized forms of political mediation between the state and civil society has created structural impediments to intercaste and intercommunal cooperation, and produced personalistic forms of leadership ill suited to governing a heterogeneous social constituency. In fact, the state that once served as the mediator of conflicts has now become the source of conflict in India. The Indian state's failure to redistribute more equitably the fruits of neoliberal growth and ameliorate the social costs of structural adjustment is largely due to its declining political-administrative capabilities—the result of the erosion of the state's institutional presence in society. As the Indian case materials illustrate, under these unpropitious political circumstances even the many well-conceived and well-intentioned poverty alleviation and long-term development programs succumb to partisan and pork-barrel distributive politics, depending on the proclivities of dominant economic interests and influential government officials.

Comparative studies make clear that the ability of a government to implement effective safety nets for the vulnerable and poor during economic transition depends not only on its commitment to poverty alleviation, but also its capacity to forge broad coalitions of support and to rise above entrenched interests to translate reformist and redistributive policies into reality. If India's democracy is indeed going to deliver the goods (economically speaking), a careful nurturing of institutions more conducive to the promotion of developmental goals are an imperative. Given the current volatility and fragmentation in the Indian political system, however, where reliance on fluctuating plebiscitarian and personalist appeal for legitimation and aggregation have become the norm, growth with redistribution faces an uphill struggle.

Notes

1. For details see *Business India,* 19 May–1 June 1997, p. 64.
2. The current account is the balance between exports and imports of goods and services. A strong capital inflow normally creates or deepens current account deficits. It encourages imports and discourages exports by increasing the supply of foreign exchange and causing the currency to appreciate. India's current account deficit as a proportion of GDP stood at the unsustainable level of 3.2 percent in 1990/91.
3. In 1991 the wholesale price index increased by 13.3 percent, of which the food price increase was 20.1 percent and the foodgrain price increase was approximately 30 percent (World Bank 1996a).
4. The Rao administration was the first minority government in India, that is, one without an ensured majority in Parliament.

5. Neoliberalism refers to an economic model that advocates a minimalist state, market allocation of goods and services, and openness to international capital and markets. To neoliberals, economic development with distribution can best take place through the discipline of the market—via the liberalization of the domestic market and pursuit of more "outward-oriented" trade and exchange rate policies and reduction in government intervention in domestic markets for goods, capital, and labor, thereby allowing prices, interest rates, and wages to find their "natural equilibrium" through market discipline (via the interaction of supply and demand). Development also takes place through the deregulation of financial markets and the opening up of restricted sectors of the economy to private investment; the dismantling of restrictive legislation, such as direct and indirect taxation; the privatization of SOEs and the liquidation of unviable or "sick" firms and SOEs; and the complete dismantling of the industrial licensing system and foreign exchange controls. In general, all the above means the conversion of a "statist" or control-bound, inward-looking economy into a market-conforming, export-oriented, or outward-looking economy. Such a market-conforming, outward-oriented strategy will enable the economy to move toward an equilibrium growth path in which patterns of production, investment, and capacity creation follow dynamic comparative advantage, thereby minimizing resource costs, increasing competition in domestic markets, and eliminating potential channels of corruption.

6. This public statement by India's former finance minister Palaniappan Chidambaram to the Indian Parliament is illustrative. "In my lifetime, I want to see India grow at 8 to 8.5 percent per annum, year after year, and so eliminate the poverty that we have known for five thousand years. In my estimate, that requires a per capita income of US$1,500. If we grow at 8 percent per year, we can reach this target in 18 or 20 years. Look, I am not talking of $5,000 or $10,000. Just a per capita income of US$1,500, which will remove poverty from this country."

7. See for example O'Donnell (1973); Sheahan (1987); and Skidmore (1977).

8. In fact, cross-national analyses conclude that authoritarian regimes have not done significantly better at sticking to either economic stabilization (Remmer 1985/86) or structural adjustment programs (Haggard and Kaufman 1995). In a recent study, Terry Lynn Karl (1997) persuasively argues that in Venezuela the democratic regime of President Carlos Andres Pérez (in contrast to the dictatorship of Jimenez) successfully shifted a greater proportion of state spending toward programs that benefited the middle and working classes. Turning the economic crisis it inherited into an "opportunity," the Perez administration took full advantage of the additional powers granted to it by the legislature to reform Venezuela's "pacted democracy" and oil-revenue dependent economy.

9. This means evidence drawn from the "developmental" authoritarian regimes, without reference to the numerous neopatrimonial and predatory authoritarian systems in Africa, Latin America, and Asia, such as Nigeria under various rulers, the Philippines under Marcos, or Nicaragua under Somoza.

10. To my knowledge this term was first used by Jorge Dominguez (1997).

11. For a concise expression of this view see Pereira, Maravall, and Przeworski (1993).

12. According to O'Donnell (1994), "delegative democracies" are elitist democracies in which the state executives make and implement policies (in particular neoliberal policies) by cutting channels of participation, limiting debate, and centralizing authority in the executive and favored "technopols." O'Donnell drew heavily from Argentina under Menem to illustrate such "Caesarist" presidential behavior. He notes that "delegative democracies" in the long run endanger the prospects for democratic consolidation.

13. According to Peter Evans (1995), who first coined the term, states with embedded autonomy are those with coherent internal organization and close links with society.

14. Frei's electoral mandate ends in 2000.

15. While most goods are freely importable on payment of the specified customs duty without licensing requirements, a small number of goods fall into the Restrictive List of imports. The restrictions are principally in the area of consumer goods, for reasons of security, health, and environmental protection, or because the goods are reserved for production in the small-scale sector, which requires low skills and employs a large number of people.

16. Under the WTO guidelines the European Union (India's largest trading partner), along with the United States, Canada, Japan, and Australia, filed complaints against India's proposed nine-year phaseout of import restrictions on some 2,700 items, mostly consumer goods. However, in late 1997 India agreed to a six-year phaseout of quantitative restrictions.

17. For example, on the basis of net profits after tax the return on capital remained below 5 percent throughout the 1980s, declining to only 2.3 percent in 1990/91 (Rao and Linnemann 1996).

18. There is no duty on capital goods imports with a minimum value of Rs 50 million (approximately $1.4 million in 1997 prices) for agriculture and allied sectors.

19. The SEBI introduced a number of enforcement measures during 1996/97, including requiring stock exchanges to implement uniform norms for imposition of circuit breakers and trading suspensions in cases where price manipulation is suspected. Further, all the exchanges are required to set up surveillance departments and have to supply to the SEBI daily settlement and preissue monitoring reports. A trading database has also been created with the SEBI for trades on the National and Mumbai Stock Exchanges.

20. India has one of the world's worst tax-collecting records. In 1995 only 12 million people (out of 960 million) paid personal income tax, and only 12,000 of them declared an income of more than one million rupees (approximately $33, 000). In 1997 the government introduced a no-questions-asked and no-penalty Voluntary Disclosure of Income Tax. Its effectiveness remains to be seen.

21. The Finance Act of 1996 introduced the concept of the MAT. Under this provision, a company whose taxable profits are less than 30 percent of its adjusted book profits (profits calculated under the Companies Act, 1956) will have to pay a minimum tax on 30 percent of the book profits at the tax rates in force. However, the provisions are not applicable for certain infrastructure projects.

22. According to Gulati and Sharma (1991), the fertilizer subsidy rose from around Rs 4 billion ($500 million) in the early 1980s to Rs 46 billion ($2.7 billion) in 1989/90; the subsidy on electricity rose from Rs 3.6 billion ($450 million) in 1980/81 to Rs 34.7 billion ($2 billion) in 1989/90. The subsidy rate for electricity was a staggering 82 percent in 1989/90. Similarly, they note that the average annual irrigation subsidies from 1974 to 1989 have been Rs 100 billion ($5.9 billion) at 1989 prices, and the average credit subsidy have been Rs 12 billion ($700 million) a year.

23. However, state governments have usually neutralized these cuts by picking up the slack. For example, when Digvijay Singh became chief minister of Madhya Pradesh in November 1993, he lost no time in announcing the waiver of electricity charges on irrigation pumps and threshers of up to five hp. The cost to the exchequer totaled Rs 375 crore annually. When Laloo Prasad Yadav came to power in Bihar in 1990 he announced a thirty-two-point welfare scheme; over the years the points have progressively increased, and now number over 3,000.

24. In 1991 the central government proposed a 40 percent hike in urea prices in the annual budget. However, under pressure from the farmers' lobby, the government subsequently lowered it to 30 percent, with exemptions for small and marginal farmers. In 1992 the union finance minister decontrolled the prices of potassic and phosphatic fertilizers, resulting in steep increases (some 80 percent) in the prices of these fertilizers. These policies had several implications. Because urea prices were still controlled, many farmers started using urea exclusively, with serious long-term environmental implications. To stop such practices, the government announced a subsidy of Rs 1,000 a ton for potassic and phosphatic fertilizers, adding another Rs 630 crores to the total bill in 1994.

25. In 1996/97 India's share in the world trade in agricultural commodities stood at about 1 percent. Agricultural exports have received special attention from the government because it sees exports as central to raising farm incomes, reducing unemployment, and earning foreign exchange.

26. For details see Government of India (GoI, various years).

27. The fact that the Indian economy has not been plagued by the macroeconomic problems facing the countries of East Asia and ASEAN illustrates the strong underlying differences between India and the others. First, India's current account deficit in 1996/97 was only 1 percent of GDP, while the current account deficit of Thailand was 8 percent and 6 percent in Malaysia. Second, India's pattern of external debt is much different in that the ratio of total external debt to GDP has been declining—from over 40 percent in 1991 to a 1996/97 26 percent. The pattern for Thailand, Malaysia, and Indonesia is just the opposite. Third, the composition of external debt liability has been heavily weighted in favor of short-term liability in the ASEAN economies. Short-term debt can be very destabilizing given the fluctuations in exchange rates. On the other hand, India's short-term liability is only 7 percent ($6 billion) of a total external debt of $90 billion. Finally, India has moved more cautiously on the path of full currency convertibility than her neighbors, thereby reducing the possibility of large-scale cross-border capital movements and currency speculation.

28. During his visit to India in January 1995, the U.S. secretary of commerce, the late Ron Brown, who was accompanied by twenty-five CEOs of major U.S. companies, announced that the Clinton administration had designated India as one of the world's biggest emerging markets.

29. It is important to note that both foreign direct investment and foreign portfolio investment (in the Indian stock markets and through Global Depository Receipts issued in Europe) have seen sustained growth.

30. These amount to roughly 350 million people. For details see Gupta (1996, 130).

31. In other words, the number of poor increased by an average of 1.76 million a year in the most recent period for which there are comparable *NSS* data.

32. For details see *India Today*, 15 February 1995, pp. 45–48.

33. For details see research by the Economic and Political Weekly Research Foundation in *Economic and Political Weekly*, 7 January 1995.

34. Indeed, there is a large body of literature that shows that when exchange rates depreciate the prices of tradable goods rise, food prices rise, and the real wages of the working population fall.

35. S. P. Gupta (1996, 132) notes that "even in terms of physical units (per kg), the total per capita cereal consumption decreased both in rural and urban areas between 1990–91 and 1992."

36. The quote is attributed to former finance minister Manmohan Singh (Rao and Linnemann 1996, 49).

37. The World Bank's SALs have been in operation since the 1980. The IMF set up the SAF in 1986 to provide concessional financial support to low-income member countries. Programs supported by SALs and the SAF, though tailored to the varied needs of individual member countries, share basic neoliberal assumptions regarding development.

38. The correlation between high growth rates and employment generation is indeed problematic. The case of China (and India) vividly illustrate that high growth rates do not ameliorate unemployment, but under some conditions may actually exacerbate it. For details on the "jobless growth" in India see Kothari (1997) and Nayyar (1996).

39. For a good overview see Kothari (1997) and Nayyar (1996).

40. This is in part due to the fact that the PDS allocations to states bear little relationship to the extent of poverty in the state. According to Nayyar (1996, 176), "it is estimated that during 1991–93, 67 percent of the total offtake from PDS was allocated to seven States while they accounted for 44 percent of the total poor. In contrast, Bihar, Madhya Pradesh, Orissa and Uttar Pradesh accounted for 40 percent of the poor, but received only 15 percent of the offtake."

41. It is well known that ration cards for the PDS are available to the whole population regardless of income. In fact, the PDS provides large subsidies to middle- and high-income households.

42. For details see Kothari (1997) and Swaminathan (1996).

43. The Asoka Mehta Committee appointed in December 1977 carried out a comprehensive review of the panchayati raj system and made detailed recommendations for its reform, including periodic elections, adequate administrative staff, and empowerment of the poor.

44. While the rules mandate elections every five years, in the event of a dissolution earlier they mandate elections within six months of the dissolution.

45. My analysis of the Chilean experience since 1973 draws on a number of sources, including Bosworth, Dornbusch, and Laban (1994); Collier and Collier (1991); Collins and Lear (1995); Edwards (1995); Graham (1994); Hojman (1993); Lustig (1995); Morley (1995); Oppenheim (1993); Petras, Leiva, and Veltmeyer (1994); Raczynski (1995); Sheahan (1997); Valdes (1995); and Weyland (1997).

46. According to Graham (1994, 25–26), "per capita spending in these areas in 1986 was only 40 percent of the 1970 level."

47. Collins and Lear (1995) note that a section of the middle class has also borne the cost of immiserization. Also see Petras, Leiva, and Veltmeyer (1994).

48. For a comprehensive overview see Hojman (1993); Sheahan (1997); and Valdes (1995).

49. The Concertación was led by the PDC in the Center, the Partido por la Democracia (PPD) on the Center-Left, and the Partido Socialista (PS) on the Left. Other parties included the Radical Party, the Social Democratic Party, the Radical Democratic Socialists, the Humanist Party, and the Party for Democracy.

50. Hojman (1993) notes that the continuity between the Aylwin government's economic policies and those of its predecessor was the result of the convergence of economic thought that included the Christian Democrats and the Right, as well as most prominent economists on the Left.

51. Scully (1996, 103) aptly notes that "institutionalized parties are certainly not a sufficient condition for explaining successful economic policymaking in new democracies, but they may be necessary."

Bibliography

Abel, Martin. 1970. "Agriculture in India in the 1970s," *Economic and Political Weekly*, vol. 3, no. 28, pp. A5–A24.

Abrol, Dave. 1983. "America's Involvement in Indian Agricultural Research," *Social Scientist*, no. 11, pp. 8–26.

Adelman, Irma, and Cynthia T. Morris. 1967. *Politics and Economic Development*. Baltimore: Johns Hopkins University Press.

———. 1973. *Economic Growth and Social Equity in Developing Countries*. Stanford, Ca.: Stanford University Press.

Adiseshiah, M. S. 1985. "The Unfinished Task," *Seminar*, no. 316, pp. 36–42.

Agarwal, Bina. 1988. "Neither Sustenance nor Sustainability: Agricultural Strategies, Ecological Degradation, and Indian Women in Poverty." In Bina Agarwal, ed. *Structures of Patriarchy: The State, The Community and the Household*. London: Zed Books.

———. 1994. *A Field of One's Own: Gender and Land Rights in South Asia*. London: Cambridge University Press.

Ahluwalia, Isher J. 1985. *Industrial Growth in India*. Delhi: Oxford University Press.

Ahluwalia, Montek. 1978. "Rural Poverty and Agricultural Performance in India," *Journal of Development Studies* 14, no. 3 (April), pp. 289–324.

———. 1986. "Rural Poverty, Agricultural Production, and Prices: A Re-examination." In J. W. Mellor and G. N. Desai, eds. *Agricultural Change and Rural Poverty*. Delhi: Oxford University Press.

Ahmad, Shahid. 1977. *Class and Power in a Punjabi Village*. New York: Monthly Review Press.

Alavi, Hamza. 1965. "Peasants and Revolution." In R. Milliband and J. Saville, eds. *The Socialist Register*. London: Merlin Press.

———. 1972. "The State in Post-Colonial Societies," *New Left Review*, no. 74, pp. 59–82.

Alexander, K. C. 1981. *Peasant Organizations in South India*. Delhi: Indian Social Institute.

Almond, Gabriel, and Sidney Verba. 1963. *The Civic Culture*. Princeton, N.J.: Princeton University Press.

Amsden, Alice. 1979. "Taiwan's economic history: A case of etatisme and a challenge to dependency theory," *Modern China*, vol. 5, no. 3, pp. 341–379.

———. 1989. *Asia's Next Giant: South Korea and Late Industrialization*. New York: Oxford University Press.

245

Anderson, Kim, and Hayami, Yujiro. 1986. *The Political Economy of Agricultural Protection: East Asia in International Perspective.* London: Allen and Unwin.

Appleby, Paul. 1953. *Public Administration in India: Report of a Survey.* New Delhi: Government of India, Cabinet Secretariat.

Appu, P. S. 1975. "Tenancy Reform in India," *Economic and Political Weekly,* vol. x, no. 33–35, pp. 1339–1375.

Apter, David. 1965. *The Politics of Modernization.* Chicago: University of Chicago Press.

Athreya, V., G. Djurfeldt, and S. Lindberg. 1990. *Barriers Broken: Production Relations and Agrarian Change in Tamil Nadu.* New Delhi: Sage Publications.

Austin, Granville. 1966. *The Indian Constitution: Cornerstone of a Nation.* Oxford: Clarendon Press.

B. M. 1974. *Economic and Political Weekly,* vol. ix, no. 21, p. 814.

———. 1980. "Appeasing the Rich Farmer Lobby," *Economic and Political Weekly,* vol. xiv, no. 29, pp. A111–A112.

Bagchi, Amiya K. 1982. *The Political Economy of Underdevelopment.* London: Cambridge University Press.

Baig, M. A. 1990. "Lie of the Land," *India Today,* 15 July, p. 77.

Bailey, F. G. 1963. *Politics and Social Change: Orissa in 1959.* Berkeley: University of California Press.

Balasubramanyam, V. N. 1984. *The Economy of India.* London: Weidenfeld and Nicolson.

Bandopadhyay, Nripen. 1975. "Changing Forms of Agricultural Enterprise in West Bengal," *Economic and Political Weekly* (April 26).

Bardhan, Kalpana. 1989. "Agricultural Growth and Rural Wage-Labor in India," *South Asia Bulletin,* vol. 9, no. 1, pp. 12–25.

Bardhan, Pranab. 1970. "Green Revolution and Agricultural Labor," *Economic and Political Weekly* (7 July), pp. 1239–1246.

———. 1984. *The Political Economy of Development in India.* Oxford: Basil Blackwell.

———, and Ashok Rudra. 1984a. "Terms and Conditions of Sharecropping Contracts: An Analysis of Village Survey Data in India." In Pranab Bardhan, ed. *Land, Labor and Rural Poverty: Essays in Development Economics.* Delhi: Oxford University Press.

———. 1985. "Poverty and Trickle-Down in Rural India: A Quantitative Analysis." In J. Mellor and G. N. Desai, eds. *Agricultural Change and Rural Poverty.* Baltimore: Johns Hopkins University Press.

———. 1989. *Conversations Between Economists and Anthropologists: Methodological Issues in Measuring Economic Change in Rural India.* Delhi: Oxford University Press.

———. 1996. "The State Against Society: The Great Divide in Indian Social Science Discourse." In Sugata Bose and Ayesha Jalal, eds. *Nationalism, Democracy, and Development: State and Politics in India.* New Delhi: Oxford University Press.

Bates, Robert. 1981. *Markets and States in Tropical Africa.* Berkeley: University of California Press.

———, and Anne Krueger. 1993. *Political and Economic Interactions in Economic Policy Reform.* Oxford: Basil Blackwell.

Bauer, Peter T. 1981. *Equality, The Third World Economic Delusion.* London: Methuen.

Baxter, Craig. 1975. "The Rise and Fall of the Bharatiya Kranti Dal in U.P." In John Osgood, Craig Baxter, and Myron Weiner, eds. *Studies in Electoral Politics in the Indian States.* Delhi: Manohar Books.

Bayly, Christopher A. 1988. *Indian Society and the Making of the British Empire.* Cambridge: Cambridge University Press.

Bell, Clive. 1974. "Ideology and Economic Interests in Indian Land Reform." In D. Lehmann, ed. *Agrarian Reform and Agrarian Reformism.* London: Faber and Faber.

Beteille, Andre. 1974. *Studies in Agrarian Social Structure.* Delhi: Oxford University Press.

Bettelheim, Charles. 1968. *India Independent.* New York: Monthly Review Press.

Bhaduri, Amit. 1973. "Agricultural Backwardness under Semi-Feudalism," *Economic Journal,* lxxxvi, pp. 120–137.

———. 1983. *The Economic Structure of Backward Agriculture.* Delhi: Macmillan.

———. 1986. "Persistence and Polarization: A Study in the Dynamics of Agrarian Contradiction," *Journal of Peasant Studies* 13, pp. 82–89.

Bhagwati, Jagdish, and Padma Desai. 1970. *India, Planning for Industrialization.* London: Oxford University Press.

Bhagwati, Jagdish. 1985. "Is India's Economic Miracle at Hand," *New York Times,* June 9, p. 4.

———. 1993. *India in Transition: Freeing the Economy.* New Delhi: Oxford University Press.

Bhalla, G. S., and Y. K. Alagh. 1979. *Performance of Indian Agriculture: A District-wise Study.* New Delhi: Sterling Publishers.

———, and D. S. Tyagi. 1989. *Patterns in Indian Agricultural Development: A District Level Study.* New Delhi: Institute for Studies in Industrial Development.

Bhalla, Sheila. 1976. "New Relations of Production in Haryana Agriculture," *Economic and Political Weekly,* vol. xi, no. 13, pp. A23–A39.

Bhambri, C. P. 1971. *Bureaucracy and Politics in India.* New Delhi: Vikas Publications.

Bharadwaj, K. 1985. "A View on Commercialization in Indian Agriculture and the Development of Capitalism," *Journal of Peasant Studies,* vol. 23, no. 4, pp. 7–25.

Bharadwaj, K., and P. K. Das. 1975. "Tenurial Conditions and Mode of Exploitation: A Study of Some Villages in Orissa," *Economic and Political Weekly,* February and June, annual numbers.

Bhatia, B. 1963. *Famines in India.* Bombay: Asia Publishing House.

Bhatia, B. M. 1988. *Indian Agriculture: A Policy Perspective.* New Delhi: Sage Publications.

Bhatt, G. D. 1990. *Rural Development Programmes in India: An Evaluation of Integrated Rural Development Programme.* Delhi: Shanti Publications.

Blair, Harry. 1980. "Rising Kulaks and Backward Classes in Bihar: Social Change in the late 1970s," *Economic and Political Weekly,* vol. 15, no. 2 (12 January), pp. 64–74.

———. 1984. "Structural Change and the Agricultural Sector, and Politics in Bihar." In John R. Wood, ed. *State Politics in Contemporary India.* Boulder, Colo.: Westview Press.

Blyn, George. 1966. *Agricultural Trends in India 1891–1947: Output, Availability and Productivity.* Philadelphia: University of Pennsylvania Press.

Booth, Ann, and Robert M. Sundrum. 1985. *Labor Absorption in Agriculture.* Oxford: Oxford University Press.

Bose, Sugata, and Ayesha Jalal. 1997. *Modern South Asia: History, Culture, Political Economy.* New Delhi: Oxford University Press.

Bosworth, Barry, Rudiger Dornbusch, and Raul Laban. 1994. *The Chilean Economy: Policy Lessons and Challenges.* Washington, D.C.: Brookings Institution.

Brandt Commission. 1983. *Common Crisis.* London: Pan Books.

Brass, Paul. 1965. *Factional Politics in an Indian State: The Congress Party in Uttar Pradesh.* Berkeley: University of California Press.

————. 1980. "The Politicization of the Peasantry in a North Indian State: I and II," *Journal of Peasant Studies,* vol. 7, no. 4, pp. 395–426 and vol. 8, no. 1, pp. 3–36.

————. 1983. *Caste, Faction and Party in Indian Politics,* vol. 1. Delhi: Chanakya Publications.

————. 1984. "Division in the Congress and the Rise of Agrarian Interests and Issues in Uttar Pradesh Politics, 1952 to 1977." In John R. Wood, ed. *State Politics in Contemporary India.* Boulder, Colo.: Westview Press.

————. 1985. *Caste, Faction, and Party in Indian Politics,* vol. 11. Delhi: Chanakya Publications.

————. 1990. *The Politics of India Since Independence.* New York: Cambridge University Press.

Bratton, Michael. 1989. "Beyond the State: Civil Society and Associational Life in Africa," *World Politics* 41, April.

Brecher, Michael. 1959. *Nehru: A Political Biography.* London: Oxford University Press.

————. 1966. *Nehru's Mantle: The Politics of Succession in India.* New York: Praeger Publications.

————. 1966a. *Succession in India: A Study in Decision-Making.* London: Oxford University Press.

Breman, Jan. 1974. *Patronage and Exploitation: Changing Agrarian Relations in South Gujarat, India.* Berkeley: University of California Press.

————. 1985. *Of Peasants, Migrants, and Paupers: Rural Labour Circulation and Capitalist Production in West India.* Delhi: Oxford University Press.

————. 1996. *Footloose Labor: Working in India's Informal Economy.* New York: Cambridge University Press.

Brown, Judith. 1985. *Modern India: The Origins of an Asian Democracy.* Oxford: Oxford University Press.

Byres, Terence. 1972. "The Dialectic of India's Green Revolution," *South Asian Review,* no. 2 (5 January).

————. 1974. "Land Reform, Industrialization, and the Marketed Surplus in India: An Essay on the Power of Rural Bias." In David Lehmann, ed. *Agrarian Reform and Agrarian Reformism.* London: Faber and Faber.

————. 1979. "Of Neo-Populist Pipe Dreams: Daedalus in the Third World and the Myth of Urban Bias," *Journal of Peasant Studies,* vol. 6, no. 2, pp. 210–244.

————. 1981. "The New Technology, Class Formation and Class Action in the Indian Countryside," *Journal of Peasant Studies,* vol. 8, no. 4, pp. 405–454.

————. 1982. India: Capitalist Industrialization or Structural Stasis." In M. Bienefeld and M. Godfrey, eds. *The Struggle for Development: National Strategies in an International Context.* London: John Wiley.

————. 1988. "A Chicago View of the Indian State," *Journal of Commonwealth and Comparative Politics,* vol. xxvi, no. 3, pp. 246–269.

————. 1988a. "New Technology and New Masters for the Indian Countryside." In B. Crow and M. Thorpe, eds. *Survival and Change in the Third World.* New York: Oxford University Press.

————. 1994. *The State and Development Planning in India.* New Delhi: Oxford University Press.

Cardoso, F. H., and E. Faletto. 1979. *Dependency and Development in Latin America.* Berkeley: University of California Press.

Castore, C. 1982. "The United States and India: The Use of Food to Apply Economic Pressure 1965–67." In S. Weintraub, ed. *Economic Coercion and the U.S. Foreign Policy.* Boulder, Colo.: Westview Press.

Chadha, G. K. 1986. *The State and Rural Economic Transformation: The Case of Punjab, 1950–85.* New Delhi: Sage Publishers.

Chakravarty, Sukhamoy. 1984. *Development Planning: The Indian Experience.* London: Oxford University Press.

———. 1990. "Development Strategies for Growth with Equity: The South Asian Experience," *Asian Development Review,* vol. 8, no. 1, pp. 133–159.

Chandra, Bipan. 1966. *The Rise and Growth of Economic Nationalism in India.* New Delhi: Peoples' Publishing House.

———. 1988. *India's Struggle for Independence.* New Delhi: Penguin Books.

Chandra, Nirmal K. 1988. *The Retarded Economies: Foreign Domination and Class Relations in India and other Emerging Nations.* Delhi: Oxford University Press.

Chattopadhyay, Paresh. 1970. "State Capitalism in India," *Monthly Review,* vol. 21, no. 10.

Chattopadhyay, S. 1973. "On the Class Nature of Land Reforms in India since Independence," *Social Scientist,* vol. 2, no. 4, pp. 3–24.

Chaudhuri, Kalyan. 1997. "The Jehanabad Carnage," *Frontline,* vol. 14, no. 25 (13–26 December).

Chazan, Naomi, and Donald Rothchild, eds. 1987. *The Precarious Balance: State and Society in Africa.* Boulder, Colo.: Westview.

Chenery, Hollis. 1974. *Redistribution with Growth.* London: Oxford University Press.

———. 1975. "The Structuralist Approach to Development Policy," *American Economic Review,* no. 65.

Chopra, K. 1986. "Dimensions of Inequality in a High-Growth Region," *Economic and Political Weekly,* vol. xxi, no. 19, pp. 491–496.

Chopra, R. N. 1981. *Evolution of Food Policy in India.* Delhi: Macmillan.

Cleaver, Harry. 1976. "Internationalization of Capital and Mode of Production in Agriculture," *Economic and Political Weekly,* vol. xi, pp. 2–16.

Collier, David, ed. 1979. *The New Authoritarianism in Latin America.* Princeton, N.J.: Princeton University Press.

———, and Ruth Berins Collier. 1991. *Shaping the Political Arena.* Princeton, N.J.: Princeton University Press.

Collins, Joseph, and John Lear. 1995. *Chile's Free-Market Miracle: A Second Look.* Oakland, Cal.: Food First.

Crane, Robert. 1959. "Leadership of the Congress Party." In Richard L. Park and Irene Tinker, eds. *Leadership and Political Institutions in India.* Princeton, N.J.: Princeton University Press.

Cumings, Bruce. 1984. "The Origins and Development of the Northeast Asian Political Economy: Industrial Sectors, Product Cycles, and Political Consequences," *International Organization,* vol. 38, no. 1, pp. 1–40.

Dahl, Robert. 1971. *Polyarchy: Participation and Opposition.* New Haven, Conn.: Yale University Press.

———. 1995. "Justifying Democracy," *Transaction: Social Science and Modern Society,* vol. 32, no. 3 (March–April), pp. 43–49.

Dandekar, V. M. 1988. "Agriculture, Employment and Poverty." In Robert Lucas and Gustav F. Papanek, eds. *The Indian Economy: Recent Developments and Future Prospects.* Delhi: Oxford University Press.

Das, Arvind. 1983. *Agrarian Unrest and Socioeconomic Change in Bihar, 1900–1980.* New Delhi: Manohar Publishers.

Dasgupta, Bilap. 1977. *Agrarian Change and the New Technology in India.* Geneva: United Nations Research Institute for Social Development.

Dasgupta, Joytindra. 1979. "The Janata Phase in Indian Politics," *Asian Survey,* vol. xix, no. 4 (April), pp. 390–403.

———. 1981. *Authority, Priority and Human Development.* Delhi: Oxford University Press.

———. 1989. "India: Democratic Becoming and Combined Development." In Larry Diamond, Juan Linz, and Seymour Martin Lipset, eds. *Democracy in Developing Countries: Asia.* Boulder, Colo.: Lynne Rienner Publishers.

Dasgupta, Pratha. 1993. *An Inquiry into Well-Being and Destitution.* London: Oxford University Press.

Datt, Gurav, and Martin Ravallion. 1995. *Why Did Poverty Increase Sharply after India's Macroeconomic Stabilization.* Poverty and Human Resources Working Paper. Washington D.C.: The World Bank Policy Research Department.

———. 1996. *Macroeconomic Crises and Poverty Monitoring: The Case of India.* Policy Research Working Paper no. 1685. Washington, D.C.: The World Bank.

Davey, Brian. 1975. *The Economic Development of India: A Marxist Analysis.* London: Spokesman Books.

DeJanvry, Alain. 1981. *The Agrarian Question and Reformism in Latin America.* Baltimore: Johns Hopkins University Press.

———, and K. Subbarao. 1987. *Agricultural Price Policy and Income Distribution in India.* Delhi: Oxford University Press.

Desai, A. R. 1966. *Social Background of Indian Nationalism.* Bombay: Popular Prakashan.

———. 1984. *India's Path of Development: A Marxist Approach.* Bombay: Popular Prakashan.

———. 1986. *Agrarian Struggles in India after Independence.* Delhi: Oxford University Press.

Deyo, Frederick C., ed. 1987. *The Political Economy of New Asian Industrialism.* Ithaca, N.Y.: Cornell University Press.

Deutsch, Karl. 1961. "Social Mobilization and Political Development," *American Political Science Review* (September), pp. 493–514.

Dhanagre, D. N. 1975. *Agrarian Movements and Gandhian Politics.* Agra: Agra University.

———. 1987. "Green Revolution and Social Inequalities in Rural India," *Economic and Political Weekly,* vol. xxii, nos. 19–21.

Dhar, P. N. 1990. *Constraints on Growth: Reflections on the Indian Experience.* Delhi: Oxford University Press.

Di Palma, Giuseppe. 1990. *To Craft Democracies.* Berkeley: University of California Press.

Diamond, Larry, Juan Linz, and Seymour M. Lipset. 1990. *Politics in Developing Countries: Comparing Experiences with Democracy.* Boulder, Colo.: Lynne Rienner Publishers.

Dick, William. 1974. "Authoritarian Versus Nonauthoritarian Approaches to Economic Development," *Journal of Political Economy,* vol. 82, no. 4, pp. 817–827.

Djurfeldt, G., and S. Lindberg. 1975. *Behind Poverty: The Social Formation in a Tamil Village.* London: Curzon Press.

Dominguez, Jorge, ed. 1997. *Technopols: Freeing Politics and Markets in Latin America in the 1990s.* University Park: Pennsylvania State University Press.

Donnelly, Jack. 1984. "Human Rights and Development: Complementary and Competing Concerns," *World Politics,* vol. 36, no. 2, pp. 255–284.

Downs, Anthony. 1957. *An Economic Theory of Democracy.* New York: Harper and Row.

Dreze, J., and P. V. Srinivasan. 1996. *Poverty in India: Regional Estimates 1987–88.* Working Paper no. 36. Centre for Developmental Economics: Delhi School of Economics.

Dubhashi, P. R. 1986. *Policy and Performance: Agricultural and Rural Development in Post-Independence India.* New Delhi: Sage Publications.

Easton, D. 1979. *A Systems Analysis of Political Life.* Chicago: University of Chicago Press.

Economic and Political Weekly. 1995. 7 January.

Editorial. 1988. "Bitter Harvest," *India Today,* 29 February, p. 5.

Edwards, Sebastian. 1995. *Crisis and Reform in Latin America: From Despair to Hope.* New York: Oxford University Press.

Eswaran, Mukesh, and Ashok Kotwal. 1994. *Why Poverty Persists in India: An Analytical Framework for Understanding the Indian Economy.* New Delhi: Oxford University Press.

Evans, Peter. 1979. *Dependent Development: The Alliance of Multinational State and Local Capital in Brazil.* Princeton, N.J.: Princeton University Press.

———. 1995. *Embedded Autonomy: States and Industrial Transformation.* Princeton, N.J.: Princeton University Press.

———, David Rueschemyer, and Theda Skocpol. 1985. *Bringing the State Back In.* Cambridge: Cambridge University Press.

Ezekiel, H., ed. 1984. *Corporate Sector in India.* New Delhi: Manohar.

Farmer, B. H. 1986. "Perspectives on the Green Revolution in South Asia," *Modern Asian Studies* 20, pp. 175–199.

Fei, John C. H., and Gustav Ranis. 1964. *Development of the Labor Surplus Economy: Theory and Practice.* Homewood, Ill.: R. D. Irwin.

———, Gustav Ranis, and Shirley W. Kuo. 1979. *Growth with Equity: The Taiwan Case.* New York: Oxford University Press.

Franda, Marcus. 1968. *West Bengal and the Federalizing Process in India.* Princeton, N.J.: Princeton University Press.

———. 1980. "An Indian Farm Lobby: The Kisan Sammelan," *American Universities Field Staff Reports.* Asia No. 17.

———. 1980a. *India's Rural Development: An Assessment of Alternatives.* Bloomington: Indiana University Press.

Frankel, Francine. 1971. *India's Green Revolution: Economic Gains and Political Costs.* Princeton, N.J.: Princeton University Press.

———. 1978. *India's Political Economy, 1947–1977: The Gradual Revolution.* Princeton, N.J.: Princeton University Press.

———. 1988. "Middle Classes and Castes in India's Politics: Prospects for Accommodation." In A. Kohli, ed. *India's Democracy: An Analysis of Changing State-Society Relations.* Princeton, N.J.: Princeton University Press.

———, and M. S. A. Rao, eds. 1989/1990. *Dominance and State Power in Modern India,* vol. 1 and 2. Delhi: Oxford University Press.

Frykenberg, Robert E., ed. 1969. *Land Control and Social Structure in Indian History.* Madison: University of Wisconsin Press.

Gaiha, Raghav. 1989. "Poverty, Agricultural Production and Prices in Rural India," *Cambridge Journal of Economics,* no. 13, pp. 333–352.

———. 1996. *Participation or Empowerment of the Rural Poor: The Case of the Panchayats in India.* Occassional Paper no. 4. University of Pennsylvania, Center for the Advanced Study of India.

Gandhi, M. K. 1957. *Autobiography: The Story of My Experiments with Truth.* Translated by Mahadev Desai. Boston: Beacon Press.

George, Susan. 1989. *A Fate Worse than Debt.* London: Penguin.

Gereffi, Gary, and Donald Wyman, eds. 1990. *Manufacturing Miracles: Paths of Industrialization in Latin America and East Asia.* Princeton, N.J.: Princeton University Press.

Gerschenkron, Alexander. 1963. *Economic Backwardness in Historical Perspective.* Cambridge, Mass.: Harvard University Press.

Ghai, Dharam P. 1977. *The Basic Needs Approach to Development.* Geneva: International Labour Organisation.

Ghosh, A., and K. Dutt. 1977. *Development of Capitalist Relations in Agriculture.* New Delhi: Peoples' Publishing.

Ghosh, A. 1988. *Emerging Capitalism in Indian Agriculture.* New Delhi: Peoples' Publishing House.

Ghosh, Suniti. 1986. *The Indian Big Bourgeoisie: Its Genesis, Growth, and Character.* Calcutta: Subarnarekha.

Giddens, Anthony. 1985. *The Nation-State and Violence.* Berkeley: University of California Press.

Gill, S. S., and K. C. Singhal. 1984. "Punjab Farmers Agitation," *Economic and Political Weekly* (6 October), pp. 1728–1732.

Gold, Thomas B. 1986. *State and Society in the Taiwan Miracle.* New York: M. E. Sharpe.

Goldsmith, Arthur. 1988. "Policy Dialogue, Conditionality, and Agricultural Development: Implications of India's Green Revolution," *The Journal of Developing Areas* 22, pp. 179–198.

———. 1990. *Building Agricultural Institutions: Transferring the Land-Grant Model to India and Nigeria.* Boulder, Colo.: Westview Press.

Goodman, David, and Michael Redclift. 1982. *From Peasant to Proletarian: Capitalist Development and Agrarian Transitions.* New York: St. Martin's Press.

Gopal, Sarvepalli, ed. 1980. *Jawaharlal Nehru: An Anthology.* Delhi: Oxford University Press.

Gough, Kathleen, and Hari P. Sharma. 1973. *Imperialism and Revolution in South Asia.* New York: Monthly Review Press.

Gough, Kathleen. 1989. *Rural Change in Southeast India.* New Delhi: Oxford University Press.

Gould, D. 1979. "The Administration of Underdevelopment." In Guy Gran, ed. *Zaire: The Political Economy of Underdevelopment.* New York: Praeger.

Gourevitch, Peter. 1986. *Politics in Hard Times: Competitive Responses to International Economic Crises.* Ithaca, N.Y.: Cornell University Press.

Government of India (GoI). 1949. *Report of the Congress Agrarian Reforms Committee.* New Delhi: GoI.

———. 1950. *Constituent Assembly Debates.* Vol. 12. New Delhi: GoI.

———. 1952. Planning Commission, *First Five Year Plan.* New Delhi: GoI.

———. 1956. Planning Commission, *Programmes of Industrial Development: 1956–61.* Delhi: Manager of Publications.

———. 1956a. Planning Commission, *Second Five Year Plan.* New Delhi: Government of India Press.

———. 1957. Planning Commission, *Report of the Team for the Study of Community Projects and National Extension Service.* 3 vols. New Delhi. Also cited as the *Balwantrai Mehta Study Team Report,* after its chairperson.

———. 1959. *Report on India's Food Crisis and the Steps to Meet It.* Agricultural Production Team of the Ford Foundation. Delhi: Ministry of Food and Agriculture and Ministry of Community Development and Cooperation.

————. 1963. Planning Commission, *Progress of Land Reforms.* New Delhi: Government of India Press.

————. 1963a. Ministry of Food and Agriculture, *Studies in Economics of Farm Management in Uttar Pradesh: 1954–5 to 1956–7.* Delhi: GoI.

————. 1964. Ministry of Community Development and Cooperation, *Community Development, Panchayati Raj and Cooperatives.* New Delhi: GoI.

————. 1966. Planning Commission, *Fourth Five Year Plan: A Draft Outline.* New Delhi: Government of India Press.

————. 1972. Planning Commission. *Towards Self-Reliance, Approach to the Fifth Five Year Plan.* New Delhi: GoI.

————. 1972a. Agricultural Prices Commission. *Report on Price Policy for Rabi Foodgrains for 1972–73 Season.* New Delhi: GoI.

————. 1976. Ministry of Agriculture and Irrigation, *Report of the National Commission on Agriculture, Pt. XV: Agrarian Reforms.* New Delhi: Manager of Publications.

————. 1978. Planning Commission, *Draft: Fifth Five Year Plan, 1978–83.* New Delhi: GoI.

————. 1980. *Basic Statistics Relating to the Indian Economy: 1950–51 to 1978–79.* Delhi: Central Statistical Organization.

————. 1981. *Report of the Commissioner for Scheduled Castes and Tribes.* New Delhi: Government of India Press.

————. 1985. *Seventh Five Year Plan 1985–90.* Vols. 1 and 2. New Delhi:

————. 1986. Ministry of Finance (Economic Division), *Economic Survey, 1985–1986.* Delhi: Controller of Publications.

————. 1988. Ministry of Agriculture, *Indian Agriculture in Brief.* 22d ed. New Delhi: Directorate of Economics and Statistics.

————. 1992. Ministry of Agriculture, *Indian Agriculture in Brief. 25th ed.* New Delhi: Directorate of Economics and Statistics.

————. 1993. Planning Commission, *Report of the Expert Group on Estimation of Proportion and Number of Poor.* New Delhi: GoI.

————. 1994. *Jawahar Rozgar Yojana: Manual.* New Delhi: Manager of Publications.

Government of Uttar Pradesh. 1994. *Rapid Census.* Lucknow: Department of Panchayati Raj.

Graham, Carol. 1994. *Safety Nets, Politics, and the Poor: Transitions to Market Economies.* Washington, D.C.: Brookings Institution.

Gramsci, Antonio. 1971. *Selections from Prison Notebooks.* New York: International Publishers.

Gran, Guy. 1983. *Development by People: Citizen Construction of a Just World.* New York: Praeger.

Griffin, Keith. 1974. *The Political Economy of Agrarian Change.* Cambridge, Mass.: Harvard University Press.

————. 1976. *Land Concentration and Rural Poverty.* New York: Holmes and Meier.

————, and A. K Ghose. 1979. "Growth and Impoverishment in the Rural Areas of Asia," *World Development,* vol. 7, nos. 4–5, pp. 361–383.

Grindle, Merilee. 1986. *State and Countryside: Development Policy and Agrarian Politics in Latin America.* Baltimore: Johns Hopkins University Press.

————. 1981. "Anticipating Failure: The Implementation of Rural Development Programs," *Public Policy* 29, no. 1, pp. 51–74.

Gulati, A., and P. K. Sharma. 1991. "Government Intervention in Agricultural Markets: Nature, Impact, and Implications," *Journal of Indian School of Political Economy,* vol. 3, no. 2.

Guha, Ranajit, ed. 1982–1985. *Subaltern Studies*. Vols. I–IV. Delhi: Oxford University Press.

Gupta, Akhil. 1989. "The Political Economy of Post-Independence India: A Review Article," *The Journal of Asian Studies*, vol. 48, no. 4, pp. 787–797.

Gupta, L. 1969. *The Changing Structure of Industrial Finance in India*. London: Oxford University Press.

Gupta, S. P. 1996. "Recent Economic Reforms in India and their Impact on the Poor and Vulnerable Sections of Society." In C. H. Hanumantha Rao, and Hans Linnemann, eds. *Economic Reforms and Poverty Alleviation in India*. New Delhi: Sage Publications.

Haggard, Stephan. 1990. *Pathways from the Periphery: The Politics of Growth in the Newly Industrializing Countries*. Ithaca, N.Y.: Cornell University Press.

Haggard, Stephan, and Chung In Moon. 1983. "The South Korean State in the International Economy: Liberal, Dependent, or Mercantile." In John G. Ruggie, ed. *The Antinomies of Underdevelopment: National Welfare and the International Division of Labor*. New York: Columbia University Press.

Haggard, Stephan, and Robert Kaufman. 1995. *The Political Economy of Democratic Transitions*. Princeton, N.J.: Princeton University Press.

Hamilton, Nora. 1982. *The Limits of State Autonomy: Post-Revolutionary Mexico*. Princeton, N.J.: Princeton University Press.

Hardgrave, Robert. 1984. *India Under Pressure: Prospects for Political Stability*. Boulder, Colo.: Westview Press.

———, and Stanley Kochanek. 1986. *India: Government and Politics in a Developing Nation*. New York: Harcourt Brace and Jovanovich.

———, and Stanley Kochanek. 1993. *India: Government and Politics in a Developing Nation*. 5th ed. New York: Harcourt Brace Jovanovich.

Harrison, Selig. 1960. *India: The Most Dangerous Decades*. Princeton, N.J.: Princeton University Press.

Harriss, John. 1982. *Capitalism and Peasant Farming: Agrarian Structure and Ideology in Northern Tamil Nadu*. Delhi: Oxford University Press.

———. 1988. "Capitalism and Peasant Production: The Green Revolution in India." In Teodor Shanin, ed. *Peasant and Peasant Societies*. London: Penguin.

Hasan, Zoya. 1989. *Dominance and Mobilization: Rural Politics in Western Uttar Pradesh*. New Delhi: Sage Publications.

———. 1989a. "Power and Mobilization: Patterns of Resilience and Change in Uttar Pradesh Politics." In Francine Frankel and M. S. A. Rao, eds. *Dominance and State Power in Modern India*. Vol. 1. Delhi: Oxford University Press.

Hayami, Yujuri, and Vernon Ruttan. 1985. *Agricultural Development: An International Perspective*. Baltimore: Johns Hopkins University Press.

Hazari, R. K. 1966. *The Structure of the Corporate Private Sector: A Study of Concentration, Ownership, and Control*. Bombay: Asia Publishing House.

Heidrich, Petra. 1988. *Agricultural Labour in Indian Society*. Berlin: Akademie-Verlag.

Henningham, Stephen. 1983. "Bureaucracy and Control in India's Great Landed Estates: The Raj Darbhanga of Bihar, 1879–1950," *Modern Asian Studies* 17, pp. 35–57.

Herrera, Genero, and Carol Graham. 1994. "Chile: Sustaining Adjustment during Democratic Transition." In Stephan Haggard and Steven Webb, eds. *Voting for Reform: Democracy, Political Liberalization, and Economic Adjustment*. New York: Oxford University Press.

Herring, Ronald. 1983. *Land to the Tiller: The Political Economy of Agrarian Reform in South Asia*. New Haven: Yale University Press.

Hirschman, Albert. 1970. *Exit, Voice, and Loyalty: Responses to Decline in Firms, Organizations and States*. Cambridge, Mass.: Harvard University Press.

Hojman, David. 1993. *Chile: The Political Economy of Development and Democracy in the 1990s.* Pittsburgh, Pa.: University of Pittsburgh Press.

Huntington, Samuel. 1968. *Political Order in Changing Societies.* New Haven, Conn.: Yale University Press.

————. 1991. *The Third Wave: Democratization in the late Twentieth Century.* Norman: Oklahoma University Press.

————, and Joan Nelson. 1976. *No Easy Choice: Political Participation in Developing Countries.* Cambridge, Mass.: Harvard University Press.

Hyden, Goran. 1983. *No Shortcuts to Progress: African Development Management in Perspective.* London: Heinemann.

India Today. 1995. 15 February.

Indian Council of Social Science Research (ICSSR) 1980. *Alternatives in Agricultural Development.* New Delhi: Allied Publishers.

Indian National Congress. All-India Congress Committee. 1954. *Resolutions on Economic Policy and Programme, 1924–1954.* New Delhi.

Indian National Congress (I). 1980. *Election Manifesto 1980.* New Delhi: Congress Party Headquarters.

Iyer, Raghavan. 1993. *The Essential Writings of Mahatma Gandhi.* New Delhi: Oxford University Press.

Jain, L. C. 1983. *Grass Without Roots: Rural Development under Government Auspices.* New Delhi: Institute of Social Studies Trust.

Jalal, Ayesha. 1995. *Democracy and Authoritarianism in South Asia.* New York: Cambridge University Press.

Jalan, Bimal. 1992. *India's Economic Crisis.* New Delhi: Oxford University Press.

Janata Party. 1977. *Election Manifesto.* New Delhi.

Jannuzi, F. T. 1974. *Agrarian Crisis in India: The Case of Bihar.* Austin: University of Texas Press.

Jha, L. K. 1973. "Comment: Leaning Against Open Doors?" In John Lewis and Ishan Kapur, eds. *The World Bank Group, Multilateral Aid and the 1970s.* Lexington, Mass.: D. C. Heath and Company.

Jha, Prem Shankar. 1980. *India: A Political Economy of Stagnation.* Delhi: Oxford University Press.

Jha, S. C. 1963. *Studies in the Development of Capitalism in India.* Calcutta: Firma K. C. Mukhopadhyay.

————. 1971. *A Critical Analysis of Indian Land Reform Studies.* Bombay: Asian Studies Press.

Johnson, Chalmers. 1982. *MITI and the Japanese Miracle: The Growth of Industrial Policy 1925–1975.* Stanford, Ca.: Stanford University Press.

————. 1987. "Political Institutions and Economic Performance." In Deyo 1987.

Johnston, Bruce F., and Peter Kilby. 1975. *Agriculture and Structural Transformation.* New York: Oxford University Press.

Jones, L. P., and H. Sakong. 1980. *Government, Business, and Entrepreneurship in Economic Development: The Korean Case.* Cambridge, Mass.: Harvard University Press.

Jose, A. V. 1988. "Agricultural Wages in India," *Economic and Political Weekly,* vol. xxiii, no. 26, pp. 46–58.

Joshi, P. C. 1973. "Land Reform and Agrarian Change in India and Pakistan since 1947: I and II," *Journal of Peasant Studies,* vol. 1, no. 2, pp. 164–185 and 326–362.

————. 1975. *Land Reforms in India.* New Delhi: Institute of Economic Growth.

————. 1982. "Poverty, Land Hunger, and Emerging Class Conflict in Rural India." In S. Jones, P. C. Joshi, and Miguel Murmis, eds. *Rural Poverty and Agrarian Reform.* New Delhi: Allied Publishers.

Joshi, S. 1983. *Kisan Sanghatana Vichar Aur Karya Paddhati.* Varanasi: Sarva Seva Sangh Prakashan.
————. 1986. *Bharat Speaks Out.* Bombay: BUILD Documentation Centre.
————. 1986a. "Scrap APC—Demand Farmers." In S. Sahasrabudhey, ed. *The Peasant Movement Today.* New Delhi: Ashish Publishing House.
Kabra, Kamal Nayan. 1981. *Land Reforms and Industrialization: Institutional Linkages and their Implications.* Working Paper. New Delhi: Indian Institute of Public Administration.
Kahlon, A. S., and D. S. Tyagi. 1983. *Agricultural Price Policy in India.* New Delhi: Allied Publishers.
Karanjia, R. K. 1960. *The Mind of Mr. Nehru: An Interview.* London: Pinter.
Karl, Terry Lynn. 1990. "Dilemmas of Democratization in Latin America," *Comparative Politics,* vol. 23, no. 1, pp. 1–21.
————. 1997. *The Paradox of Plenty: Oil Booms and Petro States.* Berkeley: University of California Press.
Kashyap, S. 1974. *Politics of Power: Defections and State Politics in India.* Delhi: Vikas Publishers.
Katzenstein, Peter. 1984. *Corporatism and Change: Austria, Switzerland, and the Politics of Industry.* Ithaca, N.Y.: Cornell University Press.
Kidron, Michael. 1965. *Foreign Investments in India.* London: Oxford University Press.
Knight, Alan. 1991. "The Rise and Fall of Cardenismo: c. 1930–c. 1946." In Leslie Bethell, ed. *Mexico since Independence.* New York: Cambridge University Press.
Kochanek, Stanley. 1968. *The Congress Party of India: The Dynamics of One-Party Democracy.* Princeton, N.J.: Princeton University Press.
————. 1974. *Business and Politics in India.* Berkeley: University of California Press.
————. 1975. "The Indian Political System." In R. N. Kearney, ed. *Politics and Modernization in South and Southeast Asia.* New York: John Wiley.
————. 1976. "Mrs. Gandhi's Pyramid: The New Congress." In Henry Hart, ed. *Indira Gandhi's India: A Political System Reappraised.* Boulder, Colo.: Westview Press.
————. 1987. "Briefcase Politics in India: The Congress Party and the Business Elite," *Asian Survey,* vol. xxvii, no. 12, pp. 1278–1301.
Kohli, Atul. 1983. "Parliamentary Communism and Agrarian Reform," *Asian Survey,* no. 23, no. 7 (July), pp. 783–809.
————. 1987. *The State and Poverty in India: The Politics of Reform.* Cambridge: Cambridge University Press.
————. 1987a. "The Political Economy of Development Strategies: Comparative Perspectives on the Role of the State," *Comparative Politics* 19, pp. 233–246.
————, ed. 1988. *India's Democracy: An Analysis of Changing State-Society Relations.* Princeton, N.J.: Princeton University Press.
————. 1990. *Democracy and Discontent: India's Growing Crisis of Governability.* New York: Cambridge University Press.
Kothari, Rajni. 1964. "The Congress System in India," *Asian Survey,* vol. 4, no. 12 (December), pp. 1161–1173.
————. 1967. "India: The Congress System on Trial," *Asian Survey,* vol. 7, no. 2 (February), pp. 83–96.
————. 1970. *Politics in India.* Boston: Little Brown.
————. 1983. "The Crisis of the Moderate State and the Decline of Democracy." In Peter Lyon and James Manor, eds. *Transfer and Transportation: Political Institutions in the New Commonwealth.* Leicester: Leicester University Press.

———. 1987. "Flight into the 21st Century: Millions Will Be Stranded," *Times of India*, 27 April.

———. 1988. *Rethinking Development*. New Delhi: Ajanta Publishers.

———. 1988a; 1989. *Politics and the People: In Search of a Humane India*. 2 vols. New Delhi: Ajanta Publishers.

———. 1988b. "Political Economy of the Indian State: The Rudolph Thesis," *Contributions to Indian Sociology* 22, pp. 273–278.

———. 1988c. *State Against Democracy: In Search of Humane Governance*. New Delhi: Ajanta Publishers.

———. 1989a. "The Indian Enterprise Today," *Daedalus*, vol. 118, no. 4 (fall), pp. 51–67.

Kothari, Smitu. 1997. "Whose Independence: The Social Impact of Economic Reform in India," *Journal of International Affairs*, vol. 51, no. 1, pp. 85–116.

Kotovsky, Grigory. 1964. *Agrarian Reforms in India*. New Delhi: Peoples' Publishing House.

Krishna, Gopal. 1966. "The Development of Indian National Congress as a Mass Organization, 1918–1923," *Journal of Modern Asian Studies* 25, pp. 413–440.

Krishna, Raj. 1978. "The Next Phase in Rural Development," *Voluntary Action* 20, 7 (July).

———. 1979. "Small Farmer Development," *Economic and Political Weekly*, no. 26, pp. 913–918.

———. 1980. *Some Aspects of Wheat and Rice Price Policy in India*. World Bank Staff Working Paper no. 3831. Washington D.C.: The World Bank.

Krishnaji, N. 1975. "Inter-Regional Disparities in Per Capita Production and Productivity of Foodgrain: A Preliminary Note on Trends," *Economic and Political Weekly*, special number (August), pp. 1377–1385.

Kurian, K. M. 1975. "Class Character of the Indian State." In K. M. Kurian, ed. *India—State and Society*. Bombay: Orient Longman.

Kurian, N. J. 1990. "Employment Potential in Rural India: An Analysis," *Economic and Political Weekly* xxi (29 December), pp. A-177–A-188.

Kurien, C. T. 1979. *Economic Change in Tamil Nadu*. New Delhi: Allied Publishers.

Kushro, A. M. 1973. *Economics of Land Reform and Farm Size in India*. Madras: Macmillan.

Kuznets, Simon. 1955. "Economic Growth and Income Inequality," *American Economic Review*, no. 45.

Ladejinsky, Wolf. 1977. *Agrarian Reforms as Unfinished Business*. L. J. Walinsky, ed. London: Oxford University Press.

Lal, Deepak. 1985. *The Poverty of Development Economics*. Cambridge, Mass.: Harvard University Press.

———. 1988. *The Hindu Equilibrium, vol. 1: Cultural Stability and Economic Stagnation, India c.1500 B.C.–A.D. 1980*. Oxford: Clarendon Press.

Leftwich, Adrian. 1983. *Redefining Politics: People, Resources, Power*. London: Methuen.

Leibenstein, H. 1954. *A Theory of Economic-Demographic Development*. Princeton, N.J.: Princeton University Press.

Lele, Jayant. 1981. *Elite Pluralism and Class Rule: Political Development in Maharashtra, India*. Toronto: University of Toronto Press.

Lele, Uma. 1975. *The Design of Rural Development: Lessons from Africa*. Baltimore: Johns Hopkins University Press.

Lewis, John. 1995. *India's Political Economy: Governance and Reform*. New Delhi: Oxford University Press.

Lewis, John P. 1988. *Strengthening the Poor: What Have We Learned*. New Brunswick, N.J.: Transaction Books.

Lewis, W. Arthur. 1954. "Economic Development with Unlimited Supplies of Labour," *Manchester School of Economics and Social Studies*, no. 22, pp. 139–191.

Lieberthal, Kenneth. 1995. *Governing China.* New York: W. W. Norton.

Lijphart, Arend. 1984. *Democracies, Patterns of Majoritarian and Consensus Government in Twenty-One Countries.* New Haven, Conn.: Yale University Press.

Lipset, Seymour Martin. 1959. "Some Social Requisites of Democracy: Economic Development and Political Legitimacy," *American Political Science Review,* vol. 53, pp. 69–105.

Lipton, Michael. 1968. "Strategy for Agriculture: Urban Bias and Rural Planning." In P. Streeten and M. Lipton, eds. *The Crisis of Indian Planning: Economic Planning in the 1960's.* London: Oxford University Press.

———. 1977. *Why Poor People Stay Poor: Urban Bias in World Development.* Cambridge: Cambridge University Press.

———. 1983. *Poverty, Under-nutrition and Hunger.* World Bank Staff Working Paper no. 320. Washington, D.C.: The World Bank.

———, with R. Longhurst. 1989. *New Seeds and Poor People.* Baltimore: Johns Hopkins University Press.

Locke, John. 1988. *Two Treatises of Government.* Peter Laslett, ed. Cambridge: Cambridge University Press.

Lofchie, Michael, Steve Commins, and Robert Payne. 1986. *Africa's Agrarian Crisis.* Boulder, Colo.: Lynne Rienner Publishers.

Lustig, Nora, ed. 1995. *Coping with Austerity: Poverty and Inequality in Latin America.* Washington, D.C.: Brookings Institution.

MacDougall, James. 1980. "Two Models of Power in Contemporary Rural India," *Contributions to Indian Sociology* 14, pp. 77–94.

Macpherson, C. B. 1965. *The Real World of Democracy.* Oxford: Clarendon Press.

Majumdar, R. C. 1962. *History of the Freedom Movement in India.* 3 vols. Calcutta: Firma K. L. Mukhopadhyay.

Malaviya, H. D. 1954. *Land Reforms in India.* New Delhi: All-India Congress Committee.

Malik, Yogendra, and Joseph F. Marquette. 1990. *Political Mercenaries and Citizen Soldiers: A Profile of North Indian Party Activists.* New Delhi: Chanakya Publications.

Malik, Yogendra. 1993. "India." In Craig Baxter, Yogendra Malik, Charles Kennedy, and Robert Oberst, eds. *Government and Politics in South Asia.* Boulder, Colo.: Westview Press.

Mallick, Ross. 1994. *Development Policy of a Communist Government: West Bengal since 1977.* Cambridge: Cambridge University Press.

Malloy, James. 1987. "The Politics of Transition in Latin America." In James Malloy and Mitchell Seligson, eds. *Authoritarians and Democrats: Regime Transition in Latin America.* Pittsburgh: Pittsburgh University Press.

Manor, James. 1982. "The Dynamics of Political Integration and Disintegration." In A. T. Wilson and D. Dalton, eds. *The States of South Asia: Problems of National Integration.* Delhi: Vikas Publishers.

———. 1989. "India: State and Society Diverge," *Current History* (December), pp. 429–432.

———. 1990. "How and Why Liberal and Representative Politics Emerged in India," *Political Studies,* vol. xxxviii, pp. 20–38.

Marcel, Mario, and Andres Solimano. 1994. "The Distribution of Income and Economic Adjustment." In Barry Bosworth, Rudiger Dornbusch, and Raul Laban, eds. *The Chilean Economy: Policy Lessons and Challenges.* Washington, D.C.: Brookings Institution.

Marshall, T. H. 1964. *Class, Citizenship, and Social Development.* New York: Doubleday.

Matin, Abdul. 1989. *Changing Agrarian Relations in Mithila, North Bihar.* Unpublished Ph.D. dissertation. Centre for South Asian Studies, University of Toronto.

McClelland, David. 1961. *The Achieving Society.* New York: Van Nostrand.

McNamara, Dennis. 1990. *The Colonial Origins of the Korean Enterprise: 1910–1945.* New York: Cambridge University Press.

Mehrotra, S. R. 1971. *The Emergence of the Indian National Congress.* New Delhi: Vikas Publishers.

Meier, Gerald. 1989. *Leading Issues in Economic Development.* 5th ed. New York: Oxford University Press.

Mellor, John. 1968. *Developing Rural India: Plan and Practice.* Ithaca, N.Y.: Cornell University Press.

———. 1976. *The New Economics of Growth: A Strategy for India and the Developing World.* Ithaca, N.Y.: Cornell University Press.

———. 1985. "Determinants of Rural Poverty: The Dynamics of Production, Technology, and Price." In John Mellor and Gunvant Desai, eds. *Agricultural Change and Rural Poverty.* Baltimore: Johns Hopkins University Press.

———. 1988. "Food Production, Consumption, and Development Strategy." In Robert Lucas and Gustav Papanek, eds. *The Indian Economy: Recent Development and Future Trends.* Delhi: Oxford University Press.

———, and G. N. Desai. eds., 1985. *Agricultural Change and Rural Poverty.* Delhi: Oxford University Press.

Mencher, Joan. 1978. *Agriculture and Social Structure in Tamil Nadu.* Delhi: Allied Publishers.

———. 1980. "The Lessons and Non-Lessons of Kerala: Agricultural Laborers and Poverty," *Economic and Political Weekly* (15 October).

Metcalf, Thomas. 1967. "Landlords without Land: The U.P. Zamindars Today," *Pacific Affairs,* vol. 40, pp. 5–18.

Metha, B. 1978. "Prices and Public Distribution," *Indian Express,* Bombay, 5 May.

Migdal, Joel. 1988. *Strong Societies and Weak States: State-Society Relations and State Capabilities in the Third World.* Princeton, N.J.: Princeton University Press.

———, Atul Kohli, and Vivienne Shue. 1994. *State Power and Social Forces: Domination and Transformation.* New York: Cambridge University Press.

Mill, John S. 1961. *The Essential Works of John Stuart Mill.* Edited with introduction by M. Lerner. New York: Bantam Books.

Minhas, B. S., L. R. Jain, and S. D. Tendulkar. 1991. "Declining Incidence of Poverty in the 1980s: Evidence Versus Artefacts," *Economic and Political Weekly,* vol. xxvi, nos. 27–28 (July), pp. 1673–1682.

Misra, B. B. 1961. *The Indian Middle Classes: Their Growth in Modern Times.* New York: Oxford University Press.

Mitchell, Timothy. 1991. "The Limits of the State: Beyond Statist Approaches and their Critics," *American Political Science Review,* vol. 85, no. 1.

Mitra, Ashok. 1977. *Terms of Trade and Class Relations.* London: Frank Cass.

Moore, Barrington. 1966. *Social Origins of Dictatorship and Democracy.* Boston: Beacon Press.

Morley, Samuel. 1995. *Poverty and Inequality in Latin America.* Baltimore: Johns Hopkins University Press.

Morris-Jones, W. H. 1964. *The Government and Politics of India.* London: Hutchinson University Library.

———. 1971. *The Government and Politics of India.* London: Hutchinson.

Mukherji, S. 1988. "The Private Sector and Industrial Policy in India." In Amiya Kumar Bagchi, ed. *Economy, Society, and Polity.* New Delhi: Oxford University Press.

Myrdal, Gunnar. 1970. *Asian Drama: An Enquiry into the Poverty of Nations.* 3 vols. New York: Pantheon.

Nadkarni, M. V. 1976. "Tenants from the Dominant Class: A Developing Contradiction in Land Reforms," *Economic and Political Weekly* (December—Review of Agriculture).

————. 1987. *Farmers' Movements in India.* New Delhi: Allied Publishers Limited.

Nair, Kusum. 1961. *Blossoms in the Dust: The Human Factor in Indian Development.* New York: Praeger.

Nandy, Ashis. 1983. *The Intimate Enemy: The Loss and Recovery of Self under Colonialism.* New Delhi: Oxford University Press.

National Institute of Rural Development (NIRD). 1995. *Panchayati Raj Institutions in India: An Appraisal.* Hyderabad: National Institute of Rural Development.

Nayar, B. R. 1972. *The Modernization Imperative and Indian Planning.* Delhi: Vikas Publications.

Nayar, Kuldip. 1977. *The Judgement.* New Delhi: Vikas Publishing.

Nayyar, Rohini. 1996. "New Initiatives for Poverty Alleviation in Rural India." In C. H. Hanumantha Rao and Hans Linnemann, eds. *Economic Reforms and Poverty Alleviation in India.* New Delhi: Sage Publications.

Neale, Walter. 1962. *Economic Change in Rural India: Land Tenure and Reform in Uttar Pradesh, 1800–1955.* New Haven, Conn.: Yale University Press.

Nehru, Jawaharlal. 1936. *An Autobiography.* London: J. Capec.

————. 1948. *The Unity of India.* London: Lindsay Drummond.

————. 1958. *Jawaharlal Nehru's Speeches, vol. 1, 1946–1949.* New Delhi: Government of India.

Nordlinger, Eric. 1981. *On the Autonomy of the Democratic State.* Cambridge: Cambridge University Press.

O'Donnell, Guillermo. 1973. *Modernization and Bureaucratic Authoritarianism: Studies in South American Politics.* Berkeley: University of California Press.

————. 1994. "Delegative Democracy," *Journal of Democracy* Vol. 5 (January), pp. 55–69.

Ojha, G. 1977. *Land Problems and Land Reforms.* New Delhi: Sultan Chand and Sons.

Olson, Mancur. 1971. *The Logic of Collective Action.* Cambridge, Mass.: Harvard University Press.

Omvedt, Gail. 1980. "Cane Farmers' Movements," *Economic and Political Weekly,* no. 16 (December), pp. 2040–2043.

————. 1983. "Capitalist Agriculture and Rural Classes in India," *Bulletin of Concerned Asian Scholars,* vol. 15, no. 3, pp. 30–54.

Oppenheim, Lois H. 1993. *Politics in Chile: Democracy, Authoritarianism, and the Search for Development.* Boulder, Colo.: Westview Press.

Paarlberg, Robert. 1985. *Food Trade and Foreign Policy: India, the Soviet Union, and the United States.* Ithaca, N.Y.: Cornell University Press.

Pachauri, P. 1988. "Power and Endurance: An Unprecedented Farmers Protest in Meerut," *India Today,* 29 February, pp. 36–37.

Paige, Jeffrey. 1975. *Agrarian Revolution: Social Movements and Export Agriculture in the Underdeveloped World.* New York: Free Press.

Palmer, Norman. 1961. *The Indian Political System.* Boston: Houghton Mifflin.

Pandey, Gyan. 1978. *The Ascendancy of the Congress in Uttar Pradesh 1926–34: A Study of Imperfect Mobilization.* Delhi: Oxford University Press.

Park, Richard L., and Irene Tinker. 1959. *Leadership and Political Institutions in India.* Princeton, N.J.: Princeton University Press.

Parthasarathy, G. 1979. "Land Reform and the Changing Agrarian Structure." In C. H. Shah, ed. *Agricultural Development in India: Policy and Problems.* Bombay: Orient Longmans.

Patel, I. G. 1987. "On Taking India into the Twenty-First Century," *Modern Asian Studies,* vol. 21, no. 2.

Pateman, Carole. 1970. *Participation and Democratic Theory.* London: Cambridge University Press.

Patnaik, Prahbat. 1972. "Imperialism and the Growth of Indian Capitalism." In R. Owen, ed. *Studies in the Theory of Imperialism.* London: Longman.

Patnaik, Utsa. 1972. "Development of Capitalism in Agriculture," *Social Scientist,* vol. 1, no. 3, pp. 3–19.

———. 1987. *Peasant Class Differentiation: A Study in Method with Reference to Haryana.* Delhi: Oxford University Press.

———. 1990. *Agrarian Relations and Accumulation: The Mode of Production Debate in India.* Delhi: Oxford University Press.

Paul, S. 1984. "Mid-Term Appraisal of the Sixth Plan: Why Poverty Alleviation Lags Behind," *Economic and Political Weekly,* vol. xix, no. 18, pp. 760–766.

Pearce, A. 1980. *Seeds of Plenty, Seeds of Want: Social and Economic Implications of the Green Revolution.* Oxford: Clarendon Press.

Pereira, Luis Carlos Bresser, Jose Maria Maravall, and Adam Przeworski. 1993. *Economic Reforms in New Democracies: A Social-Democratic Approach.* New York: Cambridge University Press.

Petras, James, Fernando Ignacio Leiva, and Henry Veltmeyer. 1994. *Democracy and Poverty in Chile.* Boulder, Colo.: Westview Press.

Poulantzas, Nicos. 1973. *Political Power and Social Classes.* London: New Left Books.

Prahladachar, M. 1983. "Income Distribution Effects of the Green Revolution in India: A Review of Empirical Evidence," *World Development* 11, pp. 927–944.

Prasad, D. N. 1980. *Food for Peace: The Story of U.S. Food Assistance to India.* Bombay: Asia Publishing House.

Prasad, K. 1977. "Foodgrains Policy 1966–1976." In C. Wadhva, ed. *Some Problems of India's Economic Policy.* New Delhi: Tata McGraw-Hill.

Prasad, Pradhan H. 1979. "Semi-Feudalism: The Basic Constraint of Indian Agriculture." In A. N. Das and V. Nilakant, eds. *Agrarian Relations in India.* New Delhi: Manohar Publisher.

———. 1985. "Poverty and Agricultural Development," *Economic and Political Weekly,* vol. xx, no. 50, pp. 2220–2224.

———. 1987. "Agrarian Violence in Bihar," *Economic and Political Weekly,* vol. 22 (30 May), pp. 847–853.

Przeworski, Adam. 1991. *Democracy and the Market.* Cambridge: Cambridge University Press.

———. 1996. "What Makes Democracies Endure," *Journal of Democracy,* vol. 7, no. 1, pp. 39–55.

Purcell, Gary, and Ashok Gulati. 1993. *Liberalising Indian Agriculture: An Agenda for Reform.* World Bank Policy Research Working Paper (WPS 1172). Washington, D.C.: The World Bank.

Putnam, Robert. 1993. *Making Democracies Work: Civic Traditions in Modern Italy.* Princeton, N.J.: Princeton University Press.

Pye, Lucian, and Sidney Verba. 1965. *Political Culture and Political Development.* Princeton, N.J.: Princeton University Press.

Raczynski, Dagmar. 1995. *Strategies to Combat Poverty in Latin America.* Santiago: CIEPLAN.

Radhakrishna, Rokkam, Kalanidhi Subbarao, Sulibhavi Indrakant, and Chagnat Ravi, 1997. *India's Food Distribution System: A National and International Perspective.* World Bank Discussion Paper no. 380. Washington, D.C.: The World Bank.

Raj, Krishna N. 1973. "The Politics of Intermediate Regimes," *Economic and Political Weekly* 8, no. 27, pp. 1189–1198.

———. 1976. "Trends in Rural Unemployment in India: An Analysis with Reference to Conceptual and Measurement Problems," *Economic and Political Weekly* (8 August, Special Number), pp. 1281–1292.

Randall, Vicky, and Robin Theobald. 1985. *Political Change and Underdevelopment.* London: Macmillian.

Ranis, Gustav. 1979. "Industrial Development." In W. Galenson, ed. *Economic Growth and Structural Change in Taiwan,* Ithaca, N.Y.: Cornell University Press.

Rao, C. H. H. 1975. *Technological Change and Distribution of Gains in Indian Agriculture.* New Delhi: Macmillan.

———, and Hans Linnemann., eds. 1996. *Economic Reforms and Poverty Alleviation.* New Delhi: Sage Publications.

Rao, Krishna Y. V. 1984. *Growth of Capitalism in Agriculture: A Case Study of Andhra Pradesh.* Vijaywala: Visalaandra Publishing House.

Rao, V. M., and R. S. Deshpande. 1986. "Agricultural Growth in India: A Review of Experiences and Prospects," *Economic and Political Weekly,* vol. xxi, nos. 38–39, pp. A101–A112.

Rao, Vaman. 1984/85. "Democracy and Economic Development," *Studies in Comparative International Development* 19, pp. 67–81.

Rastyannikov, V. G. 1981. *Agrarian Evolution in a Multiform Structure Society: Experience of Independent India.* London: Routledge and Kegan Paul.

Rath, Nilakant. 1985. "Garibi Hatao: Can IRDP Do It," *Economic and Political Weekly,* vol. xx, no. 6, pp. 238–246.

Rawls, John. 1971. *A Theory of Justice.* Cambridge, Mass.: Belknap Press of Harvard University Press.

Redclift, Michael. 1987. *Sustainable Development: Exploring the Contradictions.* London: Methuen.

Remmer, Karen. 1985/86. "Exclusionary Democracy," *Studies in Comparative International Development,* vol. 20, no. 4, pp. 64–85.

———. 1990. "Democracy and Economic Crisis: The Latin American Experience," *World Politics,* vol. 42 (April), pp. 315–335.

———. 1995. "New Theoretical Perspectives on Democratization," *Comparative Politics,* vol. 27 (October).

Repetto, Robert. 1994. *The Second India Revisited: Population, Poverty, and Environmental Stress over Two Decades.* Washington, D.C.: World Resources Institute.

Riedinger, Jeffrey. 1995. *Agrarian Reforms in the Philippines: Democratic Transitions and Redistributive Reforms.* Stanford, Ca.: Stanford University Press.

Roemer, John. 1982. *A General Theory of Exploitation and Class.* Cambridge, Mass.: Harvard University Press.

Rostow, Walt W. 1962. *The Stages of Economic Growth.* Cambridge: Cambridge University Press.

Roy, A. 1976. *Monopoly Capitalism in India.* Calcutta: People's Publishing House.

Roy, R. 1967. "Selection of Congress Candidates," part IV, *Economic and Political Weekly* (21 January).

Rudolph, Lloyd, and Susanne Rudolph. 1967. *The Modernity of Tradition: Political Development in India.* Chicago: Chicago University Press.

———. 1987. *In Pursuit of Lakshmi: The Political Economy of the Indian State.* Chicago: Chicago University Press.

Rudra, Ashok. 1971. "The Green and Greedy Revolution," *South Asian Review,* no. 4, pp. 291–305.

———. 1988. "Emerging Class Structure in Indian Agriculture." In T. N. Srinivasan and P. K. Bardhan, eds. *Rural Poverty in South Asia.* New York: Columbia University Press.

Saith, Ajit. 1981. "Production, Prices, and Poverty in Rural India," *Journal of Development Studies,* no. 17 (January), pp. 196–214.

———, and Ajay Tankha. 1972. "Agrarian Transition and the Differentiation of the Peasantry: A Case Study of a West U.P. Village," *Economic and Political Weekly* (1 April).

———, and Ajay Tankha. 1992. "Longitudinal Analysis of Structural Change in a North Indian Village: 1970–1987." *Working Paper Series no. 128.* Institute of Social Studies, the Hague.

Sahasrabudhey, S. 1986. *The Peasant Movement Today.* New Delhi: Ashish Publishing House.

———. 1989. *Peasant Movements in Modern India.* Allahabad: Chugh Publications.

Sandbrook, Richard. 1985. *The Politics of Africa's Economic Stagnation.* Cambridge: Cambridge University Press.

Sarkar, Sumit. 1983. *Modern India, 1885–1947.* London: Macmillan.

Sau, Ranjit. 1981. *India's Economic Development: Aspects of Class Relations.* Delhi: People's Publishing House.

Schultz, Theodore. 1964. *Transforming Traditional Agriculture.* New Haven, Conn.: Yale University Press.

Scott, James C. 1976. *The Moral Economy of the Peasant.* New Haven, Conn.: Yale University Press.

———. 1998. *Seeing Like a State: How Certain Schemes to Improve the Human Condition Have Failed.* New Haven, Conn.: Yale University Press.

Scully, Timothy. 1996. "Chile: The Political Underpinnings of Economic Liberalization." In Jorge I. Dominguez and Abraham Lowenthal, eds. *Constructing Democratic Governance: South America in the 1990s.* Baltimore: The Johns Hopkins University Press.

Seal, Anil. 1968. *The Emergence of Indian Nationalism: Competition and Collaboration in the later Nineteenth Century.* Cambridge: Cambridge University Press.

Sen, Amartya K. 1981. *Poverty and Famines: An Essay on Entitlement and Deprivation.* Oxford: Clarendon Press.

Sen, Anupam. 1982. *The State, Industrialization, and Class Formation in India.* London: Routledge and Kegan Paul.

Sen, Bhowani. 1962. *The Evolution of Agrarian Relations in India.* New Delhi: Peoples' Publishing House.

Shah, Ghanshyam. 1988. "Grass-Roots Mobilization in Indian Politics." In Atul Kohli, ed. *India's Democracy: An Analysis of Changing State-Society Relations.* Princeton, N.J.: Princeton University Press.

Shah, S. A. 1973. *Towards National Liberation: Essays in the Political Economy of India.* Montreal: Publisher not stated.

Sharma, Hari P. 1962. "Land Reforms in a Village in the Union Territory of Delhi." In M. S. Gore, ed. *Problems of Rural Change.* Delhi: University of Delhi Press.
———. 1973. "The Green Revolution in India: Prelude to a Red One." In K. Gough and H. P. Sharma, eds. *Imperialism and Revolution in South Asia.* New York: Monthly Review Press.
———. 1985. "Political Development and Modernization," *South Asian Horizons,* vol. 3, pp. 26–34.
Sharma, R. S. 1965. *Indian Feudalism.* Calcutta: Peoples Publishing House.
Sheahan, John. 1987. *Patterns of Development in Latin America: Poverty, Repression, and Economic Strategy.* Princeton, N.J.: Princeton University Press.
———. 1997. "Effects of Liberalization Programs on Poverty and Inequality: Chile, Mexico, Peru," *Latin American Research Review,* vol. 32, no. 3, pp. 6–35.
Shiva, Vandana. 1989. *The Violence of the Green Revolution: Ecological Degradation and Political Conflict.* London: Zed Press.
Shue, Vivienne. 1988. *The Reach of the State: Sketches of the Chinese Body Politic.* Stanford, Ca.: Stanford University Press.
Silva, Eduardo. 1997. "Business Elites, the State and Economic Change in Chile." In Sylvia Maxfield and Ben Ross Schneider, eds. *Business and the State in Developing Countries.* Ithaca, N.Y.: Cornell University Press.
Singh, B., and S. Mishra. 1965. *A Study of Land Reforms in Uttar Pradesh.* Honolulu: University of Hawaii Press.
Singh, Charan. 1948. *Abolition of Zaminidari: Two Alternatives.* Allahabad: Kitabistan.
———. *Joint-Farming X-Rayed: The Problem and Its Solution.* New Delhi: Asia Publishing House.
———. 1964. *India's Poverty and Its Solution.* Bombay: Asia Publishing House.
———. 1978. *India's Economic Policy: The Gandhian Blueprint.* New Delhi: Vikas Publishing House.
———. 1981. *Economic Nightmare in India: Its Causes and Cure.* New Delhi: National Publishing House.
Singh, Tarlok. 1974. *India's Development Experience.* Delhi: Macmillan.
Sinha, A. 1982. "Class War: Not Atrocities against Harijans." In A. N. Das, ed. *Agrarian Movement in India.* London: Frank Cass.
———. 1991. *Against The Few: Struggles of India's Poor.* London: Zed Books.
Sinha, Indradeep. 1980. *The Changing Agrarian Scene: Problems and Tasks.* New Delhi: People's Publishing House.
Sirowy, Larry, and Alex Inkels. 1990. "The Effects of Democracy on Economic Growth and Inequality: A Review," *Studies in Comparative International Development,* vol. 25, no. 1, pp. 126–57.
Skidmore, Thomas. 1977. "The Politics of Economic Stabilization in Postwar Latin America." In James Malloy, ed. *Authoritarianism and Corporatism in Latin America.* Pittsburgh: University of Pittsburgh Press.
Skocpol, Theda. 1979. *States and Social Revolutions: A Comparative Analysis of France, Russia, and China.* Cambridge: Cambridge University Press.
Smith, Tony. 1979. "The Underdevelopment of Development Literature," *World Politics* 31, 2 (January), pp. 247–288.
Solow, R. M. 1956. "A Contribution to the Theory of Economic Growth," *Quarterly Journal of Economics* 70, pp. 65–94.
Somayajulu, V. N. N. 1982. *The Rural Affluent: Nature and Dimensions of Social Change in Relation to New Agricultural Technology.* Hyderabad: Indian Institute of Economics.

Spear, Percival. 1961. *India: A Modern History*. Ann Arbor: University of Michigan Press.

Srinivas, S. N. 1967. *Social Change in Modern India*. Berkeley: University of California Press.

———. 1987. *The Dominant Caste and Other Essays*. Delhi: Oxford University Press.

Srinivasan, T. N., and Pranab Bardhan. 1974. *Poverty and Income Distribution in India*. Calcutta: Statisticial Publishing Society.

Srinivasan, T. N. 1985. "Agricultural Production, Relative Prices, Entitlements, and Poverty." In J. Mellor and G. Desai, eds. *Agricultural Change and Rural Poverty*. Baltimore: Johns Hopkins University Press.

———, and Pranab Bardhan, eds. 1988. *Rural Poverty in South Asia*. New York: Columbia University Press.

Staub, W., and M. G. Blase. 1974. "Induced Technological Change in Developing Agricultures: Implications for Income Distribution and Agricultural Development," *The Journal of Developing Areas* (July).

Stepan, Alfred. 1978. *The State and Society: Peru in Comparative Perspective*. Princeton, N.J.: Princeton University Press.

Stokes, Eric. 1978. *The Peasant and the Raj*. Cambridge: Cambridge University Press.

Streeten, Paul. 1980. "Basic Needs and Human Rights," *World Development*, no. 2, pp. 107–111.

———. 1981. *What Price Food? Agricultural Price Policies in Developing Countries*. London: Macmillan.

Subbarao, K. 1985. "State Policies and Regional Disparity in Indian Agriculture," *Development and Change*, vol. 16, pp. 523–546.

Subramaniam, C. 1972. *A New Strategy in Agriculture: A Collection of Speeches*. New Delhi: Indian Council of Agricultural Research.

———. 1972a. *India of My Dreams*. New Delhi: Orient Longman.

———. 1979. *The New Strategy in Indian Agriculture*. New Delhi: Vikas Publishing.

Sukhatme, P. 1978. "Assessment of Adequacy of Diets at Different Income Levels," *Economic and Political Weekly*, vol. 31, no. 12.

Sundaram, K., and S. D. Tendulkar. 1983. "Poverty Reduction and Redistribution in FYP, VI," *Economic and Political Weekly*, vol. 36, no. 10.

Swaminathan, Madura. 1996. "Structural Adjustment, Food Security, and Systems of Public Distribution of Food," *Economic and Political Weekly*, vol. 31, no. 26.

Swamy, Dalip. 1976. "Differentiation of the Peasantry in India," *Economic and Political Weekly*, vol. xi, no. 50, pp. 1933–1943.

Tai, H. C. 1974. *Land Reform and Politics: A Comparative Analysis*. Berkeley: University of California Press.

Tendler, Judith. 1986. *Whatever Happened to Poverty Alleviation*. New York: Ford Foundation.

Tendulkar, S. D. 1985. "The Poverty Problem," *Seminar*, no. 316, pp. 65–69.

Thapar, Romila. 1961. *Ashoka and the Decline of the Mauryas*. Oxford: Oxford University Press.

Tharamangalam, Joseph. 1981. *Agrarian Class Conflict: The Political Mobilization of Agricultural Laborers in Kuttanad, South India*. Vancouver: University of British Columbia Press.

Thorner, Alice. 1982. "Semi-Feudalism or Capitalism," *Economic and Political Weekly*, nos. 48–51.

Thorner, Daniel. 1956. *The Agrarian Prospect in India*. Delhi: University of Delhi Press.

———. 1976. *The Agrarian Prospect in India*. 3d ed. Bombay: Allied Publishers.

————. 1980. *The Shaping of Modern India.* New Delhi: Allied Publishers.
Tilly, Charles, ed. 1975. *The Formation of National States in Western Europe.* Princeton, N.J.: Princeton University Press.
Timmer, Peter. 1986. *Getting Prices Right: The Scope and Limits of Agricultural Price Policy.* Ithaca, N.Y.: Cornell University Press.
Tocqueville, Alexis de. 1966. *Democracy in America.* Edited by J. P. Mayer and Max Lerner. New York: Harper and Row.
Trivedi, K. K. 1975. "Changes in Caste Composition of the Zamindar Class in Western U.P., 1595–1900," *Indian Historical Review,* vol. ii, no. 1 (July).
Tyagi, D. S. 1979. "Farm Prices and Class Bias in India," *Economic and Political Weekly,* vol. xiv, no. 29, pp. A111–A124.
Ul-Haq, Mahbub. 1976. *The Poverty Curtain: Choices for the Third World.* New York: Columbia University Press.
UNDP. 1996. *Human Development Report 1996.* New York: Oxford University Press.
Upadhyay, K. S. 1982. *Dynamics of Rural Transformation: A Study of Andhra Pradesh, 1956–76.* Hyderabad: Indian Council of Social Science Research.
Uppal, J. S. 1983. "Agrarian Structure and Land Reforms in India." In J. S. Uppal, ed. *India's Economic Problems: An Analytical Approach.* New Delhi: Tata McGraw-Hill.
Vaidyanathan, A. 1983. "The Indian Economy since Independence (1947–70)." In D. Kumar, ed. *The Cambridge Economic History of India vol. 2: C. 1757–1970.* Cambridge: Cambridge University Press.
————. 1988. "Agricultural Development and Rural Poverty." In R. Lucas and G. Papanek, eds. *The Indian Economy: Recent Development and Future Prospects.* Boulder, Colo.: Westview.
Valdes, Juan. 1995. *Pinochet's Economists: The Chicago School in Chile.* New York: Cambridge University Press.
Vanaik, Achin. 1990. *The Painful Transition: Bourgeois Democracy in India.* London: Verso.
Varshney, Aushtosh. 1988. "India's Political Economy: Issues, Non-Issues, and Puzzles," *Journal of Commonwealth and Comparative Politics,* vol. xxvi, no. 3, pp. 234–245.
————. 1995. *Democracy, Development, and the Countryside: Urban-Rural Struggles in India.* New York: Cambridge University Press.
Veit, Lawrence, and Catherine Gwinn. 1985. "The Indian Miracle," *Foreign Policy* 58 (spring).
Vergara, Pilar. 1996. "In Pursuit of Growth with Equity: The Limit of Chile's Free-Market Social Reforms," *NACLA Report on the Americas,* vol. xxix, no. 6 (May/June), pp. 37–43.
Visaria, Pravin. 1977. "Trends in Rural Unemployment in India: Comment," *Economic and Political Weekly* (29 January).
————, and S. K. Sanyal. 1977. "Trends in Rural Unemployment in India: Two Comments," *Economic and Political Weekly* (29 January).
Vyas, V. S. 1970. "Tenancy in a Dynamic Setting," *Economic and Political Weekly* (27 June).
————. 1976. "Structural Change in Agriculture and the Small Farm Sector," *Economic and Political Weekly* (10 January).
Wade, Robert. 1990. *Governing the Market: Economic Theory and the Role of Government in East Asian Industrialization.* Princeton, N.J.: Princeton University Press.
————, and Gordon White, eds. 1984. *Developmental States of East Asia.* IDS Bulletin. University of Sussex, International Development Centre.

Wakeman, Frederic. 1975. *Conflict and Control in Late Imperial China.* Berkeley: University of California Press.

Walinsksy, Louis, ed. 1977. *Agrarian Reforms as Unfinished Business: Selected Papers of Wolf Ladejinsky.* London: Oxford University Press.

Warriner, Doreen. 1969. *Land Reform in Principle and Practice.* Oxford: Clarendon Press.

Waterbury, John. 1983. *The Egypt of Nasser and Sadat: The Political Economy of Two Regimes.* Princeton, N.J.: Princeton University Press.

Weede, Erich. 1983. "The Impact of Democracy on Economic Growth: Some Evidence from Cross-National Analysis," *Kyklos,* vol. 35, no. 1, pp. 21–39.

Weiner, Myron. 1962. *The Politics of Scarcity. Public Pressure and Political Response.* Chicago: Chicago University Press.

———. 1963. "India's Two Political Cultures." In Myron Weiner, *Political Change in South Asia.* Calcutta: Firma K. L. Mukhapadhyay.

———. 1967. *Party Building in a New Nation: The Indian National Congress.* Chicago: University of Chicago Press.

———. 1968. "Political Development in the Indian States." In Myron Weiner, ed. *State Politics in India.* Princeton, N.J.: Princeton University Press.

———. 1983. *India at the Polls, 1980.* Washington, D.C.: American Enterprise Institute for Public Policy Research.

———. 1986. "The Political Economy of Industrial Growth in India," *World Politics,* vol. xxxviii, no. 4, pp. 596–610.

———. 1992. *The Child and the State in India.* Princeton, N.J.: Princeton University Press.

Weisskopf, Thomas. 1974. "Dependence and Imperialism in India." In M. Selden, ed. *Remaking Asia: Essays on the American Uses of Power.* New York: Pantheon.

Westphal, Larry. 1978. "The Republic of Korea's Experience with Export-Led Industrial Development," *World Development,* vol. 6, no. 3.

Weyland, Kurt. 1997. "Growth with Equity in Chile's New Democracy," *Latin American Research Review,* vol. 32, no. 1.

Wolpert, Stanley. 1997. *Nehru: A Tryst with Destiny.* London: Oxford University Press.

Wood, Geoff. 1972. "Conflict and Clientelism in a Bihar Village," *Institute of Development Studies Bulletin,* vol. 4, no. 3.

World Bank. 1975. *The Assault on World Poverty.* Baltimore: Johns Hopkins University Press.

———. 1984. *Situation and Prospects of the Indian Economy: A Medium Term Perspective.* Washington, D.C.: The World Bank.

———. 1989. *World Development Report 1989.* New York: Oxford University Press.

———. 1989a. *Country Studies: India—Poverty, Employment, and Social Services.* Washington: D.C.: The World Bank.

———. 1990. *World Bank Development Report: 1990.* New York: Oxford University Press.

———. 1993. *The East Asian Miracle: Economic Growth and Public Policy.* New York: Oxford University Press.

———. 1996. *World Development Report 1996.* New York: Oxford University Press.

———. 1996a. *India: Five Years of Stabilization and Reform and the Challenges Ahead.* Washington, D.C.: The World Bank.

———. 1997. *India: Achievements and Challenges in Reducing Poverty.* Washington, D.C.: The World Bank.

————. 1999. *World Development Report 1998/99.* New York: Oxford University Press.

Wunderlich, Gene. 1970. "Land Reforms in India." In USAID *Spring Review of Land Reform: Country Papers,* vol. 1, no. PB195315. Washington, D.C.: U.S. Department Of State.

Index

Absolute deprivation, 21*n6*
Affirmative action, 11
Africa, 185*n33*, 187
Agrarian reform: Congress Agrarian
  Reforms Committee, 96, 98–99,
  121*n6*; Congress Party failures, 108;
  consequences of, 110–118; failure of
  implementation, 103–110, 140*n15;*
  institutionalist strategy, 95, 96–100,
  101–103, 120; in Japan, 105, 147;
  Marxist analysis, 104; in Mexico,
  106–107, 122*n30;* in the Philippines,
  105; policies and goals, 101–103;
  political economy of, 96–101; in
  South Korea, 105, 147; as strategic
  political resource, 100; in Taiwan,
  107; technocratic strategy, 95,
  125–126; in West Bengal, 46;
  zamindari abolition, 95, 100, 101,
  110–111, 114–115, 119, 149, 163,
  190. *See also* Rural development
Agricultural Debt Relief Scheme, 212
Agricultural Prices Commission (APC),
  135, 169, 195–197, 200, 203, 207,
  214*n19*
Agricultural Refinance and
  Development Corporation, 201
Agriculture: in Aligarh district,
  159–160; in the colonial era, 63–64;
  cooperative/collective, 101–102, 115,
  118, 128, 130; exports, 227, 242*n25;*
  government subsidies, 6; investment
  in, 129, 136–137; labor, 31, 46, 155,
  167, 168–169; Marxist reforms, 46;
  mechanization, 167; neoliberal
  reforms, 227; productivity, 99–100,

134, 164; profitability, 163; state
  impact on modernization, 25–27;
  subsistence, 166, 185*n33;*
  technological change in, 31; trickle-
  down theories, 32; types of,
  163–164. *See also* Rural
  development
Ahluwalia, Montek, 32, 148
Aligarh district, 159–160
Allende, Salvador, 233
All-India Anna DMK (AIADMK), 7
Almond, Gabriel, 34–35
Ambedkar, Bhimrao Ramji, 1, 22*n17*,
  50, 69, 186*n40*
Amsden, Alice, 85
Anarcho-communitarians, 16
Andhra Pradesh, 7, 112, 116, 145
Antipoverty programs, 27, 33,
  180–182, 236
Appleby, Paul, 50
Apter, David, 35
Argentina, 238, 240*n12*
Asoka Mehta Committee, 232,
  243*n43*
Assam, 112, 145
Association of Southeast Asian Nations
  (ASEAN), 225
Austerity measures, 220
Austin, Granville, 20*n2*
Austria, 39
Authoritarianism: in China, 59*n55;* as
  development stage, 36–37, 221; in
  Latin America, 37, 57*n31,* 233–234,
  236; under neoliberalism, 220–221,
  240*n8;* in South Korea, 221
Authority in rural society, 170–175

269

Left Front (West Bengal), 46
Lele, Jayant, 58*n36*, 81–82
Lewis, John, 127, 132
Lewis, W. Arthur, 31
Licensing, 79, 91*n35*
Lifespan of Indians, 74–75
Lijphart, Arend, 56*n23*
Lipton, Michael, 99, 104, 213*n7*
Loans: agricultural waivers, 207, 211;
by international institutions, 231,
242*n37;* government, 103;
production, 150, 165–166
Local government, 51–52, 59*n51*
Lok Dal, 215*n30*
Lok Sabha, 14, 48–49, 119, 138, 177,
199, 238

Macpherson, C. B., 36
Madhya Pradesh, 116, 140*n4,* 145,
241*n23,* 243*n40*
Mahalanobis, P. C., 76, 139*n2*
Maharajas, 97–98
Maharashtra, 116, 145, 153, 190,
204–205
Majdoors, 18
Malaviya, H. D., 113
Malaviya, M. M., 68
Malaysia, 242*n27*
Malik, Yogendra, 180
Maliks, 97
Mallick, Ross, 46
Malloy, James, 37
Mandal, B. P., 11
Manufacturing, colonial-era, 64–65
Manuvadis, 10
Marginal Farmers and Agricultural
Laborers Scheme, 176
Market access agreements, 225
Marquette, Joseph, 180
Mauryan Empire, 61, 62
Mazdoor Kisan Sangram Samiti, 173,
210
Mazdoors, 97, 209
McClelland, David, 56*n15*
Mechanization, 167
Mehta, Balwantray, 59*n50*
Mehta Study Team Report (1957), 51
Mellor, John, 32, 170, 185*n36*
Menem, Carlos, 240*n12*
Merrill Lynch, 229
Mexico, 89*n21,* 106–107, 122*n30,* 136
Migdal, Joel, 5

Minhas, B. S., 28
Minimum alternate tax (MAT), 227,
241*n21*
Mitchell, Timothy, 4
Mitra, Ashok, 185*n32,* 213*n12*
Modernization approach, 40
Monoculture, 144
Moghuls, 61, 62
Monopolies and Restrictive Trade
Practices Act (*1969*), 91*n35*
Moon, Chung In, 21*n13*
Moore, Barrington, 39–40, 65, 68, 82,
117, 122*n24*
Moral economy, 47, 63
Morgan Stanley, 229
Multilateral Investment Guarantee
Agency, 224
Muslim League, 89*n13*
Muslims: caste among, 159, 162; as
land owners, 158; political strength
of, 7, 212
Myrdal, Gunnar, 40, 118
Mysore, 116

Nagpur resolution, 115, 123*n46,* 128
Naidu, G. Narayanaswami, 205
Nair, Kusum, 115
Nanda, Gulzarilal, 139*n2*
Nandy, Ashis, 2
Nanjundaswamy, Dr., 205
Narain, Dharm, 196, 200
Narain, Raj, 213*n8*
Narayan, Jayaprakesh, 191
Narayan, J. P., 66
National Council for Applied Economic
Research, 230
National Demonstration Program,
135–136
National Institute of Rural
Development (NIRD), 177
Nationalism, economic, 65, 73, 75
Nationalist movement, 65–70
Nationalization, 195, 197–198
National Renewal Fund (NRF), 231
National Rural Employment Program,
16, 186*n43*
National Sample Survey (NSS), 16,
28–29, 96, 98, 229–230
Nayar, Baldev Raj, 77
Nehru, Jawaharlal: agrarian reform, 96,
108; as betrayer of the masses, 68;
death of, 127, 133, 135, 138;

About the Book

This broad, historically grounded study examines the relationship between democratic governance and economic development in postindependence India (1947–1998). Sharma addresses the fundamental paradox of India's political economy: Why have five decades of democratically guided strategies failed to reconcile economic growth with redistribution or to mitigate the condition of extreme poverty in which some 350 to 400 million Indians—more than 40 percent of the population—live?

Drawing on an exhaustive empirical review of India's rural development and reform policies over the past fifty years, Sharma demonstrates that the wide discrepancies between development goals and actual outcomes have been fundamentally shaped by the manner in which the various constituents of the democratic polity coexist with and are inextricably embedded in rural society. His study challenges traditional concepts of democracy and development, as well as the relationship between the two.

Shalendra D. Sharma is associate professor of politics and director of the master of arts in Asia-Pacific Studies program at the University of San Francisco.